361.7
L97   Lurie, Harry L.
a   A heritage affirmed.

Temple Israel
Library
Minneapolis, Minn.

———

Please sign your full name on the above card.

Return books promptly to the Library or Temple Office.

Fines will be charged for overdue books or for damage or loss of same.

LIBRARY BUREAU CAT. NO. 1166.3

A Heritage Affirmed

The Jewish Publication Society of
America

Philadelphia 5722 1961

The Jewish Federation Movement

in America

A HERITAGE AFFIRMED

by

Harry L. Lurie

THE
JACOB R. SCHIFF
★ LIBRARY ★
OF JEWISH
CONTRIBUTIONS TO
AMERICAN DEMOCRACY

NUMBER 14 IN THE SERIES

Preface and
Acknowledgments

Beginning with the organization of the earliest federations of Jewish charities in 1895 and 1896, down to their present expansion to over three hundred metropolitan areas and regions, this form of central welfare organization has performed important functions and has made substantial impacts on the communal life of American Jewry. The persistence of this form of Jewish welfare organization, its role in the raising of funds for philanthropic purposes, the broadening and adaptation of its functions in relation to the changes in economic and cultural life of American Jewry here and overseas merit the attention of persons concerned with communal life of the American Jewish population in its relationships to the religious and ethnic groups among whom Jews reside.

This report on the Jewish federation in the United States and Canada from 1895 to the present day does not claim to be based on comprehensive or even adequate research; but being something less, it is possibly something more. Although the writer has attempted to present the record as he understands it as objectively as possible, it is in a sense a personal document, based upon active participation in federations for the greater part of a professional career which has extended for nearly fifty years—that is, for more than three-fourths of the period of federation history.

My first contact with federations was in 1909, when as an immigrant youth with the benefit of an American public school education, I attempted to teach English to more recent immigrants, in classes organized by the Jewish Federation of Buffalo. Later I was employed as an assistant to the executive of that Federation, helping with the transients and serving as the agent of the Industrial Removal Office, with immigrants sent to Buffalo from New York City. World War I put an end to that.

After a number of years in non-sectarian voluntary and public social agencies and as a teacher of social work, I was appointed, in 1925, superintendent of the Jewish Social Service Bureau of Chicago. During that period I was also involved in surveys of Jewish communal welfare agencies in Detroit, Baltimore and Grand Rapids.

Beginning in 1930 and for the following twenty-seven years, I was the executive of the Bureau of Jewish Social Research (national) and its successor agency, the Council of Jewish Federations and Welfare Funds, established in 1932. In this capacity I had the opportunity of continuing professional contacts with forty federations which over the course of the years grew, until at present there is a federation in every city with a Jewish population of 1,000 or more, and even in many places where the population is smaller.

Under the circumstances, drawing upon personal experience, involvement and memory, but in the main on the more dependable institutional records, reports,

minutes of discussions, and interviews with federation
personnel, I here offer an account of the history and development of American Jewish federations, welfare
funds and community councils; I do not, however, pre-
sume to call this the work of a research scholar. No
attempt has been made in this history of federations to
give great attention to the important national Jewish
agencies and movements, nor to local religious and secular
activities not directly involved in the basic development
of federations. In spite of these limitations, it is hoped
that this study may be of some value for those involved
in the continuing administration of the welfare programs, to students in schools of social work, and to others
concerned with American welfare organization.

The writer assumes full responsibility for the point
of view which has determined the selection of data
and their organization, but his own learning processes
and the development of this understanding of the events
in which he has been involved derive from a great many
sources. These acknowledgments are offered therefore
without implying any responsibility for the product. For
my attempt to provide a systematic approach to one
aspect of community organization I owe most to the
sociologist Charles H. Cooley under whom I was first a
student and later an instructor in the department he
headed at the University of Michigan. For my approach
to social work, I am most in debt to Edith Abbott and
Sophonisba Breckenridge of the School of Social Administration of the University of Chicago, and to Jane
Addams of Hull House; for my initial contacts in the
field of Jewish social work to Cecil B. Wiener, Samuel
A. Goldsmith, Frances Taussig, Dorothy Kahn and Dr.
I. M. Rubinow.

The lay leaders in the federation field have had perhaps the greatest influence on me and I must acknowledge my indebtedness to the hundreds of leaders with whom I have had long association; but I believe that I learned most from William Shroder, Ira M. Younker, Sidney Hollander, Julian Freeman and Fred Butzel. Similarly, my acknowledgments to the professional associates in the federation field past and present whom I have quoted in this report, including Solomon Lowenstein, Jacob Billikopf, Samuel A. Goldsmith, Isidore Sobeloff, Morris Waldman, Harry Greenstein, Maurice Hexter, Joseph Willen and others. Finally, I want to acknowledge the contributions made by the professional staff of the CJFWF, especially by George Rabinoff and Philip Bernstein, to the sources of my information and to my development of this subject.

The first draft of this history was prepared in 1957 when I retired from the administration of the CJFWF. This present draft was completed in 1960 with the generous assistance and criticisms of the members of the staff of the CJFWF who helped to bring the factual material up to date. I therefore express my deep appreciation to Philip Bernstein, S. P. Goldberg, Morris Zelditch, David Turteltaub, Alvin Chenkin and Walter Lurie, and to Nora Donegan for secretarial help, and to Frieda Ramm for assistance as librarian.

The initial draft of this history was mimeographed and circulated by CJFWF to a group of federation leaders and others, from several of whom I received valuable criticisms and encouragement.

HARRY L. LURIE

December 27, 1960

Table of Contents

Part I: Development of the Federation Movement

CHAPTER

Part II: Federation and Jewish Community Organization

Part III: The Federation Movement Today

List of Illustrations

(following page 212)

part one

The Development

of the

Federation Movement

I

Federation Defined
by Practice and History

*J*ews have lived in North America and have maintained an organized group life for more than three hundred years. Over the years they have developed various types of welfare services to meet individual and group needs. The type of organization with which this report is concerned is the Jewish welfare federation. First established in the year 1895, federations* have since then been organized in practically every city in the United States and in Canada and have played an important role in the communal life of American Jewry.

The welfare federation is only a part, and not the whole, of a broad range of organized Jewish activities in American cities, but it has a number of attributes that are not found, or are less fully developed, in other types of associations. What are the essential aspects of the

* The term "federation" is used throughout to include *local* organizations that may be called by such titles as Federation, Welfare Fund, United Appeal, United Jewish Community, Jewish Community Council, etc. The first federations used the name "Federation of Jewish Charities"; subsequently the term "Welfare" or "Philanthropy" or "Community" was substituted for "Charity" in recognition of changing attitudes or broadening functions.

federation? What conditions brought it into being; what problems and difficulties were encountered? Which of these were surmounted and which remain to hinder or to weaken its objectives? What is the present scope of federation? What are its limits and what are likely to be the future trends? These are some of the basic questions which this record may help in part to answer.

ESSENTIAL ASPECTS OF FEDERATION

Federation is primarily a device for welfare financing and welfare planning similar to the community "chests," the community "councils" and the united "funds" which exist in nearly every American city. This form of welfare organization seems particularly suitable for maintaining cooperation on welfare objectives among a population which may vary in religion, national origin or ethnic character. The chests and councils and united funds operate largely in urban centers where size and diversity of populations have been responsible for the establishment of multiple voluntary welfare agencies, expressing the initiative and the benevolent impulses of different elements of the population.

The Jewish federation is a Jewish group philanthropy organized and operated by Jews, raising funds primarily from Jewish contributors, and serving Jews and Jewish group objectives. There are many other kinds of philanthropic agencies organized by Jews, administered by Jews, serving Jews or Jewish group interests, operating on a local or national basis or in behalf of Jews in other lands. What distinguishes the federation from other forms of Jewish welfare effort is the combination of a number of elements, several of which are absent or less prominent in other types of Jewish welfare agencies:

4

1. Federation is primarily and essentially a continuing project to collect funds on a *city-wide* (or larger metropolitan or regional) *area from Jewish contributors*. It may, of course, also derive some part of its funds from other sources, such as governmental fees or payments for services, income from non-sectarian and inter-sectarian community chests, invested funds, etc.

2. Federation raises funds for the *purpose* of *supporting a group of beneficiary welfare agencies* and *welfare programs* which carry on their services locally, regionally, or nationally or are designed to serve the well-being of Jews in other lands. The list of beneficiary agencies to which the federation contributes usually includes all or most of the *local* Jewish welfare agencies plus a number of national and overseas Jewish agencies.

3. In addition to raising funds for the operation of Jewish welfare programs, federation together with, or in behalf of, its *local* beneficiary agencies usually assumes responsibility *for the administration, direction and planning of local welfare programs*. Federation's concern for Jewish group needs may and usually does include local health and welfare planning, educational and cultural needs, and group relationships.

4. Federation is usually the *instrument* for *representing the social welfare interests* of the local Jewish population *in its relationship to other parts* of the local citizenry and their voluntary group activities.

5. Except for a few of the largest cities, where functions may be divided by agreement among two separately organized bodies, the *local federation*

combines in a single agency functions relating to local Jewish responsibility for local, national and overseas Jewish organized welfare.

6. Federation is administered by a *governing body* which is designed to be, or purports to be, *representative* of those *who contribute* the funds and/or of *the local beneficiary agencies, or of local Jewish associations with various kinds of objectives.*

The Jewish federation operates in the democratic societies of the United States and Canada, but has not yet been widely developed in other countries, even in those with similar social systems.

The American Jewish federations are unique in their current ability to obtain the cooperation of practically all groups and classes in the Jewish population, otherwise separated in their communal activities by sectarian, cultural, economic or class differences.

ORIGINS OF FEDERATION

The federation is a form of Jewish communal association which derives from earlier forms of Jewish welfare organization. Its character may be traced in historical development from the religious attitudes toward charity (*Tzedakah*) derived from biblical precepts and Talmudic Law. It is the successor, under changed political and economic conditions, of many of the welfare functions and activities of the religious bodies and synagogues. It is the counterpart of the charitable and welfare functions of the organized Jewish community (*Kahal*) in existence in European countries during the medieval and early modern periods of history.

Immigration during the three centuries of settlement brought to the New World Jews whose background involved adherence to their religious precepts concerning charity and benevolence. Over this period there were in their countries of origin various forms of communal organization carrying responsibility for the functioning of these precepts in the life of the group. During the medieval and early modern period in Europe the *kahals* were legally constituted bodies operating on sufferance of the surrounding population, in the political state, and often invested by that state with the authority of taxing the Jewish population and enforcing Jewish laws. Even after the period of the Emancipation, following the French Revolution and the Napoleonic decrees, when Jews began to obtain equal political rights with the citizens of the state in which they resided, Jewish *kahals* and the *Kultusgemeinden* (as they were called in Germany) retained authority to collect taxes from professing Jews for the religious and welfare activities of the congregations.[1]

RELIGIOUS PRECEPTS AND WELFARE[2]

In the Torah, "helping the unfortunate members of society . . . is *commanded*, not requested; . . . benevolence [is] viewed not as a matter of grace but as an imperative duty."[3]

While some of the injunctions of the Torah concerning economic justice and benevolence, such as the law of the Jubilee Year and the law of the Sabbatical Year, were applicable primarily to an agricultural economy and, according to Frisch, may have been inoperative in the post-biblical era, other provisions played a profound role in the welfare practices of individuals and of congregations throughout subsequent eras. The basic biblical injunctions were obligatory. Departure from religious beliefs and practices was unthinkable for the

7

devout and compliance was imposed by the group on the less devout. Torah set forth clearly "the basic causes of poverty and misery, namely, economic maladjustment and injustice due to human greed," and provided for definite ways of dealing with such problems.[4]

Individual helpfulness and mutual aid were natural phenomena of Jewish life in the Diaspora because the precepts of religion, and the precarious conditions of life, made such practices essential for the survival of the group as well as of the unfortunate individual in need of help. Helping the poor, hospitality to travelers and strangers, lending money and goods, agreeing to give credit without the requirement of interest, support of widows and orphans, solicitude for the disabled and the aged were matters both of individual obligation and group activity.

The principles underlying the practice of benevolence, according to Frisch, designated as the "fundamental . . . principals and ideals basic to Jewish philanthropy," were:

The poor and dependent are the special wards of God and are therefore commended to the conscience and tender solicitude of the well-to-do by their common Maker.

All goods . . . come from and belong to God, the Source of all things, their human possessors being merely custodians . . . who must share with those in want.

Derived from these basic principles was the rabbinical doctrine that "Charity—whether in gifts or loans—does not represent a favor that might be withheld, but an imperative obligation springing from elementary considerations of justice."[5]

To the practices of individual charity and of mutual aid ingrained in the mores of the group, the community added organized forms of assistance through the instrument of the religious congregation. It was the general practice for each synagogue to establish a fund (*Kuppah*) for the varying communal functions, including the funds required to assist the poor.[6]

The congregation during the medieval and the early modern periods had the authority to collect taxes and enforce laws. The Jewish community, in its enforcement of Jewish Law, exercised the right derived from biblical authority (and accepted by the political state) of imposing on individuals penalties, such as fines, flogging, and in exceptional cases excommunication, and even execution of recalcitrant members guilty of serious offenses. "It came close," says Baron, "to justifying complaints that it (the *kahal*) constituted a 'state within a state.'" The integral unity of the Jewish groups during the medieval and early modern periods of history was based on "the common ties of religion, mores and descent. This integral unity, reinforced by immemorial traditions, outside hostility and, often common economic interest, resulted in an unusual combination of voluntary allegiance and public law enforcement."[7]

WELFARE PROGRAMS OF EARLY JEWISH SETTLERS

When the first group of Spanish-Portuguese Jews, leaving South America, arrived in New Amsterdam, resistance to their settlement by Peter Stuyvesant, the governor of this Dutch colony, involved a fear that the members of this group might become dependent and a burden to the Dutch settlers. This attitude is described by Baron as "revealing complete ignorance of the Jewish communal structure of the period . . . like 'carrying owls to Athens.'"[8] It would have been unthinkable for the Jewish group to countenance that any Jew be forced to

9

appeal for aid to outsiders, and particularly to the State or to other Church groups.* This sentiment was to persist long after the separation of Church and State and the availability of governmental assistance to all the population on a non-sectarian basis, and was abandoned with great reluctance by some professional leaders in the United States even in the 1930s.[9]

The small number of Jewish settlers in the Colonial period (it is estimated that there were less than 2,500 Jews in the population when the United States came into existence) carried on their own welfare activities. Jews, like members of other minority religious sects, did not participate in the welfare activities of the dominant Church-State, but were permitted to organize themselves for the welfare needs of the members of their faith.

A number of religious sects such as the Quakers were not welcomed or tolerated in several of the American Colonies, but the open and sparsely populated character of the early settlements did not impose complete segregation on minority groups. Nevertheless, the Jewish community assumed responsibility for mutual aid, continuing the biblical precepts, with their supernatural basis of authority, as interpreted and augmented by Talmudic Law.

Until the 1870s the limited number of Jews and the relatively favorable opportunities for the early settlers obviated any sizable problem of need requiring more complex forms of communal organization. Jewish immi-

---

* Voluntary agencies currently continue to meet some needs for which public aid may be available, when such aid appears to be inadequate or of inferior quality—especially in some forms of institutional care, such as in local almshouses and hospitals for the disabled. Over the whole of the 19th and into the 20th century, Jewish philanthropists were to express satisfaction and pride that there were few Jews to be found on the public charity rolls or in the public almshouses.[10]

grants to the United States until the 1880s were to come largely from Germany and the areas in central and eastern Europe under German domination, such as Bohemia, western Poland and the Austro-Hungarian Empire. Although Emancipation in Europe had opened the ghettos and relaxed some of the economic, political and social restrictions under which Jews in those areas had been living for centuries, the traditional religious practices and forms of welfare organization continued to apply for the large majority of Jews.

The disintegration of the closely knits *kahals* had begun in central and eastern Europe even before Emancipation, but the congregational unit remained intact. The *kahal* was no longer used as the instrument for the collection of state taxes from the Jewish population. However, Jews were authorized to establish religious communities, which had the authority to impose taxes for religious, benevolent and cultural purposes on all individuals who identified themselves as being of the Jewish faith. Thus in the 19th century, and up to the Hitler period and the destruction of Jewry and Jewish communal life, the *Kultusgemeinde* continued to collect taxes from all members of the Jewish faith for the support of the synagogues, ecclesiastical functions and schools, and for charitable assistance. (The limitation of these funds to and their primary use for the religious and cultural institutions gave rise at times, as in Berlin, to the establishment of voluntary groups and associations desiring to undertake charitable and benevolent projects.) [11]
These forms of communal association and benevolent attitudes influenced the character of communal organization of the dominant German Jewish settlers during the mid-19th century. Motives of mutual aid and

11

individual benevolence, the charitable and cultural responsibilities of the congregation and the creation of secular charitable activities[12] determined the pattern of welfare organization during the latter part of the 19th century and were the matrix out of which have been created the American systems of Jewish welfare organization in existence today.

The Jewish population in the United States remained small, increasing to an estimated population of 200,000 in 1880, with relatively little diversification in communal organization. Most communities had only one synagogue. As the population increased, there were additional houses of worship, arising because of differences in social class and economic status as well as through expanding areas of residence. Dissensions and schisms developed in the congregations in some of the larger centers of Jewish population. These schisms were presumably over doctrinal matters, such as a desire for more liberal forms of ritual, the desire to substitute English for the German language in the sermons, and the like. With changing economic conditions and the arrival of new immigrants not yet culturally adapted to the American environment, there began the diversification of groups which was to be found increasingly at the end of the 19th and through most of the first half of the 20th century.

JEWS FROM EASTERN EUROPE

The migrants from eastern Europe, principally from the Russian Empire under the czars, brought other aspects of Old World Jewish culture to influence the nature of Jewish communal organization in America. The processes of Emancipation had lagged in these countries, as Jews continued to be restricted to areas known as the

Pale of Settlement, and as the hostility of the surrounding population confined them to virtual ghettos. Here too the congregation and the synagogue were the dominant factors in the organization of charitable activities with a close adherence to the biblical injunctions of *Tzedakah,* reinforced by the necessity for mutual aid. With some exceptions, the Jewish communities of eastern Europe were relatively small and, while there were variations in individual economic and social status, the groups were generally homogeneous. Until the end of the 19th century, communication among these numerous towns and villages of the Pale of Settlement and with other parts of European Jewry was limited.

When Emancipation spread belatedly to eastern Europe, changes occurred in Jewish cultural life. Sectarian differences had arisen, and the Hasidim and other dissident groups set up their own congregations and synagogues. While the central or the large synagogue of the town may have continued as the officially recognized institution, groups of individuals were establishing their own separate associations (*hevras, minyans* and charitable activities). In the larger cities there were also secular benevolent societies.

The largest centers of Jewish population in eastern Europe, such as Warsaw with an estimated 77,000 Jews in 1866 and with more than 150,000 Jews in 1895, began to develop the more complex forms of metropolitan welfare organization with which we are familiar. According to Jacob Shatzky[13] religious diversity among Jews ranged from traditional Orthodoxy and Hasidism, to the more socially-motivated religious practices of the Maskilim and to complete assimilation. Internal migration had resulted in a separate Lithuanian colony among the Polish Jews of Warsaw. These factors plus economic class differentiation, the growth of a well-to-do class and the wavering and inconsistent attitudes of government officials, were responsible for a conglomeration of Jewish welfare agencies in Warsaw in the second half of the 19th century.

The officially recognized *kehillah* of Warsaw continued to function, collecting taxes from the wealthy and contributing some funds to the support of the Jewish hospital, the orphanage and the home for the aged, the free loan society and to other welfare efforts. But other sources of funds needed by these agencies exceeded the *kehillah* in importance. An agency paralleling the non-sectarian form of voluntary organization, which was to become a factor in meeting the welfare needs of Jews in America, was also to be found in Warsaw. Called the Philanthropic Society, it was organized by Christians but received support from wealthy Jews and served some of the poor of the Jewish faith. This development in welfare systems led some of the more assimiliated Jews to espouse the plan of turning over Jewish charitable efforts to non-sectarian auspices.

The growth of philanthropic institutions "not affiliated with the *Kehillah* [was] . . . so widespread . . . that they soon surpassed those that were, in scope, vitality and even in importance . . . [thus] the centrifugal trends in Jewish life in Warsaw led to an increasing decline in the role of the *Kehillah* as the focus of communal existence."[14]

We need to keep in mind this changing situation of European Jewish welfare organization in relation to the conglomerate and disorganized picture of welfare and charitable effort to be found in the large American cities, especially New York, during the first part of the 20th century. Deriving from many parts of eastern Europe, from numerous towns and villages, the newcomers began to organize multiple group activities in their new places of residence on the basis of *Landsmanschaft* (the association of immigrants from the same place of origin). Numerous synagogues, congregations, mutual aid and benefit societies were created even in small centers of Jewish population. In New York and in some other large cities they numbered in the hundreds.

These newer associations of East-European Jews added their number to the communal agencies built by Jews of the previous migrations. While the German Jewish benevolent and charitable agencies were available to the new immigrants, they were to prove unable for many years to bridge the gap which separated them from the host of mutual aid and benevolent groups established by the newcomers. Individual clients might cross the gap, but the mass of the immigrant population was to remain apart and even hostile for a considerable length of time.

THE INFLUENCE OF EUROPEAN IDEOLOGIES

The variations in basic attitudes and forms of communal organization among Jewish immigrants in the New World were in great measure influenced by European movements and ideas. Of these the most important were the Enlightenment (which followed the Reformation and opened the ghettos in western and central Europe) and the rise of socialism. The latter was to have a profound influence in the first three decades of the 20th century on the communal life of immigrant Jews in relation to the settled population.[15]

In the late 18th and the 19th centuries the effect of the Enlightenment was felt largely in the development of Reform Judaism, which added to Jewish sectarianism but did not change the congregational basis of organization for benevolence or the lay activities of members of the various congregations. It introduced, however, a larger measure of secularism into Jewish culture and opened up to Jewish groups a greater awareness and some degree of participation in the welfare activities of other population groups. Socialism, developing in Germany in the early 1800s, was espoused by some Jewish immigrants during the 19th century, but does not appear to have stimulated a mass movement among the German Jewish immigrants.

A more pronounced factor in communal organization was the development, at the end of the 19th century, of socialism and Socialist labor unions in eastern Europe. "In many ways," according to Baron, "socialism was to the Jew of the Russian Empire what Reform Judaism was to the Jew of the Western World. Both were ideologies designed to enable the Jew to escape from the medieval world and to participate fully in Western society."[16]

The immigration to the United States and Canada, before World War I, of over one and a half million Jews from eastern Europe brought individuals of varying allegiance to traditional Orthodoxy and to the religious movements of the 19th century. It also brought a considerable number who had come under the influence of socialism and the international labor movements. The result was the dispersion of these secular ideologies, especially among the concentrated Jewish settlements in New York and in a few other large cities. Forming their own political and economic associations, these immigrants came under the influence of anti-religious and anti-clerical doctrines. An ideology which stressed class conflict served to widen the existing division between the Yiddish-speaking proletarian newcomers and the native middle class among whom were many of the employers of the immigrants. In a short time this served to create antagonism on the part of many of the new immigrants toward the communal activities that had been set up by the German Jewish "bourgeosie" whom the former dubbed "Yahudim." The attitude of the newcomers toward native Jews "was that of contempt, distrust and hostility."[17] Orthodox Jews similarly were likely to be hostile toward Reform Jews, whom they considered "assimilationists" or worse.

After the first few years the new immigrants began to drift away from the welfare and educational services operated and maintained by the native Jews, organizing themselves into fraternal groups and labor unions.[18] Through cooperatives and through the labor unions they began to develop their own medical care, sanatoria, vacation agencies and Yiddish and Yiddishist recreational and cultural projects. (The latter-day descendants of these agencies can be seen today in the well-established programs of the labor unions in housing, unemployment compensation and pensions for retired and disabled. These pioneering efforts have had a profound influence upon union welfare projects and on governmental social insurance systems.)

Not only was there hostility on the part of the newcomers to native Jews but there was conflict and dissension among the immigrants themselves. These derived from divergent political and economic ideologies—between the Orthodox and the "freethinkers," the "nationalists" espousing Zionism, the Yiddish nationalists, the internationalists and other political sects flourishing in the thickly settled Jewish districts of the New World. Changing and improving economic conditions, Americanization and acculturation, the decay of socialism as a political movement, the emergence of Labor Zionism and acceptance by the majority of the State of Israel as a desirable *fait accompli*, has led by gradual stages to a rapprochement between the new immigrants and their descendants and existing communal welfare organizations.

There has been an easing of hostility as the second generation took on characteristics of the settled population in economic status, types of occupation and cultural practice. As the new immigrant population and its descendants grew to ten times the number of Jews of the older migration and began to occupy important roles on the staffs and the boards of the established agencies, hostilities eased and differences vanished. Vestiges of the old conflicts remain in the memories of the older members of the community and occasionally arise in communal affairs. The effects both of group hostility and conflict, and of the gradual easing of tensions, are some of the factors that have determined the trends in American Jewish welfare federations.

II

Forerunners of the
Jewish Welfare Federation

*I*t is clear, therefore, that Jewish immigrants came to the New World with a long history of community organization behind them and with ingrained habits of group living. Such association was essential for the practices of Judaism. It was also an essential for social and economic survival, especially in the New World in which they now settled. It was natural for immigrants upon arrival to associate with each other and with earlier settlers in order to create the organizations necessary for their religious and social purposes. In such association one might find the warmth and congeniality so important to a newcomer in a strange land. Only a rare individual preferred or could proceed to work out his adjustment in the new country without the help of other Jews. It was the exceptional immigrant who had detached himself from the religious or communal life before his migration and who now looked upon association with other Jews as unnecessary or unwelcome. Most immigrants came to their new homes through the assistance of or with the encouragement of earlier immigrants, and involvement in the group life of these friends and associates was a natural consequence.

The history of Jewish communal association is therefore a history of organized activities in behalf of recognized group interests and needs. Some group activities were traditional and spontaneous: for example, the practice of religious rites and observances and the pursuit of communal welfare programs which the members of an immigrant group carried over to the new land. Other activities grew out of new requirements, such as the need for mutual aid in getting settled and obtaining an economic foothold. Some of the essential needs of a group, such as that for a religious congregation, could be established, maintained, and developed by a relatively small number of newcomers. Other needs, such as resettlement of as yet unadjusted immigrants, or protection of civic rights, required a more mature population and a larger and more inclusive group membership.

COMMUNAL LIFE OF THE GENERAL POPULATION
DURING THE COLONIAL PERIOD

The initial settlements on the eastern seaboard were made by groups of people generally homogeneous in national origin and religious affiliation—such as Dutch members of the Reformed Church in New York, English Puritans in New England, French Catholics in Quebec, English Catholics in Maryland, and English Quakers in Pennsylvania. The communal life for many of these pioneer settlers was a blend of political and sectarian organization; there was no sharp distinction between the local parish or vestry and the political structure of the town. Ecclesiastical and political efforts combined to operate and finance the various communal services essential for the welfare and survival of the group.

With the intermingling of groups of immigrants from various lands and the arrival of new groups, difficulties were sometimes encountered in adjusting the communal structure to fit a heterogeneous group. Individuals from a different country of origin or adhering to a separate sectarian affiliation might be refused permission to settle, or might be expelled. Gradually some of these newer elements would be accepted with reluctance and, later, with the growth of industrial capitalism and a consequent shortage of labor, invited and welcomed to the Colonies.

The religious and cultural associations which the newer arrivals established were not incorporated into the official Church-and-State structure, but might be permitted to operate as voluntary groups, sometimes with a quasi-official, but more frequently on a non-official or voluntary basis. With diverse ethnic and sectarian populations in the newly opened territories, as well as in the growing towns on the eastern seaboard, the principle of free voluntary associations became an inherent aspect of American life.

These early developments accelerated the separation of Church and State, helped differentiate between civic and religious affiliation and emphasized the distinction between compulsory taxation for the support of government on the one hand, and voluntary contributions for the support of non-governmental activities on the other. The Constitution of the United States adopted in 1783 made the separation of Church and State a cardinal tenet of community life, the Church becoming a voluntary type of association. The distinction between voluntary and governmental structure was clarified, with the State involving all inhabitants, aliens as well as citizens, the non-governmental associations only those individuals who chose to affiliate.*

The national and religious diversities of the American population resulted not only in congregations and churches on a sectarian or national basis, but also led to numerous separate mutual aid and benefit societies, schools, colleges, hospitals and other welfare agencies. The first separate voluntary welfare association on record was the Scots Charitable Society of Boston, established in 1657 to help the sick and the poor and to provide burial for deceased countrymen. Other groups followed, such as the Episcopal Charitable Society of Boston (1724) and the Irish Charitable Society in 1737. The outstanding group with welfare functions in the Colonial period was the Society of Friends (Quakers) in Pennsylvania and other Colonies, which initially assumed care for members of its own sect but soon extended some of its welfare services on a non-sectarian basis.[1]

Similarly, the early Jewish settlers established congregational associations for religious, cultural, welfare, and other purposes in a number of American cities. Religious organization was of a unitary character—all the early congregations followed the Sephardic ritual. The Ashkenazi immigrants, due largely to their small numbers, were generally affiliated with these congregations, and it was not until the very end of the 18th

* Within the framework of voluntary association, new arrivals on the American continent could organize for religious, cultural and other group needs. The states did not assign any police or taxing power to religious sects or to other voluntary bodies. Neither did they interfere with voluntary association unless it was in conflict with the laws of the land or infringed upon the rights of other individuals or groups as defined by law. The laws of the states governing contracts could be invoked when difficulties or disputes arose in the relationships of members, but there was great latitude concerning compliance of individual members of a group with the rules and regulations of their associations.

22

century that the first separate Ashkenazi synagogue was established in Philadelphia.

The number of Jewish settlers was not large enough to establish a synagogue in many towns until the 1830s and 1840s when a considerable number of immigrants arrived from central Europe. At first, charitable effort was largely individual with the more successful and charitably-minded assuming communal responsibility. As synagogues were established, the giving of charity became a congregational responsibility.[2] Individual and mutual aid continued for many years to be based on ties deriving from the places of origin or from kinship, but increasing numbers led gradually to formal organization. Specialized forms of care were developed, in addition to the societies, for extending relief to needy individuals and families. The first Jewish orphan asylum was established in Charleston, S.C., in 1801. The Shearith Israel Congregation of New York City organized the Hebrew Benevolent Society, the first family welfare agency, in 1828.[3]

The establishment of voluntary welfare agencies under nationality or sectarian auspices, which began early in the life of the Colonists and grew to considerable magnitude in the latter 18th and early 19th centuries, did not however, supplant the governmental systems of poor-relief.[4] The cost of caring for the disabled, the mentally ill, and other long-term dependents, and the prevailing attitudes of harshness toward the poor, resulted in the almshouses and relief continuing as the basic methods of assisting the destitute and unfortunate until well into the second quarter of the 20th century. The general impression from the records of these early years of American history is that few Jewish poor were on public relief or became inmates of almshouses. The

23

strong traditions of mutual aid and group responsibility, as well, perhaps, as the small numbers and the generally satisfactory economic adjustment of the early Jewish settlers, made it unnecessary for them to depart from established group mores and resort to the public poor-relief systems.

Differences of religion and of national origin led to the creation of multiple voluntary philanthropic associations, resulting in a system of Protestant, Catholic and Jewish institutions. Protestants also established schools, colleges, hospitals, orphanages, homes for the aged, and similar institutions within each of the denominations— Episcopalian, Presbyterian, Methodist, Lutheran, Baptist and others. Toward the end of the 19th century the diversity of Jewish immigrant groups was to manifest itself also in a similar form of denominational sponsorship of agencies and institutions.

JEWISH COMMUNAL ORGANIZATION IN THE 19TH CENTURY— THE BEGINNINGS OF DIVERSITY

With the number of Jews in the United States, increasing only slowly from less than 3,000 at the beginning of the 19th century to about 225,000 in the next seventy five years[5] and spread thinly over most of the settled areas of the continent, there was no necessity for a complex form of communal organization. Where the group of immigrants was small and essentially homogeneous, a common religious interest or the need for an economic foothold or for leisure time association quickly led to the organization of group activities. In these earlier small Jewish communities with their sparse populations it was expedient for the entire group, whatever its diversities, to affiliate with the single existing congregation and to participate in the few other available types of group association.

As population increased and as marked differences appeared in economic and social status, a diversity of organizations and activities developed. Differences in the tempo of assimiliation to American life led to more elaborate forms of group activity. New arrivals, even of the same European background as the earlier settlers, began to find it more and more difficult to become integrated into the existing pattern of Jewish communal association. This condition became still more complex with the arrival of large numbers of immigrants of different national origins and different social and cultural habits. This stage was marked by increasing organizational diversity, the multiplication of congregational groups and the establishment of varieties of social, fraternal, mutual aid and cultural activity.

In the Jewish communal history of the typical Jewish community of Rochester, N.Y., Stuart E. Rosenberg depicts the establishment of the "German-Jewish Community" and later of the "East-European Community" which was in its initial stages (before 1890) relatively homogeneous in character. He describes the subsequent development as follows:

The diverse national origins of the East-European Jews, numbering, among others, the Polish, Russian, Rumanian and Galician groups, tended to stimulate the creation of a separate leadership for each national cluster. . . . As we approach the new century, we find the older foundations of Jewish community life slowly being replaced by a new social order. To a lesser degree among the German Jews, but perceptibly, nevertheless, the congregations of both communities were being surrounded on all sides by new and diverse societies. The total Jewish community was now less of a community than it had been before. It was a conglomeration of organizations.[6]

The normal overlapping of generations in a period of rapid cultural change forms the basis for a diversity of communal association which may persist for a long time in certain areas of interest, even for a population group which is homogeneous in other respects. If additional immigrants of the same background no longer come in sufficient numbers to maintain the original institutions, these may gradually die out or become displaced; the children of immigrant parentage begin to find less satisfaction in the congregations and other associations of their parents, and proceed to set up their own activities which differ markedly from the associations acceptable to their parents.

Thus we have seen the disappearance of many *Landsmanschaften*, fraternal organizations, relief agencies, and other activities which in their time exhibited a great deal of vitality. Also, through the processes of change and evolution, some of the initial institutions and agencies established by immigrants begin to adapt themselves to the needs and interests of succeeding generations.

MULTIPLICATION OF GROUP ASSOCIATIONS AND AGENCIES

By 1875 Jewish immigration was expanding. Official or other dependable statistics for the period before 1881 are lacking—but from that year until the outbreak of World War I there is a record of from 20,000 to over 150,000 annual immigration.[7] With this influx the number of Jews in the larger cities increased rapidly and a stage of complexity of group organization was reached where the need for coordination, at least in the field of local charitable effort, became obvious to the hard-pressed leaders in communal service. With the multiplication of congregations and synagogues there was a corresponding growth of relief societies, loan funds and other welfare agencies associated with the congregations, or established as secular agencies. Some Jewish agencies were created on the order of the newer types of social welfare programs which other sections of the general community were establishing to meet the needs of Christian immigrants.

The *Jewish Communal Register of New York City* in 1918[8] listed 3,637 separate Jewish organizations in that city for an estimated Jewish population of 1,500,000, or an average of one organization for each 410 individuals. The list included 858 congregations, 69 schools, 101 recreational and cultural agencies, 2,168 mutual aid societies and other economic agencies, 164 philanthropic and correctional agencies, and 277 other organizations.

Other large cities reported relatively fewer agencies; but cities with smaller populations in some cases reported as many as one organization for each 75 persons.[9] Many of the associations, especially in the larger cities, seemed to be unaware of, or indifferent to, the existence or operation of parallel activities. The instruments for coordination were generally lacking, with each separate agency operating in its own self-contained universe.

AN EARLY ATTEMPT AT NATIONAL ORGANIZATION

The complexities of Jewish communal life were primarily the result of the newer immigrants having come from a variety of national and cultural backgrounds. This situation was in evidence as early as 1840 and became intensified after 1880. The organization of the Board of Delegates of American Israelites in the year 1859, when the Jewish population was mainly from central Europe, is an example of group cooperation on

both the local and the national level. This "Board" was
formed as an agency "to bring about the union of American Israelites for their common welfare" so that it "would
not alone cooperate in directing government aid to the
rescue of their oppressed brethren from dangers and
persecution, but . . . through the medium of education,
would elevate the social conditions of Israelites in the
countries where the laws discriminated against them."[10]

The Board was founded as a union of congregations, but it disclaimed all ecclesiastical functions, and
concentrated on the protection of the civil and political
rights of Jews in the United States and abroad.[11] Most
of the activities of this organization were devoted to relieving the persecution of Jews abroad. At the same time
the Board mobilized the financial support of American
Jews for the relief of the victims of pogroms, of dis-
criminatory legislation and of disasters.

The function of the Board as "an agency for uniting American Israelites in self-defense," according to
A. M. Isaacs, was never "sincerely tested." The Board,
however, was called upon occasionally to remind the
federal and state governments of discrimination against
the religion of their Jewish citizens. The Board ceased to
exist in 1878, when its functions were assumed by the
newly organized Union of American Hebrew Congregations which established a standing committee, known as
the Board of Delegation on Civil and Religious Rights,
to carry on the purposes of the Board of Delegates.

During the two decades of its existence a number of
congregations in New York and elsewhere refused to
affiliate with the Board or to join it in specific programs,
because they feared domination by other congregations
with larger memberships or of a different tradition.[12]
Soon the growing diversity of congregational and re-

ligious life was to result in a number of parallel align-
ments of Orthodox and other denominational bodies, and
the formation in the 1900s of duplicate national agencies
concerned with civic and defense problems.

AMERICAN RELIEF OVERSEAS

There are also examples of cooperation within
American Jewry during the 19th century. These are
to be found in the record of aid to Jews abroad. The
distress of Jews in the Russian Empire under the czars,
due to restrictions, persecutions and bloody pogroms,
aroused sympathy in the American Jewish population
and a determination to help.[13] On previous occasions
they had sent relief to the Jews under stress in Persia,
Morocco and Rumania.[14] It was, however, the flood of
immigrants to the United States loosed by the Russian
terror that was responsible for the nation-wide response
of organized help. Generally speaking, the new immigrants were penniless and needed immediate aid; only
much later were there some who had retained a part of
their possessions.[15]

While at that time the "Jewish community as a
whole was not organized . . . the sense of obligation was
so strong that various groups combined to form a Russian Emigrants Relief Fund. . . . In many places Hebrew
Immigrants' Aid Societies were formed for receiving
the newcomers. . . . In the West and South great readiness was shown, especially on the part of the Independent
Order of B'nai B'rith, to welcome the newcomers and
introduce them to employers."[16]

With approximately 200,000 Jews coming to the
United States in the decade of the 1880s, the new arrivals
began to outnumber the settled population which was
hard pressed to supply relief, find jobs and improve the

immigrants' opportunities for employment by providing technical schools and English classes. After the dissolution of the emigrant societies, those in need were helped by the organizations for local charity—in the larger cities primarily by the United Hebrew Charities, which were organized in the 1860s and in subsequent years.

MERGERS OF RELIEF AGENCIES

Since the growing Jewish population developed varieties of group activity, organization for social welfare purposes in the larger communities become more and more complex. The first form of simplification of agency structure is to be found in the merger of two or more local Jewish welfare or relief societies. One of the first on record, the Society of the United Hebrew Charities,[17] the forerunner of the Jewish Welfare Society, was organized in Philadelphia in 1869—this was in the same year that the Charity Organization Society of London, England, was formed. Such organizations served as the prototype of similar organizations in the United States which became the source of much of the modern social work movement in this country and the ancestor of the family welfare agencies of today.

At the time of its organization (the Philadelphia Society of the United Hebrew Charities), there were a number of Jewish independent charitable societies in existence without any attempt at cooperation. This condition ... made for duplication of effort and waste, and encouraged a few to make the rounds of the various societies, imposing upon each in turn. A number of those active in relief work came to the conclusion that this situation should be remedied and efforts were accordingly made to bring about a union of the existing relief societies.

The following societies were represented at the meeting which adopted the plan of union: United Hebrew Relief Association; The United Hebrew Fuel Society; The United Hebrew Bene-

ficient Fuel Society, organized in 1841; German Ladies' Hebrew
Benevolent Society, organized in 1845; and the Ladies' Sewing
Society, organized in 1838.[18]

A similar merger of relief agencies formed the United
Jewish Charities of New York in 1874,[19] which united
two congregational relief societies, two agencies operating under secular auspices, a neighborhood relief organization and an agency providing fuel to needy
families. Other small relief societies later joined this
organization and the United Hebrew Charities (now the
Jewish Family Service Association of New York City)
became the principal agency in that city for the care of
the Jewish poor in their own homes. The movement for
the merger of small independent relief societies into a
unified welfare agency spread rapidly to other cities. It
is significant that these early efforts at consolidation of
Jewish charitable agencies preceded the first Charity
Organization Society (COS) in the United States, which
was established in Buffalo in 1877 on a non-sectarian
(but largely Protestant) basis.

The sponsors of the early "United Charities," or
"Hebrew Benevolent Associations," were largely from
central Europe, and primarily from the same social-
economic group. These mergers represented the coming
together of kindred elements engaged in a similar or related form of welfare work. Although the consolidation
of the relief efforts of the settled German Jewish group
resulted in the development of charitable programs of a
substantial character, the establishment of such agencies
did not interrupt the trend of the newer immigrants to
set up their own separate, small relief societies. At the
1906 National Conference of Jewish Charities, a speaker
from New York City stated that

... in the city of New York, East Side, we have from three to five hundred charitable organizations, some of which have fifteen members, and some of which have two hundred members. It has become a habit in New York of a great many who come from the cities, towns and villages in Russia to incorporate a relief association to relieve those that may come from the same place, and they never apply, or very seldom apply to the United Hebrew Charities. Their own neighbors, their own relatives, their own friends relieve them.[20]

Duplications of agencies giving charity to people in their own homes was not however paralleled in the various forms of institutional care. In most cities the population was not large enough, nor was its economic condition sufficiently favorable, to establish more than one hospital, home for the aged, orphanage, or social settlement. Duplicate agencies in this field came later, when the eastern European and Orthodox elements in the population began to sponsor institutions which were in effect a rejection of some of the policies or practices of agencies supported by the older elements. For many years the possibilities for the merger of agencies engaged in the same or related fields of service were limited to family relief agencies.[21]

The earlier mergers of relief societies did not result in federations, but merely in the consolidation of the several agencies which gave up their separate identities. Mergers were induced by the need for greater efficiency, by concern for the increase in the number of Jewish poor, and by a recognition that central rather than piecemeal efforts were required to cope with the poverty and destitution in this period, when the almshouse was the major help available from public funds. Federation, defined as a coming together of agencies which continue their separate existence and autonomy but cooperate for a common purpose—such as central fund-raising or city-wide planning—was a later development. It was first initiated in Boston and Cincinnati. The reasons for this development, its nature and its progress and the spread of the method to other cities are the subjects of the next chapter.

"TEMPLE ISRAEL"

III

The First Federations

The second half of the 19th century in the United States was a period of intensive economic development. Railroads were spanning the continent and were opening up new territories for settlement. Mechanical inventions and the factory system had replaced small scale handicrafts and there were new industrial giants in mining and manufacturing, oil production, railroads, and public utilities.

By the end of the century the best land of the frontier had been exploited and good cheap land was no longer available. Immigrants were crowding into the towns where they constituted the main source of labor for the burgeoning industrial system. Slums and tenements were increasing. The prevailing philosophy, "laissez faire"—which asserted that it was immoral and undesirable to interfere in any way with the "laws" of supply and demand, and which considered labor a commodity—frowned upon factory legislation and labor organization.

There was strong resistance to public or private charity for the employable and the members of their families, or to any other program that might reduce the competition for jobs among the laboring population. Poverty, disease and delinquency were the results, and periodic business depressions caused joblessness and misery, adding to the woes of the new immigrant population. There was a multiplicity of relief and welfare societies struggling unsuccessfully against the morass of destitution. But the prevalent fear that laborers might prefer idleness and the poor might prefer charity to employment and the arduous working conditions of that day made it impossible for the community to conceive of providing economic security even for the most "worthy poor." The limit of general communal responsibility was the "poorhouse," made as harsh and as uninviting as possible in order to deter "idleness and shiftlessness."

Toward the end of that period several movements were initiated which attempted to improve welfare organization. States began to establish boards of charities for the improvement of the public agencies and institutions—the first in Massachusetts in 1863. The Charity Organization Movement, which had begun in this country in 1877, was seeking an organized method of helping individuals and families in distress. By 1892 there were COS agencies in ninety-two cities. The social settlement movement for the cultural advancement of depressed slum and tenement areas, initiated in England, began in this country in 1886.

A National Conference of Charities and Correction (now the National Conference of Social Work) had been organized in 1873, and its leaders were attempting to develop a systematic approach to the problems of poverty and dependency. Out of these movements grew the forces of modern social work, with the welfare officials promoting the extension and improvement of

the public institutions, the COS group influencing the
movement toward coordination of welfare effort and the
individualization of treatment, and the social settlement
leaders (especially those associated with Jane Addams
and Hull House, established in 1889) beginning to
espouse programs of industrial and social reform. It was
to take several decades, however, for the liberal and
progressive spirit to be able to affect the dominant economic philosophy which made progress synonymous
with a policy of non-interference with the conditions
of labor and the wage system.[1]

The beginnings of modern social work in the
United States, of which the leaders of charitable agencies
under German Jewish auspices were aware and with
which a few were involved, had a profound influence
on Jewish welfare programs. There was, on the one
hand, the negative influence of the prevailing severe attitudes to poor relief; there was, on the other hand, the
influence of the more progressive forces responsible for
the rise of modern social work, with its firm belief in
the possibility of solving the problems of poverty and
its espousal of "scientific" methods to "help the poor
help themselves." The organization of the National Conference of Jewish Charities in 1900 was stimulated by
the success of the National Conference of Charities and
Correction, improvement in the treatment of individuals and families by the COS movement, and interest
in social reform by the settlement movement.

From the outset, at least one basic distinction existed
between the Jewish and the other voluntary systems of
welfare. Inadequate or niggardly as some of the assistance given by the Jewish agencies may have been at
that time, there was no doubt in the minds of the Jewish
welfare leaders that the care of the Jewish poor and un-

fortunate was the responsibility of the Jewish community and that helping the poor was a basic group responsibility. Centuries-old traditions of communal responsibility meant that individuals in need did not, as the last resort of poverty, have to turn to the public almshouse, but could rightfully expect help from other Jews.

THE FIRST FEDERATION

A primary reason for the establishment of the first Jewish federation was the growing number of Jewish immigrants and the consequently unprecedented increase in the need for charitable aid. Max Herzberg, president of the 1904 National Conference of Jewish Charities, described the situation as follows:

The last quarter of a century has made enormous demands on the means and energies of American Jewry in the efforts to aid those coming from foreign shores. Prior to that time, the Jew in America had no especial charitable problem. The number of Jewish poor was insignificant and it was a relatively easy task to help the few that appealed for assistance. The Jew in the almshouse was unknown; in the reformatory or prison a rarity. When, however, more than twenty years ago, Russia commenced that series of systematic persecutions which caused the Jews to leave their homes, and to find in America the refuge everywhere else denied them, the questions that confronted the Jews of this country began to assume huge proportions.[2]

At the first National Conference of Jewish Charities,[3] in 1900, its president, Max Senior of Cincinnati, pointed to the need for organization required by the new immigration:

During the last fifteen years, the demands for charitable purposes have grown to great proportions and call for the expenditure of sums which some years ago would have seemed fabulous. . . . Every possible form of distress had to be

provided for: poverty, sickness, incompetence; and an alien
population had to be put into accord with American life and
American ideals as quickly as possible. For these purposes the
loose, benevolent but spasmodic organizations of the past were
not equipped.[4]

Because of the rapid increase of the Jewish population, the simple, leisurely pace of helping an occasional
immigrant could not be maintained. New immigrants
were beginning to come more rapidly than the existing
relief agencies could cope with; nor could they expand
their facilities fast enough. Each of the agencies independently was compelled to intensify its efforts to secure
more adequate funds. Occasional solicitations among
prospective contributors and the annual charity ball
which had been adequate for obtaining charity funds in
the past were now inadequate; they had to be supplemented by a multiplicity of fund-raising devices and by
incessant appeals. Bazaars, special events, raffles, ticket-
selling and other methods of fund-raising then in vogue
became more and more frequent.

Some far-sighted leaders and generous contributors
with a well-developed sense of communal responsibility
became aware of the waste in these methods, both in
the duplication of appeals, and in the time and energy
of solicitors, who often were more needed for direct
service. These individuals hit upon a logical solution
for such problems: it was to bring together the various
agencies engaged in separate fund-raising and to concentrate on a single, annual, combined subscription appeal
in their behalf.

Federation owes its origin to a small group of
philanthropically-minded people of the older, settled
population who were concerned with the social prob-

lems and the poverty of the new immigrants from eastern Europe. The pioneer groups which came together to form a federation in Cincinnati and one in Boston consisted of representatives of the settled German Jewish population, who were engaged in fund-raising in behalf of the established agencies and were active in their leadership.

The Federated Jewish Charities of Boston was organized on April 29, 1895, becoming the first formally established Jewish federation in the United States. The original affiliated agencies included a general relief agency, a children's orphanage, a free employment bureau, a women's sewing society and a free burial society. The latter was the only agency in the group that had been organized by Jews from eastern Europe. The expenses of the first year of operation amounted to $27,628.[5] Cincinnati, which held its first federated campaign in 1896, has the distinction of being the first city to assume full responsibility for agency programs and for eliminating separate agency appeals.[6]

BASIC PROBLEMS OF THE EARLY FEDERATIONS

For the new and untried method, without American tradition (the community chest movement for the general population did not begin until 1914), there was at the outset the basic question of whether a single campaign could yield as much as the continuing multiple appeals. There was no guarantee that the proposed method would be effective and that the financial results would be rewarding. The proponents, however, had little doubt about the advantages of their project. From personal experience they knew that, when individuals are called upon frequently for contributions, they are likely to have an exaggerated idea of how much they had subscribed in the aggregate to the numerous appeals during the year.

The results of the first year's effort were impressive, vindicating the optimism of the federation founders.[7] But no one could tell whether the results attained in the first year, when much enthusiasm for the new method was generated, could be sustained in the ensuing years. Subsequent campaigns removed that doubt. Optimism in the pioneer cities was reinforced by the experiences of additional cities that were beginning to develop central fund-raising federations.

As the need for closer relationships among charitable efforts was being recognized, two different theories were put forward concerning the most desirable solution: (a) a central fund-raising federation for agencies which were to remain autonomous bodies, or (b) a consolidation and merger of the several agencies into a single organization. Since there was experience with mergers of relief societies, some were proposing that all charitable agencies should be centralized into one multiple-functioning organization. This was impractical for most of the larger cities, although later a comparable unitary structure was to be utilized in some of the smaller cities in which the term "federation" was applied to what was virtually a consolidation of existing welfare agencies.

In a subsequent period a number of communities with small Jewish populations such as Dallas and Camden were to organize "functional federations." These operated as a single body, engaged in the wide range of local welfare activities, including central fund-raising for local and non-local agencies.

The principles of federation rather than consolidation were, however, those which were chosen by all the large and by most of the intermediate-sized communities.

In a discussion, "Federation versus Consolidation . . . ," at the 1900 National Conference of Jewish Charities, Professor Morris Loeb of New York City clearly and forcefully supported the federation form of organization, and outlined proposals concerning the nature of its administrative structure and functions.[8]

INCREASE IN THE NUMBER OF FEDERATIONS

In 1904, less than ten years after the establishment of the first federation, the president of the United Jewish Charities of Cincinnati, Max Senior, was able to report to the National Conference of Jewish Charities:

The movement for federation or consolidation of Jewish charities according to the needs of the individual city may be fairly said to be a success. There is no longer any reasonable doubt about it. Every claim of those who have advocated it has been established; every objection of the doubter has been met; every prediction of the pessimist has proven false. Originating in my own city of Cincinnati,* it spread to Chicago, Philadelphia, Cleveland, St. Louis, Kansas City, Milwaukee and Detroit.[9]

But in spite of the enthusiastic testimonials of the early leaders of federation and the educational value of exchange of experience at national conferences, the movement grew slowly in some cities with substantial Jewish populations. In 1904 the cities which were considering, but had not yet organized, federations included, not only New York (which established its federation in

---

* It is interesting to note that as late as the year 1904 the Boston Federation and its claim of being the first federation was not recognized at the Conference. This was perhaps due to the fact that the Boston Federation was not a member and was not represented at the Conference. For the first several conferences Boston was represented only by its United Hebrew Benevolent Association, one of the beneficiaries of the Boston Federation. Another reason may be that other cities did not look upon the Boston project as a "true" federation since its function was limited to a general appeal for funds, largely to supplement the separate efforts of the individual agencies.

1917), but Baltimore (1907), San Francisco (1910), Los Angeles (1912), and Pittsburgh (1912).

Federating brought with it many questions of organization and policy, which were resolved only gradually. Because federation depended for its major source of funds upon an annual subscription, it was necessary to assure a contributor that his contribution would cover the total solicitation of the beneficiary agencies for their regular annual expenditures. Most federations therefore began by prohibiting their constituent societies from separate fund-raising through "any play, bazaar, raffle, theatrical benefit, outing, or other forms of entertainment for which tickets are offered for sale." While not allowed to solicit contributions for their annual maintenance costs, the agencies could accept endowments and bequests.

To assure success, the early federation had to find a method of soliciting funds that would reach a larger number of potential givers. It discovered what has proved to be a persistent problem, namely, that its hardest task is the solicitation of prospective contributors. The fund-raising campaign had to be organized; the informal methods of the past could no longer suffice. Louis Wolf, president of the Philadelphia Jewish Charities in 1904, stated that:

Where formerly this was done by a handful, it is now a part of the life of our community—it is everybody's business (of course the officers of the Federation principally) to see that everybody else is as large a contributor to the Federation as his means will permit.

In the larger cities the early federations began their activities with from six to eighteen constituent beneficiary societies. For example, the Philadelphia Federation reported in 1906 that it raised about $145,000, an increase of "50% over the old system." There were twelve beneficiary institutions, including the Jewish Hospital Association which operated a general hospital, a dispensary, a home for the aged and infirm, and a home for consumptives; the United Hebrew Charities (the merged family relief society); a Foster Home and Orphan Asylum; an Educational Society; the Orphan's Guardian Society (aid to dependent mothers); a Maternity Hospital; Seaside Home for Children; Immigrant Aid Society; a Young Women's Union for Care of Children; a Sunday School Society; the National Farm School at Doylestown. The Federation in that year also gave allocations to the Denver Hospital for Consumptives and to the local branch of the Alliance Israélite Universelle. However, "an independent hospital, an orphan asylum, and possibly six or eight independent relief societies" were not affiliated with the federation.[10]

While the organization of the campaign was the primary concern, it was not the only difficult problem which immediately faced federation. How and by whom were the funds to be distributed? Fortunately for the young federations, they were not confronted with the most difficult of all budgeting problems—the budgeting of a deficit. Economic trends were generally favorable, population was increasing, conditions were improving among the settled Jewish population, and federation campaigns began to show increases from year to year. Each of the beneficiary agencies was therefore assured of at least as much money as it had been able to collect through its own efforts the previous year. Getting as much as before was therefore a basic though unwritten guarantee to the beneficiary agencies. Indeed, the theory of federation would probably have joined the limbo of good but impractical ideas if in the early years less money had been raised and if the beneficiaries had not profited from an arrangement which some had been reluctant to enter. (In the depression of the 1930s a few recently organized federations in small cities were unable to withstand the sharp drop in income and were temporarily abandoned.)

But the distribution of the excess of income over amounts raised previously in unfederated appeals was not without its difficulties. Because the federation could exercise discretion in the allotment of its funds, it became by virtue of that very fact a policy and decision-making body able to affect the fortunes of its beneficiary agencies and the development of social welfare in its community. The distribution of the funds did not turn out to be as simple as one early federation president believed when he reported to the NCJC that: "Our Federation is supreme, there being no other means of obtaining money allowed. We have increased our allotments to the societies under our financial care, as our Board of Directors saw fit."

RELATION OF FEDERATION TO ITS BENEFICIARY AGENCIES

Many new problems were to grow out of this allegedly simple matter of fund distribution: what was to be the nature of the trustees on the federation's board; what might be the relationship and the different responsibilities and privileges of the federation and its constituent agencies; what were to be the relations of federation and agencies, respectively, to the contributor; should the agency receiving the funds retain complete autonomy in the matters of program and standards, or were such matters the responsibility of the federation as the trustee acting in behalf of contributors?

These and other questions arose from the fact that

contributors were not giving their funds directly to the constituent agencies, but to the federation as a central treasury and as a representative of these agencies.

Designation of contribution preferences as a device, occasionally attempted, proved unworkable and failed to satisfy the majority of the agencies and contributors. In most instances the federation operated on the principle that designations could not go beyond the reasonable budget of an agency. It was, indeed, rare for an agency under the system to receive as much as the total of its authorized budget from designated gifts.

The beneficiary agencies were the major influences on the character of the early federations and on the policies which were evolved. Many of the federations were individual-membership organizations, with all contributors eligible for membership and responsible for the selection of the board of trustees and for the administration of all federation functions. The actual conduct of affairs, however, was not in the hands of the contributors, due either to their indifference, or to the difficulty of devising procedures for broad participation of a large number of people. In a number of cities the beneficiary agencies, invited to form a federation, insisted on a major share in the management of the federation's affairs and fashioned their federation as an association of agencies. They then selected representatives to a governing body. The boards of such federations, however, were augmented by additional directors-at-large selected in theory by, or in behalf of, the contributors as members.

Where the views of the more active contributors rather than the agencies' views predominated, federation in some cities would exclude from its elected board individuals who were at the same time serving as officers or directors of a beneficiary agency. In some cities the presidents of the beneficiaries might be invited to participate as ex officio members of the board of federation.

Both before and after the rise of federations, the welfare agencies were deriving financial support from the charitable impulses of large groups of contributors; only the rare agency was ever fully supported by a small number of founders or adherents. The contributors enlisted by the agencies, or stimulated in larger numbers or for greater amounts by the fund-raising campaigns of federation, were not at that time conscious of the need for an organization which would extend beyond the practical financial needs of the charitable agencies. Aside from public fund-raising events, most contributors failed to express an interest in participating in the management of federation or beneficiary agency functions.

There was, therefore, general acceptance of the federation's purposes and confidence in the reputation of those chosen to administer its affairs, and few contributors looked upon federation as an instrument extending beyond the scope of its fund-raising functions. But the other potentialities of federations were implicit in the situation from the outset. Limited as the early federation may have been, it did constitute a central address in the community for a common function—that of charitable aid—a function of great importance to the Jewish population of that period.

Many contributors had no contacts with their federation beyond being solicited for and paying their pledges. Others, however, used the federation office as a central address in the community for referring client and group problems and for receiving criticisms and complaints of the work of the beneficiary agencies. Through these contacts with individuals in the community, federation was to become in time the central planning as well as the central fund-raising instrument for communal welfare services.

For the most part the early federation leadership, whatever its basis of selection, recognized that a broad degree of autonomy was essential to the effective administration of a beneficiary agency. One federation president who in 1904 saw a relationship between the federation movement and general trends, remarked that "this is the age of centralization, in finance, in industry, and in many other forms of activity, and a federation of charities is but in keeping with the spirit of the age." He recognized that federation

can exist only as long as it serves the purpose for which it is formed. It is intended to be a central body empowered to collect from the Jewish citizens of the community one common fund to be distributed amongst the institutions in proportion to their respective needs. It is not intended to interfere with the autonomy of existing societies nor to dictate their administrative policies. It is calculated to do away with the unhealthy spirit of business rivalry between societies, and to instill into the minds of the members of the community an interest in all of the organizations that together constitute the general plan of charitable endeavor.[11]

Another federation president, when asked "To what extent does the federation control the subsidiary organizations?" replied:

The federation has no control whatever in the management of the subsidiary organizations—each institution has its annual meeting, elects its own officers and conducts its affairs exactly the same as before the organization of the federaiton. The only actual control the federation has is that no addition in the way of new buildings or any other addition or additions to those already occupied, or any other means used to increase their annual expenditures (of course endowed gifts are excluded), can be made unless authorized by the federation.[12]

The character of federation-agency-contributor relationships was being changed through the new experiences which derived from the work of federation. More money was being raised, thereby convincing most of the constituent agencies of the solid merits of the new method. It was generally reported that the cooperative spirit was growing among the agencies and between them and the federation. One enthusiastic president reported that "Federation, or consolidation, has so harmonized the work that each subsidiary organization works in conjunction with all others toward a common end. A spirit of unity and fellowship has taken the place of the petty bickering and feeling of rivalry which too often prevailed among the small societies."[13]

The methods of charity administration were considered strengthened: ". . . it is but natural that, with increased funds, the character of the work has improved and its scope widened. No progressive constructive work can be done when funds are not secure, and when the anxiety about raising money diverts the minds of directors from their legitimate activities in caring for the poor."[14]

Beneficial effects of a developing general communal interest were also noted. "Contributors recognize that they do not support only one or the other charitable institution, but have an interest in all forms of endeavor which aim to raise their fellow men. The evidences of the broadening spirit are numerous and gratifying."[15]

But the "gratifying" results did not, at first, extend to all segments of the community—either the contributors or the constituent agencies. Federations in some cities reported the lack of response to their solicitation for funds from well-to-do Jews from eastern Europe and the reluctance of charitable agencies recently established by such groups to federate with similar ones administered by the German Jewish group.

GROUP CONFLICT AND FEDERATION STRUCTURE

During the early years of federation, the lack of rapprochement between the mass of eastern European Jews and the smaller group of the settled and wealthier Jewish population from western Europe was a perennially unsolved aspect of Jewish life. In 1908, Professor Jacob Hollander of Baltimore described the situation which had developed after the East-European migration that resulted from the pressures of intense anti-Semitism, pogroms and massacres:

"Assistance was no longer claimed as a fraternal right and extended as a kin-like obligation" as had been the prevailing motivation of the earlier charities when the newcomers were of the same national origin and cultural background. The call for assistance had represented "the imperious demand of stricken humanity." Professor Hollander continued:

But, as the situation lost its bitter novelty and the burden settled in onerous pressure, benevolence waned and something much akin to patronage grew. The charitable association became no longer a semi-social device, whereby the more prosperous members of the community relieved the misfortunes of neighbors and associates, but a tax-like charge for the indefinite relief of the misery and dependence of a distinct class, different in speech, tradition and origin, unsought in arrival and unwelcome in presence, whose only claim was a tenuous tie of emotional appeal and an identical negation in religious belief.

It was inevitable that this should be reflected in the conduct of the institutions. Complying to the letter with the requirements of the beneficiaries, there was yet neglect of the more subtle psychological elements; it made the Russian Jew, and later, his Rumanian or Lithuanian confrere, a troublesome beneficiary of German Jewish charity. What he received was given him, too often, neither in the form to which he was accustomed nor in the spirit to which he was entitled. The hungry were fed, the naked clad, the sick were served, but incomparably more regard was paid to the material than to the intangible elements in the situation.[16]

The new immigrants did not remain for long a destitute class unable to overcome the immediate handicaps of migration. In New York City, where the largest mass of new immigrants was concentrated, the great majority of the newcomers soon possessed sufficient initiative and economic competence to establish their benefit and loan societies, their agencies for aid and shelter of the newer arrivals, their orphanages and homes for the aged, and to establish the first hospital in the United States under Orthodox Jewish auspices (Beth Israel, in 1890). In a short period of time, the immigrants from eastern Europe were establishing welfare agencies and institutions in other cities as well.

The older sections of the Jewish population for a long time considered these developments unnecessary duplications—indeed, evidences of ingratitude—rather than admirable examples of self-help. Professor Hollander, however, took a different view—that these separate and independent efforts were the natural consequence of the lack of understanding and full acceptance of the newcomers by the native Jews.[17]

With this development of parallel and duplicating agencies, the need for a more inclusive type of federation was evident. Professor Hollander advocated objectives which were to become realities fifteen years later in a number of cities.

The logical and rational development of communal Jewish activity is in the direction of an arrest of further duplication of downtown, no less than of uptown, institutions, and the unification or integration of all the charitable efforts of a community wherever located or however constituted, in that federated form which, while giving free play to individual energy and enthusiasm, will still make paramount the collective responsibility and the common concern.[18]

The cultural gap between those who administered the communal relief funds and the recipients of charity, and the patronizing attitude of some federation leaders towards the new immigrants were formidable obstacles to the popularity of the philanthropic efforts of German Jewry in the eyes of a number of new immigrants. They were important factors in delaying the attainment of satisfactory relationships with the East-European elements of the Jewish population. A discussion at the Conference of Jewish Charities in 1900, on whether dependent immigrants did or did not have the right to refuse to work on the Sabbath, illustrates one aspect of the cultural gap which took many years to resolve. "They must change their habits," said one speaker. "I do not think I can condemn a man for observing his Sabbath," was the rejoinder by another welfare leader. Failure to respect and understand the cultural habits of newly arrived Orthodox immigrants was also evident in other aspects of the situation.[19]

A growing sympathy for and understanding of the philanthropic activities of the immigrants from eastern Europe was indicated in a 1923 report on Jewish communal organization in America prepared by a group of executives, with Solomon Lowenstein, the executive of the New York Federation, as chairman. This report stated that:

The new immigration was essentially sound and self-respecting. It was not a pauper class but rather a pioneer group driven into exile but determined to take the fullest advantages of the opportunities of their new home. Thus we find the creation of new forms of associations either on a neighborhood geographical foundation or on a conception of more independent forms of helpfulness. The Hebrew Free Loan Society, Free Burial Societies, Chevroth of various types, the Hachnosas Orchim . . ."

Of chief importance, however, in the minds of the newcomers, were those agencies meeting either their direct religious needs or conditions by their peculiar (*sic*) religious desires. In addition to the synagogues . . . the school for religious instruction constituted an important and immediate form of expression. Moreover, the profound convictions in the conduct of orphanages, hospitals, homes for the aged, etc., with regard to the dietary or other religious requirements of the eastern Jews were such that as soon as their financial condition permitted, they undertook the establishment of such institutions, conducted perhaps not with the same degree of technical efficiency as the older agencies, but more nearly in accord with their own desires.[20]

The limitations of the early federations and the difficulties of establishing relationships with the new welfare agencies of the East-European group is illustrated in a survey of Jewish philanthropic organizations of a large eastern seaboard city made by the Field Bureau of the National Conference of Jewish Charities. (For excerpts from this unpublished report see note 21.)

ECONOMIC BASIS OF GROUP CONFLICT

It was not only the differences in national origin and religious practice that created the cleavage between older and newer immigrants. Many of the older immigrants had become the employers of the new group, and the prevailing conditions of low wages, intermittent unemployment, sweatshop conditions, lack of labor organization, and other difficulties acted to intensify class feeling. Elbogen[22] states that:

The preponderant majority of immigrants were tailors or other needle workers; these found and accepted work under wretched sweatshop conditions . . . Scarcely had the newcomers disembarked when they were eagerly seized upon, but their pressing need and their unfamiliarity with conditions were mercilessly exploited . . . they were forced to work endless hours under murderously unhygienic conditions for starvation wages.

While the Jewish and other welfare agencies were trying to help some of the immigrants to improve their physical conditions, they were oblivious to the economic questions involved. They tended to accept the condition of the labor market as a fixed element in the social forces of the community.*

In a report on "The Russian Jew and Charity," Harold Silver describes these conditions:

. . . organized labor (New York) objected to charity agencies on two counts: (1) the men at the helm of the agencies were hostile to labor; and (2) the agencies, particularly the Baron de Hirsch Fund and the (N. Y.) United Hebrew Charities, furnished strike-breakers and cheap labor to employers, thus undermining the union and lowering the wage standards. A considerable collection of instances and individual experiences are brought forward to substantiate these accusations.[23]

The conflicts and strains were gradually eased, however, and the social welfare leaders of the period began to learn that an effective relationship based upon a more sympathetic understanding of the cultural patterns of the new arrivals was possible.

Even as early as the last decade of the 19th century we find quite definite indications of a better understanding between the

* Later, the spirit of social reform was to permeate the ranks of the professional workers as they began to recognize that sweatshop labor and other substandard economic conditions were not fixed but were subject to social action and social improvement.

Russian and German groups and even some cooperation in charitable work, both by Russian Jews joining the existing agencies as individuals and by the two groups jointly forming new organizations.

There were three logically distinct steps that led up to this better mutual understanding between the two groups. There was, first, a realization on the part of the Russian Jews of some of their shortcomings; secondly, an appreciation of the values of organization and system that the German agencies possessed; and thirdly, a friendlier and more sympathetic attitude on the part of the German group toward the psychology, needs and struggles of the newer arrivals. While these steps can be distinguished logically they did not, of course, follow in that sequence chronologically. Nor is it to be assumed that the misunderstandings and prejudices of the two camps ceased at this point and an "era of good feeling" began.[24]

Some part of the credit for the gradual improvement in group relationships was attributed to the emergence of the professional social worker as an element in the administration of Jewish charities, as well as to the acceptance of the concepts of humanitarianism and of the value of the individual which were beginning to permeate American social work. In 1918, Felix M. Warburg, in an address to the National Conference of Jewish Charities, stated:

The social workers have wiped out class feeling in groups where such a thing seemed to be impossible. Take our large cities, and some of you may be aware of many of the divisions that existed between the Russian Jew, the German Jew, the Oriental Jew, and oh, there are so many varieties, and all of them had prejudices against the other type. These times of friction have gone. In our recent New York Federation drive all of them worked together.[25]

Progress in improvement of relationships was not rapid. In some communities it took a new generation to overcome ingrained prejudices. Cleavages in some cities persisted for sufficient time, not only for the emergence of a duplicate series of welfare agencies, but for the creation of "downtown" federations (e.g., in Chicago and Baltimore). In Baltimore the older group had established its federation in 1906, to be followed a year later by a separate "downtown" federation of the newcomers. It was not until 1921 in Baltimore and 1923 in Chicago that merger of the "downtown" and "uptown" federations could be effected.

Even when no competing East-European federation existed, representation of the newer elements was extremely limited, although one or more agency established by the eastern Europeans might be part of the central federation. A survey of a large city federation was still to find in 1923 that its "Executive Committee includes no one who might be said to represent the Orthodox group in the community, or the institutions established by the Orthodox group."[26]

As a better spirit began to prevail, and some representatives of the newer immigrant groups were being chosen for federation boards, the planners faced more directly the question of extending federation to the non-affiliated agencies established by the immigrants from eastern Europe.

There are two viewpoints among Jewish social workers. One is that these organizations, because they are generally substandard, and because they are inadequate in facilities and in funds, should either be put out of business or absorbed in the larger activities of the federation in this same field. The other viewpoint is that such organizations ought to be permitted to continue; that when there are a number of such Orthodox institutions, they might even be federated in a separate federation, and that ultimately, when the Orthodox group has learned through the expedient of necessary experience, then and only then, should these institutions be offered a place in the general Jewish federation.[27]

The conclusion reached by the speaker, however, was that

A *modus vivendi* can be and must be worked out. We must not only harmonize our charities, but must weld them into a strong and consistent whole, so that they become an instrument of real power.[28]

The view of agency inclusion in the existing federation, rather than the intermediate step of a "downtown" federation, prevailed. Communities differ, even today, in the extent to which such full federation has been achieved. In some cities it is complete or virtually so, in others more progress is still required. The fact that a considerable number of the earlier, small, private relief, benefit and mutual aid societies have disappeared, due to the broad development of public assistance and the general economic improvement, has facilitated the process, as has the dwindling of the need for orphanages for dependent children.

It was perhaps this latter factor which finally resulted in the merger of child care agencies. One such occurred in Chicago in 1942, when the Marks Nathan Orphan Home under Orthodox auspices was merged with the Jewish Children's Bureau, which included an institution for dependent children established by the German group. Both institutions had been beneficiary agencies of the Chicago Federation since its inception. However, in a few of the larger cities, an occasional hospital, orphanage or home for the aged still remains unaffiliated with the local federation.

A 1923 EVALUATION OF FEDERATION

After more than a quarter of a century of experience the results of federation were evaluated in the 1923 report of a committee of the National Conference of

Jewish Social Service. The report summarized the successes and limitations of the movement up to that time:

In the opinion of your committee, it can fairly be claimed that the federations have been successful in improving the financial methods of our communal agencies in securing a larger measure of support and a more intelligent, just and efficient distribution of the funds thus realized. It may also be fairly claimed that as a direct result of the federation movement, there has come about improved standard of the work of the various constituent organizations, amplifications of the content of their work and an expansion of the fields of activity.

It cannot be said so surely that the federations have shown themselves to be resourceful in meeting new needs, in initiative in the establishment of new organizations to solve questions insistently presenting themselves, in enlisting the efforts of existing agencies, nor providing reserve or capital funds for the rehabilitation of antiquated plants or the construction of new institutions. Nor have they been altogether happy in their efforts to secure the hearty cooperation and active participation of all the elements making up the Jewish body politic.[29]

The report did not claim for federation sole credit for the improvement of standards and for the development of professional social work in the affiliated agencies:

Contact with non-Jewish agencies, offering in many instances examples of superior method and wider vision, . . . the development of a class of professional social workers, . . . [have] been a direct influence in the development of Jewish social work. The increasing interest in social questions . . . has been shared by Jews and non-Jew alike and has much to do with the improvement of the techniques of our various agencies.[30] *

The chief cause of failure to create a comprehensive federation [is attributed to the] lack of understanding and congeniality between the different national groups within the community.[31]

There was also an awareness at that time of the broader needs of the Jewish community and of the

* See note 31 for other excerpts from this report.

problem of finding a structure of organization that would encompass these needs and create a basis for full cooperation. Some experiments in new organization had been made, as in the New York *Kehillah* (terminated in 1922 —see below, chapter IV). A few of the larger cities were experimenting with what was called "District Service," an organization of services and agencies under federation auspices on a smaller geographical basis than that of the federation itself. Also in some smaller communities, Jewish Centers were seeking to enlist the participation of many groups and stimulate interest in programs that were more extensive than the traditional recreational and cultural services of the Ys and Settlements. None of these developments seemed at the time to give full assurance of achieving the aims of comprehensive community welfare planning.

It is the definite opinion of your committee that the federation represents but a stage in our communal development and not the final form. What that form may be, it is impossible at this time to forecast.[32]

IV

The Development and
Growth of Federations

ABSORBING THE IMMIGRANT FLOOD

*L*arge scale immigration during the first two decades of the 20th century was the determining element in
the character of Jewish communal life and in the problems
and programs of federations. The Jewish population increased nearly fourfold between 1880 and 1900; by the
turn of the century it was estimated that the number had
reached one million, and more were arriving year by
year, to result in a fivefold increase in Jewish population in less than fifty years. Nearly one and one-half
million Jewish immigrants had come by 1914, at an
average rate of 150,000 annually. World War I, however, shut off the main sources of Jewish immigration
and only 75,000 Jews entered the United States between
1915 and 1920.

There was a substantial rise in Jewish immigration
for a few years in the early 1920s. In 1921 nearly 120,000
were admitted, and an average of 50,000 came annually

for the next three years. But by 1924 highly restrictive quotas, based on national origins, sharply curtailed Jewish immigration until a low point of approximately 2,000 was reached in 1933. Thus, except for the refugees of the later 1930s and 1940s (on a greatly reduced scale in comparison with the past), the historical era of Jewish immigration to the United States ended in 1925.[1]

During the years of heavy influx, federations and their agencies were concerned with the problems of absorption. Little governmental assistance was available even for the settled population for most of the period, and immigrants who received public aid within the first five years of their residence faced the threat of deportation. If these newcomers struggling to integrate themselves into the economic and social life of the country were to get help it had to be provided through voluntary sources.

Even though those were, on the whole, years of expanding American economy, arrested only by brief periods of recession, gaining a foothold was a difficult task for most of the immigrants. For those were also years of intermittent and irregular employment for Jews in the needle trades—with their seasonal layoffs and substandard earnings. Mechanized industry was demanding more skills than those which many immigrants had brought with them. It was, moreover, the period of generally low wages, lack of labor legislation and unregulated sweatshop and tenement industries. Women and children in many of the families labored in unsupervised home industries to eke out a minimal, harsh existence.

Most of the needy immigrants received help from friends and relatives or from the group benefit societies which the immigrants themselves established for mutual aid. The burden of assistance not available from such sources fell upon the organized relief societies. New relief organizations therefore mushroomed in the larger cities, even where there had been an earlier merger of relief agencies. There was at first little central planning, clearance, or communal awareness. Gradually the central family service and relief agency maintained by the federation began to be accepted as the basic agency to which the immigrant could turn when he found himself in need.

IMPROVING THE SOCIAL WELFARE PROGRAMS

The methods of giving relief, although motivated by the best charitable impulses, were at first primitive and unstandardized. The volunteer officers of the agency would meet as a group and interview the prospective clients, listen to their stories, and give or withhold assistance on the basis of prejudice and sentiment. The inadequacy of such a method of dealing with family needs was being recognized in the general social welfare movement of the period.

The established Protestant sectors of the community had founded the first Charity Organization Society in Buffalo in 1877. This movement was trying to understand the causes of poverty, while attempting to organize the formal and informal sources of material help needed. The main advance in methods of helping the poor was in the development of personal and individualized service in place of the routine impersonal procedures then in vogue. In spite of an only rudimentary recognition of the basic economic and social factors in poverty, and a negative attitude toward the organization of specific measures of supplying income to families without adequate breadwinners, the COS move-

61

ment was to play a substantial role in the improvement of social welfare work.

The pioneer leaders of Jewish charities were responsive to the new ideas of personal service which the charity organization societies were stimulating. In 1900, Max Senior paid tribute to these influences on Jewish welfare programs:

The admirable work of such bodies as the National Conference of Charities and the New York Charity Organization Society has not failed to leave its impress upon us. Through the length and breadth of the land the conviction has spread that better methods of administering charity must prevail; that above all else the manhood of the poor must be recognized, and every effort made not to break down character. The introduction of this idea into Jewish charity work has called for almost a revolution of methods. Open-handed but indiscriminate alms-giving and a cordial but unthinking welcome to the stranger within your gates have ceased to be the be-all and end-all of charity. It has come to be recognized that personal service is the cornerstone of true charity, and that a new system and new methods must be built around and upon it.[2]

American social work was not only emphasizing better methods of individual help, but was beginning to turn to social reform to solve the adverse economic and social conditions which were pressing with the greatest severity on the immigrants. These were the days of the initial steps in industrial and civic improvement, in the development of labor standards and safeguards against epidemics, accidents, and excessive exploitation of labor.

In 1908, Dr. Lee K. Frankel, then the executive head of the United Jewish Charities of New York City, acknowledged the influence of Christian social work and social reform.

We Jews must begin to realize that it has been left to non-Jews to bring to our notice—to us, the people with the wonder-

ful Mosaic legislation back of us—our duties along the line of
that brighter, nobler, higher philanthropy, which means care of
your neighbor; which means prevention of disease; which
means protection against vice; and the prevention of the exploitation of labor. We Jews have had to be taught during the
last twenty-five years by our Christian neighbors how to proceed along the lines of modern advances in philanthropy. If
there have been improvements in tenement-house legislation (I
speak of New York), it has not come from the Jewish landlord
on the East Side. If there has been legislation forbidding the
working of children and women in factories, it has not come
through the initiative of the Jewish employer of labor. In all
these constructive activities the Jew has followed in the wake,
and has not been the leader, which his training and heredity
should have taught him to be.[3]

It was not long, however, before the Jewish relief
agencies were to equal and, in some aspects, surpass the
Christian agencies in the care of the poor. A readiness to
collect a communal fund for relief needs in contrast to
the more prevalent practice of the charity organization
societies in trying to organize assistance separately for
each family—exclusively from among his relatives,
friends, societies, church groups and other sources—was
an outstanding difference between most of the Jewish
and the general charity organization societies.[4] The Jewish relief agencies were rapidly accepting the validity of
most of the policies then called "scientific" charity. What
was generally meant by that term was that it was not
sufficient to continue to provide needy and destitute
families with doles, but that an effort must be made to
discover the causes of their poverty and to use imagina-
tion to work out a constructive solution of the family's
economic difficulties.

While it was obviously impossible for the social
welfare agencies at the time to cope with the larger
problems of dependency inherent in the shortcomings

of the economic system, there were vigorous movements on the part of labor and liberal elements for economic and social reform. For the most part, however, the social agencies, Jewish and non-Jewish alike, contented themselves with undertaking the more limited programs and services within their means. Included in such services were job-finding efforts, workrooms for the unskilled (especially for women), vocational training schools, medical services and educational programs.

PIONEER RESETTLEMENT PROGRAM

Though the Jewish welfare work of the period followed rather than led in creative social welfare advance, it does have several substantial pioneer efforts to its credit. Among these a program for the reception and resettlement of immigrants was noteworthy for its scope and scale of organization.

Out of the efforts to cope with the economic problems of the early migration came the Industrial Removal Office, the IRO. This organization was founded in 1900 as a result of the growing interest in alleviating the general distress of the congested East Side of New York. Initiative for the movement—to relocate immigrants from port cities to the interior of the country—resulted from the interest of leading Jewish philanthropists, and the program was established with the help of the Baron de Hirsch Fund which sponsored and supported the project.[5]

The organized federations throughout the country assumed responsibility for helping the individual or family sent by the IRO to gain a foothold in the larger interior communities. The fraternal Order of B'nai B'rith, a national service organization with local lodges, helped the transferred people in the smaller communities.

The outbreak of World War I and declining immigration resulted in the practical cessation of the work of the IRO (it was finally terminated in 1922); but the program had been an important factor in increasing the Jewish population of many of the communities in the interior of the country. The IRO can also be credited in part with fostering the development of federations, particularly in the Middle West and South.[6]

LONG-TERM PROBLEMS OF IMMIGRANT ADJUSTMENT

Though most of the immigrants who needed help soon after arrival were quickly able to become independent and self-supporting, long-term problem cases were beginning to accumulate.

In 1900 Morris Goldstein had tabulated 200 successive applications for assistance to the United Jewish Charities of Cincinnati. He found that 25% involved sickness, 15% unemployment, 10% physical defect or old age, 10% desertion and 5% death of the wage earner. He compared this group of clients with statistics of several non-sectarian charity organizations, finding in the Jewish group a higher percentage of sickness and accident, of physical defect or old age, of desertion and of cases where there was found to be "no need of assistance." There were smaller percentages of lack of employment, shiftlessness or intemperance (20% in the non-Jewish statistics). Mr. Goldstein reported that he could find no case of intemperance in the 200 cases mentioned above, and that in the previous four years he had found only one habitual alcoholic among 1,900 applications.[7]

The United Hebrew Charities of New York in 1905 analyzed their relief disbursements as follows:

28.3% to widows and children
14.6% to deserted women
17.2% to consumptives
21.2% to other forms of illness
3.7% to applicants over 60 years of age
15.2% for other causes.[8]

These statistics would seem to point to the fact that, except for periods when immigrants were suffering from initial or temporary unemployment, federation relief agencies were a resource used largely by immigrants afflicted with long-term illnesses of the breadwinners and by families impoverished through death or desertion.

The Jewish agencies began to direct attention to the problems which were making for recurrent and for long-term dependency. Tuberculosis of the breadwinner[9] was associated with poor living conditions and rife among workers in sweatshops. It was for many years considered the main scourge afflicting the immigrant; and it stimulated the establishment of national and local Jewish hospitals for the tubercular.

Family desertion also seemed to be connected with the difficulties of immigrant adjustment. A number of men who had left wives and children in Europe were either unable or unwilling to send for their families. The husband upon arrival in this country sometimes made a new attachment which he was reluctant to give up. In some instances the deserted wife was brought over by her friends and relatives rather than by the offending husband. At times separation resulted from incompatibility after the wife's arrival.

Another widely recognized problem was that of child dependency. Some of the relief agencies were at first unable to find a desirable plan of service for the widow or the deserted wife with young children. It was felt that such women were handicapped in many ways in rearing their families, yet there was a general reluctance or inability to furnish sufficient and continuing relief so as to maintain a functioning household. The prevalent attitude resulted in the transfer of many of the children of widows or deserted wives to the orphanages.

TUBERCULOSIS

Programs to ameliorate or solve these conditions were to arise out of the newer concepts of social welfare. The National Jewish Hospital for Consumptives (now the National Jewish Hospital) was organized in 1899 and established in Denver, where the climate was then considered especially suitable for the treatment of the disease. The German Jewish philanthropic leadership and the B'nai B'rith were mainly responsible for this development. It was followed by the Jewish Consumptive Relief Society, which was organized, also in Denver, in 1904 by representatives of the East-European group; and by the Jewish Consumptive Relief Association organized in the vicinity of Los Angeles in 1912. Both these last-named institutions were supported by Jewish immigrant labor groups. The Los Angeles effort was ascribed to a variant in the climate "theory" for the treatment of tuberculosis, as well as to variations in labor ideology among the supporting groups.

Clients suffering from tuberculosis were being sent for treatment to these national institutions by the relief agencies; other patients were finding their own way to these hospitals. It was at first the practice of some of the federations to send on to Denver the wife and children of the tubercular husband, on the assumption that, if the patient were sufficiently recovered to leave the sanatorium, it would be preferable for him and for his family to remain in what was considered to be a more salubrious climate. There were arrangements between the sending community and Denver for the financial support of such families. It was not long, however, before the necessity of a specific climate for the tuberculous was questioned. Federations and special groups began establishing local sanatoria, and the practice of sending families of tubercular patients to Denver was gradually discontinued.

New York City established a sanatorium at Bedford Hills as a part of the Montefiore Home and Hospital for Chronic Diseases, in 1897; Chicago founded the Winfield Tuberculosis Sanatorium in 1908, Baltimore the Jewish Home for Consumptives in 1907. Most cities, however, continued to utilize the national hospitals. Local communities also continued to develop hospitals, dispensaries and outpatient services for the general treatment of the sick, with special clinics for the tuberculous. The most comprehensive non-institutional program in this field was developed in New York City with the establishment of the Committee for the Care of the Jewish Tuberculous, in 1913, which provided clinical, preventive and aftercare services, including special work opportunities (the Altro Workshop) for arrested cases unemployable on a full-time basis in regular industry.

FAMILY DESERTION

Family desertion was considered under the law a local problem, with the deserting husband guilty of a misdemeanor. This made it impossible to extradite deserters located in another state. Locally, moreover, the penalties for family desertion were minor and ineffectual. Successful efforts were made by social agencies to have child abandonment defined as a felony, subject to more drastic correctional treatment, including extradition of the husband across state boundaries. At first, help to the deserted family involved a mixture of harsh attitudes, reluctant and inadequate assistance to wives, and the placement of children in orphanages.

To deal with the problem of desertion, federations and local Jewish relief agencies cooperated in the establishment of the National Desertion Bureau (now the Family Location Service). The Bureau, set up in New York City in 1914, served as a clearing house for the registration of families left destitute by the desertion of the breadwinner. Through a national network of correspondents the Bureau was frequently able to bring information concerning the missing husband to his family, and to the agency supporting the family, and to assist in efforts toward family reunion.

THE TRANSIENT

Large-scale Jewish immigration had also intensified the problem of transiency, both of unattached individuals and of entire families, from city to city across the United States. The federations which accepted responsibility for local dependents were unwilling or in some instances unable to accept responsibility for extended assistance to such applicants. There was a widespread tendency to "pass on" migrants to other communities or to attempt to send them back to their original city of residence. Passing on of transients led to conflicts between communities as to which city was to be considered obligated to help the needy transient.

A solution was approached through the establishment, by the National Conference of Jewish Charities, of a committee to deal with the problem and through a "Transportation Agreement" in 1900 which adopted standard policies and regulations for achieving equity among the various local federations and charitable agencies. In disputed cases a Conference committee made decisions which the signers of the Transportation Agreement were pledged to accept.

DELINQUENCY

Every group is likely to have social offenders and lawless members and, although the number of Jews in prison was relatively low, delinquency was becoming a matter of increasing communal concern to American Jewry in the early 1900s. The problem was recognized as acute and of special concern to New York City, with its congested areas which were considered breeding grounds for the delinquent and the maladjusted. It was apparent that many of the children of immigrants were no longer amenable to the ways of life or to the discipline of their parents and some were coming into conflict with the law.

Interest in delinquency at this time was heightened by exaggerated charges about the extent of delinquency among Jewish youth made by uninformed or biased law enforcement officials and repeated at Congressional hearings on national immigration policy. Occasional crimes of a sensational character tended to magnify the seriousness of the problem.

This situation led to increased interest in providing constructive outlets through recreational and cultural services. In New York and one or two other large cities the problem was sufficiently urgent to stimulate the establishment of guidance services and, in New York, of an agency for institutional care of some of the more difficult problem children. The agencies, which were later merged into the New York City Jewish Board of Guardians, included a Jewish Big Brother Association, a

Jewish Big Sister Association, a Jewish Protectory and Aid Society, a Prisoners' Aid Bureau and the Cedar Knolls School at Hawthorne, N. Y.

In a few years delinquency began to be considered a less urgent problem within the Jewish group. The rate of juvenile delinquency among Jews has elsewhere, as in New York City, fallen considerably below the general rate.

EARLY EDUCATIONAL INSTITUTIONS

Because of the need of the immigrant to acquire a new language and for help in the process of achieving citizenship, many communities established special Americanization and educational services at which teaching English to the foreign-born served as an initial point of contact with the newcomers. Group activities for children and youths accelerated the processes of cultural change. While these efforts were beneficial to the young in their adjustment to the American community, they served to widen the gap between the generations.

The philosophy inherent in the cultural aims and interests of the established Jewish population was not always acceptable to members of the immigrant group. The services were looked upon by some immigrants as patronage or condescension arising out of depreciation or rejection of their own values in favor of the ways and habits of the settled group. The programs seemed to some to attempt to inculcate the religious and cultural ideas of Reform Judaism in the new immigrants while riding roughshod over the latter's religious and class feelings. The work of the early cultural and social welfare agencies established for the immigrants was criticized by some of the leaders of the East-European group. A point of view expressed by A. H. Fromenson, then an editor of the *Jewish Daily News—Jewish Gazette*, at the 1904 National Conference of Jewish Charities was typical:

A certain very inconsiderable minority of the great mass of human beings takes advantage of the opportunities offered by the Settlements and the Educational Alliance, but, when all is said and done, when every claim made for them by their most enthusiastic admirers and workers is conceded, the fact remains that so far as the overwhelming majority of the East Side is concerned, it is as if these institutions did not exist at all. Worse even than that, they are regarded by a very large number with absolute antipathy and by another very large number with mistrust.

Another and perhaps more serious fault of the Settlements and kindred institutions is that having come into existence they proceed at once to antagonize, instead of trying to win sympathies and cooperation of the people. Instead of shaping the work of these institutions in accordance with the real needs and desires of the people, the effort was to shape the minds of the people in accordance with the theories of those who instituted the work.[10]

Such criticisms were undoubtedly extreme; but it may be said to the credit of the Settlements and educational services that they did not remain immune to them. New lay and professional leadership was emerging, imbued with a greater understanding of and sympathy for the values of the immigrant group. The new immigrants began to develop their own cultural activities both apart from and within the existing Settlements. Also, the professional direction of the agencies was being drawn increasingly from among the younger members of the immigrant group itself.

For several decades the Jewish Settlements were rated below the quality of the outstanding examples of the Settlement movement.

A 1920 survey of Jewish recreation activities reported that:

The Jewish Settlements of New York City . . . have not developed personalities of the type which non-sectarian Settlements have developed. This is true of the Jewish communities throughout the country. The tendency has been to institutionalize rather than to individualize. Executives have been permitted to carry out policies, but within limitations circumscribed by the directors of the organizations. No distinctively Jewish organization has had executives who have possessed the freedom of individual initiative which has been exercised by Jane Addams of Hull House, Professor Graham Taylor of Chicago Commons, and Lillian D. Wald* of the Henry Street Settlement . . . personalities of influence, such as those of the non-sectarian agencies have not developed in the recreational type of social work in our Jewish communities throughout the country.[11]

The Jewish Settlement movement, whatever benefits it may have afforded to the early immigrants, was, however, destined to be a passing phenomenon. The early congested slums where the Settlement Houses were being established were in large measure transitional residential areas. Economic improvement was rapid and with it came removal of the Jewish population to the more desirable parts of the city. The Settlements began to be replaced by YMHAs, YWHAs and Jewish community Centers with clientele drawn increasingly from the middle income groups.

JEWISH EDUCATION

Initially the federations had considered Jewish education solely a congregational responsibility, outside the scope of secular philanthropic financing and planning. It was not until the Talmud Torahs were established as communal institutions and supported by the newer immigrants through various fund-raising devices,

---

* Lillian Wald was Jewish but was connected with a non-sectarian Settlement.

which included solicitation of federation subscribers, that the philanthropic aspect of Jewish education was recognized by the leaders of federations. A federation subsidy to Jewish educational institutions was rare before 1915; soon a few of the federations were beginning to include Orthodox agencies and to accept some of the communally supported educational institutions as beneficiaries.

The principle of federation responsibility for Jewish education, however, was not accepted easily. The issue became a controversial one in many communities, not to be fully resolved in some of them for more than three decades. An analysis of the place of Jewish education in the communal program of federation is indicated in the survey of the Boston Jewish Charities made in 1930. (The surveyor, Solomon Lowenstein, was the executive of the New York Federation which included a central Bureau of Jewish Education and several of the New York Hebrew Schools as beneficiary agencies. The majority of the Jewish schools in New York, however, were continuing to finance themselves independently.) The principle of federation responsibility as well as the practical problems of inclusion of Jewish education in the federation budget are indicated in the following excerpts from the survey report:

The question as to the relation of Jewish education to Jewish community organization is not one of principle . . . but merely . . . expediency. We may take it for granted that such education should not be supplied absolutely free of cost . . . complete subsidy by the community would be contrary to the spirit of Jewish tradition which has always regarded the education of the young as a first charge upon the parents; . . . a limited number of pupils . . . because of the economic disability of their parents will be unable to meet even their fair share of such cost. There will always be charges for supervision, for training of teachers, for various administrative costs, etc., which likewise will require public support.

How shall these necessary communal charges be met. Three ways are possible: first, the development of a Jewish educational program as a function of the religious congregations; second, the creation of a separate central organization devoted to this purpose exclusively; third, the inclusion of these agencies in the general program of the central social, philanthropic, educational agency of the community, usually designated by the term of federation or some similar name.

The recommendation in the Boston survey favored the third alternative. "It would seem to be logical that a proper program of Jewish education should find inclusion within the central communal organization, but with limitations geared to the financial resources of the federation."[12] Increasingly, federations have adopted this policy.

CHILD DEPENDENCY AND "MOTHER'S AID"

Child welfare services were expanding rapidly in this period, especially in orphanage facilities. The number of children who were lacking both parents was small and the orphanages housed many children of disabled or deserted fathers and those from other types of broken homes. The day of "mother's pensions" had not yet dawned and there was criticism both of the children's institutions and of the relief agencies in their policies and methods of dealing with these problems.

Leadership in developing new and improved measures for caring for dependent children came from the example of the Protestant social welfare agencies. In the Jewish field the predominant tendency at first was to defend the orphanage as the superior method of care for dependent children. Soon, however, some of the leaders in the field began to experiment with the system of placing Jewish children in family or foster homes. Dr. Ludwig Bernstein, superintendent of the Hebrew Sheltering and Guardian Society of New York (Pleasantville) had demonstrated (according to Judge Julian Mack, president of the 1906 Conference of Jewish Charities) that "good homes are readily obtained for Jewish orphans, both for adoption and for board. What holds true in New York will be found true elsewhere."[13] Apparently this plan for a different method of child care was also reinforced by experience in caring for about 500 orphan children brought to the United States from Russia.[14] Greater use of subsidies to mothers, permitting them to maintain their homes for the rearing of half-orphaned children, was also developing with Cincinnati in the lead.[15]

The change of emphasis from the institution to the family boarding home was gradual. In 1910 Rabbi Rudolph Coffee of Pittsburgh told the National Conference of Jewish Charities:

We observe that Jewish workers are defending the system of placing dependent children in large buildings or institutions, while our Christian workers have given up this method because they have found better ways to provide for children.*

In a few years the placing-out system began to be generally accepted. By 1932 the number of Jewish dependent children in family boarding homes was beginning to exceed the number cared for in institutions.[17] Many federations were active in stimulating this trend which was being endorsed generally as the more desirable method of child care.

* This was an exaggeration. Institutional care persisted in Christian welfare work and has continued to a large extent, but with increased placement of children in family homes. See note 16.

The first national White House Conference on Child Welfare, in 1910, was a landmark in American social welfare. This conference emphasized the value of the family home as the natural place for children, and endorsed the efforts of social work to keep the home intact. These sentiments were accepted by leaders of the Jewish welfare field who had begun increasingly to advocate keeping mothers with dependent children in their own homes. It also led to interest on the part of Jewish welfare agencies in the development of the governmental Mother's Aid system, which began in 1911 with a law enacted in Missouri, limited to Jackson County. Mr. Jacob Billikopf, then the superintendent of the Jewish Famliy Services in Kansas City (located in Jackson County, Missouri), took an active role in the development of a public form of assistance to mothers with dependent children. The movement spread rapidly. Within ten years Mothers' Aid laws had been enacted in forty-one states.

SPECIALIZATION OF AGENCIES AND FEDERATION PLANNING

The increasing number of immigrants and the new and complex problems which faced them called for social welfare programs of a more extensive character than before. The established agencies were enlarged and assumed new functions. New agencies mushroomed, some with a different program, others paralleling or duplicating the older agencies. Through the initiative of the agencies in federation a rough approximation to social planning was taking place. The federation, in responding to the financial problems of the constituent agencies, became an indispensable factor in this development. In many of the federations, there was a close connection between the fund-raising and the relief agency programs, a single executive serving both.

ORGANIZATION OF THE NEW YORK COMMUNITY

A. The Federation

The development of specialized agencies as well as the complexity of the welfare programs available to the huge Jewish population of New York City can be seen in the composition of the New York Federation when it was organized in 1917. It covered the boroughs of Manhattan and the Bronx; Brooklyn[18] established its own federation in 1909. The 1918 campaign of the New York Federation raised funds for a list of ninety-two constituent agencies and auxiliaries. These included a number offering some special form of relief, such as fuel or clothing, as well as agencies giving general family assistance and service, organizations for the care of the handicapped, recreational and Settlement agencies, summer camps, hospitals, outpatient services and convalescent homes, day nurseries and kindergartens, Jewish education and vocational training schools, employment bureaus, widows' aid societies, institutions for children, child guidance services, juvenile protective homes, and homes for the aged and chronically ill.

The New York Federation was established as a fund-raising instrument in behalf of these constituents, but did not interfere with the autonomy of the agencies in their programs or administration. There was no initial provision for the federation as a central planning agency. The terms of agreement between federation and the beneficiary agencies called for a basic guaranteed minimum for each agency, and left to the federation as a whole the disposal of surpluses. Since the guaranteed minimums represented the amount of funds raised in the initial year of organization, the federation soon had a considerable amount of additional funds to distribute. Following the experience in the larger cities which had established federations earlier, the New York Federation in its 1918 campaign reported income of over $3,000,000 derived from 77,500 contributors, a notable increase over the pre-federation experience both in amounts raised and in the number of contributors. Through its budgetary processes, research studies, and other procedures, the Federation in New York, as in all other cities, became an important factor in the growth and development of services. Shifts in programs, mergers of agencies, discontinuance of outmoded services and other progressive developments which have occurred can be credited to federation.

The reactions to the new Federation in New York were enthusiastic on the part of leaders of the movement, the contributors and the agencies. Its first executive, I. Edwin Goldwasser, reported in 1918 that:

The entire community has been welded into a solid unit. There is no division of uptown or downtown nor any other sort of division within the Federation. Problems of the community are considered in the broadest possible way, and the decisions are accepted by the constituent societies as the result of the most careful deliberation. The various campaigns have developed new groups of workers; men and women never before connected with Jewish work have rallied to the cause of the Federation, and have contributed in no small measure to its remarkable success.

The committees of the Federation are considering the general problems of community welfare, and for the first time in the history of the Jewish community in New York City, opportunity is given for the full consideration of problems that affect many institutions. The possibilities for coordination and cooperation are practically unlimited.[19]

Although New York did not establish a federation until 1917, the need and desire for communal planning had arisen earlier. A most interesting development in the history of Jewish communal organization was the establishment of the New York *Kehillah* in 1908, which represented the first community council specifically organized for purposes other than that of raising funds for philanthropic agencies: it concerned itself with problems of group relationships and general Jewish social and cultural problems. In 1908, ten years before the establishment of the New York Federation, Nathan Bijur, the president of the National Conference of Jewish Charities, had stated that:

New York still remains the exception to all the Jewish communities of the country in that it has rejected federation; the movement having that end in view, organized in the fall of 1906, having been abandoned in the early part of 1907.[20]

The lack of a philanthropic federation in New York was considered by many a serious gap in Jewish communal organization. Attempts to set up the Council of Jewish Philanthropic Agencies had been unsuccessful. There were, however, continuing associations of agencies of the same European national origin such as the Federation of Galician and Bucovinian Jews of America (1903), the Federation of Rumanian Jews (1908), and the Federation of Russian and Polish Hebrews of America (1908).[21]

It was generally recognized that there was no instrument adequate to deal with the complex religious, educational and philanthropic needs of the huge community. There were also troublesome problems in those years: anti-Semitic reactions and general anti-alien feelings were becoming more widespread, resulting in charges of Jewish criminality at immigration hearings, and in similar public statements by important law enforcement officials.

When unwarranted charges of criminality were made against New York Jews in the fall of 1908, it was found difficult to present the facts to the public in their proper light. This gave rise in October 1908 to the feeling that a more effective organization of New York's Jewish forces should be attempted. A first step in that direction was taken by a call for a conference of delegates of various organizations. . . . This conference . . . led to the appointment of a committee of twenty-five, with authority to consult with other organizations, looking to the creation of what might be known as the Jewish Community of New York City.[22]

The organization that developed from this conference called itself the *Kehillah* (Jewish Community) of New York City and was established as an association of delegates from synagogues, charitable agencies, mutual benefit societies, fraternal organizations, educational societies, community associations, Zionist and religious congregations and cultural societies. The purpose of the *Kehillah* as stated in its constitution was:

To further the cause of charitable and philanthropic endeavor by the Jewish community of the City of New York, with the view that organized agencies engaged in such work may, by discussion and upon the advice of this body, cooperate for mutual betterment in methods and economies of administration, and that ways and means may, from time to time, be considered and devised to cope with such conditions and exigencies affecting the well-being of the Jewish community as are not cognizable by existing organizations.

A plan of delegate representation was put into effect. At the organization meeting in February 1909 there were present about 300 delegates from 222 societies and their constituent agencies, an estimated total of 500 organizations.[23] The meetings of delegates were supplemented by the organization of Service Bureaus, whose function was to study the community problems and to make recommendations for coordination, for common planning and for effective action. The scope and functions of these bureaus, though organized primarily for New York City, extended to all Jewish problems of a nationwide character. A Bureau of Jewish Education was organized in 1910, one on economic problems (the Bureau of Industry) in 1914, one on recreation and culture and a school for the preparation of communal workers in 1914, and the Philanthropic Research Bureau in 1916.[24]

Though the work of these research and service bureaus was generally acknowledged as helpful and they were credited with having made solid contributions to the communal programs of New York, the original plan of a democratically organized, representative communal body to concern itself with all aspects of Jewish life and to project common action, failed to take root. Since *kehillahs* represented agencies and not the people directly, it was hoped to overcome this deficiency by a new procedure of direct voting and participation.[25] Before an ambitious proposal for changing the methods of the *Kehillah* could be put into effect, the organization suffered a rapid decline. Professor Salo Baron explains the decline as follows:

The New York *Kehillah* movement of the period of the First World War failed not only for accidental and personal reasons; the failure was primarily a reflection of real disorganizing forces. In any case, its operation, had it begun to operate, would have required new methods, indeed entirely new approaches, and its effectiveness would have been limited, at best.[26]

Committees of the *Kehillah* continued to function until 1922. Parts of the service program had been operating as independent bureaus and these either continued under the auspices of the New York Federation, as in the Bureau of Jewish Education, or became the nucleus of research and service agencies serving the entire country as well as New York City. The Bureau of Jewish Social Research (merged with the CJFWF in 1935), for example, was the successor to the *Kehillah's* Bureau of Philanthropic Research. The National Jewish Welfare Board was the outgrowth of the Young Men's Hebrew and Kindred Associations. With the end of the *Kehillah*, the New York Federation, concerned with the philanthropic programs, remained as the important central communal welfare agency in that city.

During this period an organization similar to the *Kehillah* arose in Philadelpha and others were attempted in Detroit and other cities. The New York experience had made a valuable contribution to an understanding of the nature of Jewish communal life, the kind of structures that could be set up for central communal service, and the scope and limitation of any organization that attempted to deal on an overall basis with broad aspects of Jewish life. The community councils which were to become established in the 1930s became the successors to this experimental phase of central Jewish communal organization.

GROWTH OF NUMBER OF CITY FEDERATIONS

While a comprehensive structure of central communal association and planning on an overall basis failed to strike root, progress was being made by the philanthropic federations, which were being widely extended. By 1919, fifty cities were reported as having established federations and by this time the movement had reached several of the smaller communities—some with fewer than 1,500 Jews.[27]

A few of the federations in the smaller communities were essentially united relief societies, but in most cities the list of beneficiary organizations included other types of health and welfare agencies as well. A few cities were also providing for the support of communal schools for Jewish education. Forty of the federations reported expenditures for 1918 totaling $6,325,000, which ranged from over $3,000,000 for the Manhattan-Bronx New York Federation to $1,800 for Dallas, Texas.

Considerable sums were being expended by the larger federations that year, with Chicago spending $750,000; Philadelphia, $245,000; San Francisco, $217,-000; Boston, 187,000; Baltimore, $150,000; St. Louis, $140,000 and Pittsburgh, $130,000.

Expenditures in 1918 were predominantly for the support of local service programs; only a few of the federations were giving subventions to national agencies, such as the national hospitals for the tuberculous and the regional institutions for children and the aged, which had come into existence during the preceding decades.

PROGRESS OF FEDERATIONS DURING THE FIRST TWO DECADES

There was thus substantial progress in the organization of communal programs and in the development of federations during the first two decades of the 20th century. Increased funds were being obtained through federated, central fund-raising, standards of service were being improved, and new agencies were being established to meet special problems. New principles of community organization were emerging to make federation an instrument in behalf of the entire system of social welfare

—not merely a device for the support of established agencies by an original group of sponsors. There were evidences of a growing rapprochement between the founders of federation and some of the leadership of newer segments of the Jewish population who were displaying increasing vigor and initiative in establishing agencies and services.

The first two decades of the 20th century were also a period of marked improvement in social and economic conditions, with enlargement of voluntary health and welfare programs throughout the country. Attention was being directed not only to giving relief to the destitute, but to the prevention of sickness and poverty. Great strides were being made in programs for civic improvement. There were advances in social legislation—factory regulations, compensation for industrial accidents, mothers' pensions, juvenile courts, child labor laws and assistance for the aged. Progress was being made in the improvement of the public school system and other public institutions. Trade union organization among Jewish workers as well as among the general American population was helping to improve the economic conditions of the immigrant as well as the native worker.

Professional workers were being employed increasingly by the social welfare agencies and they were developing a systematic body of theory and practice, along sympathetic and effective lines, to assist wherever help was needed. Schools of social work were being established to prepare the workers required by the social welfare agencies.

It was a period of general social welfare advance which was reflected in a noteworthy improvement in the work of the Jewish federations and their constituent agencies. There was also a general optimism that social conditions would be further improved in the years ahead. The conviction that poverty was an inherent aspect of an economic system based upon scarcity was giving way to the belief that poverty could be eliminated in the growing productivity of a prosperous country.

GROWING IMPORTANCE OF AMERICAN JEWRY

Profound changes were also taking place in the nature of the Jewish community. With increased immigration it had grown enormously; and with the gradual economic and social adjustment of the immigrants to American life, they were able more effectively to organize themselves as a community. World War I undoubtedly had a significant effect. Professor Salo W. Baron describes it as follows:

During the years 1914-1918 the American Jewish community grew into maturity. Until 1914, despite the tremendous increase in their population and wealth, the Jewries of the Western Hemisphere were largely the recipients of the cultural and political bounty emanating from the Old World. Even the Reform movement . . . was largely a European creation. . . . Orthodoxy and Conservative Judaism were . . . even more . . . a continuation of trends deeply rooted in the old heritage. . . . Politically, too, every important movement from Zionism to extreme assimilation, from diaspora nationalism to Bundism and labor unionism, was essentially a carry-over of ideologies and attitudes generated by Old World conditions. In international activities the leadership . . . rested as a rule with . . . European organization. . . . The Zionist Organization . . . depended for its ideological and practical progress upon the intellectual resources and manpower of continental Jewry.[28]

The development of American Jewish activity for the relief and assistance of the European Jewish population suffering from the effects of World War I was closely related to the conditions responsible for the federation movement. With this period basic changes began to appear in the relationship between Europe and America. The role of leadership in Jewish philanthropy and culture shifted from European to American Jewry. The dynamics of American Jewish communal welfare organization reflect these changing roles.[29]

V

1920 to 1930—A
Decade of Prosperity

The post-war decade of the 1920s opened with a business recession, then considered an inevitable but temporary aspect of the business cycle. In a year the recession was succeeded by eight years of increasing prosperity and industrial activity. At the decade's end, an intense and prolonged depression was beginning which was to have a profound effect on the economic and social life of the country and, especially, on its organizations concerned with social welfare.

For the Jewish community that period began with a five-year resumption of immigration from the countries of eastern Europe which had suffered from severe war damage and were now in the throes of radical changes in their political and economic structures. This was to be followed in the middle of the decade by drastic restriction of immigration. Except for the special refugee legislation of the 1940s these restrictions have continued as the basic national policy, and have been responsible for the sharp curtailment of immigration from eastern and southern Europe.

But the resumption of immigration in the early 1920s did not impose upon the Jewish communities the strains and tensions which had been experienced earlier. The new immigrants came to a more settled community, where friends and relatives were in a better position to help them. More selective in its very nature, the immigration of the 1920s brought people with skills adaptable to the American labor market. The new economic conditions were responsible for increasing the industrial population, expanding industries and building up the urban aspects of American life.

In the previous three decades an upward economic swing had moved some immigrant Jews from the factories into the middle economic group. The needle trades, peddling and small retail merchandising no longer loomed so large as Jewish means for earning a livelihood; the American-born generation was being absorbed into the professional and white collar occupations. Labor unions were successful in attaining more satisfactory standards of pay and hours in formerly substandard occupations in which many of the immigrants continued to be employed.

Better economic conditions made it possible to improve the standards of the communal institutions, to substitute competent staffs for untrained workers and to secure more money to do a better job. Absorption of immigrants was a more rapid and more satisfactory process as the group as a whole moved forward in its economic, social, and civic adjustments. Relief activities for a time continued on a considerable scale, but the decreasing numbers of the dependent group in some cities was becoming obvious.

Municipal and county governments in some of the northern cities were starting to improve their programs of public assistance. "Mothers' Pensions," the new relief method of aiding mothers with dependent children, was spreading from the voluntary to the public agencies, and Jewish communal agencies, for their part, no longer considered this form of public assistance unsuitable for eligible Jewish families. Community chests, raising funds from the general community for sectarian as well as for non-sectarian social welfare agencies, were developing throughout the country and were adding substantial funds for social agency programs.

As the settled immigrants began to reach an improved stage of economic well-being, the focus shifted away from financial support toward broader social and group interests. New synagogues were built, and social clubs established for the well-to-do. As the Settlement movement waned, YMHAs and Jewish Centers were being constructed and there was a beginning of organized communal interest in Jewish education.

The period was not without its negative factors. Anti-alienism was becoming ingrained in the national immigration policy, and native anti-Semitism reinforced by movements imported from Europe was becoming a more pervasive aspect of American life.

Although cleavages between the various sections of the Jewish population continued during the period, there was a slow but gradual improvement in relations as the cultural differences between the children of the old and of the new immigrants began to narrow. The emphasis on a single campaign, motivated by a desire to extend the federation to all sections of the community, was one of the factors which helped to develop more satisfactory relationships in philanthropy.

The problems of the war-dislocated East-European Jewish population, estimated at over 8,500,000, had aroused the emotions of American Jews, and representatives of the various elements of the community joined together and cooperated effectively in bringing their influence to bear on the shaping of certain provisions of the peace treaties. An American Jewish Congress was organized in 1917 by representatives of all sections of the Jewish population; delegates were elected by popular vote. This Congress was established as a temporary organization to unify American Jewish action with relation to the treaties of peace which followed the war. It brought to the Peace Conference the strong support of American Jewry for its efforts to establish a democratic basis of life and the rights of the minority populations in the new national states which were to be fashioned out of the Austro-Hungarian and Russian Empires and for the establishment of a National Jewish Home in Palestine.[1]

ORGANIZATION FOR OVERSEAS RELIEF

The deep interest of American Jews in assisting Jewish sufferers of the war led to the organization of basic national agencies for overseas help. Before 1914 a considerable amount of assistance was being given by individuals to their relatives and friends abroad, and the *Landsmanschaften* formed by the immigrants had maintained a fraternal interest in the welfare of the Jewish communities of their native lands. The outbreak of the war led to the formation of three national bodies for overseas relief, representing various sections of American Jewry: the Central Committee for the Relief of

Jews, organized by the Union of Orthodox Congregations; the overseas relief program established earlier by the American Jewish Committee; and the Peoples Relief Committee, representing labor groups. These three programs were merged in 1914 to establish the American Jewish Joint Distribution Committee, under the leadership of Felix Warburg. Mr. Warburg was an immigrant from Germany associated with the banking firm of Kuhn, Loeb & Co., and was recognized during his lifetime as the outstanding philanthropist and leader in Jewish communal welfare.*

The JDC was an important development in practical group cooperation, of great future significance to Jewish communal organizations. Since its establishment the JDC has been successful in securing the cooperation of local communities for fund-raising. In its first ten years JDC reported expenditures of close to $60,000,000 raised throughout the United States and distributed to war sufferers and the war-displaced populations in all parts of the globe. During the next few years it was to raise even larger sums in special programs of assistance to eastern Europe and for the program of Agro-Joint, which attempted resettlement and colonization of the Jews living in the Soviet Union.

In addition to the Joint Distribution Committee, the Zionist Keren Hayesod and the Jewish National Fund (Keren Kayemeth) were raising funds for the development of Palestine for Jewish settlement. The JDC during these years was also spending a sizable part of its funds to aid war sufferers and other immigrants who were going to Palestine. It was estimated that in the year 1923 nearly as much ($12,000,000) was being raised and

* Leadership in Jewish communal welfare was exercised for many years by Jacob H. Schiff (1847-1920), also a partner in Kuhn, Loeb & Co. and the father-in-law of Felix Warburg.

spent for overseas work as for welfare activities in this country.

While the federations in most cities at this time were not the direct instruments for overseas fund-raising, it was generally local federation leadership that took responsibility for helping to organize the JDC and other campaigns for overseas and national causes. A number of the executives of the local federations, led by Boris Bogen of Cincinnati, were enlisted by JDC for professional direction of its overseas programs in the postwar period.

The development of large-scale overseas programs and the participation of the local communities in these efforts called attention to the new problems of fundraising. In addition to the JDC, other organizations were attempting to raise funds for their special causes, and contributors were again beginning to feel the pressures of multiple appeals which they had experienced from local agencies before the organization of federations.

By 1923, therefore, proposals were being advanced that some new form of organization be established for a more systematic and permanent basis of fund-raising for national and overseas causes. It was first proposed in 1923 that the Jewish War Relief Committee—the fund-raising arm of the JDC—might assume the task of raising funds for other legitimate overseas and national agencies. It was felt that both the large contributors and the communities in general had confidence in the competence and integrity of the Jewish War Relief Committee and would welcome this broadening of its functions and would consent to cooperate in such a project. The additional sums involved would be only a fraction of what this agency was raising in its nation-wide campaign. The idea was explored but could not be realized, though a number of federations expressed general approval. The concept of a similar national welfare fund campaign was raised from time to time in later years, also without realization.

At the 1924 National Conference of Jewish Social Service, Samuel A. Goldsmith, then director of the Bureau of Jewish Social Research, proposed that an information service be established for federations, to deal with the national and overseas organizations. He also proposed the establishment of separate annual campaigns in each community for non-local causes, the funds to be apportioned by a distribution committee set up by the federations.[2] This proposal in essence was the plan which in the next three decades was to become a major phase of Jewish communal fund-raising.

THE COMMUNITY CHEST MOVEMENT

World War I also served to stimulate a greater degree of cooperation in philanthropic efforts in the general community. Borrowing from the experience of the Jewish federations, leaders in philanthropic work were beginning to support the non-sectarian or intersectarian community chest plan as a more effective method of raising funds for the multiplicity of social welfare agencies and causes. Such a method of central philanthropic fund-raising had been followed in Cleveland in 1913. The development of "war chests" after 1914 was stimulated because of the large sums needed for the expanded wartime programs of the Red Cross, local welfare agencies and the newly created community wartime welfare services. When the war ended, the emergency "war chests" and "patriotic funds" were transformed in many cities into permanent community chests.

The success of central community fund-raising during this period and the benefits of inter-group and inter-sectarian cooperation had resulted in Jewish federations in a number of cities giving up their own separate fund-raising and joining the community chests. The Jewish agencies, formerly receiving their funds from campaigns conducted exclusively in the Jewish community, became the beneficiaries of the general chests which were enlisting contributions from all sections of the population. By 1924 there were seventeen Jewish federations in community chests in cities of more than 300,000 general population.[3]

However, the only Jewish federations in the larger cities which had joined the chests before 1923 were those of Cincinnati, Cleveland, Detroit and San Francisco. There was considerable hesitation on the part of other large community federations to affiliate with community chests, and a national study was undertaken to evaluate the advantages and disadvantages of inclusion. A survey team consisting of Maurice Hexter and Samuel Goldsmith representing the Jewish Conference studied the development of federation and community chest relationships and their findings were reported to the 1923 Conference of Jewish Social Service in a paper by Dr. Hexter.[4]

After an extensive field trip the surveyors found that a real federation existed primarily in the larger Jewish communities; in many of the small cities the agency designated as a "federation" was merely a united agency for family relief. The federation of *all* eligible philanthropic agencies was as yet incomplete except in two cities. In the other communities the affiliated agencies constituted from 20% to 85% of agencies, representing from 60% to 95% of philanthropic expenditures in those cities. They noted "a strong tendency within the past two or three years to give ample opportunity to the newcomers to share fully and freely in communal responsibility."

On federation-chest relationships, the surveyors related the mixed attitudes they had found in their study on the part of the Jewish federation leaders, but stated that "it is still too early to predict any direct consequences of affiliation with community chests. The alliance is still too young." However, it appeared to be definite that "more money comes to the Jewish agencies than they received before such merger," and "the Jews partake in an active way in directing campaigns and in budgeting the income." Dr. Hexter, however, had "personally, extreme reservations about the ultimate effect of such alliance."

In Dr. Hexter's opinion joining the community chest would "not be harmful:

> a). where the community has already developed a community spirit and a rather high type organization of its own, so that the Jewish community is accustomed to large giving;
>
> b). where the Jewish community can turn over to the community fund a strong leadership and personnel for campaign purposes;
>
> c). where the Jewish community will organically provide much larger sums of money to the community chest than it in turn will seek for the support of its own enterprises."[5]

Though many leaders believed that the positive aspects of community chest affiliation outweighed its disadvantages, a negative attitude toward chests is expressed in a statement of a federation executive of a small community, who declared in 1927: "To some extent the community chest may be considered a disrupting factor in the development of Jewish community life. There is a certain feeling of pride to be enjoyed in the retention of virility by the Jewish community that is stimulated by its own instrument of money raising."[6]

Attitudes of other federation leaders, however, were increasingly favorable, and federations in many cities began to affiliate with their community chests. It seemed at first as though such affiliation meant the end of separate communal fund-raising in those cities; but this assumption was soon to be proven erroneous. In many cities non-sectarian chests did not include what were considered primarily religious agencies for which philanthropic funds had been raised in the past. For this reason some chests did not include YMCAs and Jewish Centers. This meant that federations which were supporting Jewish educational services would need to continue additional separate fund-raising activity. With the end of the war, local community chests were no longer raising funds for the several temporary national and overseas agencies which had been war chest beneficiaries. Most of the Jewish national and overseas agencies, however, were of a permanent character and had continued to conduct their own campaigns during the war period.

The favorable attitude toward community chests is illustrated in a recommendation made in 1929 in one of the communal surveys of a federation which had not yet affiliated:

The Survey, after full consideration of the issues involved in the local situation, and of the experience of other communities, definitely recommended that the Jewish agencies join the chest. Jewish organizations affiliated with chests have been treated on an equitable basis, and while chests have not been uniformly successful, they have generally attained their major financial objectives. The accompanying advantages of joinder with the chest, in promoting a working fellowship on a common

97

humanitarian task and in securing the widespread participation of the public, are important considerations because of the stimulus towards the development of a progressive community program which is of benefit to all groups.[7]

By 1930, Jewish federations in forty cities had become affiliated with their local community chests. (By 1936 this had increased to sixty-two.) No community chest had been developed in New York or Chicago; and of the other large federations, Baltimore, Boston, Buffalo, Milwaukee, Philadelphia and St. Louis were continuing their separate fund-raising for their local welfare programs. All of these cities, with the exception of Baltimore, affiliated subsequently. The New York and Chicago federations, while continuing their major direct fund-raising efforts, became participants of the auxiliary special chests when they were established later in their cities.

In some cities in which federations entered community chests, the arrangement was for the federation to receive a lump sum from the chest, with the federation retaining responsibility for budgeting and distributing the funds to the individual Jewish health and welfare agencies. In other cities, the chests determined the individual grants to the agencies, with the federations having neither fund-raising nor primary budgeting responsibilities for these agencies.

IMPROVING STANDARDS AND REORGANIZING STRUCTURES

The problem of whether to join or not to join the community chest was not, however, the only common problem which was being studied by Jewish federations in those years. The sense of pressure and emergency of the previous two decades was no longer acute and federations were able to take a longer view of their development and their current problems. Because of changing needs and shifting community conditions federations became interested in drafting plans for the future. Extensive surveys were conducted in New York, Chicago, Cleveland, Boston, Baltimore, Los Angeles and in many other communities, large and small.

The surveys found that many aspects of the program could be improved in quality of work and staff, duplication avoided, parallel organizations merged, obsolete services abandoned and the general interest broadened. The surveys in that period were to find that there were still wide cleavages between sections of the Jewish population. New Orthodox orphan asylums had been established in communities that for many years had had an orphanage or child care service under Reform auspices.[8]

Surveys also helped to stimulate the development of federation in some of the smaller communities.[9]

The changing nature of federations was coming into focus. There was a greater interest in social service coordination and an increased desire to expand the functions of federation beyond the sphere of fund-raising. The interest in coordinating social services helped to develop the idea of an over-all perspective, and federation began to concern itself with the total welfare need —rather than with an assortment of unrelated piecemeal services.

The desire of federation to unify philanthropic forces, including the non-affiliated agencies, was also focusing attention on the shortcomings of federation structure and administration. Questions were being raised by federation leadership concerning the nature of the federation, its representatives, and the extent to which participation in its administration was open to all elements of the community. Far-sighted leaders were seeing federation in a new role—as a substantial resource for supporting communal services—and they were recognizing that it should be fashioned into a communal instrument for democratic participation and policy formation.[10]

SHIFT FROM RELIEF TO PROMOTION OF GROUP OBJECTIVES

With the reduction of immigration, improving economic conditions, and the shrinkage of relief needs, federation leaders could see the possibilities of shifting community interests to an emphasis on cultural values and away from relief agencies, hospitals, and care of dependent children and aged. Programs for education and leisure-time activities could now be fostered.

Federations during the 1920s were beginning to include the community schools for Jewish education which for many years had remained outside the orbit of the philanthropic federation. Local bureaus of Jewish education were organized, in many instances as part of federation planning. They were subsidized as an aspect of the general federation interest in the coordination of agencies and in the improvement of standards. Following the lead of the New York Federation which in 1917 accepted the Bureau of Jewish Education as a beneficiary, other federations assumed responsibility for establishing central bureaus for Jewish education in their communities.

By 1932 such bureaus were constituents of federations in fourteen of the larger cities; federations in twenty-four additional large or important intermediate cities had not as yet developed central bureaus in this field but by 1936 were giving financial support to schools under communal or group auspices.[11] In many cities the desirability of federation support of Jewish education remained a controversial question, but a more positive attitude toward this problem was making headway. In a survey of a small community in which a federation was recommended, one of its advantages, it was pointed out, would be the improvement of the Jewish educational program.

The Jewish educational activities, along with the other community activities, reap the benefits of the reorganization of the Jewish federation. The inadequately organized Jewish community . . . has had its negative effect upon the Jewish educational program which, until now, has further suffered from the fact that Jewish education has not been dealt with by the leaders as the concern of the entire community. The good work that is being done along Jewish educational lines requires intensification, consolidation and coordination to the end that the problem will be dealt with as a whole, rather than through isolated efforts of this or that individual school.[12]

ROLE OF THE PROFESSIONAL

The need for competent and well-trained professional services as an essential of Jewish communal programs was not yet fully established. Initially the tasks of administering the enlarged relief societies, the institutions and the new federations had passed by necessity from the hands of volunteers to that of the "paid" workers. Social welfare work was becoming a profession. Non-sectarian "schools of philanthropy" had been established in New York and Chicago early in the century, and professional training, professional standards and professional methods were developing. In the medium-sized as well as the largest cities the employment of "paid" workers and the recognition of professional standards was being gradually though reluctantly accepted as a necessity.

Many of the early paid workers in the Jewish field

were men and women of devotion and competence, quick to learn from the experience of the workers in the related fields of philanthropy in the general community. As the schools of philanthropy developed, opportunities for training were utilized and the more forward-looking Jewish agencies became the training ground for additional qualified workers. The role of the professional in the Jewish field had been one of gradual and often difficult growth. Board members at first were inclined to look upon him as a paid employee rather than as a professional guide.[13]

As a result of increasing contacts between leaders in cities with professional assistance and those without it, more Jewish agencies were hiring professional workers. The field began to attract competent persons who would find a career in administering the social programs and serving the Jewish community. Louis Levin, the executive of the Baltimore Federation, discussing "Social Work as a Profession" stated in 1910 that:

Though the number of Jewish professional workers is still small, we can be assured that it will increase rapidly. Efficient schools of philanthropy, in the organization of which Jews have had some, but a minor and inadequate, part, exist in a number of educational centers, and will increase rapidly; boards and their supporters are rapidly coming to the point where they will accept only the worker who has adopted social service as a profession and has trained in the work, for even minor positions.[14]

It was not long after this that the increasing numbers of paid personnel, and the recognition of the special requirements of the Jewish field inspired exploration of the need for training facilities which would emphasize special Jewish aspects not being provided by the existing schools of philanthropy. An early start had been made in the School for Jewish Communal Work under the auspices of the New York *Kehillah*—which for a few years offered a program of professional training for the fields of social welfare, cultural and educational services. With the closing of this school the need for a program was considered by the National Jewish Conference, in 1922, and led to the establishment of the Graduate School for Jewish Social Work in 1925. The school was set up cooperatively with the help of several foundations and of the federations, which contributed to its support until its liquidation in 1939. Through an arrangement with the New York School of Social Work, students of the Graduate School were enabled to get a combined preparation in the general theory and practice of social work as well as special training in the field of Jewish communal services.

An additional and increasing number of Jewish social workers were being trained by the general schools of social work, and their studies were supplemented by field training or early experience in Jewish agencies. In a study made in 1942 it was learned that seven out of every eight family workers, eleven out of twelve child care workers, one-half of the recreational and group workers, community organization personnel, vocational personnel and workers for the aged, had taken courses at graduate professional schools. More than two-thirds of the entire group (fewer in the smaller cities) had such formal preparation for their tasks. In the same year, 1942, however, only a small fraction of the professional group employed in Jewish social agencies had completed the two years of graduate education now considered standard for the social work profession.[15]

THE ORIGINS OF WELFARE FUNDS

The most important organizational development during the 1920s was the establishment of the first Jewish welfare funds to finance local and non-local beneficiary agencies. While federations were making progress in joint fund-raising for local programs, the national and overseas agencies continued to depend on their separately conducted campaigns. Appeals for overseas needs for the Joint Distribution Committee, the Zionist fund, and for other agencies, as well as solicitation for an increasing number of national organizations, were not then included in federation campaigns. Competition in the local communities among these multiple nation-wide campaigns was rampant. Furthermore, ideological differences about the Zionist movement tended to split the community into warring factions.

The advent of community chests and their successful operation had meant that the Jewish federations, whose functions had been purely fiscal, now found themselves substantially without function. After several years of experience with community chests, the Jewish federations learned that the chests could not solve two basic problems facing the Jewish community: 1) they made no provision for raising capital funds for plant renewal and expansion, and 2) they did not undertake any financial obligation for national and overseas causes and for local services of a religious character.

Federation leaders were also aware of what was happening to Jewish communal organization in the community chest setting. Morris Waldman, executive director of the Detroit Federation in 1927, stated:

Financially the Jewish agencies belonging to the Fund are infinitely better off than they were nine years ago, prior to the establishment of the Community Fund,* and probably better off than they would be had there been no Community Fund. . . . Nevertheless, the affiliation of the most important social service agencies with the Fund has complicated, perhaps retarded, at any rate made more difficult though not impossible, the development of a comprehensive and effective Jewish community organization.[16]

This combination of problems led to further federation planning in fund-raising for the national and overseas agencies and for special local interests which were not included in community chest campaigns. The answer in a number of community chest cities was the establishment of a Jewish welfare fund, beginning simultaneously in 1926 in Columbus, Detroit, Indianapolis, San Francisco and Oakland.[17]

Four other welfare funds were established under federation auspices by 1931—in Cincinnati, Omaha, Cleveland and Minneapolis; and a few of the smaller federations were beginning to include some non-local beneficiaries. The plans for the Jewish welfare fund followed in many respects the relationship established between the federation and its constituent beneficiary agencies.[18]

PROBLEMS OF WELFARE FUND ORGANIZATION

Although proponents of the Jewish welfare fund were enthusiastic about the results secured from the first campaigns, it was soon learned that the central financing of national and overseas agencies brought with it a new series of problems which differed in degree, if not in kind, from the problems which federation had originally experienced in relation to local beneficiaries. In one city it was reported that the larger national organizations had

* The community chest in Detroit was called the Detroit Community Fund.

been willing to cooperate and kept their agreements on fund solicitation, but complained because the subventions did not come up to expectation. The welfare fund believed, however, that agencies had failed to recognize the saving derived from not having to send solicitors and conduct campaigns in these cities. Some of the national and overseas beneficiary agencies and welfare funds failed to live up to the conditions of the welfare funds and continued to solicit money, through various devices, after they had agreed to give up their independent campaigns when they were granted welfare fund support.[19]

THE NATIONAL APPEALS INFORMATION SERVICE

The remoteness of the local communities from the administration of the national and overseas agencies, for which funds were being raised, made it necessary to find a method of maintaining closer contacts with the needs and programs of these organizations. Unlike the local agency which could be financed and budgeted by its own community federation, the national and overseas agencies were campaigning throughout the country and were deriving their funds both from the few welfare funds that had been established and from their own independent efforts in the non-welfare fund cities. Even in these latter cities, however, contributors responding to the individual campaigns were turning to their federations for information on the outside appeals.

These needs led to the organization of the National Appeals Information Service in 1927. The NAIS consisted of an association of federations which undertook jointly to finance studies and collect information concerning the programs of national and overseas fundraising organizations. The Bureau of Jewish Social Research was employed as the study agent of the federations for this purpose. The work of the NAIS continued until 1932, when it became an essential national service carried forward by the National Council of Jewish Federations and Welfare Funds in its budget research department.

CHANGING ATTITUDES AND THEORIES OF JEWISH ORGANIZATION

During this period a question, which had sometimes been voiced before 1890, concerning the rationale for Jewish philanthropic services, was again being heard. The question of the justification for separate Jewish welfare agencies was rarely heard in the early days of federation when an unusual development of Jewish needs had led to the organization of large-scale Jewish relief agencies and Jewish federations. During the prosperous years of the 1920s conditions were changing, immigration was being restricted; the larger part of the immigrant group had worked out its own adjustment. Public welfare was developing a more modern approach and the community chests were taking responsibility for fundraising for Jewish as well as for Christian and non-sectarian causes.

During this period, also, cultural changes were proceeding rapidly, as the younger generation developed American ways stamped upon them by the pattern of the public school system and the general life of the community. Not only in social welfare and education, but in recreation and leisure-time activities, non-sectarian and commercial developments were being increasingly utilized by the Jewish population.

Religious adherence and practices were changing rapidly among the children of the immigrant generation, many of whom were finding the Orthodox practices and synagogues of their parents uncongenial.[20] Some of the early federation leaders expressed concern with what they believed was a diminishing interest in philanthropic welfare activities supposedly arising from the processes of cultural assimilation:

[We must recognize] that by reason of the process of assimilation, there is annually an increasing escape from our ranks and year by year we find ourselves losing for communal purposes an increasing proportion of those men and women who by reason of heredity, tradition and longer established residence, should for many years to come furnish the largest proportion of our active communal workers.

If the present diminution of immigration is to continue permanently, this will constitute an ever increasing weakness in our endeavors thoroughly to organize our Jewish communities.[21]

A concern for the future of the Jewish welfare organizations in the face of these changes raised questions in the minds of other thoughtful leaders. The situation was analyzed by William J. Shroder, president of the National Conference of Jewish Social Service in 1927, as follows:

What part Jewish social service is to play in the coming order of things is uncertain. Signs point in both directions—for and against the survival of Jewishness, which alone will justify the maintenance of Jewish social service. As sustaining influences, we note the recrudescence of anti-Semitism, the distress of Jews in eastern Europe and Russia, the development of Palestine, the assumption of social responsibility (notably in the fields of character-building and recreation) by temple and synagogue, the growth of the movement for Jewish Centers and the general acceptance of some program for Jewish education.[22]

The pessimists were beginning to forsee the end of Jewish social service brought about by changing economic conditions, by the assimilation of the Jewish immigrant population and by the growth of public welfare. On the other hand, some leaders of federations saw in these trends an opportunity for the "positive" development of Jewish communal life with "cultural" replacing "charitable" interests.[23] Similar views were expressed by the Jewish educators, the workers in Jewish Centers and cultural agencies, and other professional workers. As stated by Israel Chipkin, president of the National Council of Jewish Education (1928):

There is every reason to anticipate that within the life of the present generation, philanthropy will have performed its mission. When it has done so, vast resources and energies within the Jewish community will be released and will seek new channels of expression.

A motivating force which created a firm communal bond will have disappeared, and Jewish leadership will have to formulate a new program, broader in content, perhaps more vital in its contribution to Jewish life. In this sense, at least, the American Jewish community is facing the dawn of a new day.[24]

But the forecasts in 1928 and 1929 for the end of Jewish dependency and an increasing interest in Jewish cultural life were premature. By 1930, there was evidence of the onset of a large scale economic depression which brought again to the fore unsolved economic problems of the whole community. It brought with it also the increasing difficulties of raising adequate funds which affected both federations and community chests. It was to bring with it, moreover, during the next few years, an avalanche of Jewish problems overseas and the repercussions of a world-wide anti-Semitic movement in the United States.

VI

From the Depression
to the War's End

The years from 1930 through 1945 were years of tremendous issues and vigorous solutions. Great changes were taking place in world affairs. Acute economic depression, world-wide in extent, was succeeded by one of the most prosperous periods in American history, during which unparalleled scientific developments heralded the beginning of the atomic age. The period also witnessed nazism and fascism exploiting anti-Semitism as a political weapon and launching a holocaust of destruction against European Jewry.

The early post-war years brought a decisive settlement in Palestine, with the establishment of the State of Israel and the opening of its doors to a large segment of the survivors of European Jewry. The Soviet Union drew the Iron Curtain around the countries of eastern Europe and launched the "cold war" against the Western nations.

These world conditions influenced American Jewish life. There was a heightening of group consciousness and a strong urge toward group cooperation and group action. This manifested itself tangibly in many ways—in the strengthening of Jewish communal welfare organization and its spread into all centers with substantial Jewish populations; in a more generous response to Jewish needs, as demonstrated in vastly increased giving to Jewish causes and in greater numbers of givers; in the strengthening of defense efforts against anti-Semitism and a determination to improve group relations; and finally, in the expansion of programs for overseas aid. At the end of the period American Jewry, by virtue of its size and economic conditions, had become the predominant segment of world Jewry.

Before 1920, federations had been geared to meet the problems of poverty and immigrant adjustment, operating through the traditional charitable agencies in the field of health and welfare. During the prosperous years of the 1920s the extent of relief needs and immigrant adjustment requirements began to ebb. Communities again found resources for building hospitals, homes for children and the aged, and new centers for meeting the cultural and educational needs of youth. Federations entered the cultural and educational fields of service—in part because of a philanthropic interest in helping to provide Jewish education and leisure-time activities for dependent and marginal families, in part through an awakening interest in the cultural life of the total community.

The economic collapse came just as a beginning was being made in all these directions. Soon relief pressures became overwhelming, the desire of federations to turn their attention and their funds to a wider communal program had to be postponed. As the depression grew in intensity, it threatened to impoverish, not only the recently adjusted immigrant families, but practically all

111

other sections of the population. In a few years, the federations and the welfare agencies which they supported were to encounter an economic distress of a magnitude greater than any that had been experienced during the height of immigration. Not only the newly arrived were affected, but also the resident and settled population.

It was not necessary to establish new agencies for the emergency. Assistance had in fact been continuing on a substantial basis despite reduced immigration and the beginnings of local public welfare programs. For two years, 1930 and 1931, federation's fund-raising efforts continued to be successful.[1] The recognition of increased need stimulated giving on the part of those who were still able to make substantial contributions. But as the depression continued and became more severe, a decline in available philanthropic resources was inevitable. It was necessary for all social agencies, sectarian and non-sectarian alike, to undertake a greater measure of cooperation if they were not to be completely overwhelmed by the pressures and the magnitude of the economic decline. The entire community geared itself to fund campaigns and work-relief programs to try to meet the enormously increased burdens of the charitable agencies as applications from all sections of the population poured in.

With from ten to fifteen million Americans jobless, the emergency campaigns conducted by community chests or by other overall bodies eased the strain for a brief period, but they were far from adequate to cope with the needs of the unemployed. All voluntary welfare organizations were forced to admit their inability to meet the financial needs of the tremendous number of applicants for help. At first, municipalities and states tried to meet the problem by voting emergency funds to be disbursed by the voluntary relief organizations or by the public welfare departments. By 1932, with declining municipal and state income, it was obvious that only the federal government with its larger fiscal powers could be considered the final resource for meeting mounting distress. Jewish leadership as well as the leadership of other sections of the community began to look to the federal government for basic shoring up of the livelihood of American families, through federal help for the unemployed.[2]

A new federal administration in 1933 adopted a slate of new measures to bolster up the economic system and to provide some assistance to the unemployed and their destitute families. Made-work programs, grants-in-aid to the states and other measures were climaxed in 1935 by the Social Security Act which established the groundwork for a continuing policy of federal programs of social security and public assistance, with more adequate unemployment aid and other measures. The effects of the depression on the unemployed were ameliorated and an upward economic swing began.

The pressures upon the Jewish family agencies for relief began to decline. By 1934 it was estimated that between 70% to 90% of Jewish dependent families were on the public relief rolls.[3] From that year on the Jewish family service agencies assumed an ever diminishing role in providing income for dependent families. The giving of financial assistance by Jewish agencies to Jewish families before long became minimal, operating only for those to whom public assistance was not indicated or was unavailable, such as for new immigrants.

In the aftermath of the depression, an appraisal showed that in a number of cities where recently built communal institutions had been financed by mortgages, the situation had become precarious. There had been the danger of bank foreclosures as dwindling income made it impossible to maintain payments and interest charges. Most federations had little in the way of reserve funds and these were soon exhausted in meeting the increased needs of the relief agencies and in continuing the operation of other essential communal services.[4]

The depression affected Jewish communal services primarily in the decrease of funds for maintaining the communal institutions, and in the increase in relief applicants. Other results of the depression were less acute. The voluntary hospitals were reporting a decrease in private bed occupancy and a general reduction in the number of patients. As lowered incomes for families postponed needed hospital care, the number of patients served by the outpatient clinics increased.

In the area of dependent child care, the depression did not increase the number of children placed away from their homes; the number in fact declined. Twenty years of emphasis on the principle of not removing children from their homes for reasons of poverty was having its effect, and public and private relief resources were now available to maintain family unity. In 1932 the number of dependent children in foster homes began to exceed the number under institutional care for the first time in the history of Jewish child care services.[5]

To help the unemployed, federations enlarged and intensified their job-finding efforts, and Jewish vocational service agencies were established in a number of cities. (These agencies continued their services during the war, when the problem changed from that of excessive unemployment to labor shortages.) Discrimination against Jews in employment and special aspects of vocational guidance were also receiving attention, both through the vocational service agencies and the developing functions of community relations agencies.[6]

In New York City, the chronic disparity between the Brooklyn Federation and the Manhattan-Bronx Federation in their ability to raise funds became even more marked during the depression. The declining income of the Brooklyn Federation had forced it to make drastic cuts in all its appropriations. It was necessary in 1931 for the New York Federation to come to the aid of Brooklyn, if an essential communal program of assistance to Jewish families was to be maintained in that borough.[7] In 1937, after two decades of separate existence, the New York and Brooklyn Federations combined their campaigns into a single appeal, with an integrated federation for the entire city developing after several years of joint fund-raising.

FEDERATIONS ORGANIZE THE COUNCIL OF JEWISH FEDERATIONS AND WELFARE FUNDS

In 1929 there were sixty-three Jewish federations and five welfare funds in the principal cities of the United States reporting to the Bureau of Jewish Social Research. In addition, there were twenty-four other cities, mostly with small Jewish populations, which had some central organization, and where the family agency was beginning to take on some general community welfare functions.[8]

With the deepening of the depression, federations found it essential to associate more actively for common purposes. As a result of meeting together to consider the effect of the depression on Jewish communal programs, and with the experience of several years of jointly planning and supporting the National Appeals Information

115

Service (NAIS), federations recognized the need for a permanent National Council of Federations. The Bureau of Jewish Social Research in 1931 had organized a "Continuing Committee of Federation Executives" to provide opportunity for exchanges of experience and common planning on the critical problems that federations faced with the growing economic depression. Samuel A. Goldsmith, chairman of a committee which had been organized by the Federation Executives to study the problem, recommended the formation of a national council, and listed the areas of Jewish social work which called for common planning and common efforts as follows:

The relationship of Jewish federations to community chests;

The relationship of program of Jewish cultural and educational work to program of Jewish federations;

The relationship of local Jewish communities to the program of national service organizations, dealing particularly with the problems of organization of Jewish community work; and

The relationship of the Jewish family relief programs to tax relief programs locally and nationally, and to the emergency relief funds raised in the various communities.[9]

In 1932 the National Council of Jewish Federations and Welfare Funds was formally established on the initiative of fifteen federations. The Council began to develop services to communities in cooperation with the Bureau of Jewish Social Research. In 1935 the Bureau was incorporated into the Council of Jewish Federations and Welfare Funds.

THE IMPACT OF ANTI-SEMITISM

The organization of the Council of Jewish Federations and Welfare Funds and the various regional and national meetings of federations during this period were indicative of the new problems facing Jewish communities, and of the reactions of the communities to these problems and of the changing character of federations. In addition to the depression, with its adverse effect on the living standards of the population and on the financial resources of the agencies, the onset of the historic tragedy which was to overwhelm overseas Jewry had an increasing impact on the Jewish communities of this country.

With the advent of Hitler the raging anti-Semitism in Germany threatened to become a general conflagration. The insecurity and suffering of the Jews in Germany came as a shock to Jews in this country who had been assuming for generations that the virulent types of anti-Semitism were limited to eastern Europe and that Jews in central and western Europe were living in relative security. The JDC, which had been almost at the point of discontinuing its activities in Europe, was faced again with enormous problems. The efforts of Zionist fund-raising bodies to build up Palestine were seen not only by Zionist sympathizers but increasingly also by non-Zionists as affording opportunities for the resettlement of the harassed and displaced Jews of Europe.

The intensity of anti-Semitism in central Europe made it immediately obvious that the phenomenon would not be confined to the overseas countries. Its repercussions began to be felt in America through the increasing virulence of anti-Semitic activities operating in the confused and discouraging period of the economic depression. The national agencies concerned with group relationships, which had previously been dealing with far less acute problems and whose operations had been relatively small in scale and concerned primarily with the rights of Jews overseas, had to begin to expand their efforts to deal with the growing tide of prejudice and discrimination in the United States. It was obvious that Jewish communal life and organization were entering upon a new and difficult era.

STOCKTAKING AND EVALUATION

Stocktaking and evaluation were natural tendencies in a period when communities were facing such radically different circumstances. The focus in 1934 and 1935 was on the effects of the economic depression. The disaster affecting the lives of Jews in central Europe was still too recent in inception for its impact on the future of overseas and American Jews to be fully evaluated. What was the federation movement; what had it accomplished and where was it going? With federation income sharply curtailed by the depression, there was need for a critical self-examination. Such an analysis was undertaken by a committee of the CJFWF of which Dr. Ben Selekman (then executive of the Boston Federation) was chairman.[10]

The committee sought to define the programs and policies which federations should adopt as the basis for shaping their new programs during that difficult period. In a summary prepared by Dr. Selekman and published in the *American Jewish Year Book, 1934-1935,* the following basic points were listed:

> 1. In view of the increasing assumption of responsibility on the part of public agencies for relief, the federation may be expected to give a decreasing emphasis on relief functions as such, and increasing emphasis on: (a) problems of occupational redistribution to help secure a better balance for Jews in the economic life of the country; and

(b) those activities which are so specifically Jewish that none but Jews can be expected to support them . . . granting of larger appropriations than have been allotted in the past to cultural and educational work, and relatively smaller appropriations to family welfare, child care and health, the three fields which have hitherto received the bulk of federation funds.

2. The federation must assume a more direct responsibility for the proper organization of support for national and international agencies. The work of these agencies is as important to the protection and survival of the Jewish people as is the work of local agencies. Their present method of competitive fund-raising leads to disunity and to a minimum of financial results. Where the federation cannot itself assume responsibility for raising funds for national and international work, it should organize an efficient fund-raising mechanism for the purpose. The experience of welfare funds in operation in a number of communities for central fund-raising for all Jewish needs should be studied for the light it may throw on this problem.

3. The federations must review their traditional fund-raising methods for the purpose of broadening the sources of their support, by enlisting new subscribers of small and middle-sized contributions instead of concentrating too exclusively, as it has in the past, upon the relatively few wealthier members of the community.

4. Since Jews are affected by fundamental economic and social forces that affect all Americans, the federation as representative of the Jewish community should cooperate in promoting desirable social legislation and governmental action to provide security and a progressively rising standard of living for the masses of people.

5. The federation must be made the authoritative agency of the Jewish community for studying, planning, reorganizing and creating the type of instrumentality which will best serve the needs of the community. This calls on the one hand for a modification of the rights of autonomy of individual agencies, elimination of antiquated services, and

the promotion of amalgamations where desirable; and on the other hand for the democratization of the federation structure so that all groups of the Jewish community will be represented in the governing body.[11]

These proposals were translated into practical activities and were increasingly accepted by the federations throughout the country. Within the next ten years the following trends began to be marked:

1. Broadening of fund-raising organization and campaign methods resulting in an effective response by all elements of the Jewish community to the growing needs of national and overseas programs dealing with anti-Semitism and its effect upon Jews. **2.** A shift in focus of interest from emphasis on charitable services for dependents to broader aspects of welfare at home and large-scale fund-raising for overseas needs. **3.** Structural changes in Jewish communal organization with the aim of bringing larger and wider segments of the population into association for cooperative work.

RAPID GROWTH OF WELFARE FUNDS

The first two trends resulted in the establishment of welfare funds; the third in changes in federation structure and administration. These three developments were interrelated in many communities. In 1930 there were hundreds of small and intermediate-sized communities without central organization for fund-raising or for other communal services. In many of these cities an advisory council of local interest groups and associations was frequently the basis upon which a central fund-raising machinery for a welfare fund was established.

Jewish communities which had for a number of years received funds for the support of their local services from the community chests now began to develop their own welfare funds in order to achieve a community-wide response to the needs of the overseas and national agencies. Communities which had few occasions to meet the welfare needs of local families or individuals were galvanized into action in behalf of suffering Jewry overseas. Almost overnight Jewish group consciousness was becoming more profound and was being manifested in concrete programs of group action.

An increase in the number of welfare funds was the specific response to these new problems. The development was spontaneous and rapid. By 1936, thirty-five additional welfare funds had been organized, twenty-three of them since 1934. By 1941 there were Jewish federations or welfare funds in 260 cities—virtually every city with any substantial Jewish population, and many very small ones.[12]

THE WAR YEARS

World War II brought to a climax the trend in Jewish organizations which had begun in the 1930s. For Jews the hostilities had not begun with the military phase in the autumn of 1939—they had been initiated at least six years previously and had induced a vigorous development of local communal welfare organization and overseas relief programs. Practically all communities were now organized, better prepared to meet the responsibilities at home and to mobilize support for the overseas agencies struggling with the holocaust of destruction abroad.

At home the war mobilization induced heightened industrial productivity, utilizing manpower to the fullest possible extent, and sweeping away the remaining pockets of unemployment. Anti-alien sentiments which had been retarding the economic absorption of the refugee immigration were weakened in the face of war needs for full production. Nazi-inspired anti-Semitism was becoming suspect and the emergence of the Soviet Union as a wartime ally brought a temporary postponement of most of the ideological conflicts then current. Greater unity of action became the aim of our national life, helping to ease group differences.

The requirements of civilian defense and stability on the home front helped to safeguard the ongoing programs of the social welfare agencies. For the first time in more than a decade the social welfare needs were largely those arising from full employment rather than those which were by-products of economic recession. It was again obvious that our governmental and voluntary health and welfare agencies were an important element of community well-being, not only a last resort for the poor.

Improved economic conditions brought increases in philanthropic funds. The acute problems of the period were the rising costs due to wartime inflation, only partially controlled; the shortage of physicians, nurses, social workers and other employees who had mobilized for war services; shortages of available foster homes, and wartime restrictions on supplies. In the face of these shortages, there was a need for expanded social services on the home front, and increased use by an employed population of health and welfare facilities. New recreational services and programs were required in the war-intensified industrial cities and for the men and women in the training camps and on leave in the adjacent communities.

A factor in the increase of local expenditures during the war years was the organization of programs for men and women in the armed services of the United States. It has been estimated that approximately 550,000 Jews were members of the armed services.[13] The work of the National Jewish Welfare Board was expanded to provide this personnel with religious, cultural and recreational services and local communities assumed responsibility for the men and women in the nearby training camps. Federations cooperated with the JWB in a nation-wide study of the number of Jews in the armed forces and assembled information concerning their services.

WAR CHESTS

The need for additional funds and wartime services, and the organization of a National War Fund for domestic and overseas wartime welfare needs gave rise to the war chests sponsored by the non-sectarian community chests. They were designed as single inclusive campaigns for local welfare services as well as for the wartime service agencies and the overseas relief appeals. In the desire to achieve local unity among all groups and to help concentrate upon a single overall campaign, Jewish welfare funds considered the question whether to continue their separate appeals or join the war chests. Only the Jewish Welfare Board's program of services to the armed forces had been integrated into a general national agency appeal. And if war chests were to allocate funds for other Jewish national and overseas appeals, it would have to be through inclusion of local Jewish welfare funds.[14]

The position of many Jewish social welfare leaders on the question of war chests was summed up at the 1942 General Assembly by William J. Shroder:

Force of circumstances, rather than any thinking, is going to determine whether Jewish welfare funds must go into or can stay out of war chests. We should think about and determine the conditions under which we go into war chests. Our welfare funds are more than mere money collecting and distributing agencies in our Jewish community; the welfare fund is a social organization, educating us in meeting our social obligations; it harmonizes our divergent interests into an integrated plan, substituting cooperative effort for destructive competition. It is the result of twelve years of effort in developing a technique, a machinery, a platform upon which a kind of community unity, for which we all hunger, has been and is being developed.[15]

Affirmative decision to join war chests was made in twenty-four cities in 1943, including Chicago, Detroit, Cincinnati, St. Louis, Atlantic City, Buffalo and Memphis. Separate campaigns by the Jewish welfare funds were conducted by mutual agreement in other war chest cities.

The changed conditions affecting community organization resulting from the transfer of separate Jewish fund-raising organization to war chests in some cities raised doubts about the performance and stability of Jewish federations similar to such doubts as had been voiced in the early days of community chest movement. In 1927 one Jewish federation leader had stated that "Jewish leaders were already wondering if there is further need of the Jewish federation in cities in which they are connected with the chest."[16] This was obviously a short range view which experience in the 1930s and 1940s served to dispel.[17]

The experience of the Jewish federations that had joined war chests was on the whole encouraging. Conducted in the spirit of wartime unity, chests had proven to be good fund-raising instruments; and few difficulties were encountered, although some doubts were expressed on what might happen to the resumption of Jewish fund-raising when the war chests ended.[18]

The final War Chest and National War Fund Appeal in this period was conducted in the fall of 1945. With some exceptions, allocations to Jewish federations for 1946 were approximately the same as, or slightly above, the 1945 grants. Anticipating the end of the war chest period, some federations were undertaking supplementary campaigns to meet increased overseas needs.

Little difficulty was experienced in the transition back to separate fund-raising:

Looking ahead to the resumption of independent fund-raising after the completion of current war chest drives, Jewish community leaders are unanimously optimistic. It is anticipated that, far from having lost ground during the war chest period, the Jewish organizations will emerge as stronger and more effective fund-raising agencies.[19]

This turned out to be an accurate forecast proven by the events of 1946 and subsequent years.

LARGER ALLOCATIONS FOR OVERSEAS AGENCIES

There was a gradual shift in fund-raising methods by the national and overseas agencies, as more and more local welfare funds were established and assumed responsibility for obtaining financial support for these agencies. In 1935 the federations and welfare funds had contributed only 20% of the income of 32 national and overseas agencies. By 1946 this proportion had increased to an estimated 80% of all philanthropic contributions received by these organizations—about 95% of the funds received by the United Jewish Appeal, and 55% of the income of other overseas and national agencies.[20]

The outbreak of the war in Europe in 1939 also intensified the local efforts of the Jewish communal organizations. Although the new welfare funds were largely concerned with national and overseas problems, local services were accorded increased attention. During this period, Jewish family relief agencies, which had been able to show a decrease in costs due to the assumption of basic relief by public governmental agencies, were again having to make large expenditures in behalf of the refugees who were now permitted to enter this country.[21]

Since 1933 it had become increasingly evident that the situation facing Jews in Germany was a highly precarious one. Efforts of agencies operating overseas with American funds to mitigate the disaster in Germany became less and less effective, and emigration to Palestine, to the United States and to other countries was intensified. Early in 1936 the federations and welfare funds were told by representative European leaders at the General Assembly of the CJFWF that there was no future for the Jews of Germany and that emigration was the only remedy. The federations and welfare funds thereupon pledged that they would raise the largest possible sums for the immigration and resettlement work of the JDC and UPA (United Palestine Appeal) and would accept responsibility for helping all immigrants who could be brought to this country.[22]

THE ORGANIZATION OF COMMUNITY COUNCILS

As federations and welfare funds received wider support from larger sections of the Jewish community (see note 20), they also adapted their structures to this broadening of participation. The point of view expressed in 1937 by Sidney Hollander was indicative of the changing attitude:

Federation is unique as the one meeting ground on which Jews of all opinions can join in common purposes. But to achieve unity, the federation must be representative of *all* Jewry, a true *kehillah* of social purpose, and that means that all groups must meet on an equal footing. Wealth must not dominate nor social position. "Reform" Jews have no greater claim to control than "Orthodox."[23]

As a means of securing wider overall participation in the central communal programs, and of extending these programs into non-philanthropic areas, a number of cities established community councils either directly through federations or as an independent project of interested groups. The distinction between a community council and a federation became in time primarily that of structure rather than of function, and often a distinction in name only, with no real difference either in structure or in function.

The deep concern of the 1930s with problems of group relations made it possible to enlist the interest of Jewish organizations and to secure representation on the community council from a variety of non-philanthropic fraternal, Zionist, religious and other interest groups, fully supported by their own members. In a number of cities this form of structure based upon group representation was the basic design for the community councils and for the recently organized welfare funds concerned primarily with raising money for overseas and national agencies.

In a few cities where federations and welfare funds had been in existence for a number of years, a separate community council representing a wide variety of Jewish interest groups became, as in Cleveland and Detroit, the place for discussing issues other than those of fundraising, primarily in the area of group relationships— within the Jewish community, and with the total community. Such councils concerned themselves with anti-

Semitism and intra-group problems such as *kashruth* and group ethics. The federation in these cities accepted and supported the community council in these functions.

Where the community council was being advocated as a new form of communal organization, differing in structure and function from some of the existing federations and welfare funds, the validity of multiple separate communal structures was questioned. Why community councils? Why not the expansion of federation to take on the constituency, structure and functions associated with community councils?

The rationale for a community council as a separate organization was stated by Max Simon, the first president of the Cleveland Jewish Community Council, organized in 1936. Ten years previously Orthodox agencies had joined the federation, which had also established a bureau of Jewish education and had undertaken a welfare fund function to supplement community chest fund-raising. The structure of the Cleveland federation included representation of contributors and beneficiary agencies, with a provision for the participation of a number of rabbis, but without representation of other organizations. Mr. Simon stated that, "There was still needed some instrument capable of bringing together all elements of the community on a more extensive basis than had been achieved by any existing organization (the federation)."[24]

The activities of the Cleveland Council during the first year of its existence are indicative of the functions which it assumed. The Council's discussion and action embraced "any matter of general concern to the Jewish community." In the first months there had been no lack of problems. At the first meeting attention was called to the chronic practice of injecting fictitious "Jewish issues" into local political campaigns to stir up racial and religious prejudice against particular candidates, in the hope of obtaining the "Jewish vote." While the Council concerned itself primarily with group and public relations, it also considered that it had some responsibility in other areas of the communal field.

What authority was such a body to enjoy? This question arose at the outset. Was it to be merely a forum or could it take action; and if it could, what would action mean in terms of its authority over and the responsibility of its member agencies?[25]

Some of the leaders of community councils soon recognized that their organization could not act as an authoritative body since it had no ability to enforce the decisions of majorities on resisting minorities. Consequently, a council's basic function, if not the only one, would be to serve as an instrument for enhancing voluntary association and creating opportunities for group cooperation.

It was obvious at this time that federations, welfare funds and community councils were attempting to find a more incisive approach to the solution of problems confronting the American Jewish community, and that all of them were experiments in effective community structure. In some communities the establishment of a community council as an additional organization was a reflection, or a survival, of former group cleavages and conflicts. Some federations sponsored the formation of community councils, to undertake functions which the federations at that time did not consider appropriately within their own jurisdiction or responsibility. In many communities, however, the central federation or welfare fund had become sufficiently broad in concept and sufficiently acceptable to all groups in the Jewish population as to enable it to take on additional functions without the necessity of building a second structure.

Although most communities in the 1930s were successful in adapting their existing organizations to meet the pressing needs of the time, not all the conflicts among the various elements of the Jewish community were being resolved through voluntary cooperation; groups and viewpoints persisted which could not be reconciled with the action programs desired by other groups. There were some, therefore, who believed that what was required was "a scheme of Jewish self-government expressing all social, religious, economic, and other phases of Jewish life." That this was a theoretical and impractical approach was seen already in 1936.

The scheme for such self-government is not only chimerical—it is unwise. It represents the ecstatic wishes of a few who, feeling that Jewish community life is a vacuum, desire to fill the vacuum with words. . . . That the activities of the community need better organization, more planful procedure, a more dignified and more valid expression of communal purpose is, of course, apparent. Our Jewish community life in the United States is still quite young.[26]

The structures for communal organization were thus evolving during this period through experimental organization for central fund-raising for local, national and overseas needs, and for dealing with anti-Semitism and intra-group problems. An additional communal body grew in part out of the need to secure a broader base of participation in new functions which had not yet been included under the existing federation. In time a consolidation of functions and structures was to be achieved in many of the cities which had previously set up more than one central agency.

While these efforts toward central communal organization were taking place, a continuation of the cleavages resulting from group diversities was highlighted by the difficulties of achieving cooperation nationally on two important aspects of Jewish communal interest. These, to be considered in the next chapter, are: (a) fund-raising by the overseas agencies, and (b) programs dealing with anti-Semitism.

VII

Local Funds and
National Agencies

The uncontrolled and world-wide spread of anti-Semitism during the 1930s had a marked effect on the group consciousness, the group aims and the communal interests of American Jewry. In the face of external threats, the traditional divisions and separations seemed to many thoughtful observers an expensive luxury which Jews could ill afford.

On the local scene this feeling was translated into various forms of cooperative group association. The desire to close ranks was the mainspring for the formation of the many federations, funds and councils which were organized in that period. Communal agencies established in previous decades were strengthened, and the desire for unity made itself felt in many areas of Jewish interest.

With the development of local central fund-raising responsibility for national and overseas agencies, the existing federations faced new problems. It seemed reasonable and logical to the federations that the cohesiveness of groups and the cooperation of agencies which had been achieved in the local communities could be repeated among the national and overseas agencies if only the proper approach and suitable procedures could be devised.

The practical problems arising locally from the desire for greater unity and cooperation among national agencies was manifested early among the new welfare funds. "Generally speaking, local community organizations have increased the acceptance of individual responsibility for both local and national needs."[1] With funds derived from all sections of the community being allocated to a variety of agencies, what were equitable allocations to agencies which had depended previously upon the more limited number of direct contributors? How were the agencies' requests to be reconciled with the funds available, which were invariably less than the sums requested? What were the relative merits and relative needs among the different fields of work and among agencies engaged in the performance of similar or related activities? Why was it necessary to have more than one agency operating in each of the fields of health, welfare, group relations and overseas relief?

The problems were in some respects similar to those which had confronted federations in the initial stages of central fund-raising for local agencies; but there were new aspects by virtue of the fact that each local welfare fund represented but a fraction of the total area from which the national and overseas agencies were seeking funds, and the work of the latter could not be observed at first hand, as could the local beneficiaries.

These new problems and difficulties in the budgeting process were among the first concerning which welfare funds began to look for help. Since the national and overseas agencies had been established as a result of the interests of special groups, and not as a consequence of national central planning, the rise of welfare funds was bound to focus attention on this piecemeal development, with its overlappings and duplications, and to raise the question whether a more cooperative form of agency planning might be initiated.

If these questions were to be properly answered it could only be through the cooperative efforts of a number of cities.

NATIONAL AGENCIES FOR THE TUBERCULAR

The first field with which the welfare funds concerned themselves was that of the national hospitals for the care of the tuberculous. The field had been one of the largest among the Jewish charitable interests before the organization of overseas relief efforts. Though the four agencies—the National Jewish Hospital of Denver, the Jewish Consumptives' Relief Society of Denver, the Ex-Patients' Tubercular Home of Denver, the Jewish Consumptives' Relief Association of Los Angeles—were continuing to run separate campaigns in many communities, they had become beneficiaries of welfare funds in a considerable number of cities. It seemed desirable to evaluate the work of the four organizations, to consider the relationship of the national agencies to the problems and to the programs for the care of the Jewish tuberculous which had developed locally in a number of larger Jewish communities, and to determine what cooperative plans could be undertaken by the national and local hospitals in this field.

The survey initiated in 1937 was undertaken under the joint auspices of a committee representing the institutions and the welfare funds. Completed in 1938, the study recommended the creation of a joint instrument to be set up by the national agencies for the purposes of cooperative planning. The survey also suggested that it would be logical and desirable for the four institutions eventually to consolidate their efforts into a unified organization.[2]

Although the institutions were giving consideration to the recommendations, concrete measures to follow through were slow to develop. An initial logical step seemed to be the merger of the National Jewish Hospital and the Jewish Consumptives' Relief Society—both located in Denver, and both substantially concerned with similar programs of medical and social care. Proposals for merger were looked upon favorably by the welfare funds and were endorsed by the Board of the CJFWF in 1940.

Several years of conferring and of exploring this aim resulted in complete failure. The institutions therefore turned their attention to what seemed a less difficult proposal—the setting up of a council of the four national agencies to study problems of their interrelationships and to attempt to achieve a greater degree of cooperation in service and in fund-raising. A Council of National Tuberculosis Institutions was finally established in 1943 with the stated purpose of devising ways and means for a coordinated program of effort; and for two years this Council employed a professional director to promote its program. But the JCRS of Denver had from the beginning declined membership in the Council, and when no progress was made toward a merger of the JCRS with the National Jewish Hospital of Denver, the Council of National Tuberculosis Institutions was disbanded. The four agencies intensified their independent campaigning and an increasing part of their income was being secured from outside the welfare funds. The trend away from inclusion in welfare funds and toward independent fund-raising increased from year to year. In 1940, the four institutions were receiving about 15% of their contributed income from welfare funds. By 1952 the percentage had shrunk to less than 6%.[3] In effect this field of national service did not accept federation support, nor is it generally accepted, by the system of local federated financing. This experience of national health agencies preferring their independent efforts to inclusion in federated funds is similar both in the Jewish and in the non-sectarian fields.

OVERSEAS AGENCIES

The history of financing of the overseas agencies exemplified a trend opposite to that of the agencies for the care of the tuberculous. Centralized support of overseas programs became increasingly an essential part of federated fund-raising, and coordination of overseas work developed early. Though at the beginning the difficulties in this field seemed overwhelming, the nature of the overseas problems made cooperation imperative.

The two principal agencies working overseas, the Joint Distribution Committee and the United Palestine Appeal, were for many years competitive in their approach to contributors. The division of American Jewry into Zionist affiliated individuals and non- or anti-Zionists was an important element in the competition. Since welfare fund policy was to seek contributions to a common fund from all persons despite their special interests or affiliations, it was essential that both the JDC, which was concentrating its efforts on European aid, and the United Palestine Appeal, which was engaged in central fund-raising for the major Zionist programs in Palestine, should be included as beneficiaries of local central fund-raising organizations.

Like other national agencies, the agencies raising funds for overseas work sometimes took a negative attitude toward the development of central fund-raising, which would supersede their independent campaign efforts. A number of cities found them none too cordial to the creation of welfare funds. Nevertheless, as the welfare fund movement spread, the majority of national and overseas agencies began accepting participation and giving up their independent fund-raising, though frequently with great reluctance.

Rivalry in fund-raising by such agencies as stressed the enlistment of individual contributors for their specific causes was now transferred to the local central fund-raising organizations. The major ideological difference between JDC and UPA in these years was on the relative priority of aiding distressed Jews in the countries of their residence as against stimulating their migration to Palestine. Each of these organizations was attempting to obtain an allocation of funds measured in terms of the comparable funds received by the rival agency.

At the end of 1936, the welfare funds brought this situation to their national service agency, the CJFWF, and urged that greater harmony be established among the agencies competing for allocations in their communities. Differences between the two organizations at that time were too acute to make a joint campaign practicable. Some less drastic proposal for resolving the competition was required. The Council was finally successful in getting the JDC and the UPA to agree on a ratio growing out of their past experience that might serve as a guide to 1937 welfare fund allocations for each.

In the same year, the JDC reached an agreement with ORT (engaged in a vocational program in many of the countries in which the JDC was operating as the principal overseas welfare agency) by which ORT agreed to request its own separate allocation from the organized welfare funds, while JDC undertook responsibility for a grant to ORT in order to avoid an additional campaign (by ORT) in the non-welfare fund cities in which the JDC was raising funds independently. This agreement between ORT and JDC did not bring complete satisfaction; and welfare funds were raising questions as to the necessity for a separate ORT allocation in view of the close relationship of ORT's work to the program of JDC —which was also engaged in subsidizing vocational programs in a number of European countries.*

An advisory formula accepted by JDC and UPA and transmitted to the welfare funds by CJFWF for the relative proportions of the funds to be allocated to JDC and UPA operated satisfactorily in 1937. Nevertheless, the renewal of the agreement on a formula for 1938 was again attended with difficulties, and considerable time and effort were required to arrive at a percentage satisfactory to both organizations.

An additional problem in 1938 was the raising of funds for the National Coordinating Committee for German Refugees[4] which had been organized as a joint effort of a number of national and local service agencies in New York City assisting the refugees arriving in this country. The Coordinating Committee, which included HIAS and other national agencies in its membership, had established a close relationship with the JDC as the agency for immigration service in Europe; but it was in need of a separate budget in addition to the funds regularly raised by its participant agencies. An agreement was finally

* Eventually, the JDC worked out an arrangement with ORT in welfare fund cities as well as in the unorganized communities, which has continued to date, with JDC providing support for ORT, and with ORT giving up its separate campaigns.

effected for 1938 which took its financial needs into consideration.

THE EMERGENCE OF THE UNITED JEWISH APPEAL

The problems involved in working out such agreements became increasingly difficult in preparation for the 1939 campaign. The needs and goals of both JDC and UPA were greatly enlarged with the growing sense of urgency about the fate of European Jewry and the necessity for assisting German refugees to immigrate to Palestine. The CJFWF, representing the wishes of its membership, requested the JDC and the UPA to arrive at a fair agreement in the division of funds they would raise for overseas needs in 1939. As William Shroder, then president of the CJFWF, stated: "This request was based on a desire to avoid friction arising from competition for funds in welfare fund cities." But an even more practical reason for the request was that "it was based on the belief that a fair agreement would produce maximum giving."[5]

The results of the negotiations were more successful than had been anticipated. Cooperation was extended beyond the mere agreement on a percentage ratio. A United Jewish Appeal was organized which involved the two major agencies in a merged campaign with an agreed upon procedure for the basic amounts to be distributed by the UJA to its two major partners. In addition, the UJA accepted responsibility for the financing of the National Coordinating Committee for Refugees. Through the CJFWF the welfare funds were given representation on the committee which was to distribute the surplus part of the funds raised by the UJA.

The achievement of a merged campaign in 1939 did not, however, end difficulties within the UJA, which for several more years continued in a state of uneasy peace. The merged campaign was immediately successful in securing greater funds, but other problems loomed large in the minds of the partners. As time approached for a new annual agreement on the division of funds there were extended discussions as to what constituted an equitable distribution of income and what part of the funds should be given to the National Coordinating Committee (reorganized in 1939 as an autonomous agency under the name of the National Refugee Service). The representatives of the welfare funds through the Council were again a factor in establishing a formula for the distribution of funds raised by the UJA for 1940.

The reaching of agreement and the setting up of the UJA meant that from this point on the UJA would look upon the welfare funds, which were being rapidly established in small, as well as intermediate and large cities, as the instruments for securing financial support from the American Jewish community. Each agency, however, continued to feel that its program warranted a larger proportion of the funds being raised in welfare fund cities than the percentage which had been negotiated.

UJA INSTABILITY

Because of continuing and unresolved disagreements, the United Jewish Appeal was dissolved at the end of 1940. Despite extended negotiations, the JDC and the UPA had been unable to arrive at a satisfactory formula, and the two agencies announced that they would conduct separate campaigns for 1941. The main source of difficulty seemed to be in the proportion of funds to be allocated to the National Refugee Service.[6] Most of the local leaders believed that the dissolution of the UJA would be detrimental to the success of their welfare fund campaigns. The attitudes of welfare fund leadership on the desirability of a continuation of the United Jewish Appeal were clearly and sharply expressed at the General Assembly of the CJFWF held in Atlanta, Ga., February 1-3, 1941. Negotiations were therefore resumed and an agreement was finally reached in March 1941, following several months of independent campaigning by the two agencies.

UJA agreements were continued in 1942, 1943 and 1944 with somewhat less difficulty. At one point in the course of negotiations on the 1944 agreement, however, unresolved difficulties loomed so large that it looked as though the UJA might again be dissolved. Sidney Hollander, the president of the Council, and William J. Shroder, the chairman of the Board, addressed a letter on November 9, 1943, to the federations, welfare funds and community councils stressing the need for united community action and for the maintenance of their central fund-raising even should the national agencies find it impossible nationally to cooperate effectively in their fund-raising relationships with welfare funds.

The acuteness of the problem was due to ideological differences. The American Jewish Conference had been established in 1943 for the purpose not only of securing cooperative action among all Jewish groups on the European situation, but also for the purpose of adopting an American Jewish consensus about the future of Palestine. The fund-raising agencies were not themselves members of the American Jewish Conference, but they were closely related to organizations that were. At the close of the Conference's first meeting some of the national agencies which had participated in its organization withdrew from membership because of an unwillingness to accept the resolution on Palestine. Ideological conflicts within the communities now became intensified.

The difficulties for the UJA in 1944 were, however, resolved, but they became acute again at the end of the year, when it was necessary to negotiate for the 1945 campaign. But by this time the experience of the welfare funds with the UJA had inclined them strongly toward a permanent UJA. This point of view was illustrated in a resolution adopted by the West Central States Region of the CJFWF, in October 1944, which stated that:

In view of the unifying influence which the UJA has exercised not only in fund-raising . . . but in creating a greater spirit of mutual understanding and sympathy between the exponents of the several causes and within the community, we urge: (1) The continuation of the United Jewish Appeal on a permanent basis without the uncertainty attendant upon the making of annual contracts; (2) The creation of such impartial budgeting machinery within the United Jewish Appeal itself as would eliminate the need for annual bargaining by the component agencies.[7]

Late in 1944 it was announced that the JDC and the UPA had failed to come to an agreement for 1945. The agencies had appeared willing to reconstitute the UJA, but they were unable to agree on terms. Separate national campaigns were announced by the JDC, UPA and NRS; and some were already in progress. Welfare funds directly and through the CJFWF were urging the agencies to reconstitute the United Jewish Appeal; but this had not yet been achieved in February 1945 when the federations and welfare funds were meeting in the General Assembly of the CJFWF. It was not until June of that year that the UJA was again reconstituted after a series of meetings with representatives of the welfare funds and the intervention of the President's War Relief Control Board.[8] The WRCB had been established by the United States government at the outbreak of war for the purpose of supervising and coordinating numerous war relief appeal agencies which were active during the period.

Following this forced reconstitution in 1945, the UJA had been continued with gradually diminishing tensions and strains. Both the JDC and the UPA recognized that the two organizations were essential parts of an overall integrated program of overseas aid. Some problems of fund distribution remained, especially that of financing the United Service for New Americans and the New York Association for New Americans (successor agencies to the National Refugee Service). The heavy post-war refugee immigration and resulting high costs of the program was one of the major problems, finally resolved in 1949 by the appointment of an impartial chairman of a joint JDC-UPA committee for this sector of the UJA program.

At the end of 1953, the JDC and UPA, which had not previously negotiated an agreement for more than a single year, were able to conclude a five-year agreement. By this time there had been a number of years of highly satisfactory cooperative relationships on progams between the JDC and the Jewish Agency for Palestine, the major beneficiary of the United Israel Appeal (the name now given to what used to be known as the United Palestine Appeal).

COORDINATION OF COMMUNITY RELATIONS WORK

Only partial progress has been made in coordinating the community relations agencies, although much effort was expended in the attempt. The problems of anti-Semitism, which had become virulent with the Hitler period overseas, were becoming intensified in this country in the 1930s. At the beginning of the decade, three national organizations were engaged in this field of work: the American Jewish Committee, established in 1906; the B'nai B'rith Anti-Defamation League, established in 1913; and the American Jewish Congress, first established in 1917 and reconstituted in 1922. Operating with small incomes and on a limited scale of expenditures in the early 1930s (aggregating $100,000 for the three agencies in those years), the programs of these organizations expanded rapidly as American Jews in 1933 responded to the problem with intensified efforts to combat anti-Semitism. The Jewish Labor Committee also was organized that year as representative of the Jewish labor groups. Each of these organizations was independently trying to deal with the problem, so that the ideological, class and other differences among their leaders and their adherents tended to limit the areas of cooperation and consultation.

Competition for allocations from welfare funds among the four national agencies brought additional conflicts and strains to the local communities. The urgency of the problems of anti-Semitism and the need for agreement on action were evident. A desire for greater cooperation and unity among the organizations soon was voiced at national and regional meetings of federations and welfare funds. It seemed obvious to the leadership in the local communities, as well as to some of the national leaders, that the continuation of independent and unrelated efforts in this field was undesirable.

A General Jewish Council was organized in response to these sentiments in 1938, consisting of the representatives of the four national organizations. Greater unity was anticipated from this development, with resultant improvement over anything previously attempted in methods of consultation among the agencies.

The General Jewish Council, however, did not solve

the problems of competition for funds in the local communities; nor did it reduce the overlapping of rival programs. The results obtained by the General Jewish Council were reviewed in local communities, at regional meetings and at the General Assembly in January 1940, where many voiced the need for greater progress. One local community leader stated:

> . . . there seems to be particular dissatisfaction with the present arrangement. Each local community is called upon through budget committees or boards to evaluate the work of the respective national agencies. Competition often leads to acrimonious local dissension. If the General Jewish Council is not prepared to be the fiscal agency of the four organizations, it might at least determine, in either amount or percentage, the reasonable requirements of the four agencies in their public appeals, to guide local federations in their allocations for civic-protective purposes.[9]

The representatives of communities also found that the Anti-Defamation League did not look with favor on the local community relations councils which had been developing in a number of the larger cities in an effort to bring together all local elements for joint action to meet local problems. Although several of the other national agencies were less negative,* some of their leaders took the position that local public-relations programs should preferably be organized by and as part of the programs of the individual national agencies. It was evident that there was no basic agreement between the national agencies, on the one hand, and the local communities on the other, on the kind of local structure and program which were needed in this field of interest.

The differences on policy, program, and fund-raising among the national agencies continued to engender a

---

* The American Jewish Congress in general supported the theory of local community council.

desire in the local communities for coordination superior to that being obtained through the General Jewish Council. A merger of the programs and finances of the several agencies was proposed by some national as well as local agency representatives. Among the questions discussed were the possibilities of achieving agreement on programs through a unified structure or through combined fund-raising; but the discussions were inconclusive.

Some of the welfare funds wanted to resolve the matter by making a combined allocation to the four national defense agencies. Such welfare funds wanted to leave it up to the General Jewish Council to decide on the distribution of a lump-sum grant to its four national constituent agencies. Though the General Jewish Council was strongly urged to undertake a joint fund-raising campaign in 1941 in behalf of its major agencies, it felt itself unequipped to do this or to attempt to make suggestions to guide welfare funds on the allocation of money to its constituent agencies. Henry Monsky, president of the B'nai B'rith, reported regretfully at the 1941 Assembly "that the GJC had not accomplished what it set out to do. In the matter of joint fund-raising and joint planning," he stated, "the partnership has not been effective."[10]

The difficulties in relationship among the four national agencies continued to grow and there were no tangible results from the discussions of merger and combined fund-raising possibilities. While these inconclusive discussions were going on, the American Jewish Committee and the Anti-Defamation League, in 1941, organized their Joint Defense Appeal. Thereupon, because of the failure to arrive at a more inclusive form of fund-raising for the national defense agencies, the American Jewish Congress withdrew from the General Jewish

Council. It raised four specific charges against that organization: These were:

1. The Council has not achieved a coordination of activities of its member agencies, and its member agencies have not seriously desired such coordination.

2. The Council has done nothing to organize or to coordinate the defense work of local communal organizations.

3. The Council, by its failure to guide local communities in their defense work, has added confusion to the work of defense in many of the communities.

4. The Council, unwilling to assume control over the defense situation, has stimulated competition on the part of its own member agencies on a scale never before witnessed in the United States.[11]

The three remaining agencies, however, continued to maintain the General Jewish Council and publicly expressed regret at the withdrawal of the American Jewish Congress.

With the withdrawal of the Congress, the local communities and the welfare funds experienced even greater dissatisfaction with the lack of unity in this field. A plan to remedy the situation presented to the 1943 General Assembly by a committee which had been set up the previous year, had met with the four agencies and had examined various aspects of the problem. The plan, known as the Wertheim Plan after its proponent—Mr. Maurice Wertheim, then president of the American Jewish Committee—proposed the merger of all civic protective work conducted by the four agencies in the United States; it suggested central fund-raising and other forms of coordination.

Before the Assembly met, three of the organizations —the American Jewish Committee, the American Jewish

Congress and the Jewish Labor Committee—had indicated approval of the general principles of the committee report. The fourth organization, the B'nai B'rith Anti-Defamation League, had rejected one of the basic points —that of having a joint operating body—but had expressed a willingness to cooperate on other recommendations, including the transfer of some limited functions from the individual organizations to the central body.

Discussions and committee work continued throughout 1943, culminating in the creation of the National Community Relations Advisory Council at the 1944 General Assembly of the CJFWF.[12] The four national agencies were joined before the end of the first year by the Union of American Hebrew Congregations and the Jewish War Veterans and by fourteen local community relations councils which were able to meet the criteria of membership in the NCRAC. Subsequently other local community relations councils were established and qualified as members of the NCRAC. It was the opinion of some of the officers and leaders of the NCRAC, as well as of others, voiced at the meeting of the CJFWF, that several of the national member agencies of the NCRAC were resisting the development of activities clearly within the stated aims and objectives of the organization.[13]

Despite its limitations, the formation of NCRAC resulted in some concrete achievements in agency cooperation. Conflicts and difficulties, however, continued both in the area of fund-raising and in the ability of the agencies to agree upon joint planning so as to avoid duplicate and parallel functions. When the Large City Budgeting Conference of welfare funds was organized in 1948 for joint consideration of welfare fund budgeting problems, the difficulties in arriving at equitable decisions on fund allocations to the national defense agencies, based upon an accurate appraisal of their work, was among the first of the major questions considered. The LCBC held a series of conferences with the national agencies in order to arrive at a better understanding of their programs and budgetary needs. Conflicting claims among the agencies made it impossible to make clear decisions without more detailed study. Accordingly, an intensive survey was recommended, which the NCRAC agreed to sponsor together with the LCBC in 1950. The subsequent developments from this survey generally referred to as the MacIver Study, from the name of the survey director, Robert M. MacIver of Columbia University, belong in another chapter of this history.

ANOTHER ATTEMPT AT SOLVING NATIONAL-LOCAL RELATIONSHIPS— ADVISORY NATIONAL BUDGETING

The history of the "national advisory budgeting proposal," twice a controversial issue in the annual General Assemblies of the CJFWF, like the history of the American Jewish Conference and the NCRAC, is pertinent to the story of how the pressures of anti-Semitism and the traumatic Jewish experience in this country during the period from 1933 to 1945 compelled unity and coordination among welfare organizations. At the same time, it illustrates the extent to which group conflicts and divided group interests continued in spite of these pressures.

It had seemed theoretically possible that external threats and dangers might overcome traditional differences, and that a structure for Jewish communal action might evolve on the national scene somewhat analogous to the local federations and community councils. In 1943 this was attempted in the short-lived American Jewish Conference. While the tide of sentiment toward unity

149

and cooperation in Jewish communal affairs ran vigorously in the 1930s and 1940s, resulting in considerable coordination in programs and activities, many of the underlying group suspicions and rivalries persisted. The failure of the various proposals for unity may be attributed to the reciprocal fears of accepting a national structure which might make communal domination possible by Zionists or non-Zionists, by Reform, Orthodox or Conservative elements, by East-European or central European Jews, by local over national agencies, by one group of national agencies over another group of national agencies, by one or another ideology. Less general but no less decisive was the unwillingness of the leadership of some national and overseas agencies to jeopardize their official status or give up any of the traditional prerogatives of agency autonomy.

On one score a defense of these resistances is possible. Federation, with its central planning, fund-raising and budgeting could operate successfully on the local scene because it was easier to allay group suspicions and individual rivalries and to achieve group cooperation on the basis of face to face association within a limited geographical area, even in the very large metropolitan areas. But on the amorphous national scene, with its great distances, its sectional differences resulted in an inability to overcome the limitations inherent in the derivative kind of representation necessary for the action of national bodies.

"National advisory budgeting" was a proposal developed in the CJFWF and by many of its local constituent agencies. It was designed to achieve a unified national procedure for assisting local welfare funds to make equitable allocations among the numerous national and overseas beneficiaries of central campaigns.

In the local communities there were many partisans

of the rival agencies, but a considerable number of contributors were responding, on an overall basis, to the whole range of important Jewish causes, without overriding interest in any one of them. The communities were seeking more information, asking for enlightenment on the work of the agencies, and looking for guidance on the competitive claims of the various organizations. If there could be a merger or coordination of agencies in the same or related fields, the welfare funds would be spared the task of determining the special merits of one or another agency in the same field, each enthusiastically promoted by national and local pressure groups. Because of the slow progress being made in coordination, or in mergers of agencies with similar functions, other solutions were being explored.

In the initial stage of extending central fund-raising to national and overseas agencies, the federations had set up the National Appeals Information Service (1927), to report on the work and finances of the nationally organized agencies that were appealing for community support. The studies and data which resulted from this service, however detailed, seemed to many of the welfare funds to offer them insufficient aid for making equitable budgetary decisions. Member agencies of the CJFWF asked repeatedly for some better approach, beyond that which could be achieved by their local budget committees and local budgeting procedures, to determine the needs of the many appeals.

One frequently offered suggestion was that the budgets of the national and overseas agencies appealing to welfare funds be reviewed by an impartial national body which would make recommendations on agency needs and equitable local responsibilities. Spurred on by resolutions at regional meetings of welfare funds, a committee was established by the Board of the CJFWF in May 1940 to study these proposals. After completing its study, the committee recommended that the principles and procedures of a national review process be established in the form of a National Advisory Budgeting Service.[14]

A plan for the setting up of an impartial national committee to undertake an intensive process of budget review was adopted by the Board of Directors of the Council, and this recommendation was submitted to its 1941 General Assembly. At this meeting, the decision was made to submit the question through a mail referendum of the member agencies of the CJFWF.

For several months the pros and cons of the proposal were debated by the member community agencies. There was general agreement on the need for improved fact-finding. But there was also considerable opposition, both by some of the local and some of the national agency spokesmen, to this setting up of a national committee to evaluate the programs of the agencies and to determine how much should be apportioned to each of the applicants.

Those in favor of the measure believed that only a national committee could give competent advice on the competitive claims of the numerous agencies and that an impartial body could be set up for this purpose. Those opposed were strongly convinced that an objective and unbiased appraisal of needs and of recommendations for funds required by the various agencies was impossible at this juncture in American Jewish communal organization. They believed that everyone who might be enlisted for the national budgeting service, no matter how well-intentioned, would have a specific ideological approach to Jewish life; that the economic, social and cultural heritage of all such persons would color their judgments, with undesirable consequences to agencies with a purpose or background not in accord with the prejudices or inclinations of the majority members of a national review committee.

Though the proposal involved only the making of advisory judgments, with local welfare funds retaining full freedom and autonomy of action to accept or reject that advice, and with no restrictions on the educational and promotional efforts of the national and overseas agencies, the opponents believed there would be a tendency to accept such recommendations as authoritative rather than advisory; and this in their opinion might be unfair to specific organizations.

The opponents of the plan were also assuming that they could expect more equitable allocations by continuing to influence local welfare funds through their national leaders and local sympathizers without the intervention of an evaluating procedure. They therefore preferred that the budgetary allocations should continue to be made locally, city by city, without the influence of recommendations backed by the prestige of a national review body.

A referendum among the member agencies of the Council resulted in a slight majority in favor of the National Advisory Budgeting proposal. However, because of the sharp controversies that had been engendered and the intensity of the opposition, the Board of the CJFWF decided that it would not proceed with the project, but instead would try to enlarge the fact-finding services of the CJFWF on the work and financial experience of the agencies without suggesting amounts or ratios of allocations.[15]

Such a decision, however, could not settle the problem. The annual difficulties in constituting the UJA, the lack of progress in the General Jewish Council, the setting up of the Joint Defense Appeal and the withdrawal of the American Jewish Congress from the General Jewish Council, the continuance of multiple campaigns and competitive national fund-raising even stimulated further interest in the possibility of working out a more satisfactory approach to local budgeting problems. Welfare funds continued to urge action beyond the enlarged budget research services of the CJFWF, and local federations and regional meetings again passed resolutions requesting advisory services from a national source. At a New England Regional Conference in November 1944, for example, the CJFWF was asked "to take a larger part in determining which national and overseas agencies are worthy of participation in local welfare funds and to suggest the extent to which these agencies should participate in local funds."[16]

To meet this urge for better procedures the Board of the CJFWF agreed in 1945 once more to submit the question of national advisory budgeting to the federations and welfare funds; it made preparations for a new discussion of this question at the 1946 Assembly. A poll of the sentiment of the Board's members had indicated that a considerable majority was in favor of instituting a National Advisory Budgeting service. Both the proponents and opponents of the measure were given an opportunity to present their views to the welfare funds. Although unresolved ideological differences were still a factor in the controversy, it became obvious even before the scheduled meeting of the General Assembly that a number of national agencies which had been noncommittal or lukewarm when the project was first presented in 1941 were now opposed to the plan.

The opposition to the proposal was effectively organized and was now even more convinced that the plan was undesirable. Sharp controversies arose in local communities over this question, and it seemed to many of the welfare fund leaders who were favorable to the plan that it was inadvisable to proceed with its execution in the face of the vigorous opposition of a part of the local leadership even if it consisted only of a minority. The project, which in 1941 had been able to obtain a slight majority in a referendum of federations and welfare funds, was, therefore, overwhelmingly defeated at the 1946 General Assembly. It was obvious that national agency rivalries and the sentiments of local partisans which these engendered were too acute to permit the resolution of the welfare fund budgeting problem through such national action.[17]

In retrospect, it can be seen that the difficulties which had been encountered in establishing advisory national budgeting illustrated the unresolved group conflicts and diverse group loyalties of the period. The adherents of the American agencies with Zionist or Palestine programs were convinced that the federations and welfare funds were still dominated by representatives of the older immigration and were imbued with non-Zionist attitudes. They felt that, if not the officers of the federations and welfare funds, at least the large contributors were so imbued, and they believed that the Board of CJFWF was largely made up of such representation. While there had actually been a gradual transformation of the local leadership from that which had obtained several decades before, that development was perhaps too recent to have been fully visible.

There was also the general reluctance of nationally organized agencies, with many of their leaders resident in New York City, to entrust their financial future to a consolidated central body representing hundreds of local welfare funds in all parts of the country. While local central fund-raising had been accepted in practice, many of the agencies were reluctant to give up their direct contacts with contributors. Agencies in welfare funds sought increasingly to develop some form of local membership for maintaining and, if possible, strengthening their influence within the local federations.

The community chests and councils had been able to achieve in 1942 a national advisory budgetary service, in the relation of non-sectarian chests to a group of national agencies, but Jewish communities had to look for other ways of solving their budgeting problems. Some improvement in the situation was brought about through the growing cooperation of the JDC and the UPA in the United Jewish Appeal, which after 1945 received a very large part of the funds raised by the local communities. The Committee on National-Local Relationships set up by the CJFWF frequently found piecemeal solutions for some of the difficulties—through mergers of programs, agencies and appeals, and through various other forms of cooperation. A more intensive type of study and report on the overseas problems was developed through the research and evaluative work of the Institute on Overseas Studies set up by the CJFWF in 1947.[18]

Federations continued to urge cooperation in programs and, where appropriate, the merger of related or parallel agencies. For several years large city planning conferences organized by CJFWF for the exchange of experience and the discussion of common problems with overseas and national agency representatives helped toward better understanding.[19]

The problem of multiple campaigns in the overseas field was one of the most serious problems in the post-war period, and federations and welfare funds were urging that a central plan be formulated for fund-raising especially for Palestine.[20] One concrete result of these requests by welfare funds was the establishment by the Jewish Agency in 1949 of a Committee on Authorization and Control of Appeals in behalf of Israel, which prevented the rise of numerous special campaigns for projects of doubtful validity or urgency.

Another important step in intercity cooperation on a national basis was initiated at the suggestion of Harry Greenstein, executive of the Baltimore Federation, when nine of the larger welfare funds outside of New York formed the Large City Budgeting Committee. As pointed out above, the LCBC began, in 1948, to explore means of establishing a cooperative basis among the larger welfare funds for the consideration of their responsibilities to the national and overseas agencies, with the CJFWF serving as secretariat. (By 1958, the LCBC had been extended to a membership of twenty-three of the largest welfare funds.)[21] Organized as a voluntary association and joining in reviews of agency budgets on a cooperative basis, the LCBC helped to disseminate greater understanding of selected agencies, to find a basis of agreement with a number of them concerning their proposed annual appeals, to work out procedures for the presentation of operating budgets, and to reach a consensus on the validity of the sums being requested for their annual programs.[22] It was thus in a practical manner carrying out some of the objectives of the National Advisory Budgeting proposals.

Nationally, through the CJFWF General Assembly and through complementary local actions, communities established principles and guideposts for minimizing the number of competing agencies and dealing with multiple appeals. They developed criteria for the relationship of local leaders and individual contributors to national agencies; they set up liaison arrangements for developing closer relationships between the welfare funds and the national and overseas agencies; they developed standards and procedures for obtaining and utilizing budgetary information; they called for mergers and for more coordinated planning by agencies in the same fields and they took a number of other steps to ease the budgetary problems.

All of these activities and developments were an indication of the growing conviction among communities that their concern for meeting national and overseas needs did not end with raising maximum sums. On the contrary, it involved responsibility for the wisest expenditure of these funds through careful budgeting and allocations and for the most effective service in terms of avoiding waste, duplication, and substandard quality of programs. They reflected, indeed, the growing importance of the local federations as the key element in the communal life of American Jewry.

part two

The Federation and Jewish

Community Organization

VIII

The Post-War Period

SUBJECT TO CORRECTION

As in all human concerns only what is past in Jewish communal association is known or at least knowable. The past can be evaluated from today's perspective; it can be arranged in chronological order and theoretical designs fitted to the sequence of events. Today's events are more difficult to evaluate. If we regard them in relationship to the years which have passed, it is from a contemporary point of view; the future may view today's happenings in a very different light. We can only speculate on whether what we observe today is the end of a trend, the beginning of a new one, or an accidental and ephemeral occurrence. Even the description of main events, which is attempted here, runs the risk of questionable selection and faulty interpretation. An analysis of the current scene must, therefore, be prefaced with the cautionary phrase, "subject to correction."

THE END OF THE WAR

Events after the year 1945 seem to represent not one, but two basic trends: first, an acceleration of tempo in some major phases of welfare organization, and second, a following period of diminishing intensity. The programs of Jewish federations involved two main elements: responsibility for the work abroad, and for the maintenance and development of domestic programs.

With the end of World War II, some form of central federation had been achieved in practically all cities with a sufficient number of Jews for such formal association. The stresses of the previous two decades, and the consequent deepening of group consciousness, had fostered the establishment of federations, welfare funds and community councils throughout the length and breadth of the land. New forms of organization had emerged which had brought into association practically all segments of the Jewish population for central fund-raising and for joint responsibility for some of the more urgent problems. Even small cities had achieved organization and had developed a consciousness of the need for continuing communal activities. In a few regional areas, such as southern Illinois, a federation had been established for a sparsely settled Jewish population; elsewhere, large city federations were serving their metropolitan areas and surrounding districts.

Whatever the temper of Americans generally at the end of the war about relaxation from the pressures of the emergency, American Jews recognized that victory over the enemies of the country and of humanity would not mean the end of the responsibilities which the communal bodies and the national agencies had assumed. Instead, it was evident that even wider opportunities for constructive work were at hand, and that American Jewry would respond to these opportunities.

With the victory over Hitlerism and nazism, the surviving remnants of the Jews of Europe were emerging from the nightmare which had hung over them for more than a decade, a tragic phase in history which had decimated their ranks and shattered their centuries-old Jewish communal life. American Jewry, which had been spared this tragedy, had a compelling urge to undertake whatever programs and remedies were now feasible. Opportunities opened for rescue and rehabilitation abroad— causes that were to elicit the deepest and most vigorous response of philanthropic sentiment American Jewry had known. For a number of years the mobilization of constructive help for Jews abroad was to be the major outlet and direction for American Jewish philanthropic sentiment.

American Jews felt themselves capable of assuming tasks beyond any undertaken before, and these feelings were soon to be translated into the greatest and most significant philanthropic fund-raising effort in the history of the American community. Extensive programs were about to be undertaken in Europe by the United States and by the United Nations for the war displaced populations and the refugees; but large areas of need remained for supplementation by voluntary programs.

During the war, all Americans had been mobilized for the nation's war effort. Though large sacrifices had been involved, and there had been a considerable number of casualties, the end of hostilities found the nation in the midst of a more vigorous industrial development than when the war began. The country, as a whole, had not suffered physically from the ravages of war which had been inflicted on allies and enemies alike in Europe and in the Pacific. The remarkable economic advance of the country in response to war mobilization had removed the last vestiges of the depression of the thirties. The United States had shown a remarkable capacity for organization and economic development and now became the world's leading power.

Similarly, American Jewry, less than one-third before the war, now numbered about half of the world's Jewish population, as a result of the ravages of war and of Hitler's diabolical destruction of European Jewry. The old centers of European Jewry, which for more than a century had been the fountainheads for American Jewish cultural development, were now virtually destroyed, or were, as in the Soviet Union, in eclipse and officially detached from the rest of Jewry. Paralleling the emergence of the United States as the primary power in world affairs, American Jewry found itself occupying the leading role in world Jewry. Jews overseas looked to America for help in rebuilding their shattered lives and for the resources required to develop Palestine as a place of settlement for the surviving Jews of Europe and North Africa.

The opportunities which faced American Jews at home were also of compelling importance. First the depression and then the war made it impossible to give attention to long-range communal needs. During this period, the normal welfare, health and cultural programs were maintained, but institutional plants had deteriorated and could not be improved because of wartime building restrictions.

The war had temporarily halted refugee immigration, and peak industrial development had helped in the absorption of those immigrants who had come before. Movement of Jewish population from older to newer areas of residence had continued, with the result that many of the basic Jewish institutions were now located in districts of dwindling Jewish population. In the next ten years, a further movement of Jewish population took place to the outlying parts of the city—and to suburban areas—intensifying the problem of relocating or improving the religious and welfare institutions. Jewish communities, therefore, faced the necessity of raising unprecedented sums both for aid overseas and for the building and maintenance of their own communal life.

There was, fortunately, increased ability to meet these obligations and challenges of the post-war period. With the depression receding into the background, the nation was entering a new period of economic prosperity. The common experience among Jews of participating in the war effort and of closing their ranks against the onslaught of anti-Semitism had greatly strengthened group solidarity and group consciousness. Further, the ever-increasing recognition of the extent of the tragedy which had befallen European Jewry shocked American Jewry into a greater sense of urgency and group responsibility. The sharp contrast between the wealth and security of Americans and the poverty and destruction suffered by the Europeans stimulated a vast program of aid on the part of the American government and led to a similar undertaking on the part of American Jews to mitigate the distress of overseas Jewry.

At first, however, the release of tensions occasioned by the approaching end of war again brought to the fore the unresolved problems of group differences among national agencies; and this had local repercussions. In 1945, the UPA and the JDC experienced the sharpest difficulties of the uneasy decade of partnership when they tried to agree on the relative priorities of their programs. The American Jewish Conference, which was thinking of continuing as a permanent organization to concern itself with central planning on the domestic problems of Jews, experienced a growing opposition on the part of some of its former adherents. On the other hand, the NCRAC, which had been established in 1944, began its first year with the promise of developing a co-operative program on the part of its constituent agencies. During the next decade, some of these differences were to be resolved, others were to be continued, and new conflicts and difficulties were to arise.

DEMOGRAPHIC CHANGES

As a number of the Jewish communities undertook to examine themselves by means of surveys and demographic studies, they became aware of profound changes. Immigration restrictions had resulted in the gradual aging of the foreign-born elements and a decline in their numbers which were not offset to any large extent by the refugee immigration. The segment of the Jewish population derived from the original immigrants from central and western Europe was estimated to constitute less than ten per cent of the Jewish population in 1950. The largest part of the Jewish population was made up of immigrants from eastern Europe and their native-born children and grandchildren.[1]

The American Jewish population of East-European origin, had progressed both economically and in social status, and was exceeding the earlier groups, not only in the number of contributors to philanthropy, but in potential giving capacity and amounts of giving as well. There were marked changes in occupations between the native-born generation and their immigrant parents. Except in the largest centers of population, such as New York and Chicago, where a significant part of the Jewish population was still to be found in industrial employment, the majority of the Jewish population had moved into what is called the "white collar" group, involving the managerial, professional, and clerical occupations.[2]

The change from an immigrant to a native-born population, and the accompanying educational and occupational changes, were also having a marked effect upon the cultural life of the community. A greater homogeneity was to be expected from the native-born generations of American Jewry, which would make possible a more uniform pattern of cultural life. The different national origins of immigrants, a constant factor in American life for more than sixty years, no longer operated as a dominant cultural force—though economic and social class differentiations might take their place as factors in group relationships.

These changing aspects of Jewish life in local communities were reflected in the nature of group cooperation during fund-raising campaigns and in many aspects of communal planning. In 1948, when fund-raising efforts reached their peak, it was estimated there were over 1,300,000 contributors to Jewish federations and welfare funds. Considering the proportion of young children and the fact that the average size of the Jewish household is probably around three (the parents and one child), this record indicates that the central agencies were able to base their support upon exceedingly broad mass participation. Although there has been some decline in the number of givers as well as in the amounts raised since 1948, the record of the number of contributors to welfare funds is still estimated at more than 1,000,000.

MILESTONES IN THE FUND-RAISING RECORD[3]

With a rapid upward trend from less than $30,-000,000 raised in the 1941 campaigns, American Jews in 1945 raised between $115,000,000 and $125,000,000 in philanthropic funds for local, national and overseas purposes. This total includes $35,000,000 in local capital fund campaigns, $35,000,000 for the United Jewish Appeal (as compared with $27,000,000 in 1944), and approximately $10,000,000 by other overseas agencies.

In 1945, the central welfare funds of the federations had raised $71,000,000—or 60% of the annual contributions to American Jewish philanthropy. The amount raised by federations and welfare funds in 1946 was almost double that of the previous year. A total of $131,000,000 was reported in response to the unprecedented needs overseas for relief and rehabilitation. (The United Jewish Appeal reported 1946 campaign results of $101,000,000 as against $35,000,000 in 1945—almost all of it from federations and welfare funds.)

In 1947, federations and welfare funds raised approximately $156,000,000. In 1948, an estimated $201,-000,000 was reported raised by local central community campaigns,* the all-time high in Jewish philanthropic fund-raising. All the factors required for successful results were of a positive character. The period of post-war economic adjustment and reconversion had been brief, and the country was experiencing a continued economic development. Employment and prosperity were increasing. Enlarged opportunities for immigration and other constructive solutions of the displaced Jews of Europe were broadening, and the establishment of the State of Israel and the opening of its doors to a flow of Jewish immigrants aroused widespread enthusiasm. All of these factors spurred the communities on to better campaigns and moved the overseas agencies toward more vigorous and effective programs.

---

* These campaign results are exclusive of funds raised for buildings and other capital purposes.

The high-water mark of fund-raising reached in 1948, called forth in part by the assumption that this was a year of emergency giving, could not be maintained. But it became evident with each succeeding year that the need for vast funds would continue, that contributions could not be considered "one-time" gifts, and that large-scale giving would have to be maintained. In 1949, however, there was a mild economic recession continuing into 1950, and the economic outlook was clouded. The totals obtained in the fund-raising of the centrally organized campaigns began to decline.

(It is not known, however, since complete data are lacking, whether Jewish philanthropy since 1948 has declined, or whether it is being maintained but is being distributed through various channels that are not included in the current compilations. A considerable part of the unrecorded fund-raising may be made up in part by causes not included in the annual Jewish federation and welfare fund campaigns. There are indications that there have been considerable contributions to capital funds conducted as separate campaigns in behalf of synagogues, community centers, hospitals, homes for the aged and other communal institutions, gifts to universities under Jewish auspices, gifts by Jews to non-sectarian institutions and causes, and the like.)

In 1951, the project for the sale of the State of Israel Bonds was launched and secured approximately $365,000,000 in the United States by the end of 1959. There were large investments in, and other types of aid to, Israel.

The results of central fund-raising campaigns, and the share allocated to UJA, were as follows:

Year	Total Raised (in millions of dollars)	Allocated to UJA
1949	170	103
1950	142	86
1951	136	80
1952	121	68
1953	115	65
1954	108	58
1955	110	57
1956	130	75
1957	138	82
1958	123	68

In addition, national and overseas agencies other than the UJA, during this period, were raising between $27,-000,000 (1949) and $50,000,000 (1958) annually from independently conducted campaigns exclusive of allocations from welfare funds.[4] The facts behind these results are discussed later in this chapter.

OVERSEAS PROGRAMS

During this period, federations and welfare funds were responding to the post-war-created opportunities for constructive service abroad by assuming the enlarged fund-raising goals which were being sought by agencies engaged in overseas programs. Practically all of the contributors to central local funds, were responding generously to the call for vastly larger resources which these programs needed, and could utilize, in bringing help to the war sufferers.

At the beginning, the greatest interest was focused on helping two groups: the survivors of the Nazi concentration and death camps, and the slave laborers who had been released by the victorious armies and now constituted a large volume of displaced persons without homes or prospects. The armies of occupation, especially

those of the United States, the intergovernmental
agencies, the International Refugee Organization (IRO)
and the United Nations Relief and Rehabilitation
Agency (UNRRA) were beginning to take primary responsibility for helping the entire group of displaced
persons and war sufferers, estimated at over 20,000,000
persons. But, a great deal of additional voluntary help
was needed if effective programs of rehabilitation were
to be found for this huge group of war casualties. It was
estimated that there were 1,400,000 Jews in Europe outside of the Soviet Union who had survived the Nazi
extermination program. This number included the Jewish nationals of the countries of eastern and southeastern
Europe, and of western Europe which had been under
Nazi domination during the war.

The overseas agencies were facing prodigious tasks.
In central Europe, the displaced people were being assembled into refugee camps. Their number was augmented by refugees from the countries of eastern Europe
who had been unsettled by adverse conditions, such as
recurrent pogroms in Poland, and spurred on by the
hope of finding these camps a way-station to immigration
to the Western World or to Palestine. At the beginning,
immigration possibilities to countries outside of Europe
were limited. The Palestine White Paper of 1939 had
attempted to freeze immigration after 1944, and sharp
restrictions were being made, resulting in attempts—
many of them successful—by Jews to enter as "Illegals."
While President Truman's directive had opened the
United States again to quota immigration, not more than
8,000 were able to gain entry in the first year after May
1946. Opportunities for immigration to other countries
were similarly restricted.[5]

There was movement of displaced persons from

and to the camps and it was estimated in 1948 that there were still close to 200,000 Jewish displaced persons in the official camps established for them in central Europe and Italy. This took no account of the unsettled additional hundreds of thousands of the uprooted living outside the camps in various parts of Europe.

The UJA appeal for $100,000,000 for 1946 was completely successful ($101,000,000 was actually raised, as compared with $35,000,000 the previous year). The JDC and the UPA were now able to assume large responsibilities with the assurance that the Jewish federations and welfare funds were alert to their objectives and were willing to undertake vigorous fund-raising campaigns in their behalf. In 1946, the JDC was the principal beneficiary of the UJA, receiving 57% of funds available for distribution to the UPA and JDC. In the search for constructive solutions, the JDC and the Jewish Agency for Palestine (both supported by UJA) cooperated effectively, especially in the field of migration to Palestine—the Jewish Agency assuming responsibility for enlisting and selecting immigrants for Palestine and for their care and resettlement upon arrival, the JDC taking responsibility for helping the immigrants en route to their destination.

As more displaced persons were able to leave the camps for overseas countries and for Palestine, the relative costs of the programs of the two organizations shifted. With the opening up of large-scale immigration opportunities in Palestine, which followed the creation of the State of Israel, it was natural for the UPA agencies to emerge as the largest phase of the overseas program. By 1950, with the displaced persons in Europe further reduced in number, and the areas of need for the JDC services outside of Israel shrinking because of gradual adjustment of Jews in the countries of western Europe, the JDC embarked upon a program of welfare services (Malben) in Israel, initially planned with the Jewish Agency and the government of Israel. Since 1946, the task of adjusting the available UJA funds between the programs of the JDC and the UPA has no longer encountered the ideological differences and agency rivalries which had previously made the preparations for an annual UJA campaign a thorny procedure. As the displaced persons began their trek to Israel and other countries, the JDC, which had been the major beneficiary before 1948, required less than one-third of UJA funds to finance its programs in 1953.

The question of allocation of UJA funds to the United Service for New Americans (USNA) and New York Association for New Americans (NYANA) serving the new immigrants in this country, was, however, a problem in 1948 and for a few years thereafter, when refugee immigration to the United States under the Displaced Persons Act increased. This was settled through the appointment of an impartial chairman acceptable both to the JDC and the UPA. With the expiration of the Displaced Persons Act, and the beginnings of the more restrictive McCarran-Walter Immigration and Nationality Act of 1952, and with growing self-support by refugees already settled here, the funds required by the two immigrant aid agencies in the United States declined from a peak of close to $14,000,000 in 1949 to approximately $926,000 in 1955. (These agencies received 14.2% of UJA funds in 1949 and 2.9% in 1955.) In 1954, cooperative relationships between the JDC and UPA were underscored by the adoption of a UJA agreement for a five-year period.

While the United Palestine Appeal, formed jointly

by the Keren Hayesod and the Keren Kayemeth, was the principal fund-raising agency for Israel, and has been able to reduce the number of separate appeals through subsidies to several other fund-raising efforts under Zionist auspices, a complete integration of fund-raising efforts in behalf of Israel has not been achieved. Hadassah, the National Committee for Labor Israel, and Pioneer Women have continued to conduct their own national campaigns; as have the American Fund for Israel Institutions (now the American Israel Cultural Foundation), the Federated Council of Israel Institutions, Hebrew University, Technion, Weizmann Institute and several other smaller agencies.

In the general overseas field (outside of Israel) the number of multiple appeals has been considerably reduced since the war years, when various religious and labor groups (such as the Vaad Hahatzala and the Jewish Labor Committee) conducted independent campaigns unrelated to that of the JDC. With post-war stabilization in Europe, these separate fund-raising efforts have been discontinued or have dwindled considerably.

The improving relationship within the partnership which constituted the United Jewish Appeal was a gain to the welfare funds in that it removed a constant source of friction between the local partisans of the once rival agencies. Both groups could now devote themselves to the common task of the UJA compaign and of supporting its claims for an equitable share of welfare funds. This cooperation did not, however, solve residual difficulties, such as those which arose from the separate appeals of other agencies operating abroad, which conducted independent campaigns outside the UJA. For all of the welfare funds and for all of the agencies there remained the perennial question of what part of the funds raised in a central campaign was to be allocated among the respective overseas, national and local claimants.[6]

MULTIPLE APPEALS

The desire to resolve the problems of the multiple appeals for overseas causes resulted in a variety of proposals and recommendations which, one hoped, would simplify the appeals and produce constructive results. Among those which were suggested and endorsed by the communities were:

1. That a single, unified appeal for philanthropic aid to Israel be established with the cooperation of the fund-raising agencies and the assistance of Israel authorities.

2. That if a single combined Israel appeal could not be achieved, at least there be an agreement among the agencies on a joint budget which would establish priorities of function and relative program needs. Such a joint budget would help guide local welfare funds on the valid claims of the competing appeals, serve as a basis for local fund distribution, and channel American Jewish philanthropic aid to help meet Israel's most urgent social problems.

3. That short of a complete Israel philanthropic budget, agreement should be reached on relative needs and formulae for fund allocation for selected agencies in related fields, such as the three advanced educational institutions in Israel: Hebrew University, Technion, and Weizmann Institute.

4. That some authoritative body should be established to determine the validity of new or recently organized philanthropic appeals and to regulate the fund-raising procedures.

While sympathetic consideration was given in both this country and Israel to proposals 1 and 2, and they were repeatedly discussed at conferences and by committees, progress, thus far, toward their realization has not been noteworthy. Many of the organizations have a long history of independent existence, some pre-dating the establishment of the welfare funds. Then, too, some were sponsored by Zionist and some by non-Zionist groups in addition to which there were fears that reduced funds might follow a unified campaign. Further, agency rivalries did not facilitate the ability to reach agreement on a common Israel budget. The government of Israel was still too new and had too many other major tasks before it to assume a role of leadership in establishing full cooperation among the philanthropic agencies financed by foreign funds which were operating in Israel.

Substantial progress, however, was made on proposals 3 and 4. In 1950, the three institutions for advanced education voluntarily agreed on a unified campaign in the United States—the UIT. When united action was discontinued, in 1952, it was succeeded by recommendations of a formula for welfare fund distribution for maintenance needs of these three agencies. This proposal, made by Dr. Giora Josephthal, then treasurer of the Jewish Agency, at the request of the welfare funds through the CJFWF, also led to the establishment, in 1954, of a joint committee for the three institutions set up by the government of Israel and the Jewish Agency for Palestine.

By the beginning of 1955, further progress toward the coordination of the separate fund-raising activities of the three institutions had been achieved. The Hebrew University and the Haifa Technion had decided to combine their appeals to local welfare funds for their annual maintenance needs. The Weizmann Institute had discontinued its appeals to welfare funds and to the general public for maintenance and capital needs (except for an annual dinner and continued efforts to attract investment capital). Financing of the Weizmann Institute was to be assumed by the Jewish Agency and the government of Israel.[7]

Although the Jewish Agency, which had been constituted by the various Zionist organizations, did not undertake a fully combined or unified philanthropic campaign for Israel in the United States, it did combine the appeals of several organizations—Keren Hayesod, Keren Kayemeth (through 1960) and the welfare programs of the General Zionist, Mizrachi, Agudath Israel, and Revisionists. Separate campaigns were continued, however, by the Labor Zionists, Hadassah, and several other organizations.

In order to prevent a multitude of new welfare and cultural agencies from being launched (a likely prospect at the time the State of Israel was founded), the Jewish Agency, in 1949, set up procedures for the authorization of fund-raising campaigns and relationships between the separate campaigns and the United Jewish Appeal. A committee on Control and Authorization of Campaigns was established under its aegis, in which the CJFWF and UJA participated, with the number of campaigns for Israel limited to thirteen. It set conditions to govern appeals; it required financial reports and reports on the transmission of funds to Israel; and it defined the priority of the UJA campaigns in the matter of publicity and timing. The committee did not, however, pass on the budgets of the authorized agencies nor set priorities among their programs.

REORGANIZATION OF THE JEWISH AGENCY FOR ISRAEL

In April 1960 a further reorganization of American Jewish philanthropic aid for Israel took place through transformation of the American section of the Jewish Agency for Israel into an autonomous body. While retaining the name, Jewish Agency for Israel, Inc., this body came under the administration of a governing board of twenty-one persons. Seven of these were designated by the International Jewish Agency—six Americans and one Israeli (the treasurer of the international Agency)—and the other fourteen were American Jewish leaders, designated nominally by the United Israel Appeal.

The plan of the reorganization included the following provisions:

1. Final and complete authority for the allocation and expenditure of funds provided by the United Jewish Appeal, and channeled through the United Israel Appeal for needs in Israel, was vested in the reorganized Jewish Agency for Israel, Inc. This was in compliance with the position taken by the Internal Revenue Service of the U.S. Treasury Department, requiring American control of tax deductible contributions to all agencies if used overseas.

2. All such funds were to be used solely for resettlement and absorption of immigrants and related purposes.

3. Staff appointed by, and responsible to, the Jewish Agency for Israel was to examine the needs and assure compliance with the decisions taken.

4. Expenditure of the funds and administration of

the program in Israel would continue to be carried out by this International Jewish Agency by contact with the Jewish Agency for Israel, Inc., in the United States.

5. Grants made by the Jewish Agency to the "Constructive funds" of the political parties for their welfare and educational activities in lieu of campaigns in the United States were to be discontinued as of January 1, 1961. Instead, a plan was developed whereby the Jewish Agency, Inc., would pass on the application of each institution and project, and make direct grants to those approved, without going through the party channels.

6. Cultural, educational and public relations activities in the United States, conducted and financed by the Jewish Agency, were transferred to the administration of the American Zionist Council, with financial responsibility to be transferred on April, 1, 1961.

Among the first tasks undertaken by the new board was the development of a plan for systematic reduction of the debts which had been accumulated by the Jewish Agency both in the United States and overseas as current income failed to meet the cost of the care of immigrants in Israel, and for which debts the Jewish Agency for Israel, Inc., retained legal responsibility. Another task of the new board was to develop long range plans for helping the immigrants achieve self-support rather than year-to-year projections of such aid.

The provision for the above reorganization was to continue through the period of the current United Jewish Appeal agreement, that is, through 1963. It was indicated that, in the meantime, consideration would be given to the expressed wish of Jewish federations for more direct and broader community representation on the governing body, in formulating further revisions.

COORDINATION OF SERVICES FOR IMMIGRANTS

Four organizations had been operating for many years in another field of overseas work, that of services to immigrants. They were the United Service for New Americans and the National Council of Jewish Women in the United States, and HIAS (working both in this country and abroad), and the Joint Distribution Committee, which operated overseas immigration services. With the organization of the National Refugee Service, the predecessor of the USNA, complete integration was established in the national immigration services of the National Refugee Service (NRS) and the National Council of Jewish Women (NCJW). Parallel activities, however, were continuing between HIAS and the JDC abroad and HIAS and USNA in the United States. To welfare funds and federations it was obvious that coordination in this field would be highly desirable. Over a period of ten years, various attempts were made among the organizations involved and through the National-Local Relations Committee of the CJFWF to effect a unified program in this field. Early in 1954, the national agencies announced that a merger of services had been adopted, and a United HIAS Service formed the overall agency. It incorporated the work of the USNA and HIAS in the United States and the work of HIAS and the immigration services of the JDC abroad.[8]

FUND-RAISING AFTER 1948

With the peak of federated fund-raising occurring in 1948, evidence was soon to appear that this unusually high level would not be maintained. As compared with 1948, funds raised in central community campaigns declined by 21% in 1949 and by another 10% in 1950. Decreases in subsequent years were smaller. The result, however, was that by 1955 the welfare funds as a whole were raising only 55% of the amounts obtained in 1948. The major reasons for the drop in welfare fund achievements, beginning in 1949, seems to be that large contributors had given on a "one-time emergency" standard in 1945-48 and did not feel they could maintain the same amounts annually as a continuing obligation. Then, too, overseas needs were less dramatic compared with the refugee camps in 1946 and the struggle for Israel's survival in 1948. In addition, after delays in raising capital funds during the two decades of depression and war, there was a tendency among givers to channel more of their philanthropy to synagogues, hospitals, community Centers, homes for the aged, and to non-sectarian capital fund and maintenance campaigns. The launching of the sale of Government of Israel Bonds and other investments in Israel offered additional avenues for the channeling of funds made available for Israel from American Jewry.

Not all aspects of community fund-raising seemed to be affected after 1948 in the same way. The non-sectarian community chests, which had maintained a stable level of campaign results over most of their history, showed small but steady increases in funds obtained during this period. The Jewish federations and local Jewish agencies which were receiving their major support from community chests were therefore not affected as seriously by the drop in welfare fund results. However, because of the limitations in community chest funds, more marked in some cities than in others, the Jewish welfare funds were supplementing some community-chest-supported agencies operating on less than the amount of funds required for their normal programs. The welfare funds also undertook increasing responsibility for financing communal services, such as Jewish education, local community relations, and refugee relief, which were not usually included among community chest beneficiaries. Inflationary tendencies during this period meant that more dollars were needed to maintain even the same level of local services, placing an added strain on communal funds. The national agencies were similarly affected by inflationary factors and needed more dollars for their work.[9]

The trend of financing and distribution of funds is apparent in the table of receipts of the New York UJA and of other welfare funds and the proportions of the total income devoted to the UJA and to other causes.[10] In examining the following table, it is pertinent to note the corresponding figures for income of the New York Federation which is devoted exclusively to local welfare services. In the New York Federation, the trend of fund-raising differs markedly from the trends in welfare fund cities, but it is comparable to the financial experience of federations which derive some of their funds from local community chests.

CHANGING PATTERNS OF GIVING

An examination of the contributions to welfare fund campaigns during this period indicates that the change in results may be attributed to the changing pattern of giving.

In 1948, 0.6% of the givers contributed $5,000 and over, and were responsible for 40.3% of campaign re-

Welfare Fund Income (exclusive of New York)

Year	Total Income	UJA Allocations	%	Other Allocations and Costs*	%
1945	$ 34,940,000	$20,070,000	57.4	$14,870,000	42.6
1946	87,148,000	62,426,000	71.6	24,722,000	28.4
1947	106,362,000	76,789,000	72.2	29,573,000	27.8
1948	135,564,000	93,642,000	69.1	41,922,000	30.9
1949	106,962,000	63,078,000	59.0	43,884,000	41.0
1950	91,987,000	55,132,000	59.9	36,855,000	40.1
1951	87,848,000	48,349,000	55.0	39,499,000	45.0
1952	78,097,000	40,336,000	51.6	37,761,000	48.4
1953	75,520,000	39,197,000	51.9	36,323,000	48.1
1954	69,554,000	33,851,000	48.7	35,703,000	51.3
1955	69,595,000	33,687,000	48.4	35,908,000	51.6
1956	82,609,000	46,741,000	56.6	35,868,000	43.4
1957	89,881,000	52,736,000	58.6	37,145,000	41.4
1958	78,359,000	41,856,000	53.4	36,503,000	46.6

* *Other allocations* column included "shrinkage" allowance for non-payment of pledges, campaign and administrative expenses, and contingencies or other reserves, as well as allocations to local and national agencies.

New York Federation Income[11]

Year	Total Income
1945	$10,466,000 (plus $14,264,000 for capital fund)
1946	12,500,000
1947	14,000,000
1948	13,841,000
1949	13,000,000 (plus $11,000,000 for capital fund)
1950	14,500,000
1951	14,750,000
1952	14,500,000
1953	14,750,000
1954	15,300,000
1955	16,500,000
1956	17,000,000
1957	15,197,000
1958	16,891,000

sults. Givers of $500 and over, representing 6.4% of the contributors, accounted for 76.3% of campaign totals. In 1952, with gradual changes in the giving pattern in the intervening period, the corresponding figures are: 0.3% of contributors of $5,000 and over being responsible for 31.9% of welfare fund income; and givers of $500 and over, representing 4.5% of all contributors, contributing 70% of the total raised. In 1954, 0.3% of the givers contributed $5,000 and over, and were responsible for 30.6% of campaign results. Givers of $500 and over represented 4.2% of contributors and accounted for 68.7% of campaign totals.[12]

The shrinkage in welfare fund results was due largely to the reduction of the amounts contributed by givers in the top brackets. The middle-income bracket of givers did not show the same rate of decline; in many cities they held to previous levels of giving. Only a small part of the reduction has been due to the shrinkage in the number of givers. The drop-out in annual contributors is reported to be mainly of givers in the less than twenty-five-dollar bracket.

Whatever may have been the reasons for the drop in giving, the shrinkage of funds brought with it serious problems of fund allocations. The UJA, which had benefited most from the increased giving in 1946-1948, experienced the sharpest decline in allocations, and this was of concern to those responsible for overseas programs, since the need for funds continued to be very great. While United States grants-in-aid, German reparations and improvement in the economy of Israel have been of tremendous help to the Israel causes, Israel's economic position is still on a deficit basis, requiring large philanthropic aid from abroad. The UJA has been seeking, in various ways, to maintain the level of welfare fund allocations, or at least, not to have them fall more precipitately than total campaign results. It has tried to achieve this by negotiating pre-campaign formulae on UJA's share of the proceeds. While this has been partly successful, it has not solved the problem, since other beneficiaries of welfare funds exert similar pressures.

Then, too, support for Israel's welfare needs is derived in other ways that supplement the philanthropic gifts obtained through the welfare funds. A conference held in Israel in September 1950, in which a number of representatives of American welfare funds participated, resulted in the formulation of a program of aid for Israel which would involve philanthropic giving through the UJA and other sources, promotion of private investments in Israel's economy and the launching of the sale of an Israel Bond issue.[13]

The response to the Israel Bond Drive has yielded approximately $365,000,000 in the United States between May 1951 and the end of 1959. In 1954, the UJA appealed to the communities for loans totaling $75,000,-000, to help Israel overcome the difficulties of its short-term debt problem. The short-term debt had been so pressing, that from month-to-month unusual efforts had to be undertaken to meet payments, with additional costs of high interest rates. Communities joined in cooperative efforts which netted approximately $65,000,000 in loans borrowed by local welfare funds, largely on a five-year basis. The funds made available were known as the Consolidation Loan of 1954, and served to ease Israel's current financing difficulties and to speed measures toward self-support. The UJA agreed to meet the payments of these loans as they occurred.*

* The UJA asked for renewal of the loan and for major new borrowing from the local welfare funds in 1956, 1958 and 1960. The net

The focusing of attention on the overseas problem fostered the development of special studies undertaken in behalf of the welfare funds by the CJFWF. Such studies, organized under its Institute on Overseas Studies, have been helpful in throwing light upon Israel's economic and welfare needs. They have pointed to available resources, improvements in the economy and in the operations of the welfare agencies for the absorption of immigrants, and have projected plans to decrease the need for outside aid.

---

result of loan repayments and new borrowings was to bring the total of outstanding loans back to the 1954 figure of $65,000,000.

IX

Building and Expansion
of Services: 1945-1960

SYNAGOGUES

Even while the communities moved in the post-war period to provide the funds to rebuild the shattered lives of European Jewry and to support the building of a Jewish community in Palestine, they were at the same time manifesting an increased interest in domestic needs.

Since 1945, the largest area of building has been in the construction of temples and synagogues. Older synagogues, located in the older centers of Jewish population while their congregants now lived in areas at some distance, needed new facilities; newly organized congregations called for buildings; there were moreover, synagogues inadequate in size and facilities that had to be replaced. Obsolete buildings now were unsuitable for their functions and fell below the standard appropriate to the new economic and social status of their memberships. There is no detailed inventory of the spurt in synagogue building, but it was obviously very extensive

—not only in the large cities, but in many small ones. The trend toward new synagogue building continues with the movement of large numbers of Jews to developing suburban areas.

The building of synagogues in the newer sections of the cities and in the suburban areas has been accompanied, to a considerable extent, by a change in the nature of their facilities. No longer limited in use, as were most of the early buildings, to the functions of worship and religious study, the newer buildings are planned with facilities for social, educational and recreational functions. Provided with classrooms, auditoriums, swimming pools, indoor and outdoor equipment for leisure-time activities, the new synagogue buildings are physically equipped to function as social centers for the families of the congregation.

Some of them are also attempting to provide the staff services needed for the operation of a social center. These developments are raising the question of the relationship of Synagogue Centers to the movement for Jewish Centers organized on a communal and non-denominational basis which has been developing vigorously for more than four decades in the majority of American cities.[1] In very small cities and suburban areas the synagogue center is frequently the only existing institutional basis for Jewish communal activity.[2]

HEALTH AND WELFARE INSTITUTIONS

In the health and welfare fields in which federations generally assume direct responsibility, planning for new construction began early. In some cities it started in the last year of the war when, with victory in sight, there was hope that the lifting of wartime restrictions would permit the resumption of peacetime building. Among the first to anticipate this prospect, and to recognize that careful study was necessary in order to avoid sporadic piecemeal efforts by individual agencies, was the New York Federation. This body took several years to make an intensive study of needs before launching a campaign, in 1945, for $21,000,000 to expand and modernize its $70,000,000 plant of seven hospitals, a score of neighborhood centers and numerous other agencies.

Similarly, other communities began to determine what changes were needed in their health and welfare programs and what institutional building these changes required. In 1945 a total of twenty-seven cities reported campaigns for capital funds.[3] Detroit embarked on a campaign to secure funds for building the first Jewish hospital in that city; Cincinnati, Kansas City and Pittsburgh started to raise funds for hospitals or facilities for the chronically ill; and Oakland, Youngstown, Syracuse and Chattanooga ran campaigns for new community Centers. Chicago, Philadelphia, Boston, Baltimore, St. Louis, Cleveland and other large cities engaged in fund-raising for the improvement of their Jewish hospital facilities, with Miami and Minneapolis organizing their first Jewish hospitals in this period. New or improved hospital facilities, new or enlarged homes for the aged, new and improved facilities for community Centers, were planned and built in many cities.

With the post-war period the changes, which had been under way for some time, in the purposes and motivations of Jewish philanthropic institutions became more evident. The main change was in the shift of the focus of philanthropy from a concentration on the problems of poverty to a concern for the welfare of the group as a whole. Where previously the emphasis in family service and child care agencies, in homes for the aged, in Jewish education and Settlement Houses and, to a large extent, in hospitals, was on the needs of the dependent groups—those unable to pay for health and welfare services—the trend was now to serve the whole population, in their health, welfare, educational and institutional needs.

It was recognized that hospitals were needed for the rich as well as the poor—and for the practice of medicine by Jewish physicians—and that recreational centers were essential for all sections of the community, not merely for the indigent and the immigrant. It was also becoming accepted doctrine that communally-supported services—homes for the aged, homes for the chronically ill, family and child guidance agencies and vocational adjustment—were in many respects more satisfactory than those to be privately secured and should be made available to people of all income levels.

The synagogues and recreational and educational centers, the health facilities, the programs for families, children and the aged were recognized as important factors in maintaining a community of Jewish interests. Federation leadership began to see that institutions and services to meet general needs added essential values to Jewish communal life and that the nature and quality of these institutions and services would in turn help to determine the character and quality of the Jewish community. The realization of these influences was beginning to move philanthropy into the larger areas of mutual aid and self-help.

Though services-for-everyone involved a change of attitude from charity given to one of payments for services received it was found to be true that few agencies can exist on service income alone. Therefore federated funds remain an essential factor in the maintenance of communal institutions. More important is the fact that the organization of common services, their administration in terms of building and equipment can only be successfully attained by the cooperative efforts of the whole community.

The record of institutional building and expansion of services is indicated in the following facts:[4]

Hospitals

Between 1945 and 1960 the number of beds in 74 hospitals under Jewish auspices increased from 13,800 to 18,283. The increase in number of beds does not adequately portray the replacement of old by new facilities nor the advance in standards and corresponding costs as hospitals were reacting to the current advances in medical science, were developing university affiliation, research and teaching facilities, special care of the chronically ill, psychiatric services and other specialties. Philanthropic support for the maintenance of 65 Jewish hospitals, which reported their 1959 operating receipts, amounted to $18,827,000, representing 11.6% of total receipts. Of this total, Jewish federations supplied close to $9,000,000. In addition, funds from governmental agencies supplied over $12,000,000 to the operating receipts of Jewish hospitals. Payments for services amounted to over $125,000,000 representing 77% of operating receipts.

Aged and Chronically Ill

The care of the aged and the chronically ill also required considerable expansion of facilities. The proportion of individuals 65 years of age and over in the general population had increased since the 1920s. This age group constituted 4.8% of the total population in 1920; by 1954 the proportion had increased to 8.4%. The more effective work of the public assistance agencies and the availability of Old Age Assistance and Old Age Insurance programs first established under federal auspices in 1935 had made it possible for many aged persons to remain in their own homes, but it had not decreased the number of aged

193

persons who needed special institutional care either because of their disabilities, or because of unavailable family homes. With the substantial rise in the number of aged Jews, increased pressure upon institutional facilities continued despite the growing number of able-bodied aged who were receiving public assistance and were continuing to live in their own homes.

The need for Jewish homes for the aged and their bed capacity have been increasing steadily. In 1945 the total bed capacity of the 63 Jewish homes for the aged was approximately 6,000, representing an increase of approximately 25% over 1930. By 1960 there was a bed capacity of 12,428 in 74 Jewish homes for the aged and plans were under way for further expansion in a number of cities. For 1959, 64 homes for the aged reported philanthropic income of approximately $5,000,000, representing 22.7% of total receipts. Payments for service accounted for 73.7% of operating receipts.

New planning for the aged was not limited to the building of facilities to house those unable to be cared for in their own homes. It involved also the extension of programs of social service, recreation and health adapted to the needs of the aged, and greater efforts for home care of the aged who were not sufficiently disabled to require institutional and nursing treatment. In many communities a program of caring for the aged began to be extended through the family service agencies, community Centers and hospitals. The latter in addition began to take a greater interest in medical care for the chronically ill which included a large proportion of aged persons.

In 1956, a four-year study of coordination of local Jewish health services for long-term illness was initiated by the CJFWF, financed by a grant from the United States Public Health Service. A series of reports have been issued dealing with the findings of this study.[5]

The original aim of the study, as set forth in the application to the U.S. Public Health Service, was "to study in detail recent efforts to coordinate the facilities of a general hospital with the resources of other medical and related community services." The results of the study which have elicited widespread interest in medical and welfare circles throughout the nation have important implications for the program of health institutions, homes for the aged, family and vocational service agencies, and for local and national health and welfare planning. There are indications that the study will help to stimulate more effective and more desirable community planned programs for serving patients with chronic illnesses.

Jewish Centers

In 1943 the National Jewish Welfare Board reported 293 constituent organizations with 390,000 individual members and annual expenditures of $5,700,000. In 1955 it reported the affiliation of 348 Centers and branches reaching an estimated total of 565,000 individuals and expenditures of over $16,000,000, with new buildings undertaken since 1948 valued at $41,400,000. Additional buildings are in the planning stage in other cities. (See chapter XIII on group work and recreation.)

Jewish Education

There are no statistics available for the building costs of Jewish educational facilities during this period. Many schools for children and youth are housed in congregational facilities as well as in Centers and other communal buildings, but a few facilities especially designed for Jewish education were built in various cities. The record of development is perhaps better illustrated by enrollment figures which were estimated at nearly 553,600 in 1958 compared with 239,000 in 1948. According to Uriah Z. Engelman of the American Association for Jewish Education, "Enrollment in Jewish schools has increased faster in the past half-century than the Jewish population." In 1959, the AAJE estimated that American Jewry was spending over $51,000,000 on operating Jewish schools; that there were 3,367 school units of all types compared with 2,200 Jewish schools, with annual expenditures of approximately $6,000,000 in 1944. The part of this total cost derived from philanthropic funds has not been reported. However, it was estimated that the federations spent approximately 12% of their allocations for local services on Jewish educational agencies.

For the year 1958, enrollment in Jewish schools was distributed as follows: Orthodox 21.0%; Conservative 38.6%; Reform 28.1%; Yiddish 1.3%; other or multiple (noncongregational) 11.0%.

Child Care

There was no substantial building for child care services in this period. Principles of child care had moved from a primary dependence on congregate or cottage plan institutions to an emphasis on providing care for children in their own homes or in substitute private family homes. As a result there had been a decline in the number and the capacity of child caring institutions from 60 in 1930 to 23 in 1960. In 1930, the institutions cared for 60%; in 1959 only 26% of all the children under care were in institutions. During this period there was also a decline in the total number of children under care, from 7,833 at the end of 1940 to 4,169 at the beginning of 1960.

The shrinkage in the number of dependent children requiring care has been attributed to several factors, including (a) the improving economic position of the Jewish population and the pre-war reduction of the birthrate which facilitated the maintenance of family homes and the absorption by relatives of children from broken homes; (b) the improved methods of child care service which resulted in a shorter period of care away from their own families being required by children who were placed; (c) increasing use of foster homes rather than institutional care; (d) the improvement in case work service on the part of family and children's agencies which made it possible to serve in their own homes children who might otherwise have been removed because of inability to adjust within the family environment; and (e) the availability of public assistance through the program of aid to dependent children and other social security measures.

A long-time trend in the decline of numbers of children under care had begun to level off in 1952. However, the statistics for 1959 (compared to 1954) indicated a further drop in the number of admissions. While no new institutions for dependent children were being built or old ones enlarged, attention has been directed to the special needs of the emotionally disturbed and other problem children who could not be adjusted in their own homes and for whom the available foster homes were not adequate for the therapeutic treatment they required. New York, Chicago and Bellefaire at Cleveland led in creating facilities for residential treatment of emotionally disturbed children. A number of other cities including Detroit, Los Angeles, Boston, St. Louis and San Francisco have set up, or are in the process of developing, specialized small group residential centers.

The per capita costs of treatment of emotionally disturbed children in residences are high on account of the intensive psychiatric, supervisory and case work services such homes require. The number of children suitable for a particular type of residence is not apt to be large. While the smaller communities can provide care under their own auspices for a great variety of children, they need to turn to Jewish agencies outside their own communities, or to agencies under non-sectarian or public auspices, for appropriate treatment for special child care problems.

Family Service

Family service conducted through office procedures did not require new building during this period. In a number of cities, however, office facilities were improved corresponding to the changed nature of the functions of these organizations. By the end of the acute period of the depression of the 1930s the major function of the Jewish family agencies was no longer in terms of financial assistance, which had been taken over by public facilities.

Between 1945 and 1954, however, most of the Jewish family service agencies were involved in helping the new immigrants to adjust and were expending considerable amounts for relief of this group. Resident families not eligible for public assistance and those whose assistance needed to be supplemented were a small factor of the

197

family agencies' relief costs during this period of high employment. In 1950, when the Jewish family service agencies were spending about $4,000,000 on relief, 80% of this amount was being devoted to immigrant families. However, though the refugee load was absorbing a good part of the energies of the Jewish family agencies they were also extending services to individuals and families other than the dependent or marginal group. The total number of clients being served by Jewish family agencies has remained fairly stable over the last ten years. The declining refugee and immigrant group load has been replaced by service to the resident population. For a number of years many of the Jewish family service agencies had been concentrating on solving the problems responsible for dependency and maladjustment. Many of the problems were those of individual and family pathology not different in kind from those to be found among people in all economic classes. The agencies had been able to develop skills which they were now making available to families other than those in the dependent or marginal group. Counseling and help in the adjustment of family and children's problems were tending to become a significant phase of the work of the family welfare agencies in many of the larger communities. (The child guidance services may also be one of the factors in the decline of the volume of children requiring placement outside of their own family groups.) The family agencies during this period began to receive fees from those able to afford payment. Counseling services were developed especially in New York (where the care of refugees was being assumed by a separate organization, the New York Association for New Americans), and were becoming a significant phase of the work of most of the other Jewish family service agencies which employed professionally trained case workers.

For the year 1959, 70 family service agencies reported total operating receipts of approximately $9,500,000 of which 82% originated in federation or local community chest support. Payments for service added 5% to agency receipts.

In 1959, 78 Jewish family service agencies reported receiving close to 44,000 applications, of which 1,800 or
7.3% were made by recent immigrants. The agencies
reported a monthly average of approximately 13,500
active cases of whom 17% received financial assistance
amounting to $2,205,000 during the year. Of this amount
30% went to immigrant clients. (The New York Association for New Americans accounted for one-half of all
reported financial assistance to immigrants throughout
the United States and Canada being given by the family
service agencies.)

COSTS OF PROGRAMS

During the post-war period there were substantial
changes in the relative costs of the parts of the functional
programs which federations and welfare funds were financing in behalf of their communities. These changes
are indicated in the table which gives the distribution of
local funds by functional fields for the years 1946 and
1956 (the latest available data). All costs rose substantially: in 1956 the communities were spending more than
twice as much on their local programs as in 1946, and
all fields were receiving larger funds, ranging from a
35% increase for the field of community relations to a
215% increase over the 1946 allocations to aged-care
agencies. The increases were 136% for recreational
agencies, 129% for health and hospitals and 130% for
Jewish education.[6]

THE DEVELOPMENT OF OTHER LOCAL SERVICES

There were improvements and extensions of other
communal services under federation auspices which did
not involve extensive buildings or capital funds. Among
the more important of the services which required only
office facilities were the developing programs to promote
better inter-group relationships, help in vocational adjust-

Distribution of Federation* Allocations
for Local Services in 60 Communities—
1946 and 1956
(amounts in thousands of dollars)

| | 1946 | | 1956 | | Index Of Change 1946-1956 |
	Amount	%	Amount	%	1946=100%
Health	$ 3,034	26.4	6,948*	28.7*	229.0
Family & Child Services	2,918	25.4	4,893*	20.2*	167.7
Recreation & Culture	2,047	17.8	4,829*	20.0*	235.9
Jewish Education	1,234	10.7	2,833	11.7	229.6
Aged Care	538	4.7	1,694*	7.0*	315.0
Refugee Care	579	5.0	1,105	4.6	190.7
Employment & Guidance	415	3.6	804	3.3	193.8
Community Relations	477	4.2	642	2.7	134.6
Other	256	2.2	437	1.8	170.8
Total**	$11,497	100.0	$24,185*	100.0*	210.4
Sources of Income					
Federations**	6,801	59.2	$15,310	63.3	225.1
Community Chests**	4,696	40.8	8,875*	36.7*	189.0

* Includes both federation and community chest funds; however *direct grants* from community chests to agencies not included except where reported by federations.
** Slight differences due to rounding.

ment, and provision for non-institutional medical home care, recreational and cultural programs for the aged and extensive community Center programs.

AGENCIES DEALING WITH RELATIONSHIPS OF AMERICAN RELIGIOUS AND ETHNIC GROUPS

One of the most extensive developments during this period was in the field of group relations. During the acute period of anti-Semitism in the 1930s and early 1940s, a number of cities had organized active committees or special agencies to concern themselves with this aspect of community life. It had become increasingly evident that the problem of anti-Semitism did not involve merely coping with overt incidents, but required a positive program of studying the relationship of Jews to other groups in the community and exploring the areas of civil rights and of democratic practices generally. This approach resulted in the development of broad programs of community education and of methods for facilitating constructive inter-group participation on the part of religious bodies and the creation of other forms of group association. In a number of cities, local committees on interracial and inter-group relations were being established under governmental or voluntary auspices frequently stimulated by the experience and the interest of the Jewish federations.

When the NCRAC (National Community Relations Advisory Council) was organized in 1944, it established criteria for defining the nature and extent of a local community relations agency suitable for membership in the NCRAC. Fourteen local agencies qualified at the beginning of that program. (By 1960, the number of local community relations councils which were members of the NCRAC had increased to 52—some of them covering state-wide areas.) In addition to the members of the NCRAC, other communities also developed similar programs through local committees, with the result that guiding principles for the improvement of group relations are inherent in the work and policies of many central Jewish community organizations and their constituent agencies. In 1958, it was reported that approximately $722,000 was being spent on such local services, involving 2.5% of federation allocations for all local programs in 93 communities. In addition, local welfare funds were contributing $2,600,000 or 2.6% of their annual allocations to the national agencies in this field.[7]

The desire to achieve close integration between the work of the national agencies and the local communities, and among the national agencies themselves, continued to receive attention. A basis for limited forms of cooperation had been achieved in this field with the establishment of the NCRAC in 1944; there still remained, however, considerable competition and undesirable forms of rivalry among some of the national agencies. The Large City Budgeting Conference and representatives of other communities were hopeful that a more effective relationship might be attained. With the cooperation of the NCRAC and its agencies, a survey was undertaken in 1950 under the direction of Professor Robert M. MacIver of Columbia University.

The report which Dr. MacIver submitted in 1951[8] was subjected to considerable study and discussion within the NCRAC and by the agencies and communities. There was unanimous acceptance of a statement of principles contained in the report, suggesting joint program planning, with logical and practical division of labor; reassessment of strategy; community consultation and other improvements in the coordination of the services of the agencies. However, full agreement could not be obtained in 1952 on a specific plan for putting these principles into operation. Following the adoption of a plan of operation acceptable to the members of NCRAC, with the exception of the American Jewish Committee and the Anti-Defamation League, these two agencies withdrew from the association and are no longer affiliated with NCRAC.[9]

The NCRAC, however, has been enlarged by the membership of additional national and local agencies and has extended its services of joint planning of programs, reassessment of objectives and methods, and cooperative relationships among its affiliated national agencies and local community relations councils.

VOCATIONAL SERVICES

There were significant developments in the organization of vocational services under Jewish federation auspices during this period. Before the 1930s, vocational services were largely engaged in trying to find jobs for new immigrants and for marginal workers. With the rise of anti-Semitism and large-scale unemployment, the vocational agencies began increasingly to concern themselves with the broader aspects of Jewish vocational problems: occupational distribution, discrimination in employment, and adjustment to jobs.

The Jewish Occupational Council, a national service agency for this field, reported that twenty-six Jewish vocational service agencies under federation auspices were providing individual educational and vocational guidance and job placement services. Most of these had psychological testing facilities and a large number were conducting group-guidance programs. They were also involved, in a number of cities, in the operation of sheltered workshops for the handicapped and for vocational rehabilitation. With the growing interest in service to the aged, the vocational service agencies intensified their vocational guidance and placement services for this group.[10] In 1958, employment and vocational guidance agencies received over one million dollars from federations, representing 3.4% of federation's total allocations.

There was a marked development of standards during this period. In addition to the improvement of the facilities of hospitals, homes for the aged, and community Centers, new and improved methods of service were attained in practically all other fields. Where previously development of standards was a sporadic process dependent upon the personnel of the individual agencies, the 1945-1960 period indicated an acceptance of the need for conscious and systematic planning on the part of federation and its agencies in a unified approach. Most of the larger, and many of the smaller, federations set up central planning committees of qualified representatives of the agencies and of the community. These standing central committees are engaged in studying needs and agency programs, and are attempting to work out improved cooperation in order to bring the resources of the community to bear on needs and on long-range planning.

Out of this organization of communal planning grew such developments as mergers of related and parallel agencies, central bureaus for the care of the aged, extension programs of community Centers, home-care programs for the chronically ill and non-institutional methods of providing suitable care for the aged. Communities have also planned Golden Age Clubs for the older population, camps and nursery schools, psychiatric services, and have moved ahead in many other aspects of educational and welfare services.

The dynamic period of post-war development in

Jewish communal work, the enlargement of overseas programs, the growth and spread of central community organization, and the extension and improvement in functional agency services directed attention, again, to the need of Jewish services to be administered by a competently prepared professional group. Since the closing of the Graduate School for Jewish Social Work, special facilities for professional education for Jewish personnel has been lacking. There has, however, been an increase in the number and enrollment of schools of social work under general auspices and a large increase in the number of Jews preparing for social work in these institutions.

When the war ended, there was a shortage of trained and skilled workers and, it was believed, a lack of orientation on the part of Jewish graduates of general social work schools to the special characteristics of the various fields of Jewish social work in which there were positions to be filled. Plans were developed through the cooperation of a number of the national organizations for a training program designed for the supplementary preparation of qualified workers for top executive and administrative posts in Jewish welfare programs. A Training Bureau for Jewish Communal Service[11] was established for this purpose in 1947 and it conducted courses for selected students for several years.

The Training Bureau was discontinued in 1951. The chief reasons for its closing were: the difficulties of attracting mature students able to finance themselves in post-graduate training, the cost of the program in relation to the limited number of enrolled students and the deficits in funds needed, the slackening of demand for additional personnel in the higher echelons, and lack of agreement on the special supplementary types of training required by social workers who already had general professional preparation and some years of experience in Jewish organizations.

While a formal resource of this kind for the special preparation of professional workers for the field was available for only a few years, Jewish agencies have made substantial progress in the character of their professional personnel and in their utilization for advancing the standards of Jewish welfare programs. One example is the increase in the number of federations employing professional executives, from less than sixty cities in 1940, to more than twice that number in 1960.

Although the Training Bureau was discontinued, a program of education for social work, begun several years earlier at Yeshiva University, has been continued and expanded. In 1959, Brandeis University initiated its special advanced doctoral program, the Florence Heller School of Social Welfare Administration.

SOCIAL PLANNING

An Advisory Committee on Social Planning established by the CJFWF in 1950 has devoted itself to central planning for the care of the aged, the relation between hospitals and federations in financing and planning, problems of emotionally disturbed children and facilities required for meeting their needs, the relationship between federations and community chests, relationships between Jewish Centers and federations, the rationale, scope and functions of the family service agency, and the formulation of guiding principles for central planning by federations.[12]

There has been a growing interest also in community planning for Jewish education, with central bureaus established in at least forty-five communities. In 1958, Jewish education was receiving $3,450,000 in support from Jewish federations, which represented 11.7%

of federation funds. Federation allocations to Jewish education have thus more than doubled since 1946. The Large City Budgeting Conference encouraged its members to undertake increased support of the American Association for Jewish Education, a national service agency in this field, which, in 1952, undertook an intensive study of Jewish education in the United States looking toward improvement and development of one of the basic areas of Jewish communal interest.

THE NATIONAL FOUNDATION FOR JEWISH CULTURE

The organization of the National Foundation for Jewish Culture in 1960[13] is an example of the growing interest of Jewish federations in programs concerned with some of the more general aspects of American Jewish life.

For a number of years, national agencies dealing with Jewish history, research, archives, publications and scholarships experienced great difficulty in obtaining the required interest and support of their programs. Competition with welfare agencies and the greater appeal of such programs to the charitable sentiments of the Jewish population, the obstacles of apathy or indifference, the pressures of more immediate issues had greatly limited the work of agencies concerned with cultural needs and services. The attempts of such organizations to interest the federation and welfare funds in the value of their activities and in their need for financial support had met with only a meager or token response over the years.

The piecemeal efforts of a score of unrelated agencies and the growing dissatisfaction of the federations themselves with this condition led the Large City Budgeting Conference in 1954 to recommend that a national survey of Jewish cultural endeavor be undertaken in the United States. Such a comprehensive study was undertaken in 1958 by the CJFWF with the cooperation of the agencies concerned. Centered on fields of cultural interest and extending beyond Jewish agencies to encompass the programs of universities, commercial publishers serving these interests, and others, the study[14] emphasized the importance to the Jewish communities of a greatly intensified American Jewish cultural development.

The report, presented to the 1959 General Assembly of the CJFWF, was enthusiastically received, and the Assembly called for the prompt implementation of its major proposals. This mandate was carried out in 1960 with establishment of the National Foundation for Jewish Culture, together with the National Council of Jewish Cultural Agencies as a planning arm. The Hon. Herbert H. Lehman, former governor of New York and U.S. senator, accepted leadership as its honorary president, with a governing board composed of distinguished men and women drawn from all sections of the United States and Canada.

The purpose of the Foundation is to provide assistance and leadership to the national agencies and communities in strengthening Jewish cultural development in North America. It undertook to mobilize support for scholarship, research and other programs which do not come within the scope of individual agencies, to coordinate and extend archival resources, to enrich the quality of publications, to help the national agencies meet the priorities of their major unresolved needs, to develop periodic comprehensive assessments and guides for the field as a whole. The funds required for the operating expenses of the Foundation and the Council were assured for the first three years by special grants from the major federations and welfare funds.

X

Sectarian and Non-Sectarian Welfare Agencies

ORGANIZING THE JEWISH COMMUNITY

*H*ow does federation relate to the various proposals on how the Jewish community should be organized? Adherents of various theories on the future of Jewish life in the modern world have been most concerned with this subject. They have questioned whether a specific federation, or the federation movement as a whole, is in line with their aims of developing an association of American Jewry on a unitary and overall basis. In these discussions opinions have been expressed on whether the existing federations are properly imbued with the sentiments favoring, or are satisfactorily performing the functions necessary for, "Jewish survival"; whether they are furthering the aim of "positive Judaism" or are accelerating or retarding the processes of "assimilation." The varying theories of the future of Jewish communal life that have been held by the lay and professional leadership of federations, and by other critics and observers, are pertinent to the history of federation activities.

OBJECTIVES OF COMMUNAL ORGANIZATION

Aims and programs for communal organization have been advocated by individuals and are inherent in formal movements. The religious denominations which promote doctrine and principle to guide individual behavior may also have more or less specific ideas concerning group and communal organization. Still other proposals are made by movements that are primarily secular, such as the several Zionist or non-Zionist organizations, as well as by other associations with a particular ideology.

These various movements and the ideas and the designs for the Jewish future that they advocate are often in conflict with one another and have led to sharp controversies among workers in the Jewish welfare field. The social welfare agencies have occasionally served as the arena in which these conflicting ideologies have met.

Without attempting a catalogue of the objectives of all of these formal and informal movements—which range from what has been designated as complete assimilation to extremes of Jewish separatedness—it may be helpful to set forth those aims which are relevant to the continuing programs of federation:

1. To organize the Jewish community for the purpose of promoting the welfare of individuals and to help individuals, families and groups to adjust to the conditions of their environment.

2. To organize the Jewish community in order to assure the continuity of the traditional Jewish culture and Jewish religious beliefs and practices and to counteract tendencies toward loss or abandonment of Jewish cultural values and traditions.

3. To organize the Jewish community in order to

facilitate the processes of cultural evolution and of adaptation to American life. Such programs may at the same time strive for the integration of the historical continuity and traditional values of Jews with the conditions of a multicultural environment, or to the evolution of current religious ideas.

4. To organize for the protection of Jews in what may be considered an unfavorable or hostile environment; to help avoid the undesirable aspects of prejudice and of discrimination; to improve group relationships and help resolve the difficulties arising from minority status.

5. To organize the community in order to retain, continue and expand the close group association of Jews, so that they may effectively assist Jews in other lands, and to help the state of Israel cope with its problems and difficulties.

It is obvious that a specific program or movement may involve more than one of these purposes or additional objectives. On the other hand, several of the movements that apparently promote the same or similar aims may differ on the meaning of their objectives and on the kind of communal organization required for their attainment. Some objectives are based upon or seek the support or adherence of all, or the greatest possible number of, Jews in the population; other movements may be intended for and may be successfully carried on with relatively small groups of people. There are some programs which aim to imbue individuals with particular sentiments concerning the desirable future for the life of Jews in the modern world, while being opposed to any mass movement and rejecting the need for organizing a "Jewish community."

Until relatively recently, federations have usually limited their community organizing efforts to the first objective—that of promoting individual, family and group welfare. This objective, weighted originally in the direction of material well-being and physical health, has more recently involved concern for psychological well-being, social adjustment and the attainment of more satisfactory relationships with other groups in the population. The latter objectives bring the welfare programs closer to some of the proposals and movements that are primarily concerned with the religious and cultural life of Jews.

Although federations may not have specific cultural objectives as a conscious design, the work of the federation and the programs of their beneficiary agencies frequently parallel the cultural goals of some of the formal movements; they are likely in general to reflect the prevailing sentiments of the dominant supporters and the administrators of the agencies. On the other hand, the desire of the federations for successful fund-raising impels them to reach all elements of the Jewish population in the largest numbers possible.

To accomplish the fund-raising aim, it is imperative to avoid the negative reactions of any group of potential givers. As a consequence, federation usually tries to steer clear of controversial ideological questions and forgo identification with one or another partisan cultural objective. The more homogenous the Jewish population, the more the federation is likely to find itself in accord with the dominant cultural preferences of the group; the more the community is diversified, the more will federation attempt to remain as neutral as possible among conflicting objectives. The non-controversial character of most of the welfare agencies and welfare programs helps

1. The Joint Distribution Committee at an early meeting. Seated, left to right: Felix M. Warburg, chairman; Aaron Teitelbaum; Albert Lucas, secretary; Mrs. F. Friedman, official stenographer; Boris D. Bogen, executive director; Leon Sanders; Harry Fischel; Sholem Asch; Alexander Kahn; Jacob Milch; Miss Harriet E. Lowenstein, comptroller; Col. Moses Schoenberg; M. Z. Margolies; Israel Friedlander; Paul Baerwald, associate-treasurer; Julius Levy; Peter Wiernik; Meyer Gillis; Harry Cutler; Cyrus Adler; Arthur Lehman, treasurer; Jacob H. Schiff. Standing, left to right: Abraham Zucker, Isidore Hershfield, Meyer Berlin, Stanley Bero, Louis Topkis, Morris Engelman.

2. Ellis Island Ferry, 1906. On board, a group of young Jewish girls who fled from Russia to escape being sent to Siberian prisons for revolutionary activities. At boat rail, volunteer workers of the National Council of Jewish Women, who look after the welfare of the newly arrived immigrant girls. Known as the "Port and Dock Department" of the Council, this service became the historic NCJW Service to the Foreign Born. The service was initiated in 1903 at the request of the United States Government, to prevent white slavery, exploitation and sweatshop labor that were the lot of many immigrant girls arriving alone and penniless in America.

3. New York, 1906. An investigator sent by the National Council of Jewish Women visits a home to which several immigrant girls have been released by the Ellis Island authorities. Several thousand such visits were made, in cooperation with other organizations, as an outgrowth of the Council's Port and Dock Department volunteer service.

4. Morale work for Jews in the U.S. Armed Forces. The predecessor of the National Jewish Welfare Board religious and morale program. The scene was photographed on the Mexican border, 1916.

5. Members of the JWB Executive Committee, 1918. Seated, left to right: Rabbi Maurice H. Harris, Louis Marshall, Col. Harry Cutler, Dr. Cyrus Adler, Gustave Hartman. Standing, left to right: Chester J. Teller, Rabbi David de Sola Pool, Mortimer J. Schiff, Israel Unterber, Henry J. Bernheim, Joseph Rosenzweig.

SURVIVORS OF THE **TITANIC**

In care of the Hebrew Sheltering and Immigrant Aid Society

די גערַאטעוועטע פון דער שיף טיטַאניק

אונטער די אויפזעהונג פון די חברו שעלטערינג אין אימיגרַאנט אייד סַאסייעטי

Photo by Ph. Kravitz, 578 E. Houston St.

6. Survivors of the Titanic. In care of the Hebrew Sheltering and Immigrant Aid Society

7. Passover Seder, 1918. Jewish immigrants at the home of the Hebrew Sheltering and Immigrant Aid Society of America, 229 East Broadway, New York.

8. JDC activity in Russia, 1920. Begun as early as 1914, it included relief, feeding, child care, medical aid, reconstruction and vocational training. Between 1914 and 1924, JDC spent approximately $14,300,000 for the relief and rehabilitation of Jews in Russia.

9. Farming colonies in Russia, 1925. By 1938 there were 215 Agro-Joint colonies, with 100,000 persons, engaged in farming. From 1924 to 1938, Agro-Joint provided some $16,000,000 for these activities.

Events of the past several years have brought an ever-increasing burden of responsibility for welfare activities to Jews throughout the United States. The scope of such responsibilities has widened greatly and the nature of the responsibilities themselves become more complex.

It is the purpose of the Conference to throw added light on these problems, to consider the means by which federated and unorganized groups may deal with them and how individuals may relate themselves to such programs.

1935

NATIONAL CONFERENCE
on JEWISH WELFARE

•

CONGREGATION EMANU-EL
COMMUNITY HOUSE

1 EAST 65TH STREET

NEW YORK CITY

JANUARY 3RD THROUGH 6TH

UNDER THE AUSPICES OF

NATIONAL COUNCIL OF JEWISH
FEDERATIONS AND WELFARE FUNDS

(Address All Communications to the Office
71 West 47th Street, New York City)

PROGRAM

•

Thursday—January 3rd

12:00 M.—Luncheon

Presiding Officer: JOSEPH M. PROSKAUER

I. Subject: THE AMERICAN SCENE—JEWISH NEEDS AND JEWISH WELFARE FACILITIES TODAY

Speaker: *Solomon Lowenstein*

II. Subject: PUBLIC WELFARE AND SECURITY

Speakers: *Paul Kellogg*
Samuel A. Goldsmith

3:30 P. M.—General Session

Presiding Officer: PAUL BAERWALD

Subject: AMERICAN AID TO JEWS OVERSEAS

1. Eastern and Central Europe
Speaker: *Neville Laski*

2. Agricultural and Settlement Developments in Russia
Speaker: *Dr. Joseph Rosen*

3. Refugees and Organized Aid
Speaker: *Dr. Bernhard Kahn*

7:00 P. M.—Dinner

Presiding Officer: FELIX M. WARBURG

I. Subject: THE PLACE OF THE NATIONAL COUNCIL OF JEWISH FEDERATIONS AND WELFARE FUNDS IN AMERICAN LIFE

Speaker: *William J. Shroder*

II. Subject: TOLERANCE AND THE REFUGEES

Speaker: *James G. McDonald*

(Albert Einstein, Judge Alfred Talley and Raymond Moley will address this meeting on Good Will and Understanding)

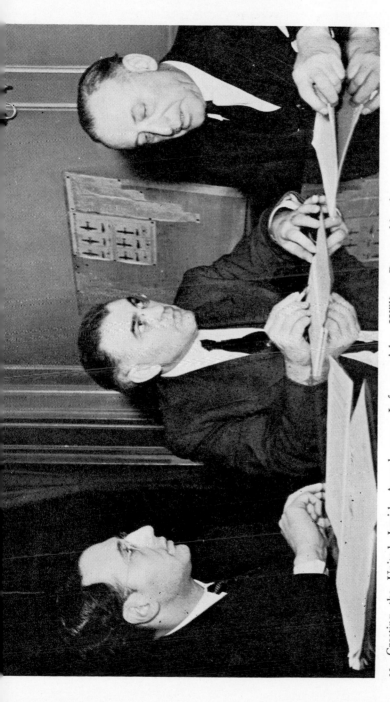

11. Creating the United Jewish Appeal, 1939. Left to right: William Rosenwald of New York, representing the National Coordinating Committee for Aid to Refugees and Emigrants Coming from Germany; Rabbi Abba Hillel Silver cf Cleveland, representing the United Palestine Appeal; Rabbi Jonah B. Wise of New York, representing the American Jewish Joint Distribution Committee.

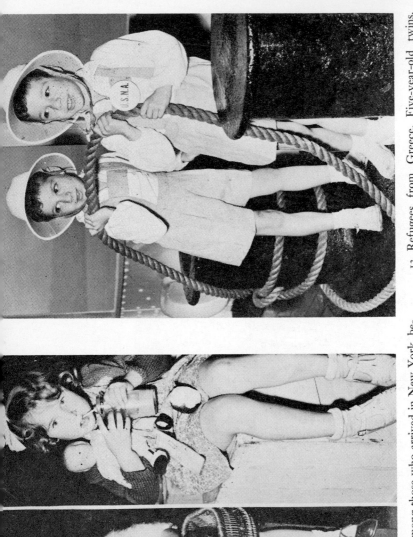

12. Refugee children. Among those who arrived in New York, between 1946–48, aboard the "Serpa Pinto," are Alice Gottlieb (left), who fled from France with her parents, Mr. and Mrs. Solomon Gottlieb, and Antoinette Steuer, who came alone, among 50 children brought from Europe by the U.S. Committee for the Care of European Children.*

13. Refugees from Greece. Five-year-old twins, Jock and Max Sarfaty, among the first Greek refugees to arrive in the U.S. after the war, sailing into Houston, Texas, on the "La Guardia."

* This committee operated on a non-sectarian basis, with funds supplied by the National Refugee Service.

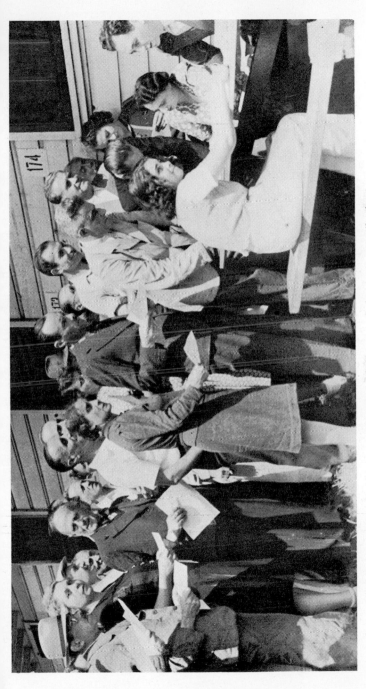

14. Refugee camp in Oswego, New York. Some of the refugees admitted temporarily into the United States under a special ruling by the President, early in World War II. They were helped by the National Refugee Service and United HIAS Service, who provided for their welfare and counseled them on resettlement. Most of them were eventually admitted to the U.S.; others emigrated to Canada and other friendly countries.

15. Refugee children from France and Portugal. Arriving in the United States after being rescued by the JDC from Europe in 1948. The same agency provided for the emigration of 93,000 persons from Europe to the Western Hemisphere and Palestine after the outbreak of World War II.

16. Leaving a DP camp, 1949. Bound for Israel.

17. NCRAC Panel of CJFWF General Assembly, Chicago, 1948. Left to right: Isaiah Minkoff, executive director NRAC; Henry Epstein, chairman NCRAC; Lester Jaffe, Cincinnati, Secretary NRAC; Dr. John Slawson, executive vice-president American Jewish Committee; Bernard P. Kopkind, New Haven, vice-chairman NRAC.

18. The William J. Shroder Award Presentation. For merger of JDC migration services, United Service for New Americans and HIAS, into the United HIAS Service. Left to right: Edward M. M. Warburg, Mrs. Louis Broido, Mrs. Mortimer May, Edwin Rosenberg, Ben Touster, Mrs. Irving Engel.

the federation to remain detached from conflicting cultural issues. Issues may nevertheless arise; and such matters as a hospital's dietary provisions, Sabbath observance at a social center, nationalist ideals inculcated at Jewish schools, the political aspects of the support of welfare programs in Israel, and many others, may demand the attention of the federation's leadership.

ON THE MEANING OF THE TERM "COMMUNITY"

Before proceeding to discuss the ways in which federations have related themselves to the various theories of community organization, it will be useful to consider the nature of community and what the "organization of the Jewish community" means in the setting of the multiple sectarian and ethnic groups in the American population.

Man is a social being with an inherent need to and a preference for living in aggregates rather than as isolated individuals or family groups. Out of the complex of human relationships and interactions and the mobility of populations there have developed forms of group association for which we use such terms as: society, community, state, nation, church, faith, fellowship, association, neighborhood, etc.

"Society," or the social order, is the broadest and most general term encompassing all phases of social living. The term "community" is most frequently applied to all the residents of a defined geographical area who are assumed to constitute a social unit by virtue of shared interests and basic interrelationships. With the primacy of governmental organization in contemporary life, sections of the habitable areas are divided into nations, states, cities, counties, townships, villages, wards, etc. The term "community" is applied to these politically constituted aggregations of people who are assumed to be involved in common responsibilities and to share common interests.

In addition to this primary form of "community," there are groups and associations with more or less formal structures, such as social clubs or fraternities, business groups and corporations, neighborhood councils, philanthropic societies and many other associations with specific social or group objectives. The term "community" is popularly used for voluntary groups (which may include only a fraction of the geographical community) that are likely to have some degree of permanence and that involve the participants in a more or less complex series of relationships and interactions and which lead to more or less sustained feeling of being part of a recognizably distinct segment of the population. The term "community" on this basis is an apt description of the interactions and interrelationships of the American Jewish population.[1]

While the communal life of individual Jews involves their association with other Jews in varying degrees, many contacts between Jews—their business contacts, for example—may not induce any special Jewish relevance. The persons involved may not be aware that the matter in hand is between persons with Jewish antecedents or, if aware, are not likely to give it any special meaning. It would therefore be desirable to limit the terms "Jewish communal activity" and "Jewish communal life" to those personal and group interactions which are imbued with Jewish relevance, that is, with an actual or potential recognition that some Jewish group objective or interest is involved.

VARIATIONS IN COMMUNAL LIVING

Some of the factors that may be responsible for the differences in sentiment and in the nature of the political and the voluntary forms of communal relationships are: size of population (relationships are obviously different among the residents of a small village than of a large metropolis); historical, ethnic, racial, religious, linguistic and cultural differences; economic and class distinctions; intellectual and educational variations, and other facets of individual and group character. Close bonds of interest or sentiment do not necessarily follow geographical lines. With modern ease of communication and transportation, specific political boundaries do not determine or limit the basis of group association. Nevertheless, face to face contacts are frequently essential for many aspects of communal living and for the maintenance of important communal institutions.

Two basic factors affect the existence and the character of association among any group of people. The first is group consciousness. If this is weak or nonexistent, individuals will not be impelled to seek group association. The second is the need to meet individual problems through group action. Without specific needs and interest which require group cooperation, a consciousness of group identity may exist only as an awareness of a shared historical background rather than as a concrete element of contemporary relationships. In the American Jewish community both elements are present —a strongly implanted and persistent group consciousness and continuing domestic and overseas needs which can be dealt with effectively only on a group basis.

JEWISH IDENTITY AND GROUP ASSOCIATION

The nature of Jewish group association in modern times reflects the Jewish historical background, with its sharp differentiation of people on the basis of their religious affiliation and religious practices. A recognition of the variations in group identities has persisted with greater or lesser intensity throughout Jewish history, depending upon the extent to which the cultural characteristics of Jews differed from those of their neighbors and the intensity of adherence to these differences on both sides.[2]

There have been times and places in Jewish history when the term "Jewish community" could mean all the residents of a self-contained geographical area, and when separation between Jews and other people was physical and legal, not merely psychological or functional. There are no such separations in the Western World today, and on this account group association among Jews must be considered the voluntary organization of group interests within the larger community. Jewish group association and communal life is a category of activity which for most persons constitutes an intensely important, though not necessarily large, portion of their existence as members of a multi-structured community. The role of an individual as citizen, worker, employer and consumer may involve little if any aspect of Jewish group association.

In the early stage of its settlement in America an immigrant group would be likely to huddle close together and to form a compact neighborhood. The majority had few or no personal contacts outside the membership of their own group. This condition tended to change during the processes of Americanization. But the tendency to form separate neighborhoods is persistent for many sectarian and ethnic groups, both because of externally imposed patterns of segregation and because of desires within the group for close association with their fellows. In due time the immigrant colonies begin to be considered by others, if not by themselves, as identifiable segments of the general population, rather than self-contained communities. The urge to be considered Americans or Texans or Pittsburghers begins to take precedence over the values surrounding the place of birth, as immigrants and their descendants or the newcomers into a locality join in the common processes of living together. Compact areas of residence in a city or suburb by people with similar interests or origins may thereafter merely help to emphasize the groups' former communal history and traditions.

VOLUNTARY SECTARIAN AND NON-SECTARIAN ORGANIZATION

There are strong tendencies toward group association among American Jews. During many centuries of residence in various lands, Jews developed organizations for religious, philanthropic, economic, and welfare purposes, for meeting the problems of relationships with other religious and ethnic groups, for the well-being and fate of fellow Jews living in other lands, and for many other important interests. At the same time, Jews share with other groups in the community needs and interests which cut across religious and ethnic lines, and they join members of other faiths in inter-sectarian or in non-sectarian interests such as political parties, business and professional groups and labor unions, scientific bodies, local neighborhood associations, fraternal associations and inter-faith welfare and educational bodies.

Separate group organization on a sectarian, racial or ethnic membership base for political or economic purposes is considered contrary to the democratic aim and spirit. In the past there have been economic and political groups organized along specific nationality or sectarian lines, sometimes with hostile attitudes toward the excluded groups, but largely as a device for organizing newcomers speaking different languages into labor unions, beneficial societies and other interests.

Some types of exclusive membership organization, though accepted as legal and traditionally valid (such as fraternities on a university campus which are open only to members of specific religious or ethnic groups) are beginning to be questioned in relation to what are believed to be the valid goals of a democratic society. On the other hand, there appears to be general acceptance of the validity of separate religious denominations and their related associations. There are proposals for uniting the sectarian and denominational groups, as in the movements for unity of Protestant sects or a unified Christian Church; but these do not seem to be making rapid headway.

There is no sharp dividing line of opinion, though there are differing views, as to what forms of communal activity on the basis of religious, racial, linguistic or ethnic group divisions are proper. The tendency, however, has been to accept associations with functions that are primarily concerned with the attainment of specific group objectives not invidious to the well-being of other groups, and to question separatedness on the type of restricted group basis which involves the general welfare of the population. The justification of a sectarian basis for what appears to be largely a non-sectarian function is sometimes questioned by members of the group itself as well as by others.

But the validity of sectarian organization is a relatively new issue. In the past the question has been rarely raised about philanthropic, cultural and fraternal organizations.[3] In fact, many of the existing Jewish organizations owe their origin to the group prejudices and discrimination of Christian associations as well as to the sentiments for group solidarity and group survival among Jews (called "ethnocentrism" by the social scientist and "clannishness" by the unfriendly lay critic).

SECTARIAN AND NON-SECTARIAN ASPECTS OF JEWISH WELFARE AGENCIES

The original aim of Jewish welfare efforts was to develop Jewish sponsored and financed agencies for the purpose of serving Jewish clients and to develop Jewish professional personnel. The latter objective was especially pertinent in fitting Jewish sponsored hospitals to the needs of the Jewish physician, who had difficulty in obtaining opportunities for internships and for practice in hospitals that were not under Jewish auspices. The rationale for Jewish welfare agencies was also to be found in the need of Jewish patients and clients to be served by health and welfare agencies that understood his special cultural habits and his problems and were in sympathy with them. Over the years, and especially within the last two decades, there have been changes in the availability of health and welfare agencies under other than Jewish auspices to serve the needs of Jews, changes in the cultural requirements of Jewish clients, changes in the areas of residence of Jews and in their economic status. These factors have affected the clientele of Jewish sponsored welfare agencies. There is also a general trend in Jewish medical institutions and in some of the case work and guidance agencies to serve an increasing number of non-Jews.

A provocative paper on the subject of what type of philanthropy is preferably sectarian and what non-sectarian was presented to the 1959 General Assembly of the Council of Jewish Federations and Welfare Funds by Joseph Willen, an executive vice-president of the New York Federation.[4] His thesis was that profound social changes in the general community and among the Jewish population made it imperative to reconsider the sectarian aspects of our social welfare and health agencies. Our social agencies, he declared, "had been formed because of rejection, out of our own needs and our religious practices . . . we built hospitals because we felt rejected—and we were rejected—in the medical world of America," . . . because "voluntary hospitals did not accept Jewish boys in internships or residencies." There were rejection, quotas, segregation.

Looking at the American scene today, Willen finds progress being made toward the democratic ideal and equality of rights. There is less discrimination, and the new economic and social order is bringing and requires "great adjustments."

Among the changes, Willen sees hospitals "now serving a large non-Jewish population"; case work agencies dealing largely with a native-born clientele "whose problems are rarely uniquely Jewish"; and community Centers, once "the meeting rooms and the classrooms of a Yiddish-speaking minority—now the living rooms of a people whose tastes, upbringing, outlook and recollections are American." Willen cites statistics on non-Jews in Jewish hospitals and Jewish interns and residents on the staffs of non-Jewish hospitals. He questions the validity of sectarian auspices for case work services that are essentially non-sectarian. He notes the presence of Jewish case workers on the staffs of non-Jewish agencies, and the use of non-sectarian agencies by Jewish clients.

Willen believes "that the goal of Jewish agencies should be to look forward to the day when they drop the strict sectarian practices which were born out of the failure of our American society to develop its ideals. . . . Let our agencies retain their Jewish character, observe the Jewish holidays and festivals . . . but let them also reflect on their boards and on their staffs the composition of their clientele. . . . [The Centers] should focus on Jewish culture, but none of this need negate an open-door policy so that persons of any race, creed or color who want to use the Center facilities can do so." . . . "Let us not confuse the function of the community Center with the synagogue," said Willen, rejecting the idea "that Jewish youth must be segregated in order to retain Jewish values":

I am convinced that only those who are skeptical of the "staying quality" of Judaism would wish to promote it by retaining sectarianism in secular institutions. . . . We Jews need fear no disintegration or disappearance of the Jewish community if we undertake the infinitely difficult steps on the road to finding Jewish meanings in our daily lives. Let us not think we keep our identity intact through the mechanical device of sectarian welfare institutions.

Other speakers at this session of the General Assembly of the CJFWF expressed fewer doubts about the validity of the current policies of Jewish sponsored health and welfare agencies. Lewis Cole, of Louisville, which had a population of only 8,500 Jews in a total population of 600,000 but maintained a Jewish hospital serving a large proportion of non-Jewish patients (for example, only 10% of the patients in 1959 were Jews), considered the question an academic one and foresaw no problems in the calculable future, since the pattern of sectarian welfare services was an accepted policy in Louisville. Mrs. Charles Lakoff of Detroit spoke of the value to Jews of services offered by Jewish agencies, such services being more personalized than the services available on a generalized mass basis. She also pointed to the close interrelationships of agencies in the present structure of multiple agency auspices. "The Jewish agencies," said Mrs. Lakoff, "nurtured and prepared me, and then sent me out into the general community as their representative. Whatever strength and influence I had in the general community flowed from the importance and strength of the agencies I represented."[5]

At the 1960 General Assembly of the CJWF, Benjamin B. Rosenberg, the executive director of the Boston Federation, succinctly posed the questions facing the Jewish federation movement as follows:

What are the special needs, if any, which would support the rationale for maintaining and for further strengthening of Jewish agencies, which serve large numbers of non-Jews?

What is the rationale for maintaining services which have become wholly non-sectarian as to the people served and the nature of the services rendered?

Is it possible to serve these needs while the agencies move toward opening their board and committee structures to more non-Jews, and toward eventual non-sectarian auspices and control?

Questions on the role of Jewish agencies and Jewish leadership in their relationship to other sectarian, non-sectarian and public agencies in our community [said Mr. Rosenberg] spring out of the concept of cultural pluralism as the underlying characteristic of our American social structure. It is within this tradition that health and welfare services have developed along sectarian lines. This trend seems to become more marked as the American community stratifies its religio-cultural structure along the lines of the three major religions. How do these developments affect the relationship of Jewish agencies, their leadership, their staff, their clientele, to the general community?

   1. Does our overriding concern with sectarian services impede opportunities for constructive relationships with the general community?

   2. Do sectarian services strengthen or weaken the structure for inter-group cooperation and planning?

3. What is and what should be the role of Jewish agencies and Jewish leadership to other sectarian, non-sectarian and public agencies?[6]

The issue of sectarianism or non-sectarianism in voluntary welfare organization currently being raised will not be generally accepted as immediate or pervasive. Nor will such issues be resolved rapidly if accepted as matters of policy requiring action. They are the long term, basic questions which impinge on our institutional structure, and the response to them will fluctuate with the times and with adjustments to the values of a democratic, pluralistic society.

In the history of American philanthropy there have been many instances of welfare agencies, health and educational institutions initially developed for sectarian purposes, gradually becoming non-sectarian in purpose, clientele and administration. This has taken place most notably in hospitals, welfare agencies and colleges that were initially Protestant sectarian institutions. This trend toward non-sectarianism, as well as the large number of different Protestant denominations, may help to explain the fact that the community organization of American Protestants in the field of welfare services is much less developed than among the Catholic and Jewish elements of the American population. In many cities with Jewish and Catholic welfare federations, there is no Protestant federation, although there are Protestant child care organizations, homes for the aged, hospitals and other welfare institutions.

POSITIVE AND NEGATIVE STIMULI

The issue of sectarianism will probably be determined in the long run by general American cultural trends. The changing nature of the American community has at all times affected the traditional expressions of Jews in meeting their group needs and in organizing group associations to meet them. A general atmosphere of sectarianism dominated many parts of the welfare and recreational fields for most of the period between 1875 and 1925, during the initial phases of Jewish group organization in this country. Beginning in 1930, acute problems of anti-Semitism both here and abroad and the devastating consequences of the Hitler period impelled a more intensive Jewish group association, dealing with the vital problems of defense of political rights, rescue of the unfortunate Jews of Europe and re-establishment of the displaced Jews in Israel and elsewhere. The traumatic effects of this period aroused a keener sense of group responsibility and a greater need for solidarity in discharging these responsibilities. These experiences have fostered a resurgence of interest in many forms of religious and cultural expression. The effects of war and post-war conditions are said also to have influenced a revival of church activities among other denominational groups.

Though many of the acute conditions of the 1930s and the 1940s no longer exist, we are still very close to the emotions of that period. Group responsibility must continue to be maintained for the necessary welfare programs initiated during that period and for coping with post-war problems. Some observers point to the strong tendencies toward sectarianism now current. They see, as the result of the acculturation of the successive generations of the immigrant groups of white racial stock, a diminution of the potency of nationality differences along with an intensification of the religious factor into three major group divisions—Protestant, Roman Catholic and Jewish.[7] If this is a correct appraisal (and there are a number of signs pointing in this direction), the continuation of this trend will foster Jewish group association.

Changing social and economic conditions among Jews, more perhaps than changing attitudes on the question of sectarian welfare organization, are responsible for the shifting emphasis in the field of Jewish welfare organization. Federations' greater interest in cultural needs and religious programs seems to be concurrent with the diminution of poverty among the Jewish population and the government's assumption of responsibility for the solution of problems resulting from poverty.[8]

MULTIPLE JEWISH GROUP ASSOCIATION

While differences among the American Jewish population arising from the differing cultures of the countries of origin and varying periods of migration are perhaps diminishing, important group differences remain. These are due to variations in cultural interests and backgrounds and arise also from varieties of economical and social experience, rate of acculturation and emotional and other psychological factors. For these reasons varieties of Jewish denominational and faternal, social, cultural and other group associations continue, resulting in a diffusion of interests and multiple and unrelated groups.

GROUP PARTICIPATION

How many adult Jews participate in organized Jewish group associations and for what purposes? No statistics are available for a definite answer to this question. For the population as a whole, there are studies of a sample cross section which have thrown light on the differential factors of age, education, family income, occupation and social status, which determine the nature and extent of participation in formal group associations. In a Detroit study it was found that approximately two-thirds of the total population were members of formal groups, and that one-third were not members of group activities. Comparatively few people belong to more than one group. The study also found that higher incomes and higher education were factors which increased the incidence of group participation.[9]

A study of the Jewish population of New Orleans[10] in 1953 is one of the few made of a Jewish community which obtained some information on the extent of participation in Jewish associations. From 70% to 85% of the various age groups, 15 years and over, informed the interviewers that they were members* of one or more Jewish organizations.[11] Of the men aged 30 and over, from 25% to 40% reported themselves as members of men's clubs attached to the synagogues; from 40% to 62% of the women in the same age group were members of sisterhoods.

Participation in the different kinds of Jewish institutional activity varies greatly, depending upon such factors as the size of population and the communal structure of the area. Membership and activity in synagogues is probably the largest type of participation in many suburban communities today. In most cities the number of individuals who contribute to the central federation or welfare fund greatly exceeds the number of members to be found in any other form of organization.[13]

* This may not mean formal membership; in some cases the individual may have attended services or had held membership in previous years but was not formally enrolled in 1953. The factor of participation rather than formal memberships may perhaps also apply to the reported figures for other associations, such as synagogue clubs, Hadassah, B'nai B'rith, etc.[12]

INTER-GROUP COOPERATION AND JEWISH "UNITY"

The functions or activities of some Jewish groups which parallel or relate to the interests or purposes of other Jewish groups provide the conditions for inter-group contacts; other groups may be isolated from each other because of their specialized function. For example, a number of social clubs can exist in the same neighborhood or community without any occasion arising for inter-group cooperation or consultation. Interaction among such groups, however, may take the form of competition, in open or unconscious group rivalry. Divergences of ritual or belief may act as a bar to contacts between congregations on religious matters, but may not obstruct cooperation in other areas of interest. Thus in a sizable Jewish population there may be various congregations or fraternal groups, and other associations, among which there may be an awareness of each other's existence, various forms of rivalry and competition for membership and for financial support, but no substantial desire for formal relationships.

There are, however, activities and interests which operate to overlap orbits and impel toward some degree of interaction. Separate associations, although apparently self-sufficient, frequently tend to get in each other's way. This, for example, was most notable in the past in the field of charitable effort. We have seen how a lack of exchange of information among independent relief societies resulted in confusion and unwise duplication of effort. On the simplest level, separate organizations with distinctly different functions find that they have some duplication of membership and that a procedure for clearance by means of a community calendar is a useful undertaking.

In many instances the factors which bring about a closer association among various Jewish groups grow out of the promotional efforts of such activities as seek to involve all members of the Jewish population. Primary among these factors has been the organization of campaigns in behalf of agencies and causes whose appeal rests upon acknowledged common interests. This has been especially pertinent in fund-raising campaigns for local, national or overseas aid.

There have been many unsuccessful attempts to achieve cooperation among Jewish groups and to create closely knit and unified communal organizations. To a considerable extent the major reason for failure to achieve a replica of the tightly managed and authoritarian forms of community organization, which at one time existed in Europe and elsewhere, has been attributed to the effect the American environment has had on the communal life of Jewish immigrants and the logic of the American doctrine of separation of Church and State.[14]

With both centrifugal and centripetal influences on Jewish group participation, the degree of Jewish "unity" or consensus on communal objectives and programs is highly variable and fluid. Thus far, no continuing unitary body has been developed. The stage of cooperation attained has covered only one or more phases of communal interest, not its totality, and has been for some of them of limited duration. Dissident groups and individuals, lack of interest in one or another form of group association, a relaxation of tension, and other conditions, may be said to have pulled the rivening strings, making of Jewish group expression a composite pattern of varying—and at times conflicting—strands, rather than a recognizable pattern of cooperative relationships. External threats such as anti-Semitism, have been more potent in bringing about cooperation in group affairs than has the desire for the continuation of Jewish culture and Jewish group values.

IDENTIFYING "FEDERATION"

Cooperation among groups and agencies which extends over a period of time, as in the federation, tends to take on structural form and become a recognizable central agency. The federation is an association of groups, a "central body," which approaches Jewish unity in a limited area. It includes a number of distinct and separate group organizations in various forms of relationship. In most cities federation emerged as an organization set up by charitable agencies with a common goal, usually to raise funds. In other cities federation was formed by groups of individuals who wanted to be relieved of the burden of multiple appeals. Sometimes its establishment involved the beneficiary agencies, interested individuals, or other Jewish bodies who wanted a federation but did not themselves wish to become beneficiaries of its fund-raising campaigns. In practically all instances, federation upon its establishment tended to take on the character of a separate autonomous agency, though its beneficiary and/or non-beneficiary constituents might continue to have a major role in its administration.

A central agency for specific group interests does not pre-empt the field of communal activity. Indeed, it frequently stimulates the development of new agencies and groups concerned with various other aspects of communal welfare. In addition to the federation and its beneficiary agencies, there are in nearly all communities separate agencies, such as religious congregations, fraternal groups, ideological groups, organizations concerned with specific functions, such as those concerned with Israel, and a great variety of other formal and informal group associations. Where the central body has developed through membership, or participation of organized groups, the basic relationship of the central body with such groups may revolve about special functions that do not duplicate and are not closely related to those of their constituent non-beneficiary agencies. Although a federation or a community council may be widely accepted for its essential functions, many individuals may consider some other association to have greater importance, eliciting greater personal involvement. For many, the federation involves merely the once-a-year donation of their contribution. They acknowledge the federation as a useful device serving the interest of the various agencies and their programs, or they might even consider it merely a single agency in the constellation of organized Jewish activities.

The successful development of the federation movement has been due primarily to the intensification of needs and problems with which the Jewish community as a whole has been concerned. It is doubtful whether federation, originally established for the coordination of relief agencies and for improvement in fund-raising, would have survived the development of public assistance, if it had not had to face constantly increasing and new types of communal problems. Within the past three decades, American Jewry has been a part of an intense situation, world-wide in its repercussions, which has added depth and poignancy to the life of all Jews.

A further important factor in the development of the federation movement has been the successful promotion and dissemination of the idea. This has been due to the natural contacts between the population of the various Jewish communities and has been furthered by the establishment of conferences and forums which facilitated the processes of inter-group education. The establishment of national organizations, such as Community Chests and Councils, Inc., in 1918 (later to become United Community Funds and Councils) in the general field of community chests, and the Bureau of Jewish Social Research in 1917, and in 1932 its successor, the Council of Jewish Federations and Welfare Funds, in the Jewish field, have been among the important factors making for the growth and maintenance of the federation movement.

XI

Theories and Problems

The Jewish immigration to the New World was certainly not undertaken for the purpose of changing cultural habits or the nature of Jewish group life. The expressed aims of most of the immigrants were likely to be economic improvement, political liberty and the practice of their religion in freedom. If the emigrants sought to escape from the ghetto, they were not trying to break with other Jews. Their prevailing ideas on group living seem to have been to reproduce, as far as American conditions permitted, the communal life of the European religious congregations.

The fact that there were bound to be changes in ways of earning one's livelihood, in language, customs and manners, was inescapable, but it was hoped that most aspects of the traditional culture could be maintained. The prevailing attitude or hope of those concerned with communal affairs was that the established institutions of the new communities would serve to perpetuate the inherited culture of the group for that and for the coming generations.

Religious and cultural conditions during the 18th and 19th centuries, however, were exceedingly fluid.

232

The attainment of Emancipation and the departure from the ghettos, the industrial revolution and urbanization, the spirit of scientific inquiry and experimentation were all conducive to cultural change and religious variation. The mingling in America of immigrant groups stemming from different cultures and different countries intensified the processes of acculturation. Individual practices were modified and communal relationships altered. There were, however, bound to be great individual variations in the tempo of change and in the eagerness or reluctance to discard the old and espouse the new. Different personal and social factors influenced ritual practices and cultural behavior to a different degree in almost each individual.

Generally, the longer the period of residence and group settlement, the wider have been the processes of change. As a consequence, later waves of Jewish immigrants deriving from different countries and backgrounds found upon arrival in this country preceding Jewish groups that had undergone considerable cultural changes. Thus, East-European immigrants bearing traditional patterns of religious Orthodoxy encountered Reform, and later Conservative Judaism, as the prevalent religious practices of many of the socially established and economically more prosperous sections of the population. Following the upswing of revolutionary movements in eastern Europe, some immigrants in the 20th century were imbued with socialistic and anti-religious ideas. The development of Zionism after 1900 was to add still another element to the crucible of theories and aims for Jewish group living. The subsequent experience of the Jewish population with rapid economic changes, Hitlerism and virulent anti-Semitism, the creation of the State of Israel as the culmination of Zionist aims, the emer-

233

gence of American Jewry as the largest section of surviving Jewry and the coming to this country of the refugee remnants of Orthodoxy and talmudic scholarship—all of these have contributed to the multiple influences which impinge today on American Jewish culture.

EARLY ATTITUDES

At its inception, federation was not conceived as a broad design for communal living or as a marked departure from the prevailing institutional pattern; it had been established solely as a technique for improving welfare agency financing and social welfare planning. In the first two decades, the views expressed and the questions under discussion were focused on practical, not ideological issues—for example, how these new techniques would affect the independence and autonomy of the beneficiary agencies; what changes had or might take place in the underlying attitudes of givers; what would be the relationship between the givers and the welfare agencies included in the federation program; how to improve the relief programs.

There was little concern at first over how federation was related to the Jewish "community" and its underlying objectives. The term "communal" was not yet being generally applied to the affairs of the Jewish philanthropic agencies. There was a greater concern with the organization of religious life of the community, with denominational rivalries and the decline in religious participation, an area of interest which seemed to be in a different compartment from the field of philanthropic activities. The essence of the Jewish community throughout these earlier years was a matter of attitudes and feelings, not of organization and agencies.

For several decades, federations centered their attention on what were considered to be the immediate welfare problems of the increasing numbers of new immigrants: assistance and guidance in relating themselves to the conditions of American life, and on the strains and stresses which were arising in their lives. As has been pointed out, federation initially represented the philanthropic efforts on the part of the older immigrants and the established part of the Jewish population. For this reason, most representatives of the eastern European immigration did not look upon federation as a phase of communal organization in which they were represented or in which they participated on any other basis than that of clients, but merely the private effort of a group of philanthropically minded individuals. Philanthropy was taken for granted as an obligation of the well-to-do for the less fortunate, sanctioned by religious teaching and reinforced by centuries of custom and tradition.

SECTARIAN WELFARE AGENCIES

The Jewish federation and its beneficiary agencies were an expression of sectarian separatism in the welfare field, but few Jews or Christians at that time were likely to question the validity and appropriateness of sectarian philanthropic imperatives. There were some efforts toward coordinating the voluntary welfare activities of the overall community, but the agencies and their leadership were largely separated from each other on the basis of religious affiliations. Some welfare activities were in existence or were being developed on a non-sectarian basis, but many of these were non-sectarian in their intention rather than in their management or their constituencies.

In the Jewish group, it was rare to find any objection to federation on the ground that separate Jewish work was sectarian and therefore divisive in character and that welfare programs on a non-sectarian basis should take their place. The so-called non-sectarian charity societies were largely created by Protestants, serving Protestants and sharing responsibility for Catholic clients with Catholic parish organizations. The "nonsectarian" agencies usually accepted the policy that Jewish welfare societies were the appropriate agencies to serve Jewish clients.

PUBLIC RELIEF PROGRAMS

Similarly, the idea that any function of the federation agencies could become general public responsibility and be performed by governmental agencies seemed remote and illogical. In the early days of federations, the status of public welfare was low, with services aimed at deterring rather than relieving poverty. Not only did everyone justify voluntary sectarian and non-sectarian welfare organizations as being superior to public effort, and in the nature of things, but people also gave additional reasons for accepting Jewish responsibility for Jewish needs. The slogan "Jews take care of their own" was widely advanced, with the further rationalization that separate Jewish welfare work should be continued —harking back to the demands which Peter Stuyvesant was supposed to have made in the 17th century so that the Jewish poor should not become a charge on the general community.

COMMUNITY CHESTS

The community chests (organized after 1913)* represented a form of cooperation among sectarian and

* There were a few cooperative funds established before that date in the general community (e.g., Liverpool, England, in 1873; and Denver, Colo., in 1887), but the Federation for Charity and Philanthrophy in Cleveland, 1913, is generally regarded as the first American community chest.

non-sectarian agencies, and acceptance of the chest movement by Jewish federations was in a sense an acceptance of inter-sectarian cooperation for limited purposes rather than replacing of sectarian by non-sectarian organizations. The individual agencies and federated groups which joined the chests retained their original character, whether sectarian or non-sectarian. There was, however, sufficient group cooperation in the central fund-raising, central budgeting and other chest activities to satisfy some of the Jewish proponents of non-sectarianism, and at the same time to dispirit those who saw the community chest as a force weakening the separate development of Jewish communal services and as a further stimulus to assimilation.

BROADENING ASPECTS—DEMOCRATIC PARTICIPATION AND EFFICIENCY

With growing population, Jewish welfare agencies increased in extent and in number and in the sums of money spent. Federation and its agencies began to assume broad functions in the health and welfare field. Growth in size and importance tended to draw to federations the interest and attention of individuals who were concerned with other Jewish interests. While no one as yet equated federation with central communal organization, some observers began to consider federation as an example of, or the matrix of, such organization.

Emphasis began to be placed upon the need for greater democracy in serving Jewish welfare interests and for appeals to wider groups of contributors for financial support. This was a natural reaction on the part of those who were originally not of the limited social and economic group represented by the founders of federation who constituted its corps of leadership for many years. The newer elements of the population, as they attained economic security, constituted a significant source of support for philanthropic agencies, and they began to concern themselves with the structure of federation and to show a desire to participate in the management of its affairs.

Changes in federation structure and functions were also being precipitated by pressures from another angle: the demand for greater efficiency. Like those concerned with democracy, these critics were also asking that federation achieve a wider base of financial and moral support and that it have a structure which would assure greater effectiveness in the programs of the local services which federation was supporting. In these approaches, federation was not generally looked upon as the central communal organization, but rather as one aspect of a series of associations for various specific purposes—such as for religious objectives, cultural interests, sociability, and the like. If it was assumed that these activities were interrelated, few contended that the best interests of the Jewish population could be served through their integration. It was enough that the various segments of organized Jewish interest should become aware of each other and strive for cooperation on an *ad hoc* basis where it seemed essential.[1]

THE BEGINNING OF GENERAL THEORIES ABOUT FEDERATION AND JEWISH COMMUNITY ORGANIZATION

The proposals for the communal organization of Jews involved theories that were discussed in relation to the organization of the New York *Kehillah* in 1909 and the American Jewish Congress in 1917. It was, however, not until toward the end of the 1920s and the beginning of the 1930s—a time of acute strains and stresses both here and abroad—that general theories of

Jewish community life began to be voiced within federations or directed to them. The theories came from various sources: from people whose philosophy of Zionism or of Diaspora Nationalism was beginning to reflect on the nature of American Jewish life and on the forms and tendencies in Jewish community organization, from those who were concerned with the Jewish aspects of the culture of the American-born generation, and from others animated by still other ideas. Religious educators were finding what they considered disintegrating tendencies in the cultural life of the younger generation. They began to discuss the meaning of federation in relation to their aspirations for Jewish life.

The amorphous character of Jewish institutional life and the disintegrative forces of acculturation were analyzed and programs were offered to offset them and to strengthen the desire for what was being called "Jewish survival." The exponents of these objectives were considered by themselves "survivalists" or "positive Jews." They referred to the theorists who believed that the processes of acculturation had not gone far enough, or that the processes of cultural change were inherently desirable and inescapable, as "integrationists," "assimilationists" or "escapists." Yet some common elements ran through these approaches, with shadings between them. They were not all polarized as may be noted in the papers and articles to be found in the proceedings of Jewish welfare conferences and other publications.*

"OVERALL" COMMUNAL ORGANIZATION

Evaluating the federation, with its limited welfare functions, as an incomplete or partial form of Jewish

* In one of the debates, Professor Morris Raphael Cohen asked, "What is 'Positive' Judaism? If there is a positive, there must also be a negative, but what kind of Judaism [is] . . . 'Negative' Judaism?"

community organization, led to the concept of an inclusive agency with broader functions. What some meant by organizing the Jewish community on an overall basis is illustrated in the statement of a Jewish educator given at a National Conference in 1933:

We can consider the organization of Jewish community life partly as an immediate objective. What we aim for ideally as an ultimate end may be very difficult to achieve now, but it ought to be clear to us as to where we are trying to go. I would conceive of the Jewish community as an all-inclusive organization of Jews, democratically represented, in which the community supplements that which the individual Jew cannot do for himself, whether it is in charity, education, the life of the synagogue or economic life; that the community must help in matters of discrimination and negative affairs, as well as in the positive aspect of life; and that the community should be ultimately supported in ideal fashion on a system of self-taxation in accordance with individual income.[2]

Attempts to define the goals for federation development had been frequent in the period following World War I and took on larger significance in the 1930s. Few of the advocates of comprehensive central Jewish community organization at that time believed that the existing federations, limited as they were in the scope of their activities and functions, were the proper matrix for the proposed organization of the Jewish community. In fact, federation was not considered an appropriate vehicle for this development, both because of the shortcomings that observers seemed to find in its structure and functions and because a large part of its lay and professional leadership was considered hostile or indifferent to the goals for which the Jewish community was assumed to be organized. The advocates of central communal organization generally thought of some new central instrument for the numerous religious, cultural and philanthropic institutions to weld them into an interrelated structure.

Some of the proponents of an overall organization hoped at first to achieve communal organization through a *national* body. There had been attempts in the past to organize such a national Jewish association, but all of them had been short-lived. The American Jewish Congress, organized in 1917, however, had demonstrated that a body representative of a variety of Jewish groups and geographical areas could operate effectively on important issues and with general approval or acquiescence. Some hoped, therefore, that this American Jewish Congress, though specifically established as a temporary body, might be accepted as a permanent institution and become the basis for a national community organization concerned with the important interests of American Jewry. With the failure to achieve this objective in the early 1920s, some of the supporters of this idea turned their attention to organizing local communities as the first step toward the development of national Jewish communal organization in the United States.

The thesis of the desirability of central communal bodies was not necessarily at variance with the attitudes of federation leaders. A few at that time were actively espousing the idea of a local organization of Jews concerned with religious and cultural as well as with welfare needs. Others, who may not have considered these proposals practical or desirable, were nonetheless aware of the interrelationship of federation's work with the total range of interests of the American Jew.[3]

In 1933, Dr. Ludwig Bernstein, then executive director of the Pittsburgh Jewish Federation, and impressed with the values of the *Kultusgemeinde* of central Europe, presented a plan to his agency whereby all

Jewish groups would voluntarily combine to appoint an administrative body which would allocate funds to all units. In this proposal, the administrative council would establish three main divisions: Religious Organizations, Educational and Cultural Organizations, and Social Welfare and Related Organizations. The plan involved such features as taxation of kosher food products, and centralized charges for synagogue and temple attendance. It also called for enrolling all individuals as members, taxing for all communal expenditure, securing of a city ordinance for the control of *shohetim*. A field report of the CJFWF stated that:

The plan has been widely discussed and vigorously approved by some of the larger contributors who see in it the possibility of spreading the community financial load, the establishment of a spokesman avoiding the use of Jewish representation by unauthorized groups . . . elimination of competitive religious elements, and provision of necessary machinery not now available for Jewish education, religious purposes, etc.

Although the plan was widely favored, opposition came from fear of inclusion of "radical" elements, fear of self-segregation, dangers of arbitrary control of resources by the central body through its taxing and fundraising functions. Most active in opposition was one of the long established synagogue groups which voted against the plan, though other synagogue bodies had acted favorably. This rejection by a group which included a number of the most active communal leaders prevented further action. Dissension within the Orthodox groups also prevented progress on the plan for *kashruth* control and a tax for communal purposes on kosher food on which Dr. Bernstein had been working and which he considered a first step in achieving the more elaborate range of purposes to be involved in the proposed General Community Council.

To some federation leaders, proposals of this nature seemed to be at variance with the goals of American democracy, and were viewed as an attempt to transplant European forms of organization to an unsuitable environment.[4] Other federation leaders agreed that the proposals being advanced for organizing the Jewish community were beyond the scope and capabilities of federation, which was only a segment of the important activities in which various Jewish groups and agencies were involved. It was recognized that, in addition to the activities carried on by federation, there existed within each community, separate organizations for religious, labor, economic, social, cultural, ideological and other interests. These phases of community life were generally operating without formal interrelationships, but with a few informal contacts. It was a natural question "whether all these forms of functional manifestations of organization . . . are capable of being merged into one distinct organized community, functioning as a self-conscious unit, both with relation to the group itself and its inner problems and in relation to the larger activity without."[5]

While federation leaders accepted the fact that the scope of federation was limited and that it was a part of, and not the totality of, Jewish activities, it was, nevertheless, agreed that within its scope it was functioning as an important communal institution and that it was perhaps capable of developing into an even more important aspect of Jewish communal life.[6]

The aims of survival as understood in the early 1930s referred largely to the religious culture which was changing under the impact of the new environment. Fears were expressed of an eventual loss of identity

243

through this process. Moreover, it was not yet imagined at that time that, in a few years, the Jews of Europe would face physical annihilation by the evil force of nazism. Consequently, the major problems during the first years of the depression seemed to be the economic welfare and the social and economic standing of American Jewry and its cultural tendencies.

A leading exponent for many years of the desirability of organizing the Jewish community was Rabbi Mordecai M. Kaplan. Excerpts from his paper, which was given in 1935, exemplify the deepened awareness of the acute nature of Jewish problems—during the most serious economic depression that this country had experienced and a few years after Hitler's accession to power, when the potential evils that were to be unleashed on the modern world began to be perceived.

American Jewry is far from being healthily and creatively adjusted to the American environment. The philosophy of adjustment . . . is obsolete . . . the great issue today is to secure . . . an equal share of economic opportunity. . . . The political equality which exists in theory has been nullified and rendered valueless by the existence of gross economic inequalities . . .

Today, no minority group has a right to consider itself adjusted to the life of the majority unless it is culturally differentiated and economically assimilated. In actuality, American Jewry is culturally almost assimilated and economically very much differentiated.

To be economically assimilated means to be proportionately represented in every phase in the economic setup of the country—in the agricultural, industrial, financial and professional aspects of its life.[7]

Rabbi Kaplan's attitude in 1935 was extremely pessimistic:

The Jews of America cannot experience the sense of status by identification with the life of the American people.[8]

To meet the fears of occupational discrimination which, because of the economic depression might reduce Jews to penury and—of equal, if not greater importance —to avert the pressures toward assimilation which seemed to some of the analysts of American Jewish life to threaten to wipe out Jewish cultural distinctiveness, the remedy proposed was to organize the Jewish community.

A precedent condition to a normal adjustment of American Jewry to the economic and cultural life of the country is for all who want to remain Jews to accept and implement the ideal of an organic Jewish community. Now that the rest of the world is, for good or for ill, becoming collectivist, Jews must respond with a collectivism of their own; otherwise they are doomed to economic and moral disintegration. . . . The alternative of assimilation is closed, since the Gentiles do not wish to assimilate the Jews.[9]

It was proposed that the Jewish community organization, to be capable of satisfying the need for "Jewish status, self-respect and cosmic orientation," must envisage the problem of Jewish life in its entirety. The functions to be performed by the proposed organic Jewish community were considered under five headings: (1) administrative functions, (2) economic functions, (3) cultural functions, (4) social service functions, and (5) political functions.

Administrative functions would be: community registration upon payment of nominal annual dues of every adult Jew who wished to identify himself as a Jew; the raising of all funds for Jewish communal purposes and the proper apportionment of the budget for all Jewish needs; employment of professional, executive, clerical and other personnel; provision for the training of rabbis, cantors, educators, social workers, institutional executive personnel, etc.; an agency for the registration of Jewish marriages, divorces, births, deaths, and other important personal data; and provision for social research.[10]

The economic functions were to include efforts to achieve an occupational redistribution of American Jewry and the combating of economic discrimination against Jews. The cultural functions would aim to provide Jewish educational facilities for the child, adolescent and adult, to encourage every form of Jewish literary and artistic creativity, and to provide for public worship and other forms of religious activity. The social service functions were to embrace most of the activities which were then the main concern of our local philanthropic federations. Among the political functions, foremost importance must be given to the organization of local support for the establishment of the Jewish national home in Palestine and to political activity to defend Jewish rights both here and abroad against the assaults of anti-Semitism.[11]

If the Jews were thus organized and their communities were officially represented in a national body for the defense of Jewish rights, it would be possible, Rabbi Kaplan believed, to give to Jewish demands the force of a mass movement, and this would enable Jewish leaders to bring tremendous pressure to bear in the assertion of Jewish rights.[12]

Along with individual adult membership on registration and payment of nominal dues not to exceed $1.00 per year, a "Governing Council of the Jewish Community Organization" was proposed, "elected by the various Jewish organizations whose members are enrolled in the Jewish community."[13]

These proposals for the "organic community" and other variations of the basic theme of a voluntary constituted community organization with broad functions and authority have continued to elicit considerable interest on the part of those concerned with the theories and principles of Jewish communal life. Little support, however, is now voiced for the theory that the normal economic life for American Jewry must necessarily involve a proportional distribution of Jews in the occupational statistics of all American citizens, or that identification with the general American community is impossible or undesirable. There is also less interest in developing certain administrative functions, such as in the area of vital statistics, although the need continues to be felt for demographic data.

On the other hand, coordination and integration of Jewish group activities have gone farther than those proposed as "utopias" in 1935. Welfare funds have been developed since then as the central source of support for a variety of local, national and overseas causes. There are still considerable funds raised separately for Jewish causes, but to a large extent the bulk of philanthropic funds in most cities are being channeled through the established federation. While there has been little progress in the coordination of religious activities—nor have these become closely aligned with central community organization or federation in many cities—there has, nevertheless, been considerable progress in the cultural field. More and more, communities are developing programs for Jewish education through the instrumentality of the federation and through its constituent agencies. Many communities also have coordinated local Jewish activities concerned with group relationships.

FEDERATION LEADERS STIMULATE LOCAL COMMUNAL ORGANIZATION

An important factor in the strengthening of Jewish community organization has been the attitudes and interest of the leadership of the CJFWF and the leadership of many progressive local federations and welfare funds. A notable spokesman for inter-group cooperation was the founder and the first president of the CJFWF, William J. Shroder. His views were stated on many occasions, at General Assembly meetings, board meetings and in addresses to local federation. The following excerpt is characteristic:

Basically, the solution of all these questions rests on cooperation not only between the various sections of the Jewish group, but also between the Jewish and other groups in the general community, to the end that our Jewish work may be more effectively related to general programs.

There is no doubt that the efforts of the local communities toward group cooperation are inherently correct. The failure of national agencies to maintain and extend the gains heretofore made by them should not be permitted to discourage the development of harmonious action in local communities.[14]

Increasingly, especially in the smaller communities, this cooperation was being furthered through a structure for federation consisting of representatives of a variety of interest groups known at that time as the community council form of organization.

THE AMERICAN JEWISH CONFERENCE

In 1942, the acute condition brought about by the European tragedy and World War II led to the organization of an American Jewish Conference, to concern itself with the problems arising out of the war and with the establishment of a commonwealth in Israel. Again, as in 1920, some of the participants hoped that the wide-spread cooperation secured by the Conference from many national agencies and local communities, and the large majorities obtained for the policies and proposals developed by the Conference, might carry over and become the bases for a permanent national Jewish organization concerned with a broad range of communal problems. One of the leading supporters of the Conference, Rabbi Abba Hillel Silver, stated:

American Jews are at last finding themselves under the necessity of doing that which Jews in the old world have always had to do—consciously to orient themselves as Jews in a non-Jewish environment and realistically to face all the implications of their status as a minority group.

It is not unity which is essential, but *organization*, democratic organization in which all points of view can find their legitimate expression and by means of which the majority can properly receive its authority to speak and act for the entire community.

... The Conference demonstrated that great sections of American Jewry had matured sufficiently to welcome and accept the disciplines of organized community life. But it also demonstrated that there are groups and organizations which are not yet ready for a truly democratic organization of American Jewish life.[15]

SECESSION AND COUNTER-SECESSION

When the American Jewish Conference, initiated in the hope of furthering organizational unity, left an aftermath of secession and counter-secession, the Board of Directors of CJFWF directed its president, Sidney Hollander, and its board chairman, William J. Shroder, to write to member agencies urging the continuance of cooperation in joint fund-raising and community organization despite differences of affiliations and of beliefs.[16]

Thus, with the increasing realization, in the 1930s,

of the intensity and severity of the problems which Jewish organizations were facing, there was apparent a greater urgency to achieve increased cooperation among all groups in order to facilitate common objectives. While the existence of many forces in the community tending toward conflict and disagreement was recognized, there was equal recognition of the need for developing forms of community organization which could facilitate compromise, mutual understanding and cooperative action.

In trying to determine the most effective way to group cooperation, a basic question was "to what extent should majority rule prevail and override minority decisions." Experience had indicated that no compulsion was possible in group action and in fund-raising. In a symposium on this subject held at a CJFWF regional conference in 1940, Jerome N. Curtis of Cleveland had affirmed that "numerical majorities can hardly dictate community action to the exclusion of minority views" and that "the object of good community organization is the balancing of majority and minority influences without recourse to dictation or threats."[17]

At the same conference, the differing philosophies of Jewish community organization were defined as being:

1. that Jews should act only as individuals and should have no community organization, or—
2. that community organization should be limited to cultural and educational programs, or—
3. that Jewish community organization should concern itself with all Jewish interests.

The speaker felt that current conditions made it desirable to adopt the third attitude.[18]

A symposium in the CJFWF publication, *Notes and News*, on developing community harmony presented the views of a Jewish federation leader, of an Orthodox rabbi, of a representative of Jewish labor, and of a leading Zionist and a sociologist.[19]

There was general agreement that harmony and unity were desirable goals, but there was considerable divergence on functions and methods of community participation and group action. Excerpts from this article indicate the range of views and interests.

The community leader set forth his views:

A single organization (in a smaller or middle-sized community) can serve for both community planning and fund-raising. All that is needed is a democratic source of control, springing from a community-wide membership with close collaboration by all responsible welfare and religious societies. . . . However, it would be a backward step for the central body or its component organization . . . to take a separatist interest in nonsectarian affairs. The aim of our people should be in the direction of individual participation, not as Jews, but as Americans, in those enterprises which deal with general civic, political and international affairs. Let us have a renaissance of the *kehillah* but without a ghetto trend. . . . Moreover, the merging of communal effort should be primarily in the fund-raising and only sparingly in the functional field.

A related attitude on the limits that need to be imposed on the functions of central Jewish community organization was stated by the sociologist:

The people who constitute the Jewish group are not only Jews but Americans, business men, laborers, golf players, capitalists, Republicans, and a lot of other things. . . . We can't proceed to organize Jews on the assumption that their Jewishness is equally significant and means the same thing to all of them. . . . Cooperation between Jewish groups ought obviously to be extended as far as possible without destroying the character of the cooperating groups or reducing the resulting cooperation between them to merely a formal and empty affair.

A somewhat similar view against elimination of special group organization was expressed as follows:

We favor the fullest measure of cooperation between all Jewish groups. But cooperation does not necessarily mean the complete merger of all Jewish groups into one centralized organization.

A basic defect of current community organization was seen in the affiliations of the leadership by the rabbi:

The leadership consists primarily of prominent Reform Jews, a few Conservatives, several Zionists and occasionally one or two Orthodox Jews. . . . A community organization in this way is largely ignorant of or indifferent to the traditional Jewish spirit and customs, and cannot, therefore, conceive of Jewish needs from an Orthodox viewpoint.

A similar plea for a greater representation was voiced by the representative of labor:

To avoid the danger of mechanical centralization, the central agencies must be built on more democratic organizational foundation. The Jewish masses should be encouraged to participate in the work of the central agencies, as groups and not merely as individuals.

The negative influence of the rival national Jewish agencies on local community harmony was stated as follows by the Zionist leader:

The building up of local communal unity was made almost impossible by the national agencies that invaded the communities . . . regarding them as merely the clientele from whom financial or moral support was to be gotten.

However, he continued, the development of local community organization had done much to counteract these effects:

The welfare funds have succeeded in establishing a form of communal unity which few of the national agencies are able to break through; they run their own campaigns and make their own allocations. . . . In cities like Los Angeles, Chicago, Detroit, St. Louis—to mention only a few—the defense work is in the hands of a single committee in which all groups are represented; they are doing excellent work. . . . These are the beginnings of a new *kehillah* movement.

END OF WAR EASES COMMUNAL TENSIONS

The proposal for a "democratic'" organization which would be empowered by majority action with "authority to speak and act for the entire community" seemed to some like an attainable objective under the stresses and strains of the period of Hitler aggression and World War II tensions. Some important individuals and groups, however, objected strenuously to such a proposal, which they saw as an effort to impose majority will on minority groups, thus circumscribing their right of dissent and separate group action. The basic issue at that time was that of Palestine, a touchstone to the variety of views which were then prevalent about the place of Jews in American society. With the end of the war and the release of tensions, the problems of Jewry both here and overseas seemed less pressing. Indeed, there was a hopeful outlook that the basic problems were on the way toward a solution that did not require new forms of Jewish communal organization or greater "unity." Under this atmosphere of relaxed tensions, there was a reduction of the emotional differences over ideologies, and a consequent development of group cooperation on some important practical Jewish programs.

RELIGIOUS AND SECULAR ORGANIZATION

While stronger and more inclusive forms of central Jewish communal organization have been developing

253

through the federation, a unitary form of Jewish community organization, operating in the religious as well as in the secular field, has not come to fruition. In a few small communities, however, where favorable circumstances existed, there has been experimental development along the line of a single organization serving all religious denominations.

One example is the Norristown, Pa., Jewish Community Center. In this community of fewer than one thousand Jews, a YMHA and a synagogue joined their facilities in 1936 to form the Jewish Community Center. For a membership fee, the individual or the household is entitled to participate in all the religious, educational and cultural services made available in the Center. Through the election of a Board of Governors, members participate in the administration of the philanthropic, religious, educational, recreational, social, welfare and whatever community relations activities may be undertaken. Under the auspices of this single organization, Reform, Conservative and Orthodox services are provided on a cooperative basis. The Center plans a single, unified fund-raising campaign each year to meet local, national and overseas Jewish responsibilities.

Some observers believe, however, that for a long time to come there will continue to be a separation of religious and secular affairs.

Factually speaking, the only way the local communities have organized themselves as total communities, with minor exceptions of perhaps several small communities, has been on a philanthropic basis; that is, for the purposes of meeting the needs of the Jewish population in the general areas of social welfare, medical service, overseas relief and rehabilitation, community relations, Jewish education.

From an organizational standpoint, the Jewish religious institutions present a chaotic picture. Here and there attempts at communal planning for Jewish religious organizations and institutions have proved entirely fruitless.[20]

Perhaps the new suburban areas, with a Jewish population more or less homogeneous in social status and cultural preferences, may show further tendencies toward structural integration of religious, cultural and philanthropic functions. Starting with a synagogue and Jewish school, these facilities may foster social and other group activities; and the Jewish population of these suburbs may find this association a natural channel for the assumption of a varied range of communal activities.

As for the large, intermediate, and most of the small centers of Jewish population, Jewish communal life reflects various group interest, associations and functions, rather than the blueprint of a single "overall" organization. Nevertheless, the circumstances which will determine the nature of Jewish communal organization are not static.[21]

FEDERATION'S ROLE IN COMMUNITY ORGANIZATION TODAY

We can expect substantial progress in community organization through the federation movement which has demonstrated a capacity for adaptation in structure and functions to deal with broad areas of communal interest. Deriving its importance from its central fundraising functions, federation has provided the auspices for services which are not specifically related to philanthropy—such as programs for group relations and for educational objectives. Reviewing the situation in 1949, it was the opinion of the writer that:

The concept of federation is our American contribution to the problem of Jewish community organization. As a concept and as a symbol it has great potency, since it has demonstrated through experience that it can enlist the interest of practically

255

all sections of the population that are concerned with some Jewish problem. . . . The progress of federation has been determined in the past and will be determined in the future by the urgency of the problems which face us and by the functions that can be developed that have some reality to the solution of these problems.[22]

An analysis by Henry Zucker, executive of the Cleveland Federation, of the current stage reached by federation in Jewish communal organization illuminates the practical nature of federation in relation to the theories that have developed on Jewish communal organization both inside federation leadership and elsewhere:

The basic functions of the central communal agency are:

1. Joint fund-raising for the federated agencies.

2. Coordination of the work of the federated agencies and of the other communal agencies and organizations.

3. Community planning—an overview of the needs of the community, discovery of lacks and gaps in program, and action to meet these lacks and gaps. Budgeting and research, which relate closely to the planning process.

4. Public relations to further the discharge of the three basic functions.

The joint fund-raising function has been extended to include more and more agencies and even different types of agency. The health and welfare agencies were a beginning point—now community relations, educational and cultural agencies are included, and occasionally others. Coordination and community planning have progressed from an exclusive interest with beneficiary agencies to an interest in all Jewish communal programs, whether or not they are embraced in the central fund-raising machinery. Public relations programs have reflected the broadened concept of these original functions, as for example, in the development of forums and in other ways, there has developed a growing appreciation of the fact that the central communal agency represents a central meeting point for all Jews, where they can explore problems which are a matter of concern to a substantial majority of the community.[23]

For the most part, local federation organization has met with general acceptance on the part of the Jewish population. There are relatively few who are in sharp disagreement on an ideological basis with its aims and policies. However, some observers, for example, the advocates of a centralized form of organization with a complete roster of functions, believe that the current developments in a central communal organization do not go far enough. At the other extreme, there are those who are disturbed by the current tendencies in federation, who see in them too much centralization and who believe that a central authority in Jewish affairs is dangerous.

Federation leaders would appear, in general, to be following a practical rather than a doctrinaire policy. They do not seek to fashion federation in accordance with some pre-fabricated blueprint. In fact, the position taken is that the structure of federation must be adapted to the circumstances of American life and cannot be predetermined in accordance with patterns of organization of Jewish communities in other lands and other times. Samuel A. Goldsmith, executive of the Chicago Federation, says that:

The central problem that we really face is the development of a Jewish communal structure that is indigenous to the United States and is the outgrowth of our living in what has proved to be one of the longest lived and most competent political, economic, and social democracies in the world. If we try to impose upon our American communities any other structure than that which is indigenous to them, and which they will develop, we shall find ourselves, as human beings, unable to accommodate ourselves to the life around us and unable to cause to flower that inner community life of the spirit and an outer physical

257

community life which will make us a blessed Jewish community to ourselves and to the people of the country.[24]

In a similar vein, Zucker inveighs against the use of terms which are ambiguous and which become slogans rather than exact definition of any present or future reality.

Certain terms which have some currency in discussions of central communal organization, such as "kehillah," "democratically organized community," and "organic community" . . . are ambiguous and loosely used terms. They do not help to clarify what we are striving for in American Jewish communal life.[25]

That the nature of Jewish comunity organization is determined in large measure by the conditions of the American environment is a frequent theme of federation leadership in analyzing the nature of federations. According to Isidore Sobeloff, Detroit Federation executive:

Jewish community organization has characteristics which are peculiar to the conditions of the American environment. Israel and its developing society may furnish us with an enriching factor, but its influence for us may not be dominant. One of America's major aspects has been an expanding and open economic and social system permitting Jews as individuals to achieve greatly in almost every field of endeavor. Another feasible factor has been the pattern of voluntary association, involving a high degree of free choice in the selection of social, cultural and civic activities. As a result of these conditions, the group life of Jews in America has not been restricted to any particular mold, either by external pressure or by internal authority. American Jewry will go where it will wish to go and those who will not wish will fall away, but those who live together and organize together will continue to live by compromise and by accommodation.[26]

part three

The Federation
Movement Today

XII

Organization and
Structure

FORMS OF COMMUNITY ORGANIZATION

Some form of group association among Jews exists
in practically every American community. The kind of
structure within a city depends upon the size and complexity of its Jewish population. Other determining factors are the experiences of the community, the impact of
other cities and of national agencies, and the quality of
its local leadership concerned with group problems and
group interests. Community structures, especially within
the past three decades, have shown a rapid rate of
change, and reflect a continuing process of self-examination.

The forms of organization within the different
localities range from that of an amorphous or unstruc-
tured pattern of group interactions to a closely welded
central association which enrolls practically all members
of the population and which performs a large number
of functions for which there is an evident group concern.

To constitute a Jewish "community" requires a

minimum number of resident families, but there is no dividing line of size of population between cities that have and those that lack a continuing formal structure. Some form of central organization, such as a single religious congregation, is possible even for small units of population, and group activities with other specific purposes may be organized in such localities. However, one cannot speak of a "Jewish community" as being organized until the number of Jewish families is large enough to establish and maintain a place for worship. This requires a stable population usually with a minimum of from twenty to twenty-five families, though there are some towns with larger numbers without an organized congregation.

Informal association may exist even in the absence of an established congregation as individuals maintain contacts with other individuals in a nearby community for religious and cultural interests or merely for general sociability. In sparsely populated areas with no communal facilities available in accessible adjacent areas, individuals may be brought into association with Jewish life through national fund-raising campaigns, memberships in national organizations and through various other means. Modern methods of communication and ease of travel have considerably decreased involuntary isolation from Jewish affairs that would otherwise occur in rural areas and small towns.

Communities that are large enough to possess a place of worship are usually able to provide children with formal Jewish education, and to accept responsibility for raising funds for the campaigns of the popular overseas and national agencies. With a somewhat larger population to draw upon, it is possible to form special group activities, such as one or more social clubs, lodges or chapters of fraternal bodies, a branch of a national women's organization, a Zionist group and the like. In small towns these activities are carried on on a voluntary basis with occasional professional help from a larger neighboring community, or from the field staffs of national organizations.

THE FIRST STAGE

With the establishment of a congregation the initial stage of Jewish communal organization has been reached, and no additional communal structure may be needed by small populations. In a one-synagogue town the activities of the congregation may be limited to religious functions, including youth education, or may involve various other cultural and social activities. The gathering of funds for national and local appeals in these cities is usually undertaken by the local residents, as they respond to requests from the headquarters of national agencies. Contacts among individuals representing various interest groups are likely to be informal; in a small population there is considerable first-hand knowledge about individual and group affairs and much interlocking membership and leadership for these activities.

In many small towns one person or several may assume initiative for the various fund-raising efforts and for other group activities. Communal affairs are conducted on a highly personal and informal basis, usually with passive acceptance of the activities carried on by the self-impelled leaders. In this type of community the initiative taken by one or more active individuals will determine the quality of Jewish communal life. In the small community, the death of an individual who has been the mainspring of group activity, a waning interest or a departure of the key leader may spell the difference between vigor and apathy in communal affairs. In such situations it may be difficult to find an able successor willing to assume communal responsibility.

When the sparsely populated communities become large enough to afford the services of a resident rabbi, the formal organization of communal functions other than religious may be facilitated, providing the rabbi is interested in such activities and is able to obtain the co-operation of his congregation. About a dozen cities in this category have achieved formal organization of sufficient stability to qualify for membership in the CJFWF. No question is raised in these cities whether the existing communal organization is under religious or secular auspices; the two are closely interrelated. The Jewish population in these small towns is usually on the same cultural, if not the same economic, level and there is a large personal element in all communal activities. The conflicts that arise are likely to center on personalities, not on ideologies. As in the larger communities, there are variations in the degrees of interest or apathy which are shown in communal affairs. Some exhibit a trend toward greater interest and intensity of their Jewish group activities; others show signs of a growing indifference. But judging from the field reports of the CJFWF, there is at the present time a developed group consciousness in nearly all of them.[1]

THE SECOND STAGE—INTERMEDIATE-SIZED POPULATIONS

Few of the larger communities resemble this pattern of the one-synagogue community. While some small comunities, as well as the large ones, may have been settled by Jews of different origins and from different backgrounds, the bulk of the Jewish population in small cities will probably have arrived at about the same period of migration, usually in the 1890 to 1920 period. (Exceptions include some of the newer southern and western communities.) Those arriving at later times from different backgrounds are often rapidly integrated into the majority group. If the small community was originally settled at an earlier period, the few descendants that remain may be aloof from the newer settlers and may take little interest in the communal activities which the newcomers establish.

In the larger communities, on the other hand, there have been continuing waves of migration, settling at different periods, responsible for the persistence of a greater group diversity. In these cities the natural processes of assimilation which would in time create a more homogeneous population have not yet run their course. Religious life is on a denominational pattern—Orthodox, Conservative and Reform.

Where there are several congregational groups it has not been possible to organize community welfare activities around the synagogues. However, in some cities one congregation (usually Conservative or Reform) may include a large majority of the Jewish residents, with the minority denominational groups passive or neutral elements. In such cases the dominant congregation may, for all practical purposes, serve as the vehicle for community welfare organization. This, however, is not a static situation. Experience has indicated a trend either toward greater integration or to the emergence of group conflicts which can be resolved only on the basis of more open participation by all elements. In most communities of this type the federation is not a formal part of the congregational structure. It is separately organized; but there are close contacts between those who carry on its functions and the rabbis and the leaders of the congregations.

There is no example thus far in the multiple congregational communities of the emergence of an inter-congregational form of central community organization. This is not due to lack of cooperation among the members of the various congregations on a great many common interests and programs. On the contrary, all the congregations may be represented and be associating harmoniously in a community council form of central organization.

The reason why the inter-congregational form of central community structure has not been established in any multiple denominational community probably rests in part on the fact that generally speaking synagogues have not assumed direct responsibility for the functions that federations have performed. There is, besides, the patent fact that large numbers of Jews, though deeply interested in Jewish need and responsibilities, are yet not members of or active in synagogues. There may, however, be substantial cooperation among synagogues on religious matters. In the larger cities local boards of rabbis of various denominations have worked in unity on questions of religion in the public schools and similar subjects.

There are more than 250 cities in the United States in which the complex of congregational affiliation has led to organization in the Jewish community of a central communal welfare association which is based on a more inclusive structure than the synagogue. This form of organization, first developed in the larger cities, was designed to undertake important functions, community-wide in nature, which were not being met through the congregations.

In most of the smaller communities the federated agency undertakes direct responsibility for the basic fund-raising and welfare functions, but separate auxiliary agencies may continue in existence. These may include a volunteer relief society, a free loan society or other traditional voluntary welfare organization. The federation may have an interest in cultural needs, especially those of youth; but with no professional personnel available, this function is usually left to the synagogue. In some of the smaller cities, Jewish Centers may have developed as a community project some years before the synagogues began to extend their interest from the religious education of children to cultural and recreational needs of all age groups.

In somewhat larger communities a home for the aged, a family and children's service and a group concerned with the difficulties and the improvement of group relationships may also have been established. With increased population and activities the point is reached where communities find it necessary to engage professional help, not only for the service agencies but for the central organization itself, since the volume of work involved in fund-raising and administration quickly reaches beyond the effective capacity of volunteer workers. There are about 125 cities in this category of central community organizations with full-time professional executives.

THE THIRD STAGE—CITIES WITH CONSIDERABLE JEWISH POPULATIONS

There are no substantive differences in the structure for communal welfare between the small city—which has an organized federation, a full-time professional executive, and annual expenditures and allocations of around $50,000 or more—and the larger metropolitan center—which may have scores of specialized agencies, numerous professional personnel and financing which reaches or exceeds the million dollar mark. The differences are only in the volume of services. In the larger communities, however, instead of one central organization, there may be two organizations, such as a federation limited to local functions and a welfare fund for the support of national and overseas appeals. Or there may be a combined federation and welfare fund and an independent organization on communal relations, with coordination established through the employment of a joint executive and staff. Usually, the larger the city, the larger the number of specialized agencies, including institutions for the aged, hospitals and recreational centers.

STRUCTURES OF CENTRAL COMMUNAL ORGANIZATION[2]

Objectives and Purposes

The objectives of these federations and other forms of central organization, as stated in their constitutions and by-laws, are generally set down in abstract terms, such as "the promotion of the general welfare," "to deal with all matters of general concern to the Jewish community," "working in the best interests of the Jewish community," "supporting American and World Jewry." Objectives, however, have also at times been stated specifically, for example, "to coordinate fund-raising," "to operate communal services," "to foster unity and cooperation in communal affairs," "to assume responsibility for establishing programs to meet recognized Jewish needs," and the like.

The stated objectives frequently indicate the scope of interests current at the time the federation was established. The earlier federations are more specific on such functions as fund-raising and disbursement of funds, evaluation of the merits of beneficiary agencies, coordination, supervision and central planning of welfare services.

It is the newer federations and those which have recently undergone a process of reorganization whose by-laws stress broader and more abstract aims.

The Structures of the Central Organizations

Basic variations in the structures of the federations, welfare funds and community councils are to a considerable extent the result of a proces of adapting structure to functions. In many cases, where the original functions have been broadened and developed and new functions added, the original structure has been modified or altered to fit them. The original federations, concerned primarily with the philanthropic agencies and their financing, usually had a membership consisting of individual contributors or were constituted by associations of the local beneficiary agencies. Some of the federations combined agency and individual memberships. In a few instances these federations recognized an additional group interest, such as provision for rabbinical participation on the board of federation (as in Cleveland); but usually representation of congregations and other important groups was secured for the federation through informal procedures.

In addition to a membership body composed of individual contributors, beneficiary agencies, or both, there has been a tendency in the last thirty years in the larger cities to base the structure of the central organization on the organized group associations of the community—congregations, welfare agencies, fraternal groups, Zionist bodies and other forms of adult group association which have some aspect of Jewish communal interest. This type of structure was fostered by the development of community relation functions within the federation or under the auspices of a separate community council. It was

271

also stimulated by the development of central fund-raising for national and overseas agencies as a device to help secure the interest of all elements of the Jewish population for an overall fund campaign.[3]

The pattern of organization in some of the larger cities from 1930 to 1945 was to have two, and in one case three, separate bodies which divided between them the functions performed by a single organization in other communities. In the last two decades, there has been a vigorous concern to simplify the organizational pattern by establishing a single central body which would combine the functions of separate agencies for local financing and welfare planning, for support of national and overseas agencies, and for programs of community and group relationship. This has resulted in mergers of separate communal agencies for these purposes in many cities, recently in such major cities as Los Angeles, Philadelphia, Pittsburgh, Boston, Cleveland and San Francisco. These mergers were motivated by a desire to make better use of leadership, manpower and funds; eliminate overlapping functions and duplicating committees; short-cut cumbersome procedures; centralize related responsibilities; broaden perspectives. Other cities that have been operating with a single central organization for many years have made changes in membership provisions for the purpose of achieving greater participation of individuals and groups and more effective community action.

In Indianapolis, Buffalo and other cities, the newly combined central agency structure included representation of beneficiary and non-beneficiary agencies and individuals at large elected by a community membership. Where mergers have taken place, a single board has replaced the former separate board structures for the enlarged central organization, but the beneficiary as well as all other constituent agencies retain their autonomous character and independent structure.

Some of the smaller and intermediate-sized cities, such as Dallas and Camden, operate what are called "functional" federations, where family and child care programs, community Center and public relations program are operated as departments, directly administered by the central organization. These "federations" are usually based upon individual memberships, but in a few instances may have agency members. The "functional" type of federation seems to have become established in communities which did not have the usual complement of functional services at the time the federation was created, or are outgrowths in the smaller communities of family service agencies which gradually took on the additional functions of community organization.

INDIVIDUAL AND AGENCY MEMBERSHIPS

Eligibility for individual membership is often based on an annual contribution which ranges from $1.00 to $5.00 in most cities (a few have a $10.00 minimum). Organizational memberships may be limited to the beneficiary, constituent or participating agencies which receive financial support, or may be extended to agencies broadly defined in one city as "any organization of adults with twenty-five or more members having an interest in Jewish life . . . [and] which has been in existence for at least one year." In welfare funds which are broadly inclusive, the constituent members, in addition to the local service agencies, may include local branches or chapters of a number of national and overseas organizations which receive allocations from the welfare fund campaign.

ADMINISTRATION

A large individual or agency membership requires the creation of a smaller body for purposes of administration. Procedures for the selection of a board of directors or of an executive committee usually involve an annual meeting open to all members to elect the officers and members of the board. An organization which is based on constituent agencies without any individual membership usually has an administrative body composed of the delegates from its constituent agencies in accordance with specified procedures—individual contributors to the federated funds are technically not the direct members of such structures. The limitations of an administrative body based exclusively on delegates from the constituent agencies has been recognized by some cities where board members "at large" are elected at an annual meeting or added by board selection.

Where the organization has both individual and agency memberships, an intermediate type of board organization is usual. A nominating committee names a slate for a part of the board, which is then submitted to the individual membership at the annual meeting, or in some cities through a mail ballot. Other places on the board are filled through direct designation by the constituent member organizations. The prevailing term for board members is from one year to three years.

Some of these constitutions spell out the powers and functions of the board of directors in detail, among them the adoption of by-laws and amendments, appointment of committees, coordination of fund-raising, allocation of funds, appointment of the executive, preparation of an annual report, election of officers, action on applications for membership in the organization; supervision of the budget of constituent organizations.

COMMUNITY ORGANIZATION IN NEW YORK CITY

The City of New York is in many respects unique in its communal organization. It has an estimated population of 2,500,000 Jews, spread over the five boroughs and in the larger metropolitan areas of Long Island, Westchester County and nearby Connecticut who are closely tied to New York City through economic, social and cultural affiliations. The very magnitude makes for differences in organization even where the aims and purposes are similar to those developed in smaller communities. There are considerable variations in scope and content, not only between New York and the small cities, but even with cities of relatively large Jewish populations, such as Chicago and Los Angeles.

Whereas other large cities may have between 15 and 25 Jewish social welfare and health agencies and from 300 to 400 other Jewish group associations, there are well over 100 Jewish welfare and health agencies in New York City and thousands of voluntary group associations, including congregations and synagogues, *Landsmanschaften* and mutual aid societies, fraternal groups and welfare societies.

Districts and neighborhoods in Manhattan, Brooklyn, Queens and the Bronx may have a larger Jewish population than Cleveland or Detroit. The concentration of a large working population and the growth of the Jewish labor unions were responsible for communal labor activities which are not duplicated, except on a limited scale, elsewhere. The fact that New York is the seat of practically all of the large Jewish national organizations (often operated mainly by New York residents) has made the activities of these national groups an important element in the communal life of the New York metropolis. New York has active chapters of the American Jewish Congress and the American Jewish Committee, Zionist groups, the B'nai B'rith, Jewish Labor Committee, ORT, Council of Jewish Women, and others. Group associations such as the New York Board of Rabbis and the Jewish Labor Committee seek to bring together representatives of a specific functional interest, but since the ending of the New York *Kehillah* in 1922, there has not been any vigorous attempt to duplicate that ambitious plan for a unified communal structure.

There are three organizations in New York City which parallel the development of the federation movement in other cities. These are the Federation of Jewish Philanthropies, the United Jewish Appeal of Greater New York, and the Jewish Community Council of the Borough of Brooklyn. The Federation was established in 1917 to cover Manhattan, Bronx and Queens, and was later merged with the Brooklyn Federation of Charities which had been established in 1909. The Federation has been concerned solely with local needs. New York has never developed a comprehensive unified fund-raising campaign for a substantial number of national and overseas agencies. (The New York UJA, established in 1939, conducts a joint campaign for a few agencies, in addition to serving primarily as the local representative of the national UJA.) The Brooklyn Jewish Community Council, also established in 1939 and operating mainly in matters of inter-group and intra-group relationships, is similar in its objectives for a section of the city to the Jewish community councils of Detroit and Washington, D.C., which are city-wide in character.

THE FEDERATION OF JEWISH PHILANTHROPIES OF NEW YORK

The New York Federation is a combination of constituent beneficiary agencies and individual contributor memberships. The primary structure consists of the constituent agencies for whom the Federation raises funds and to whom the funds are allocated. Subscribers of a minimum of $10 in any year are considered the regular members of the Federation for the ensuing twelve months. Individuals under the age of 21 who pay at least $5 are considered junior members but do not have the regular membership privileges.

The structure of the Board of Trustees of the New York Federation indicates the relative importance of the beneficiary institutions and agencies as compared with individual members. Each of the constituent agencies receiving an allotment of not less than $20,000 is entitled to name a member of the Board. If the allotment from the Federation is in excess of $100,000, such agencies can be represented by two trustees. Several agencies which receive less than $20,000 can combine to name a trustee.

In addition to a differential based upon amount of allotment, the trustees so designated by the beneficiary agency are entitled to one vote, if named by beneficiary agencies receiving less than $50,000 annual allotment— and up to five votes, if they represent beneficiary agencies whose allotment amounts to $200,000 or more.

The Federation also provides for trustees-at-large elected by the membership at the annual meeting. (The annual business meeting of the membership requires a quorum of 50 members.)[4] The number of trustees-at-large is limited to one-half of the total number of votes to which the trustees designated by the beneficiary agencies are entitled. Trustees-at-large are named by a nominating committee, but other nominations can be made by petition of not less than 100 Federation members. The trustees-at-large cannot be members of the board of directors of beneficiary societies.

The New York Federation seeks to enlist contributors through business trade groups and neighborhood organizations, but campaigning among small givers is limited both by the magnitude of the problem and through an arrangement with the Greater New York Fund (a city-wide non-sectarian and inter-sectarian fund-raising agency engaged in soliciting contributions from employees and from publicly held corporations, and aiding over 400 agencies.) In this arrangement the Federation has agreed not to solicit contributions from employees earning $5,000 or less a year.

In addition to the Board of Trustees, the constitution of the Federation provides for a Businessmen's Council, which is the active fund-raising body. Activities of this Council are directed by an executive committee with a minimum of 25 members appointed annually by the trustees of Federation after consultation with the chairman of the Businessmen's Council. Other parts of the apparatus of fund-raising in Federation include the Women's Division, various trade groups, etc., of which there is a large number, and in which a considerable number of volunteers serve. Budgeting the funds and social welfare planning are the responsibility of the Distribution Committee, the Communal Planning Committee and various other committees responsible to the Board of Trustees.[5]

THE NEW YORK UJA

The New York UJA has an inter-agency structure exclusively. Contributors are not *ipso facto* members of the corporation. It was established in 1939 by three national organizations: The Joint Distribution Committee, the United Palestine Appeal (now the United Israel Appeal), and the National Refugee Service. In 1959 the funds obtained in the campaign, above general expenditures, were allocated to its parent body, the national UJA, which in turn finances the United Israel Appeal and the American Jewish Joint Distribution Committee. (The United HIAS Service has replaced the National Refugee Service, and has been receiving support for "emergency" needs from national UJA, and a contribution toward its total budget from the New York UJA.) The American Jewish Congress and the National Jewish Welfare Board also have been sharing in the New York UJA campaign on the basis of a percentage of the total income, annually negotiated. Other national agencies receiving funds from the New York UJA in previous years now conduct independent drives.

The New York UJA allocates by far the major portion of its receipts to national UJA. In the event that there might be no national agreement in any one year among the partners, an allocation committee of the New York UJA is authorized to establish a formula for the distribution of funds to the national UJA constituents.

The national UJA, which receives approximately 30% of its funds from the New York UJA, also contributes directly to the New York Association for New Americans, a local New York agency.

The United Jewish Appeal of Greater New York, Inc., is the legal corporation of the New York UJA. The membership of the corporation consists of three groups, equal in number, each originally appointed by one of the three organizations involved in its establishment. There is an annual meeting of the corporate body with each member entitled to one vote in person or by proxy. The corporate membership elects a Board of Directors (of not less than 45 nor more than 150, the number always being a multiple of three), with three groups of board members, each elected by its corresponding corporate membership group.

The Board of Directors elects its officers from among its members and has the authority to create additional offices to which it may elect individuals who need not be members of the board. The Executive Committee appoints a nominating committee of five members and the by-laws also provide for nominations by petition of 25 board members. The board may also appoint an Executive Committee of from 12 to 25 members (taking "into consideration proper representation of the interests" of its three constituent agencies) and other committees and subcommittees.[6]

THE BROOKLYN JEWISH COMMUNITY COUNCIL

Although the possibility of organizing borough-wide councils of Jewish organizations in New York City has been under discussion from time to time, such an agency has thus far been established only in Brooklyn, which has the largest unit of Jewish population in New York, estimated at approximately 900,000 persons.

The Brooklyn Jewish Community Council was organized and incorporated in 1940 in response to an active interest in problems of group relationships and in recognition of the desirability of group cooperation in dealing with these problems on a local basis. Since the national offices of the American Jewish Committee, the American Jewish Congress, B'nai B'rith Anti-Defamation League, and the Jewish Labor Committee are located in New York City, it was natural for activities dealing with anti-Semitism and group relations to be concentrated largely in the offices of the national organizations, reinforced by their local chapters and interested participating individuals. The Borough of Brooklyn, with its very large Jewish population and numbers of Jewish organizations, seemed to be a suitable area for the development of greater local participation in carrying out these group relations functions.

The preamble of the constitution and by-laws of the Brooklyn Jewish Council states that the object of the association is to unite Jewish organizations into a representative council, to act as a collective unit in matters pertaining to the welfare of the Jewish population, to foster mutual understanding among all groups, "all races and all creeds," to combat the forces of racial or religious discrimination and to safeguard rights. Though dues are received from the member organizations, the budget of the BJCC for a considerable period of time was subsidized by the American Jewish Committee and the B'nai B'rith Anti-Defamation League.

The membership of the Brooklyn Jewish Community Council consists entirely of Jewish organizations and local neighborhood Jewish councils. A number of delegates is selected by these groups, depending upon their size and the range of local units. The organization is administered by a Board of Directors which consists of up to fifty-one individuals, including the officers who are elected at the annual meeting by the delegates and those nominated by the neighborhood councils which are constituents. The services performed by the BJCC are considered to parallel those of other local community relations agencies throughout the country, and also to afford some additional functions which in other cities are usually performed by federations (such as concern for Jewish education, youth programs, etc.)[7]

Since the Brooklyn Jewish Community Council represents the most ambitious attempt to develop a central structure for other than philanthropic activities among a very large Jewish population, it may be pertinent to indicate the extent to which the broad aims of this organization have been achieved.

In an Evaluation Report made in July 1949 by the executive director, progress was reported on the development of interrelationships among the various local agencies and success was noted in breaking down the sense of isolation among the group organizations in Brooklyn. However, the report states:

The sense of identification of local constituents to local councils is weak and the sense of identification of local units of local councils to Central Council almost nonexistent. We are, therefore, to a great extent in reality still a PAPER ORGANIZATION.

Knowledge of the existence of the BJCC, its aims, purposes and program is lacking in the general community as well as within our individual constituent organizations.

This problem will be with us for a long time since it is fundamentally a problem of community education.

The report also indicates the lack of organic unity of the various activities. "There are odds and ends of activities engaged in by local councils and the Youth Council—some very worthwhile, others insignificant"; the lack of an integrated or planned program is mentioned.

With the reduction and termination of support received from the two national agencies, the finances and the activities of the Council have been reduced.[8] Considering Brooklyn's large Jewish population, nearly three times as large as Los Angeles, the work of the Brooklyn Council would seem to be limited in scope and extent. Its history again points to the difficulties encountered in attempts to organize New York Jewry for other than fund-raising purposes.

NEW YORK IS DIFFERENT

It is apparent from the foregoing that there are striking differences in structure between the communal organizations in New York and those established in cities with smaller units of Jewish population. This is especially true in dealing with non-local needs and responsibilities. There is no welfare fund in New York, and therefore no joint campaign for the scores of national and overseas agencies which continue to conduct their independent campaigns. There is no center for city-wide public relations programs. In the field of local welfare there is central planning and financing similar to other communities through the Federation.

These differences arise primarily from the magnitude of the Jewish population. There is, in fact, less difference in function than in structure between New York and other large cities, as well as in the character of administration and direction given by boards and professional staffs of the various operating agencies. There is as intense a personal involvement on the part of board members and volunteers in New York as in other cities, and this manifests itself in the spirit of the campaigns and in the conduct of agency affairs. In a recent survey based on interviews with Federation's board members, it was reported that "to most of the people we talked to the organization is more than an administrative body which collects and allocates funds. They endowed the organization with a collective personality guided not only by

283

statutory laws but by motivations as if it had a personality of its own." The largest motivating influence was the concern for Jewish status and Jewish group interests, indicating a large amount of communal concern.

Pilot studies in three small cities—Albany, Camden and New Britain—indicated that face-to-face contacts make for relatively widespread activity in membership bodies and permit greater participation in the conduct of communal affairs.[9] In all types of communities, however, there is a recognition of the problem of leadership, its continuation and replacement, which is discussed elsewhere in this volume.

XIII

The Aims and Functions of Federations

The range of its activities, the functions it performed, its role as a channel between the contributors and the program of communal services, have bestowed great importance on the federation as a communal institution. In small cities the federation is most significant because it is the center and focus of practically all group activities. In the large cities it is important because its functions, though more limited in scope, are extensive and essential. It is especially important in cities where it operates an inclusive program of fund-raising for local and non-local purposes.

There may be other institutions able to enlist more intense devotion from some elements of the population, whose activities, being less broad in application, provide a greater appeal to special groups. But federation more than any other local organization, has the advantages of an appeal to the Jewish population as a whole, an inherently generic appeal in which the humanitarian motivation is the basic component. Federation today is in most cities potentially, if not actually, the center of broad Jewish communal interests.

A HERITAGE AFFIRMED

Factually speaking, the only way the local communities have organized themselves as total communities, with minor exceptions of perhaps several small communities, has been on a philanthropic basis; that is, for the purposes of meeting the needs of the Jewish population in the general areas of social welfare, medical service, overseas relief and rehabilitation, community relations, Jewish education.[1]

DIRECT AND INDIRECT FUNCTIONS

The functions performed by federations fall into two main categories. The first consists of its administrative operations, the activities which pertain to organizing people for the support of welfare and cultural programs and to enlisting the cooperation of individuals and groups for communal action for a broad range of interests and problems. Involved are a variety of procedures in fund-raising campaigns or in providing funds through other sources, in allocating the funds to the agencies engaged in communal service, in considering conditions and problems, in planning for services in accordance with needs and changing conditions, in interpreting the work of the federation and its beneficiary agencies to the people of the community, in providing for a continuity of effort through long-term fiscal policies and enlistment of leadership, and in serving as a center for channeling changing and diverse group and individual interests into cooperative group action.

The second set of functions performed by federations are those undertaken by the beneficiary agencies or by other organizations affiliated with or related to the federation, such as agencies engaged in health, welfare, civic, educational or cultural services. Federation has direct contacts with the local agencies in these fields through its role in fund-raising, budgeting and local welfare planning, or through the relationship established by

286

federation with non-sectarian chests and with governmental bodies which utilize the services of voluntary welfare agencies.

The agencies engaged in local services are generally independent organizations with their own separate boards.* They may have their own special membership of a number of contributors to the federation or to the non-sectarian community chest from which the agencies derive their funds. But whatever the structure of the functional agencies, they are usually affiliated with or closely related to federation, for purposes of financing, coordination and community planning.

The federation which raises funds for regional, national and overseas agencies also has a relationship to these non-local agencies as a trustee for the people who have contributed the funds. This role involves the federation in the procedures of campaigning, budgeting and interpretation and places it in a liaison position between the contributors and the non-local agencies for a variety of administrative and planning responsibilities.

ADMINISTRATIVE FUNCTIONS

Fund-Raising

Nearly all federations have the function of providing funds for the support of local and/or non-local Jewish agencies.[2] Fund-raising may still be considered their primary function, in continuation of the original purpose for which federations were established. It has become, indeed, an increasingly extensive area of federation activity, in view of the enlarged programs of the national and overseas agencies. In addition, the importance of local

---

* In some small and intermediate-sized cities, as noted, the local federation operates many or all of the local services and is known as a "functional federation."

287

services has been growing. As pointed out previously, in nearly all of the smaller and in most of the intermediate and the large communities, a single organization is now responsible for raising the funds for the local, national and overseas agencies that have agreed to become beneficiaries of the central fund.

The degree to which the federation remains the basic source of financial support for local Jewish agencies depends on the number and types of welfare and cultural agencies which draw the major share of their funds from it, on the extent to which such Jewish agencies are financed by the non-sectarian community chest, and on the number of Jewish agencies dependent on philanthropic funds, but not affiliated either with Jewish federations or with community chests. In some cities—Baltimore, for example —practically all of the local Jewish agencies are beneficiaries of the federation and receive their support from that source. In New York and Chicago the Jewish federation's source of income is supplemented to a very limited extent by funds from what have been called "partial community chests." In some cities—Los Angeles and Newark are two such—community chests provide only a small fraction of the deficits of the local agencies, while in other cities the funds received from chests constitute a large share of the income of the constituent local Jewish agencies of federations.[3]

The extent to which the federation or the Jewish welfare fund includes national and overseas agencies varies in different cities. In some communities the federation includes most of the bona fide non-local agencies which seek funds. In other cities, some or many of the national and overseas agencies remain outside of the federation and conduct their own campaigns either through preference, or because they fail to meet the eligibility standards of the local fund, or cannot gain inclusion for other reasons.

Some of the larger overseas agencies, such as the United Jewish Appeal, receive their support through the local federations in practically every city where such an organization exists. They raise funds independently only in the smallest communities, which are unorganized or which have an informal type of group fund-raising. On the other hand, some national Jewish campaigns, such as Brandeis University's, are recipients of joint funds in only a few communities, preferring independent campaigns. Some national campaigns, such as that for Histadruth, are beneficiaries of federations in some cities but conduct their compaigns independently in others.

The raising of funds is the most important and frequently the most pervasive activity of the federation. The task of organizing for the campaigns is one of the major responsibilities of the executive, and usually the most pressing problem of the leaders and officers of the federation. It is generally understood that the fund-raising campaign must be repeated annually in order that the overseas, national, and local causes continue to carry on their important programs, since the renewal of annual contributions is not automatic. The fund-raising apparatus must be set in motion (it is, in fact, a continuous planning and organizational process in many cities) solicitors assigned, the purposes and goals publicized and the proper climate established for the annual campaign.

The questions of campaign organization must be answered satisfactorily if the campaign is to be successful. Success depends on the prestige and ability of the individual who accepts responsibility as campaign chairman, whether the key givers can be persuaded to increase over last year or kept from making substantial cuts;

whether successful volunteer solicitors for the key gifts, can be found; and the like.

Organization for fund-raising depends essentially on community organization procedures, and its results are frequently an index to communal health and to the ability and loyalty of communal leadership.

CAPITAL AND RESERVE FUNDS

Federations initially limited their fiscal responsibilities to meeting the annual maintenance costs of their beneficiary agencies, while the capital funds required for major improvements or additions to institutional plants continued to be raised by the agencies themselves. Endowments and bequests were generally given directly to the agencies rather than to the federation, usually as a matter of local policy. Since the funds raised annually were for operating budgets, this meant that the federation was not developing reserves. But over the years the increasing maturity and stability of the federations has led them to assume responsibility for securing the capital funds required by their health and welfare agencies and to accumulate reserves. Increasingly, endowments and bequests are being given to the federation as well as to the beneficiary agencies.

A study was made[4] of the endowment fund programs of the Jewish federations and welfare funds in thirteen large cities in 1959. (For the purposes of the study the term "endowment fund" was defined as "all the assets of the organization other than operating funds.") The *book value* of the total endowment funds of these thirteen cities increased from $22,650,000 in 1948 to $46,500,000 in 1958. Since the major share of these funds, approximately 80%, is invested in securities, their market value was considerably higher. These funds have more than doubled in ten years with the major growth during the last five years. Of the total, the Chicago Federation accounted for about $11,000,000, and the New York Federation (exclusive of the New York UJA which does not have the policy of accumulating reserve funds) accounted for approximately $17,000,000.

The number of purposes for which endowment funds are accumulated by federations has increased somewhat during this period. The major consideration remains achieving the ability to meet crisis situations, such as periods of economic recession. The next most important use of endowment funds is to provide income for operating needs of federations or their beneficiary agencies on a continuing basis, to supplement the amounts available from campaign sources. Some use portions of their endowment fund income to assist in financing capital needs. There is also some special, though minor, use made of endowment funds to finance research studies and other projects not customarily undertaken through the regular operating budget.

Among the communities reported on, the promotion of endowment fund programs and the solicitation of bequests for such programs have become well planned year-round activities. The methods used range from newspaper advertising and general mailings to specialized tax seminars and handbooks for attorneys and accountants to direct solicitation of potential donors.

The major source of endowment fund income continues to be bequests and legacies. Other income is derived from memorial donations, savings from operating budgets and, most recently, life insurance contracts and living trusts. The results of this intensified promotion of endowment fund income over the ten-year period surveyed have been impressive. In 1948 each of five federations had endowment funds of over $1,000,000. In 1958 eight federations were in this category.

THE ALLOCATION OF FUNDS—BUDGETARY PROCEDURES

In most federations and welfare funds the budgeting function is second in importance only to that of the fund-raising campaign. Just as the varying amounts of funds raised are an indication of federation's financial effectiveness, the way in which the funds are allocated demonstrates its communal quality.

Individual contributors who are affiliated with or are in strong sympathy with particular agencies may express preferences concerning the relative merits of the beneficiary agencies. On the other hand, many contributors, and the number is probably increasing, are apparently willing to accept federation's decisions, both on the inclusion of agencies and the amounts allotted to each of them. Conflicts, however, are likely to arise among the partisans of specific agencies. Thus, for example, in communities where funds from a central campaign are distributed among non-local as well as local beneficiaries, some contributors may favor local against the overseas appeals, and vice versa. National and overseas agencies may enlist the influence of outstanding local givers or of active federation leaders.

Through interpretation, publicity, enlisting of memberships, organization of chapters and other recruiting devices, the beneficiary agencies present the merits of their appeals on a competitive basis. Partisanship in behalf of specific agencies involves pressures which the local budget committees must resolve.

The problems rising out of these situations stimulated the organization of the Large City Budgeting Conference, in which an attempt is made by twenty-three major welfare funds, to explore cooperatively the needs of some of the key national and overseas agencies which receive funds in local communities. The organization by the Council of Jewish Federations and Welfare Funds of its Budget Research Department, its Committee on National Local Relations, its Institute on Overseas Studies and other research and committee services, are further means of attempting to solve budgeting problems.

From its inception the CJFWF has developed a series of national services designed to help local communities with their budgeting problems. These include basic independently-analyzed financial and program data on agencies appealing to welfare funds for support (budget digest reports), summaries of allocations made annually by welfare funds, budget workbooks for communities requesting such help, special reports on national and overseas agencies and formulation of best practices and principles in budgeting procedures.[5]

The organization and procedures of local budget committees have received considerable attention from federation leadership. It is generally acknowledged that the personnel of the budgeting committee must be sufficiently representative of the various groups and agency interest among the contributors to avoid distortions or partisanship. The mingling of various interests in the membership of the budgeting councils is considered effective in leading toward a cross-fertilization of partisan views.

Other generally accepted principles are: that budgeting committees must rely on factual data rather than on opinion or hearsay; that the group must be willing to devote considerable time adequately to discharge the responsibility it has assumed, considering each agency individually and allowing, if necessary, time for hearings with agency representatives.

The size of the budget committee varies—in some

cities a large number of key individuals is involved, with sub-groups established for separate fields of agency service, and with final action by the budget committee as a whole. The large committees are considered valuable as a means of broadening interest and understanding; but other cities have felt that a relatively small group of from five to twenty-five members has proved to be a more efficient method of procedure. Usually the recommendations of the budget committees are accepted by the governing body of the federation, which has the final authority in most communities.

INFORMATION SERVICES

With the knowledge of communal needs and services derived from the budgeting processes, federations have increasingly become a central source of information for statistics of Jewish population, on the work and finances of the local, national and overseas agencies under Jewish auspices, and on many other matters. Jews and other members of the community seeking information usually turn to the federation. Since 1945 forty cities have undertaken detailed studies of Jewish population by one or another method of sampling or census. Jewish population estimates have been made by consulting federation lists of potential and actual contributors, and other data, which are valuable for fund-raising purposes, but which are also now found to be of increasing importance for other aspects of organized communal planning.[6]

CENTRAL PLANNING

The role of the federation as a central fund-raising instrument and the processes developed to guide the allocation of funds have produced an increasingly formal and systematic approach to community planning. While the local beneficiary agencies, especially those in the intermediate and larger cities, are autonomous, and have their own boards and often their own separate memberships, the need for determining the appropriateness of funds supplied by federation has stimulated the development of an attitude of inquiry and the desire to arrive at logical rather than arbitrary decisions.

It is the annual budgeting procedure that discloses the changing conditions which must be taken into account if the allocation of funds is to be more than giving the same amount or the same percentage of the funds available each year to the same list of agencies. Year by year prices of commodities and the costs of personnel change, and there may be more or fewer families or children, or aged, or patients being served. Neighborhoods change and populations shift. Buildings depreciate; newer and more desirable methods of dealing with recognized problems are advanced; the economic conditions of the population improve or deteriorate, influencing ability to pay for the health and welfare services available. Not all of these changes are readily apparent, and systematic efforts must be made to ascertain the relevant facts through periodic reports, studies and surveys.

For many years the role of federation in community planning was not primary but auxiliary to the constituent agencies. From the beginning, however, the budget committees of federations could not escape making judgments concerning the work of the beneficiary agencies. The willingness or reluctance of the federation to respond to changes in services and to their costs was an important element in the quality of programs available to the community; and it was, further, an index to the quality of communal leadership.

The competence, range of interests and initiative of the professional director of a federation, as well as of the key individuals, has been at times the major factor in community action. Their initiative might take the form of general studies or surveys conducted by local or outside experts for an appraisal of needs and as a guide to federation policies. Sometimes these studies are undertaken with the aim of economy, or are related to doubts as to the effectiveness and appropriateness of the services which are being financed by federation. At other times, insistence on the part of beneficiary agencies for increased funds has been the impelling motive.

Gradually a more systematic approach has been developed, and in the majority of the larger and intermediate cities there are now continuing arrangements and procedures for studying local agency needs and problems and for equipping federation with the necessary knowledge to make practical budgetary decisions. There is still, however, little basic research being undertaken under the auspices of local federations, into the nature and causes of the social problems of the community.

The form of organization for community planning today depends primarily upon the size of the community. The larger federations employ a professional staff under the direction of the federation executive to search out up-to-date information about the work of the beneficiary agencies. In smaller communities, this function becomes one of the tasks assumed by the professional director. Some of the larger federations have research study committees consisting of lay members of the federation board and of the professional and lay representatives of the beneficiary agencies; they associate themselves with and utilize the staff services for their assignments.

The research and fact-finding involved is usually based upon periodic reports from the constituent agencies on their fiscal experience as well as on the volume of functional services. Definitions and schedules for agency reporting have been developed over the years on a nationwide scale under the auspices of United Community Funds and Councils, the U.S. Children's Bureau, and the Council of Jewish Federations and Welfare Funds. Information from local communities on their Jewish agencies is gathered by the CJFWF, and is analyzed and tabulated in reports which enable local communities to relate their experience to those of other cities, especially those in the same population group. The CJFWF also supplies its member agencies upon request with special information collected on various aspects of the problems which are of concern to the local federation.[7]

In most cities there are councils of social agencies on a community-wide base in which the Jewish federation and its constituent agencies participate. These local councils frequently undertake studies and engage in cooperative local planning and develop standards which are useful guides for the service agencies. On occasion, community chests and councils have taken the initiative in recommending that studies be made of the Jewish agencies which they help to finance.

SOCIAL WELFARE PLANNING

Because social planning is a joint responsibility of the federation and the functional agencies, the device of an established and continuing planning committee has been adopted. Such planning committees, or Advisory Planning Councils, usually consist of representatives of

297

the beneficiary agencies and of the federation board. They are useful in bringing together the separate agencies for joint consideration of problems, and have acted as a basic spur to community improvement in many cities.[8] The trend is toward increased acceptance of this planning responsibility of the central agency in cooperation with the constituent agencies. Extending beyond the purely fiscal relationship, these developments give expression to a mutuality of interests in progressive administration of current programs and in meeting new needs.

MEETING NEW NEEDS

The development of systematic planning within federation and its constituent agencies has led to comprehensive analyses of community needs and to a responsive attitude toward problems and programs which are outside the functions of the current beneficiary agencies. This broadening of communal interest on the part of the federation is responsible for such developments as the inclusion of Jewish education, which was organized independently of federation but has gradually become an accepted function. Similarly, federations have become concerned with cultural problems and other new needs. One of the major concerns in recent years has been with group relationships and a trend toward responsibility for programs in this field.

In most cities where a definite program for group relations has been established, it functions as a constituent and beneficiary agency of federation, or is carried on by a federation committee with services from the federation's executive's staff, or as a department of federation with a professional staff member serving under the direction of the executive. The separate agency for community relations is the usual pattern of organization in the larger

cities. Among thirty-three cities in the intermediate
size group, eighteen carried on the program as a department or committee of the central agency, and that is the
usual structure in the smaller cities.

Federations have been undertaking other communal
activities or functions which were not formerly considered as being within their field of responsibility, such
as maintaining a community calendar, publishing a Jewish weekly newspaper, holding lecture forums or similar
functions of communication and education. Federations
sponsor arts, music, and book promotional campaigns,
hold holiday observances, arbitrate intra-Jewish disputes,
and make efforts to raise the standards of business practices. The federation frequently represents the Jewish
population in local civic observances. In most cities the
federation assumed responsibilities in 1954 and 1955 for
arranging local programs in celebration of the Tercentenary of Jewish Settlement in North America, and in
1958 for civic tributes to the tenth anniversary of Israel.[9]

INTEREST IN PUBLIC AFFAIRS

As a central agency, the federation directly and in
association with beneficiary agencies is concerned with
the range of problems related to its functions and to the
programs of its member agencies. This generally involves
contacts with the public welfare and health departments
of the locality and with the voluntary agencies in these
fields. Relationships with governmental and voluntary
health and welfare agencies are also channeled through
the council of social agencies of which the federation is
a member.

Federations are also concerned with state and national aspects of social legislation in the areas of health,
social security and social insurance. Of special interest

to federations have been the use by the local governments of voluntary agencies to give medical and welfare services to dependents and to pay for such services; the assistance programs available to the clients or potential clients of the Jewish welfare agencies; the public subsidies for construction of hospitals; the Old Age and Survivors Insurance systems; the need for public provisions of medical care for the aged, and other programs.[10]

In recent years federations have been actively concerned with: the investigation and combating of subversive and anti-Semitic groups, the question of religion in the public schools, the advisability of released time for religious training, and programs for cultural education. Federations have also been active in promoting legislation on fair employment practices (FEPC) and in improvements in the federal immigration provisions. Federations which raise funds for overseas agencies are also frequently interested in matters affecting overseas and refugee aid, and in national actions related to economic aid to and progress of Israel.

In dealing with general public affairs, local federations avail themselves of the information and advisory services available from the National Community Relations Advisory Council and from the national agencies in the field of interest. Forty-eight communities are members of the NCRAC, either directly through their federations (if they operate a public relations department which meets the eligibility requirements of the NCRAC), or through a separately organized local public relations agency which is a member of the federation family.

XIV

Programs of the
Constituent Agencies

The constituent agencies of federation reflect the nature of the services which have been organized on a community-wide basis for American Jews. There are two general types of service: those which serve individuals and those which serve the community in general.

The first category includes provision for help to individuals and families in distress, guidance and care of children, and help to the aged, the disabled and other handicapped people. Related specialized services under Jewish auspices include vocational guidance and placement, homemaker and housekeeping services, counseling on marital and parent-child relationships, legal aid and many other kinds of personal service. The larger cities have built general and special hospitals, and provide outpatient services for physical and mental health. Federations in many cities are likewise involved in financing and planning various group programs for Jewish education and for recreational and cultural activities.

The second category of programs, which do not involve individuals directly but are of a general character affecting the entire Jewish population, may be carried on by the beneficiary agencies or by special departments of the federation. These include programs relating to the status of Jews as members of the general community and the maintenance or improvement of relationships among the various Jewish groups, agencies and associations. In addition to operating public forums, assuming responsibility for the publication of community newspapers and providing facilities for arbitration of intra-group conflicts, some federations also take responsibility for *kashruth* supervision of food supplies and cooperate with other welfare organizations in supporting and developing governmental welfare programs.

The degree to which all of the services are provided on a formal and systematic basis depends, to a considerable extent, upon the size of the Jewish population and its financial resources. Even the smallest organized community will usually attempt, on a volunteer basis, to help individuals in distress and to provide some cultural programs. Small communities may also undertake activities dealing with group relationships through the federation board or through a special committee.

Of the 133 cities of under 5,000 Jewish population included in the membership of the CJFWF in 1959, 62 employed a professional worker; the balance depended on volunteer and clerical help. The small communities often utilize their single professional worker for the direction of the community Center and for case work services to individuals and families, as well as for general administration and assistance in raising and collecting funds.

Cities with large Jewish populations provide family and children's services under professional direction and have established institutional facilities for group and recreational activities, communal programs for Jewish education and residences for the care of the aged. With a single exception, cities with a Jewish population of 30,000 and over have built institutions for medical and hospital care. In fact, even cities where the Jewish population is 20,000 or less have set up a number of institutions for the aged and several have established hospitals.

The auspices under which these various activities are being carried on in specific communities vary directly with the size of the community and with the extent of professional development. In the smaller communities, and in some of intermediate size, a single integrated federation will undertake all the services which can be performed out of an office or with the use of simple institutional facilities. Even in some of the cities having from 7,500 to 15,000 Jewish population, family and children's services, recreational and group work, Jewish education, community relations programs and, in a few instances, a home for the aged, will all be administered by a federation directly through committees rather than through separate agencies. In most of the intermediate and in all of the larger cities, however, these programs are operated by autonomous agencies with their own boards and sometimes their own special memberships enrolled also as members of the federation and participating in its administration.[1]

In some cities, primarily the very largest ones, there are, in addition, Jewish agencies and programs that are not beneficiaries of the local Jewish federation or of the community chest, but continue to raise their funds independently. In some instances these agencies enroll as associates in federation or in the community council for purposes of cooperation and central planning. Non-affiliated agencies may be incligible for federation financial

303

support because they fail to meet the standards established by federation or because they duplicate the functions of long-established beneficiaries.[2]

GROUP WORK AND RECREATION

Practically all federations which employ a professional worker, as well as some federations which operate entirely with volunteer services, include cultural and recreational activities for youth and for other age groups. In many of the smaller cities, and certainly in the intermediate and larger communities, there may be one or more Jewish Centers supported by federations or receiving funds from community chests. In 1958 community chests provided 17.5% and Jewish federations 25.5% of Center income.[3] Professional help and other assistance may also be made available from the federation-supported agency to synagogue Centers and other independent cultural programs to be found in the metropolitan area. Centers carry on educational, cultural and recreational activities including the operation of day and summer resident camps. At the beginning of 1959 the Jewish Welfare Board reported "over 600,000 members of Jewish community Centers. Children under 14 (34%) and adults over 25 (48%) were the largest membership categories by age groupings."[4]

In the smaller communities the group work services may be closely related to the federation, with one executive serving both the Jewish Center and the federation; or there may be separate boards and separate professional staffs for federation and Center in other small cities. In most of the intermediate cities the Centers are separate and autonomous agencies. Most of these group work agencies are constituents of the federation; for example, in 34 intermediate communities 25 Centers are constituents, 9 are non-constituents of federation. In all of the large cities the group work agencies or the major units are constituents of the federation receiving their major support from that source.

Jewish community Centers have their roots in the Young Men's and Young Women's Hebrew Associations and in the Settlement House movement for the Americanization of immigrants. The Jewish Welfare Board, national service agency in this field, has tended to define its objectives in terms of *"Jewish* cultural survival" and has stated as one of the primary functions of Jewish Centers: "service as an agency of Jewish identification."[5] These objectives were reinforced by the survey of the Jewish Welfare Board and the community Centers conducted by Oscar I. Janowsky and published in 1948.[6]

The Center movement has also been influenced by the theories and methods developed by the "social group work" profession, on the basis of such principles as, "The groupworker aims to affect the group process so that decisions come about as the result of knowledge and the sharing and integration of ideas, experience and knowledge rather than as the result of domination from within or without the group."[7]

The problem of reconciling the philosophy of social group work in an institution in a Jewish setting and under Jewish auspices, but in the midst of a heterogenous community, with the maintenance of Jewish culture has been engaging the attention of the professional and lay personnel and is of concern to the federations. There remain for clarification such questions as the availability of the Jewish Center and its facilities to the non-Jewish populations of mixed neighborhoods, inter-racial clientele, and inter-cultural programs under Jewish auspices.[8]

A more pervasive question in some of the larger

A HERITAGE AFFIRMED

and intermediate cities has been the choice between a community Center program operating in a large general Center and in neighborhood branches, or a decentralized program with separate autonomous units under a variety of local auspices (synagogues, separate agencies, neighborhood groups, fraternal associations, etc.). In a number of cities a central service program has been established patterned on the community service programs of the Chicago and New York federations.

The difficulties in the matter of coordination in recent years have been indicated by David M. Goldenberg, associated with the Metropolitan section of JWB:

I am sorry to report . . . that the vast majority of Synagogue Centers affiliated with JWB consider the affiliation meaningless. In philosophy, ideology, and in their daily activities they do not consider themselves a part of the Jewish Center movement.[9]

The movement to the suburbs and the diffusion of the Jewish population in metropolitan areas, and the tendency for newly built synagogues to have institutional facilities for cultural and leisure time programs, have become challenges to federation communal planning in the community Center as well as in other fields. The improving economic status of the Jewish population utilizing Centers has also raised the question of how far these programs should be financed by the membership rather than through philanthropy.[10]

In many communities, federations and welfare funds also contribute to the support of other recreational and leisure-time programs, such as B'nai B'rith youth services. Some of the latter utilize the facilities of Jewish community Centers.

COMMUNITY RELATIONS ACTIVITIES

The programs designed to improve and maintain desirable relationships with other elements of the wider community have taken on greater importance in recent

306

years in practically all large and intermediate-sized cities, and in many of the organized smaller cities as well.

In the small and intermediate communities central federations usually conduct the public relations program under their own auspices. Many of the intermediate-sized and largest cities have established special agencies for this function. Of 40 small cities, 32 have formally organized programs—27 of these under federation auspices. Among 33 intermediate-sized communities, 18 have undertaken community relations activities through a department of a federation. Separate community relations agencies are financed by and are constituent members of the federation in 11 cities. In four cities, the community relations agency is organized separately and is not a constituent of federation; and it raises its own funds.

In three of the 12 largest cities—Cleveland, Los Angeles and Newark—the community relations agency is a part of the central federation. In Chicago there is no central public relations agency; the local program is conducted by the national agencies. In the other large cities the community relations function is organized as a separate local agency with federation support and financing. In New York City local programs are undertaken by the national community relations agencies, whose main offices are located in that city, and by the Brooklyn Community Council for that borough.

Although nearly all of the communities with a central communal structure engage in programs of community relations directly or through a constituent agency; there are wide variations in program. These depend upon the nature of local problems and of local interests. In some cities the program is limited to occasional activities; in others year-round education is undertaken to improve the climate of relationships among all religious, racial and cultural groups in the community.

Among the programs and activities reported by the various communities were: interest in local, state and federal health and welfare legislation, including measures against discrimination in employment; measures on immigration, refugees, and relations with Israel; released time in the public school for religious education; a concern with anti-Semitic incidents as they arise; investigation and combating of subversive groups and the support of a sustained program to promote intercultural education and desirable forms of interaction among local groups. Some of the programs also include activities concerned with internal Jewish group problems, such as studies and administration of *kashruth*, Jewish Arbitration Courts, improvement of business ethics and standards, and attempts to deal with allegations concerning a "Jewish vote."

A major problem was created for federation in the community relations field, when the program to coordinate national and local agency programs failed, resulting in the withdrawal of the American Jewish Committee and the B'nai B'rith Anti-Defamation League from the National Community Relations Advisory Council. The American Jewish Committee and the ADL maintain independent contacts with the local communities directly and through the Joint Defense Appeal, their common fundraising instrument. The MacIver Report, referred to in a previous chapter, reinforced the idea of a national center for public relations work and gave added influence to the NCRAC as such a center. The NCRAC's membership has grown to an association of six national agencies, forty-six local community relations councils, and three state-wide organizations helping to set standards and coordinate the work of local and national programs.

Competition for funds has continued among national agencies in this field of service, and the programs—nationally, regionally, or of local chapters—are not always effectively coordinated with the central local programs.

JEWISH EDUCATION

While the field of Jewish education is a relatively recent area of federation responsibility, it has become an accepted function of most of them within the last two decades. Federations sponsor and support Jewish education in about half of the cities with less than 5,000 Jews, conducting it either directly or under synagogue auspices. Three out of every four federations in the intermediate-sized cities of from 5,000 to 15,000 Jews support Jewish education through constituent agencies or departments of federation. Where Jewish educational agencies are separately organized and financed, the federation maintains a sympathetic interest in their programs, recognizing them as an acknowledged phase of community organization. Practically every federation in cities with over 15,000 Jewish population makes grants to Jewish education. Central bureaus for Jewish education are maintained and financed by federations in all of the large cities.

Since there are denominational variations in the local programs of Jewish education, federations generally do not identify with any particular school—Reform, Conservative, Orthodox, or Yiddish—but seek to aid in the development of common services and joint planning. The majority of the Jewish educational programs are conducted after public school hours or during weekend periods, but there has been some development of all-day programs on the pre-school and elementary school level and in at least one case (Philadelphia) on the secondary level too.

Jewish religious schools receive support from the congregations or other bodies under whose auspices they are conducted, the separate fund-raising activities undertaken through these auspices, and from payments for tuition. Many of the schools are completely financed by these methods; others have deficits. Federations supply funds to help meet these deficits in a number of cities.

Subsidies to the Jewish schools have raised in some communities the question of policy in regard to the all-day schools. In some places this has remained an unresolved issue. In others, the question has been met by the policy of limiting federations' responsibility for the deficits of the all-day schools to that part which arises from the Jewish rather than from the secular subjects in the curriculum.

However, in a recent examination of a community's responsibility for Jewish education, the Study Committee appointed by the Cleveland Jewish Community Federation recommended that within

normal budgetary limitations the policies applying to every other institution should also apply to the all-day school, and that the entire school program should be supported and not the Jewish studies alone. Difficulties in disentangling costs partly explained the reason for this decision, but more compelling was the feeling in the committee that, once committed to support of the all-day school, the community must be interested in high standards for the entire operation, since neither the Jewish nor the general education could exist in isolation.[11]

It cannot be predicted that this theory will soon become the basis of operation in other cities in the face of strong sentiments that persist against encouraging the growth of the all-day schools. The opposition cites the principle that secular education of Jewish youth should remain the province of the public school system.

Aside from this controversial question, the position that Jewish education is an important aspect of communal life, related to the whole range of communal interests and activities, is generally accepted. Federations are concerned with and are seeking to solve such problems as the shortage of qualified teaching personnel, the modernization of school programs, the improvement of standards, the extension of programs to the entire Jewish population and to all of the denominational groups, and the liquidation of school deficits. Federations have organized and financed local bureaus for Jewish education for overall services to this field and for the development of cooperation among competing denominational groups. Allocations for Jewish education more than doubled between 1946 and 1956 and have continued to increase.[19] Federations are increasing their support of the American Association for Jewish Education, the national service agency in the field.

A basic question involved in federation support of Jewish education is what part of the cost of education should come from tuition fees. Parents vary in their economic ability, but there is a shrinking fraction of students coming from dependent and marginal families. Charging tuition fees and getting support from synagogue funds have become the uniform practice of schools under congregational auspices. Should parents pay full costs; and should the communal financing be limited to raising standards and absorbing deficits which arise when scholarships are bestowed and when tuitions are lowered for children of low income families? On these points, the principle enunciated in the Cleveland study was the following:

Parents ought to bear a reasonable share of the cost. . . . Assessing the full per capita cost would make costs to the parents

311

difficult and in some cases prohibitive. Since the community has a vital stake in keeping as large a number of children within the school as possible, it is suggested that the parents and the community be considered partners. . . . The schools should realize in fees from parents as much of their costs as possible without depriving any child of the right to a Jewish education.[18]

The gradual evolution of basic principles of federation's responsibility for Jewish education has left unresolved many questions concerning the character and content of the courses of study and their aims. There is concern for the number of children who fail to attend or who receive very little instruction in terms of number of hours a week or duration of schooling. According to a recent survey undertaken by AAJE, Jewish education in the United States is "a mile wide but only an inch deep."

The principles of federation's responsibility which are the product of local experiences have not yet extended to the question of an integrated structure for the various Jewish school systems. Leaders in at least one large community, with a variety of new congregational schools beginning to supplant a previous structure of communal schools, believe that "it is desirable and feasible to develop a communal school system" on a generic basis and that "a communal system merits more generous support by the total community than do the variety of separate schools."[14] The trend, however, seems to be in the opposite direction in most cities, especially those with large suburban developments.

MAINTENANCE OF HEALTH AND WELFARE INSTITUTIONS

Institutional care under Jewish auspices for special classes of dependents has been a long-time tradition of Jewish populations. This has been particularly evident in the care of the dependent aged, the disabled, and dependent children. The majority of the organized communities assume responsibility for providing homes for such groups, either through congregate residences or other forms of care. If the group needing care is sufficiently large, special institutions are established or the federation assumes financial resonsibility for placement in homes under Jewish auspices in some community which has such facilities. Where homes under Jewish auspices arc not accessible or available, federations may, directly or through a constituent agency, assume responsibility for payment for such care in available private institutions. Free public institutions are occasionally utilized for the indigent, rarely for the dependent aged or children, somewhat more frequently for the disabled chronically ill. Treatment of mentally disturbed Jewish patients is generally obtained through state hospitals. In a few cities (primarily New York and Philadelphia) there are one or more special psychiatric hospitals developed for experimental services rather than for custodial care or long-term treatment.

The following is a current picture of Jewish welfare and health agencies and federation relationships:

HOMES FOR THE AGED

There are over 80 Jewish homes for the aged. Of these homes, five have been established in communities with less than 5,000 Jewish population; three of these are under federation sponsorship. There are 40 homes for the aged in 58 intermediate-sized cities (27 of these homes provide regional service) and 20 of these are constituents, beneficiaries, or members of the federation. There are 41 homes for the aged in 16 cities of over 40,000 population (13 of these homes provide regional service). Institutional services for the Jewish aged are being expanded in small and intermediate Jewish communities both through the building of a residence for such a purpose or the enlarging of an existing home. Of the 17 homes for the aged in New York City, three of the largest are beneficiaries of Federation and others are affiliated with the Central Bureau for the Aged, established and supported by the Federation.

Federations initially included only the homes for the aged that had been established under German Jewish and Reform group sponsorship. Homes under Orthodox and East-European group auspices were usually independent. A few of these homes were included in the federations in the 1920s and 1930s, either by conscious planning or by the merger of the newer and older groups. More recently, with the easing of class and group differences, homes established under Orthodox auspices have become constituents of local federations.

Homes for the aged under the auspices of religious or nationality groups were one of the last of the welfare institutions to respond to the influence of modern social work. Established as an improvement over the public almshouses, they bore a close resemblance to them for over a century. They generally did offer, however, a more acceptable environment for the homeless and dependent aged unwilling or unable to continue to live in their own homes. But medical care was either completely lacking or grossly inadequate and the social and leisure-time requirements of the aged were largely neglected.

An important factor impinging on the programs of the Jewish homes for the aged came through the family service agencies which were willing to provide funds to enable aged persons to remain in their own homes. In the more progressive federations, such aid in the 1920s began to be utilized for the ambulatory aged as a substitute for the institution. Offering to continue to support applicants for institutional care in their own homes where this form of care was more suitable, the family service agencies began to request the institutions for the aged to accept the disabled and chronically ill, and undertook to make case studies of the needs and resources of the applicants. The institutions were at first reluctant. But later, under federation influence, such relationships between the homes for the aged and the family agency were developed. In the large city with multiple agencies available for services to the aged, central bureaus or committees for the aged have been established to assure a growing cooperation among case work, institutional and medical services in behalf of the aged.

For a long time it had been the policy of homes for the aged to accept for care only the relatively able-bodied, and to reject physically disabled applicants. The institutions wanted to remain residences for the aged rather than become infirmaries for the chronically ill. However, as a natural consequence of the processes of aging, the homes rapidly filled with the disabled and senile chronically ill. It began to be obvious that the disabled even more than the able bodied, were not receiving proper care from the community. Beginning in the 1930s and the 1940s the development of governmental old age assistance and social security insurance made it possible for an increasing number of aged to remain in their own homes, with resources to pay for their care if they wanted a boarding arrangement, or to live in a private home for the aged.

There has been an increase of income for homes for the aged paid for by the residents. It derives from two factors:

1. As homes for the aged have improved and refined their services, they are increasingly serving persons of means, who choose to enter the homes because the standards on which they are run are now exceptionally high.

2. Public assistance, through old age assistance and public old age insurance programs, is serving an increasing proportion of persons in homes for the aged. Currently, something over 50% of all residents of Jewish homes for the aged, for example, are recipients of old age assistance. The proceeds of these public programs are paid to the homes for care of the residents.

More favorable economic conditions make it possible also to improve the physical plants and the living conditions in the communal institutions. Homes for the aged began to add beds for an increasing number of people, organize improved programs for social living, and add occupational therapy and recreational programs. They began also to pay more attention to health and medical needs and to obtain modern preventive and therapeutic medical services for improving the condition of their residents.

Homes for the aged are serving a substantial number of mildly senile persons, in some instances because of their admission policies, in others because of deterioration of residents after admission. Information available to the CJFWF indicates that between 20% to 40% of residents in Jewish homes for the aged may be classified as mildly senile.

Homes for the aged, family agencies and federations are increasingly concerned about the needs of older persons who require opportunities for more independent living than is provided in such homes. Several communities have already developed apartment house or residential club programs, thereby meeting primarily the need for housing and social life for older persons. A number of other communities are considering how the Jewish community can best discharge its responsibility in this area by exploring the facilities available under public and private auspices and the financing methods offered by governmental and other sources.

The manager and housekeeper type of home superintendent is being replaced by a professional with social welfare or hospital training and experience. A number of the more advanced homes for the aged have begun to develop improved infirmary departments and are accepted as institutions available to the disabled and chronically ill, as well as to the more able-bodied aged for whom institutional living is a satisfactory arrangement. A number have received accreditation as hospitals eligible for use by public welfare departments, under the provisions for assistance to the chronically ill. In two decades, Jewish homes for the aged under federation auspices have assumed leadership in their communities as outstanding examples of progressive development in this field of social welfare.[15]

HOSPITALS

There are approximately 80 Jewish-sponsored hospitals and other specialized medical institutions in operation in the United States and Canada, located in 35 cities or their outlying metropolitan areas. The list of these hospitals reporting to the CJFWF comprises 41 general and seven tuberculosis institutions (several of these are open to patients with other diseases), nine long-term, six psychiatric, and 15 other types of special hospitals and

317

institutions.[16] All cities with Jewish populations of 30,000, with the exception of Washington, D.C., have established a general hospital under Jewish auspices, as have also three cities with less than 15,000 and eight cities with from 14,000 to 40,000 Jewish population. In addition to Denver, where several Jewish national hospitals are located, there are two or more general and special hospitals or institutions in Baltimore, Boston, Chicago, Cincinnati, Cleveland, Louisville, Los Angeles, Montreal, Newark, Philadelphia, Pittsburgh, Toronto, and New York (which has 26 hospitals and institutions). Where there is more than one local hospital or specialized medical institution not all of them may be affiliated with the federations.

Medical services under federation auspices today represent the largest expenditure of the federation budget for local needs. The percentage of the federation budget spent in this field has been steadily on the increase. For the year 1959, close to 25% of the total funds available to federation for local purposes were spent on hospitals and other medical programs. Total Jewish hospital expenditures in 1953 had doubled over 1947, while patient day care had increased during the same period by only 21%.[17]

Private philanthropy, however, was responsible in 1959 for supplying less than 15% of the total cost of operating Jewish hospitals. Three-fourths of the cost is derived from payments received from patients able to pay for their care, and from third-party sources such as the Blue Cross. Some of the hospitals also receive public funds directly, this being an important fraction of the income of hospitals concerned with long-term care of psychiatric or tuberculous patients. (Public funds supplied 7.5% of operating income in 1959).

Changes in the nature of the Jewish hospital have

been both along scientific and economic lines. On the economic side, the community planning emphasis for hospital services in behalf of the indigent has shifted to the care of private patients, as the volume of totally free patient care has declined. The extent of payments for services ranges from 82% of the operating costs of the general hospitals, to 30 to 50% for the long-term and psychiatric hospitals (to less than 2% in the national hospitals for the tuberculous which have the policy of free care).

These changes on the economic side are leading to a re-examination of the basis of Jewish communal support. A conclusion reached by a recent conference of Jewish hospital leadership was that:

The rationale for a Jewish hospital has been enlarged. . . . It is now recognized that Jewish community needs for comprehensive and integrated medical care of good quality are a major determinant in planning health services under Jewish auspices. Adequate provision of such care requires a general hospital interested in and capable of extending medical care into many new directions. . . . Changes in program or emphasis are affected by general community health services as well as by Jewish communal needs.[18]

The same conference also concluded that Jewish hospitals were accepting increasingly the goal of scientific objectives for their institutions through teaching and research functions. They noted that expanded medical services were being demanded by many social agencies, especially homes for the aged and children's agencies, which may develop duplicating medical facilities unless the hospitals met these needs adequately; and that new arrangements were urgently needed to facilitate the transfer of patients between hospitals and other institutions.[19] A general recognition of the interrelationships of the communal medical and other welfare institutions, especially for adequate care of persons with long-term disabling illnesses, led to a study by the CJFWF of the coordination of facilities under Jewish auspices and community planning for the chronically ill, which was financed for a four-year period beginning in 1956 by a research grant from the United States Public Health Service.[20]

The concentrated attention being given to communal planning in the health field has been accompanied by a developing lay interest and a growing competence of the lay leadership to cooperate with the professional medical groups in the administration of health institutions.

The trustees of federations and hospitals have become major forces in shaping hospital services in the overall community interest. . . . The role of the welfare federation has expanded from financial support to planning for the overall community interest.[21]

With the recognition that an effectively coordinated medical and social welfare program would provide more satisfactory and more adequate care, and would be enabled to reach a larger clientele, federations have turned increasingly to the integration of medical services and the development of cooperative relationships among the various medical and social welfare agencies. There have been mergers of the physical and administrative resources of several medical institutions, as in St. Louis; the development of medical centers through administrative mergers, as in Philadelphia; or by collaboration, as in Baltimore and Chicago.

The general hospitals under Jewish auspices, in line with community practice, have a non-sectarian admission policy—as have some of the special hospitals on a more limited basis. Nevertheless, the prevailing attitude is that

programs of agencies

they are "sectarian institutions with a non-sectarian in-
take policy."[22] This raises the question of how to measure
the proper share of responsibility of the Jewish community for the medical needs of the Jewish population
and those of the total community. Contributions to voluntary hospitals under other than Jewish auspices are
derived from the community as a whole, including the
Jewish population; the latter, in turn, uses such institutions for medical care.[23] While some cities have attempted
to develop organized hospital planning and "Master
Plans," medical institutions in others have remained
largely individualistic and uncoordinated. There is for
this reason a basic interest in the research being conducted by CJFWF (referred to above) to analyze the
theories and experience in community planning and integration of facilities.

SERVICES TO FAMILIES AND INDIVIDUALS

Agencies under Jewish auspices which provide case
work and related services to families and individuals are
active in over one hundred cities. These agencies receive
support either from federation or through the local community chest with which the federation is affiliated
(from both sources in cities where chests assist "ongoing'" programs and federations refugee services—or
where there is other sharing). In addition to agencies
which operate with one or more professional workers,
family services are available on a limited basis in practically all other federations through either volunteers,
or are provided by the federation or Center executive.

In addition to case work and counseling services,
family agencies sometimes offer visiting housekeeper and
homemaker services, free loans, special aid in setting up
self-support projects, and educational scholarships. In

321

fifty-two cities the family agency and the child care agency, in many cases previously under separate auspices, are now combined in a multiple service agency which assists families and children in their own homes or places children in suitable boarding homes, provides adoption services and makes other special arrangements.

Providing economic assistance to families has been a declining aspect of the programs of family service agencies. A large part of their effort is now devoted to helping individuals and families solve various personal difficulties. Following the establishment of a national public aid system, the relief-giving role of the Jewish family service agencies has perceptibly decreased. For a number of years the refugee immigrants made it necessary for large-scale programs of relief; but with the decline of refugee immigrants, the giving of relief has again become a smaller aspect of the work of these agencies. For the year 1959, receipts of 70 family service agencies reporting amounted to over $9,466,000, of which 82% came from federations and community chests. Less than one-fourth of the income was disbursed as financial assistance or for payment of services obtained by agencies from various sources; about one-third of this amount was assistance to recent immigrants.[24]

A number of questions concerning the development of family services are receiving consideration; among them the following:

1. With the decline in the function of financial assistance, and with current emphasis on helping families with problems that are not necessarily economic in character or origin, what is the relationship of the family service agencies to child guidance and mental hygiene clinics, to the psy-

chiatric programs of hospital and outpatient services, and to other personal services available under various auspices?

2. What are the relationships between the family service agencies and case work services being made available in homes for the aged, community Centers, hospitals and outpatient clinics, special child care institutions, etc.?

3. Are case work and counseling services by Jewish agencies, like patient care in Jewish hospitals, a type of non-sectarian service available under sectarian auspices, or are such agencies invested with special responsibility for advancing Jewish cultural interests?

4. The developing tendency on the part of case work agencies to charge fees for service from those able to pay (this has not yet resulted in any large development of self support—about 3% of total income in 1959), and the rise of private case work practitioners in the larger cities, may in time necessitate definition of the functions of case work agencies under communal auspices and of the role of individual practitioners in psychiatry and psychology.

With the focus of interest today on family and individual personal and emotional problems, on husband-wife and parent-child relationships, on behavior problems of children and other aspects of personal maladjustment, it is obvious that there is a continuing need for programs of service seeking to help people with these difficulties and to represent the interest of the community in people and their needs. In 1958, the family and child care agencies received 22%, the recreational agencies 23% and the hospitals and health agencies 24% of the federation's funds spent for local purposes.[25]

There have been differences of opinion among the leaders of family agencies, and between federations and family agencies, as to whether concrete assistance programs and facilities could be considered as primary and as basic as their counseling services. With the evolution of theories of case work which recognize the validity of the family service agency offering both counseling and tangible aids to adjustment (such as the installation of homemakers, special loans, home-finding, etc.), which are not otherwise organized and available in the community, this question is being resolved. The use of case workers in institutions for the aged, and in hospitals and other agencies, has made it possible for case work to be integrated with some medical and residential services.

CHILD CARE SERVICES

In the majority of cities services to children, involving placement in foster homes, are available from the combined Jewish family and children's service agencies. Separate agencies for children are still to be found only in ten cities. In addition, there are three agencies serving children on a regional basis and one national institution open to children with special problems.[26] There are today only 20 institutions under Jewish auspices, located in 12 cities, serving on a local or regional basis. Several of these are small special treatment homes with from three to 18 children. In 1929, there were 60 institutions.[27] There has been a continuing decline in the number of children served by both institutional and foster home agencies.[28]

Child serving agencies are increasingly assuming

responsibility for seriously disturbed children—through psychiatric services in clinics and residential treatment centers, through special day care programs, and through specialized foster homes and group homes. In a number of cities the institutions for child care services are concentrating on children with such special problems. Other cities, lacking institutions for the seriously disturbed children, are utilizing the regional agencies or the specialized institutions in the larger cities which accept a limited number of such children at the expense of the referring community.

Payment for services to children (mostly for placement) has been increasing, amounting to 50% of total operating income, including 42.6% from public funds and 7.5% from payments for service. Public welfare departments are assuming an increased responsibility for paying the cost of care for dependent children placed under voluntary agency auspices.[29]

The sharp decline over the years in the number of Jewish children that needed to be placed outside of their own homes or homes of relatives has been attributed to: improved economic conditions, the low birth rates of the 1930s, lower mortality rates among adults in the 20 to 60 year age groups, and the availability of public assistance to needy families. By 1960 there has thus far been no sharp rise in the volume of children under care, in spite of an increase in the birth rate since 1945 and the subsequent increase in Jewish population. This is explained by the continuance of favorable vital statistics, economic and other factors. Some observers, however, believe that while the number of children requiring special services will decline still further, the rise in the birth rate of the last ten years may reverse the trend in another ten years.[30] Agencies, however, are reporting a higher incidence of difficult problem children being referred to them, and increasing costs of providing adequate care for such problem cases. For this and other reasons the maintenance of an adequate program of child care services continues to be a major responsibility of federations, especially those located in large centers of population.

ADOPTIONS

The agencies serving children also utilize the procedure of adoption for children whose parents are deceased or, as in the case of the unmarried mother, willing to give up guardianship. A number of agencies are licensed to provide adoption services. In New York, there is a separate agency, the Louise Wise Services, specializing in the care of the unmarried mother and the adoption of children. Agencies receive a considerable volume of requests from prospective adoptive parents. The number of Jewish children available for adoption has been very small, largely because of the low incidence in the number of children born out of wedlock to Jewish mothers. Some agencies are seeking ways to make available children who might otherwise be placed through non-social-agency channels, the so-called black or gray markets, and are also placing some older or handicapped children formerly not considered suitable for adoption.

VOCATIONAL SERVICES

Federations help to finance Jewish vocational service agencies with full-time professional staffs in twenty-one communities, thus constituting a major focus on the economic adjustment problems of Jews in those places. These agencies supplement the placement services of the state public employment systems and the vocational guidance programs being developed in the public schools. Although they aim to serve the entire community, there is usually priority for the clients of social agencies and the difficult-to-place job seekers. In cooperation with community Centers, synagogues and other groups, group guidance programs are made available. In a number of cities sheltered workshops and special rehabilitation services are undertaken directly or in cooperation with other local service agencies.

In the current period of economic prosperity, the interest in the maintenance of special vocational services has been sustained. But concern is less than in the years of the business depression, when anti-Semitism and discrimination appeared as greater threats to the occupational careers of Jews than they do today. The current emphasis of these agencies, which accounted for 3.4% of local federation costs, is on economic objectives and appears to have little of Jewish significance.[31]

OTHER SERVICES

In addition to the categories listed above, other services received 1.8% of federation funds in 1958. Included in this group are the Free Loan Societies that were established by practically every Jewish community as the expression of mutual aid and philanthropy which had been developed over many centuries by congregations in Europe and were then transplanted to this country. In a few cities these loan societies, which by Jewish Law and tradition charge no interest, receive subsidies from federation. Some have been merged with the family agency, but they are mainly separate organizations.

Improving economic conditions have made free small loans less important for family and personal needs, but they still are a useful source of funds for small business ventures and self-support activities, and of real advantage as a substitute for commercial small loans with their high interest rates. The practice of making free loans available only on endorsements from acceptable sources limits the range of such free loan programs.

With improving economic conditions, shelters for transients (another survival of traditional European communal philanthropy) are now also more limited in character and extent. There are programs for transients under municipal and other auspices, utilized to a limited extent by Jewish transients, but shelters under Orthodox auspices continue to function in a number of cities. Services to transients under federation auspices in most cities do not consist of special institutional facilities, but may include case work services, occasional financial aid, and the use of hotels, boarding homes, and non-sectarian shelters.

In many cities there is a considerable amount of help given to transient applicants at Orthodox synagogues and from unorganized sources. In general, it is indicated that the volume of the dependent transient population has sharply declined during the post-war period. Jewish family agencies in 1958 gave a little over 1% of their relief funds to the transient group.

Student and scholarship funds are limited, but are given allocations from federations in a number of communities. Fifty-four federations in 1959-60 joined in financing a joint National Scholarship Fund established by the CJFWF, to recruit students for graduate schools of social work, to help overcome the severe shortage of personnel in Jewish welfare agencies. Other scholarships have been established by individuals or groups and have limited programs. A number of scholarship funds operating on a non-sectarian basis have also been established by Jews.

XV

Federation and the
Local Community

Over the course of years the federation has thus been an important communal institution serving vital interests through a broad range of activities. Its economic function, that of obtaining and distributing philanthropic funds, has made it the focal point of welfare programs. In small cities it has an important role because it is frequently the only vehicle for Jewish group expression. In the many cities where the functions of raising funds for local and for non-local purposes are interlocked, federation again plays a major role. In large cities, where the multiplicity of groups presents a danger of haphazard organization, the federation stands out as a beacon light of cooperative action.

Federation's role impinges on many people: on all who are solicited for contributions and on those who contribute, on the corps of volunteers assisting in the processes of fund-raising, on the members of boards and of committees engaged in supervising and guiding the services financed by federation, on the unaffiliated agencies with programs related to the functions of the federation and its constituent agencies, and on the personnel of the federation and its constituents. All of these relationships involve personal factors and many different kinds of formal and informal associations. As a natural consequence of these relationships among agencies and individuals, federations have become aware of the need to avoid difficulties and to foster constructive interactions. For these reasons some federations have been charged with timidity and with lack of aggressive initiative.

RELATIONSHIP TO CONTRIBUTORS

The function of federation as a fund-gathering agency rests on the assumption that it has a legitimate and socially sanctioned role as an instrument of philanthropy in behalf of all individuals who identify themselves as Jews. Giving is voluntary; no one can be compelled legally to contribute to federation; the individual must be motivated to do so on the basis of inherent or external stimuli. Studies have been made of the contributor and the non-contributor to Jewish philanthropy and to philanthropy in general. It would appear from these studies that, while the exercise of the charitable response is rooted in the history and traditions of practically all religious and secular groups, there is considerable diversity in the extent and nature of the philanthropic habit, that is, how much the individual contributes, to what causes, and in what ways.[1]

Organized forms of individual help and group services can be considered substitutions for and extensions of what might, in a simple form of society, be person-to-person activity. To perform the same service in our contemporary urban society an individual must become a member or contributor in a complex pattern of social welfare activities. If the social agency is to be accepted as the intermediary in this function, those who are responsible for its operation must meet the requirements of trusteeship. They must represent the cultural values and attitudes of the individuals whom they seek to enlist, as well as be able to assure them that they will conduct the affairs of the agency honestly and competently, and serve group rather than personal interests. From these requirements has come the policy of having unpaid volunteer boards of trustees to assume the obligation of being answerable to all the actual and potential contributors. Functioning under the conditions set by the general community and incorporated under state laws, welfare organizations must also meet standard legal requirements of purpose, program, responsibility of officers and boards, and of fiscal practices, in order to qualify as welfare agencies established on a non-profit basis.

The personnel and composition of the board therefore must be such as to elicit the confidence of the contributor that these basic requirements are being met. The values that the individual board members personally represent, the variations and range of these values (if the contributing group is more or less heterogeneous in composition), the length of tenure of officers and trustees (to correspond to the emergence of new groups and new attitudes) are among the factors that determine acceptance or rejection of the trusteeship group.

There is a tendency for large organizations, that have for a long time held the confidence of the public, to take on an impersonal character and for the title of the organization rather than the names on the letterhead to become the touchstone to general acceptance. The way in which such an organization develops will then depend upon the character of the administrative group itself. This may make for a relatively static condition—until some issue arises, through changing external factors, such as may affect the prevailing attitude toward what was formerly fully accepted agency function or program. Among the Jewish federations few, if any, even in the largest cities, have reached this stage of impersonality of organization; in most cities a direct personal interest is maintained on the part of large numbers of contributors in the federation program and affairs.

The two categories of procedure developed by federations to assure vital, constructive and continuing relationships with contributors and potential contributors are the following: one, various forms of publicity and communication; and, two, the process of selecting officers and board. Few federations limit their publicity to the fund-raising campaign period to stimulate interest in the causes and agencies for which the federation seeks funds. Instead, they engage in an all year around communication program, in which they seek to advise the public of the needs and work of the federation and its constituent and beneficiary agencies.

Utilized are printed items, photographs, the general and Jewish press, special periodicals, radio and television. Many federations publicize their allocations to beneficiary agencies and their other administrative actions; publish lists of contributors and other data; organize visits to agencies, plan study groups, lectures, forums, and make use of other devices for fostering closer contacts between themselves, their agencies and the public.[2]

There are special sections of the community for whom a more intensive program is undertaken. These include the corps of solicitors, the key givers, the active personnel in trade and neighborhood groups, the leadership of congregational and fraternal bodies, women's, youth and other group organizations. It is among these elements that the federation obtains its active workers and from which it recruits its leadership. The currents of opinion engendered within such active leadership groups will generally determine the attitude that will prevail in the general population toward federation and its program.

While the procedures for the selection of officers and boards vary among federations, an annual election is the most common practice. Some constitutions provide for independent nominations as well as for selection by a committee appointed by the board. The selection by the nominating committee is publicized in advance. When there is a contest arising from an independent slate, the by-laws provide for a direct secret vote at the annual meeting; but in practice, contests have been rare, and the choices of the nominating committee are usually accepted by a voice vote.

The tenure of officers is usually for one year, and some federations limit re-election to not more than three consecutive terms. Three years is the prevailing term for board membership, except in the case of directors of beneficiary agencies, who are usually chosen on a one-year basis. Many federations limit board membership to two consecutive terms of three years.

MOTIVATIONS OF CONTRIBUTORS

The basic factors which underlie the philanthropic responses of a population are both intrinsic in the nature of the programs of the supported agencies, and extrinsic, relating to the many different kinds of psychological reaction arising from the individual and group interrelations. When the program of the federation was concentrated upon giving monetary assistance through agencies for family, child care, aged and medical services, the basis of the response to philanthropy was simple and direct, ingrained in the traditions and history of the Jewish group. The giving of charity was a virtue (*mitzvah*) and the federation and the agencies served as the means for expressing this virtue.

The federation does not face the obstacle of divided group allegiances for its program, since practically all federations now include agencies under Orthodox, Reform and other group sponsorship. There may be greater interest on the part of some contributors in the program of a hospital, or of a home for the aged, or of a children's or family service, and representatives of such special interest may seek to influence the processes of fund allocation to favor their particular interest; but this allocating usually remains within the administrative group and does not affect the general run of contributors. Most contributors are likely to have a vague and diffuse interest in all the programs. This was illustrated in a study of contributors' attitudes to the New York Federation, where motivations for giving were shown to be associated with feelings of general communal obligation. The study also revealed that concern for the status, responsibility and dignity of the Jewish community outweighed the responses of contributors deriving from specific satisfactions felt in helping people in need.

With the extension of federation to programs of Jewish education, youth services, community Center and leisure-time activities and community relations, and with the wider use being made of hospitals, homes for the aged and other service agencies by all sections of the population, the charitable function has been enlarged and now includes self-help and mutual aid motives. With this change have come problems of ideological differences, especially concerning Jewish education (which have now been resolved in practically all communities).

There was danger also of conflict in welfare fund development: over the national and overseas programs which brought to the fore the issues between Zionists and those who opposed Zionism, between the supporters of Orthodox and of Reform agencies; but these have become much less important during the last decade. Some of the contributors may have a deep interest in some agencies that conduct independent appeals, and these appeals may enlist the participation of selected groups in the population as campaign workers and as givers. For the most part, however, the supporters of independent appeals continue also as the workers and givers to the federation campaign which raises funds for similar and sometimes for the same agencies on a partial budgetary basis.

RELATIONS TO LEADERSHIP GROUP

The attitudes toward federation that may be vague and diffused among the general contributing group become sharpened and articulate within the leadership group, including both those in the family of the federation and its constituent agencies and those in the leadership of other groups concerned with Jewish interests. This was evident in studies of a cross section of the leadership group in Albany, Camden and New Britain.[3] While there were some differences in the attitudes expressed, the studies reported "a general acceptance of the central community organization as the agent of the community for meeting common needs" and "genuine respect" for the central body, which was "given credit for bridging many group conflicts" and fostering cooperation among various elements.

The central agency in these cities was generally considered to be representative and to tend toward wide inclusion of all responsible groups; but some felt that there was an inherent tendency toward giving undue weight to wealth and social position in the selection of leadership. The democratic qualities of the organizations were generally acknowledged, although there were complaints about apathy and weariness in the population, lack of clarity concerning the objectives of the central agency and over-organization. There were also complaints that the service programs of federation were too often considered secondary to the concern with fund-raising and that the leaders were usually selected on the basis of their giving ability or campaign activity rather than because of their knowledge of or interest in the program of federation services.

There were differences of opinion also in the leadership group about the opportunities for participation in the affairs of federation. The majority believed that the opportunities were ample for all those who desired to be active. On the one hand, some of the board members believed that opportunity to lead was open for those who wanted to work, but because of campaign fatigue "there is far too little participation and response to the federation's need for workers," leaving the task always "to the same small group." On the other hand, there was criticism of the lack of opportunity for the younger group to succeed the veterans in charge of affairs, and an assertion of the need for a conscious effort to recruit and enlist new leadership. It was also mentioned that there was little opportunity for public discussion and debate of the issues.

The present scope of central agency activities was generally approved. In one city there was general approval of present aims, but opposition to further extension of federation functions. The exactly opposite view, however, was held by some individuals in this and in the other cities, who suggested new functions and programs for their federations.

The pilot studies of leadership attitudes were made in two cities of 9,000, and one of under 4,000 Jewish population, but it is believed that the findings are typical not only for other small and intermediate-sized cities but also for considerably larger ones. What is evident is that there is a community leadership group both in federation and outside of it sufficiently concerned with Jewish affairs to have an active interest in and definite views about many phases of community life. It is probable that their interest is shared, perhaps to a lesser degree, by many others. In any event, it is through these leadership groups, and the overt or implied expression of their attitudes and views, that the federation becomes aware of underlying currents of opinion to which it needs to respond if it is to continue as a dynamic agency.

In answer to a questionnaire received from sixty officers and trustees of federations, welfare funds and leading national agencies, considerable dissatisfaction was expressed that "we have made little progress in the creation of dynamic forums of public opinion and in securing a wide base of involvement in arriving at community decisions."[4]

DEVELOPMENT OF LEADERSHIP

With the American environment conducive to fluid and changing conditions, the agencies and institutions take on tremendous importance in the cultural life of the group. Under modern conditions cultural traditions are only partially transmitted within the family, and each new generation must be related to the group culture through other institutions. The difficulties in obtaining interest in and support for the agencies and institutions that serve the cultural aspirations of a group are not nearly so great as those involved in securing and maintaining a leadership able and willing to devote the time, talents, and enthusiasm which are necessary to institutional vitality and growth. The communal agencies offer opportunities for status and prestige for individuals from an ethnic group or religious denomination that cannot attain these as readily in other phases of civic or social life.

It is not sufficient that a leader be imbued with the will to maintain the agencies and institutions, or that he enjoy the group's approval for his willingness to assume group responsibilties. In a changing and dynamic situation, the leader can only perform his tasks effectively and responsively if he is sensitive to group values and aspirations, and able to relate these to the current necessities of individual and communal living.

This fact was clearly recognized by those who, in response to the question whether community organizations were keeping pace with the communities, expressed a fear that there may be a widening gap between the federation and the daily interests of its members.[5] This results, perhaps, from the problems of the federation in securing and maintaining the interest of the "alert and keen young people" absorbed by other interests than those involved in Jewish communal organizations.[6] One national leader stated that he was "more worried about the absence of thoroughly informed, properly motivated and zealously devoted leaders in our community than about almost anything else that I can think of at the moment."[7] However, the identification of this need and the continued devotion of the present leadership were thought to afford the hope that a vital relationship could be maintained between the communal institutions and a potential key leadership required for the community's future.

Federations have not been content merely to hope for new leadership. In scores of cities they have developed carefully planned and intensively executed programs to recruit able young men and women for community service, have organized training programs to inform them of the needs and services of the federations and their beneficiary agencies—local, national, and overseas—have arranged for them then to take their places on the committees and boards of the federations and their constituent organizations. Some of the current officers and campaign chairmen are the products of these efforts.

The recruitment has come from the ranks of campaign solicitors, and from persons who have been neither solicitors nor contributors. Concentration in some cities has been on interesting "young executives"—men in their late twenties or thirties—who already have demonstrated outstanding achievement in their businesses and professions. Their training has included monthly meetings where they: hear about the work of major agencies or fields of service from the lay and professional leaders, raise questions about their programs and policies, visit the agencies to observe their work at first hand, meet with the staff and officers of federation to discuss their special personal interests in communal service, so that these can be considered when the young people are considered for appointment or election to a committee or board post.

To foster and assist this progress throughout the country, the CJFWF in 1958 established a national Committee on Leadership Development. Composed of representatives of such programs in over forty cities, the committee collects and distributes information on the

most successful local leadership programs, brings together new young leaders for direct exchange of views in
regional and national meetings, and issues periodic reports on leadership development.[8]

A growing number of communities—twenty-seven
by the end of 1960—have established special awards to
outstanding new young leaders, enabling them to go to
the General Assembly of the CJFWF and share with
leaders from other cities of the United States and Canada
in pooling their experience and judgment on major
communal responsibilities.

These special leadership development programs are
in addition to the efforts which federations have been
making for the past two decades to help educate youth
regarding communal needs and services through programs in religious schools, young adult divisions in campaigns, and year-round activities for high school and
college youth.

THE FEDERATION AND ITS CONSTITUENT AGENCIES

While the relationship of federation to its general
public may be diffuse, relationships with individuals responsible for the operation of the constituent and beneficiary agencies are manifold and direct. The objectives
of the federation and those of the functioning agency
programs must be brought into some kind of compatibil-
ity, the ability of the federation to raise funds must be
reconciled with the legitimate aspirations of the agencies,
and cooperation must be developed between those who
have an interest in one or another specific program and
those with wider interests.

As the ideal of an integrated program of community
services replaced the earlier concept of unrelated agencies, federations have faced their responsibility for

achieving this goal. Efforts previously limited to *ad hoc* by-products of the budgeting processes have been reinforced by measures taken to provide continuing study of and specific devices for getting agency and federation representatives together for achieving a high degree of mutual understanding and cooperation.

A large share of responsibility for coordinating federation and agency aims falls upon the federation executive, whose function in communal planning is being recognized as having importance as great as his functions in fund-raising. In some large cities there may be a division of responsibility among the executive personnel, with some concentrating on welfare planning and others on the raising of funds. In the smaller communities the volunteers may assume more responsibility for fund-raising, leaving the executive free to devote himself to the planning function, or vice versa.

On the basis of experience, federations have generally arrived at a working relationship with the constituent agencies. The details of agency administration, technical procedures, responses to scientific progress and professional development are left to the autonomy of the functional agencies. The federation accepts responsibility for financial trusteeship and auditing, and for maintaining a constant awareness of the nature of and the shifts in the program activities of the agencies.

There are differences of opinion about matters for which the federation and the agency both have responsibility, such as: what elements of the population should be served and what conditions laid down for eligibility for service, what policies followed on payments for service and/or free care, what will be the range of services and what the relationship of services under Jewish auspices to services under public or non-sectarian auspices.

It is frequently difficult to reconcile differences of opinion that arise over such questions, as well as over the constant obligation of federation to distribute its funds equitably among the various claimants for communal support.

The fact that the agencies have given up their supporting contributors, or never had them, and that they therefore fear that they have no alternative but to accept the fiscal decisions of the federation, has tended to place some agencies in what they consider to be a weak bargaining position. Most federations recognize, however, that a healthy agency needs public acceptance and an active and effective board, and are willing to assist the agency in meeting these needs. Generally the condition of mutuality is recognized: the agencies need the federation, and the federation is inherently a structure built for the needs of the agencies. This growing recognition of mutuality is the underlying basis which helps to reconcile differences and to achieve the compromises necessary to perpetuate a continued healthy functioning of the federation structure and its parts.

FEDERATION-SYNAGOGUE RELATIONSHIPS

Observers have noticed that areas of common interest which are shared by the Jewish federation and the local synagogues have been increasing in extent and importance. This arises from the changing nature of Jewish congregations and their synagogue functions, and the growing concern of federation with the agencies engaged in Jewish education and cultural services. From this confluence of interests we may expect developments in the nature of communal organization that have not been in evidence in American Jewish life since the 1880s.

For nearly three-quarters of a century problems

of great importance to Jewish communal life have been intensified by the rapid increase of the Jewish population and the complexity of its problems. The need of newcomers for health and welfare services, economic and social absorption and cultural adjustment to American life, the community's need for group defense against anti-Semitism and the large demands for overseas help impelled organization on a community-wide rather than on a congregational basis. For many decades the great diversity and number of religious institutions, related to countries of origin and periods of immigration, were an effective obstacle against utilizing congregations as units of communal organization. Further, many Jews were not affiliated with congregations. The federations which organized plans to meet the needs of these programs were therefore not established on an inter-congregational basis. During this period synagogues concentrated on religious, cultural and ethical areas, with emphasis on facilities for worship and group ritual.

The division of responsibility for these many years between the federations and the congregations seemed logical, and for the most part operated acceptably to both types of institutions. The cooperation of congregations was obtained by federations and by welfare agencies for fund-raising campaigns and for moral backing and support. Leaders of congregations, temple and synagogue sisterhoods and brotherhoods were mobilized for a variety of voluntary services in behalf of the welfare programs. A discussion at the 1935 General Assembly of the CJFWF by two leading rabbis and a layman indicated a growing dissatisfaction with the sharp separation of functions, and forecast the process of realignment which was beginning to take place.[9]

In the post-war period the factors underlying these

relationships were beginning to show evidences of change. Denominational differences among the synagogues were becoming less acute, and older small synagogues were being replaced by larger institutional units. Residents in new suburban areas were organizing and establishing synagogues and congregations to function as the centers of Jewish communal life. It was natural for such congregations to develop increasing responsibility for Jewish education and for recreational and cultural activities.

At the same time that these developments in congregational and synagogue functions were taking place, federations were extending their interest in Jewish education and federation agencies were becoming more deeply involved in cultural aspects in general. Where previously the focus of Jewish Centers had been on the social adjustment of recent immigrants, there was now an increasing emphasis on the Jewish content of the recreational and educational activities, on informal Jewish education, on advancement of group interests, and on personality development.

These trends may be said to add up to a period of transition during which there are signs of an increasing rapprochement between the federations and the synagogues. There are difficulties to be overcome in working toward mutually satisfactory relationships. But both in Jewish education as well as in social Center activities improvements in professional quality of personnel and in economy of operation can be achieved if such programs are planned on a community-wide basis rather than unilaterally by a multiplicity of synagogues.

Federations are starting to meet the challenge of separate congregational activities by extending services from the welfare agencies in the center of the city to the suburbs and outlying areas. There is a gradual recognition of the values of both communal programs and congregational units. We are beginning to see the possibilities of developing federation as a general instrument for communal organization which will include more pervasive and more direct relationships with synagogues. Perhaps, in the future, congregations, especially in the suburbs, may become the district units of the metropolitan federation. There is already a very close relationship between the synagogue and the welfare federation in many small communities.[10]

EXTERNAL RELATIONSHIPS

Federation also operates in the setting of the general American community. There are, therefore, important relationships with the public and non-sectarian agencies operating in the field of the federation's range of interests. The field includes the community chests and councils of social agencies, the agencies for local economic and social planning, and the general public which is concerned with communal welfare and constitutes the contributors to the various philanthropic programs. While all of these relationships exist, there are considerable variations in the degree of awareness of them both within the Jewish community and among the various segments of the general population and their social institutions.

COMMUNITY CHESTS, UNITED FUNDS AND COUNCILS OF SOCIAL AGENCIES

The creation of community chests, united funds and councils of social agencies (patterned after Jewish federations established two decades earlier) extending since 1914 to all parts of the country—nearly 2,100 chests and united funds were members of UCFC in 1960 —has given practically all cities a form of organization relating to and in part overlapping those of the Jewish federations. Most federations or local Jewish service agencies organized on a professional basis receive allocations from their local chests. Federations operating local services on a volunteer basis may receive chest funds for relief or other special purposes in some of the smaller cities.

The importance of the community chests and united funds in the financing of local Jewish health and welfare agencies and Jewish Centers is indicated in the statistics of federation financing. Excluding Jewish education, chests in the year 1958 provided 47% and Jewish federations 53% of the funds allocated by 93 federations to their local beneficiary agencies. (The relative percentages vary considerably among the various cities and a number of federations in smaller cities are not in chests.)

Out of 79 cities with Jewish populations of under 5,000, Jewish agencies in 33 received annual allocations of funds from their local chests in 1958. Since chests generally limit their scope to health and welfare agencies and exclude support of religious programs, Jewish educational agencies are not eligible for chest support. In some cities chests likewise do not help finance recreational programs under sectarian auspices, such as YMCAs and YMHAs. Allocations are given by chests to hospitals for inpatient services in only a small number of cities.

The fiscal and planning relationships between chests and Jewish federations vary in different communities. Of 45 intermediate cities with Jewish populations of 5,000 to 40,000, Jewish agencies and federations receive funds from the local chests in 43. In some, the chest-grants go directly to the individual agencies; in others, the chests transmit the funds to the federations for distribution to the agencies, or the funds help meet part of the federations' own administrative costs. There are similar variations of procedure among cities of over 40,000 Jewish population, with perhaps greater recognition by the community chests of the role of the federation as the central Jewish planning, fund-raising and budgeting instrument.

The original basis on which community chests were organized, namely, that they would assume financial responsibility for all legitimate local services requiring philanthropic support and thereby obviate the need for separate fund-raising campaigns has not materialized in most cities. The community chests usually limited themselves to welfare agencies and excluded the essentially religious institutions. Jewish federations therefore found that they could not look to the chests for the financing of Jewish educational agencies or other agencies with a basically religious orientation, or of new agencies such as Jewish vocational services established in some cities after the original inclusion of Jewish agencies by the chests. In adition, the limits of chest funds have made it necessary for Jewish federations to supply a part of the annual maintenance costs even for chest-included agencies and for other Jewish agencies—such as hospitals—outside the scope of some chests.

Nevertheless, most chests do not consider themselves partial or supplementary sources of support for welfare agencies, except for those in New York and Chicago which are organized on that limited basis. They do consider themselves central fiscal and planning bodies. While variations in agency auspices are recognized, as is the justification for differentials, there are difficulties in applying flexibility to the criteria for determining needs

347

and costs of the programs of their beneficiary agencies.

It is difficult for the chests to accept the fact that a health or welfare program costs more under one than under another type of auspices, or to acknowledge that the Jewish federation should be given priority in planning for a Jewish family service, recreational Center or home for the aged.

While a *modus operandi* has been established between Jewish federations and community chests in most cities, it is not necessarily one that completely satisfies either party. In some cities Jewish federations were organized later than the chests and after chest relationships to beneficiary Jewish agencies had become established. On account of these factors, federations in some cities of 15,000 to 40,000 Jewish population report "a lack of clear-cut relationship" between the chest and the Jewish agencies subventioned by it. Out of this have come a number of unsettled questions concerning relationships between the federation and the beneficiary agencies. Some federation leaders believe that the chests have an incomplete understanding of the scope and objectives of the central Jewish communal agency. In spite of the unresolved problems and lack of clarity existing in many cities, "no changes in chest relationship were contemplated."[11]

There are variations in the way that federated fund-raising by chests and social welfare planning by councils of agencies are organized. In some cities the chest and the council are integrated; but for the most part, they have separate structures. Even in the latter case the chest and council may share the same executive staff. In general, the leadership of Jewish federations and Jewish agencies participates actively in both chests and councils,

348

with many serving as officers and on important committees.

Federations and their constituent agencies cooperate with other local welfare groups in maintaining and developing effective relationships between the voluntary and the public systems of social welfare. They are concerned with the planning, extension and improvement of the governmental health and welfare services, the adequacy and effectiveness of public assistance measures, payments for the services which voluntary agencies render to individuals for whom the public agencies have accepted financial responsibility. There is close cooperation among the members of councils of social agencies in promoting federal and state action on welfare measures, tax exemptions for philanthropic gifts, social insurance proposals, housing and slum clearance and the basic programs of health, education and welfare.

The CJFWF has recognized this role of federations through the establishment of a national committee on public welfare, to analyze public welfare and health developments and proposals affecting Jewish agencies, to recommend national and local action on them, and to assist federations in setting up similar committees and programs of their own.[12]

In common with the social welfare systems under other voluntary auspices, Jewish programs have adapted themselves to the responsibilities and functions which governments have assumed for health and welfare. However, differences have arisen on some matters—for example, as to whether voluntary agencies should supplement assistance given by public agencies which have assumed responsibility for providing income on the basis of theoretical family budgets. (Some public departments will compute the assistance given by voluntary agencies on the same basis as help from relatives and subtract such amounts from the relief grant, thus effectively preventing such supplementation.) In other cities voluntary agencies may agree not to supplement public assistance, either because they lack the resources or on the assumption that in refraining they somehow induce the public welfare system to become more adequate.

While there is an acknowledged basis for the division of responsibility between voluntary and governmental agencies and between Jewish agencies and public and non-sectarian programs, it has been frequently suggested that certain health and welfare functions now performed by agencies under Jewish auspices could properly be transferred to government or to non-sectarian groups. Such criticism is usually directed to functions performed under Jewish auspices which do not involve any considerable element of what has been called "Jewishness," that is, where the nature of a professional service involves little, if any, differentiated cultural component. Thus, it is conceded that a sectarian environment is desirable for housing aged persons and essential for rearing children. The need, however, for separate Jewish institutions or outpatient service for general medical care, child or family counseling or recreational facilities, is sometimes questioned.

A widespread tendency among Jewish individuals and families to utilize health and welfare services under public or non-sectarian auspices is frequently offered in support of such criticisms. On the other hand, the need of opportunities for professional development, such as in hospital internships, the requirements of group responsibility and prestige, the objective of utilizing institutions as a means for Jewish communal living rather than as ends in themselves are given as arguments for continuing the types of health and welfare programs under Jewish auspices which bear a very close resemblance to or duplicate services under non-sectarian or public auspices.[13]

XVI

Intercity Cooperation and Relations with National Agencies

Although each federation was initiated locally and related itself primarily to its own area, it is not locally limited in the range of its interests; nor is it isolated from other localities. Each city wants to know what is taking place elsewhere and to share in regional, national and overseas responsibilities; consequently, there have been continuing contacts and relationships among the lay and professional leaders of federations. These have produced a cross-fertilization of ideas and attitudes and have led, from time to time, to groups of federations working together on specific activities. Conferences, meetings, reports and publications have brought the geographically separated federations into close communication with one another.

It was only a few years after the establishment of the first federations that their leaders helped establish a National Conference of Jewish Charities (the first general meeting was held in 1900). The aims of this Conference were described as "educational, corrective, stimulating, suggestive." Lingering fears on the part of local representatives that the Conference might attempt to usurp local initiative and autonomy were dispelled by the assurance that it would not "interfere in any manner with the local work of any constituent society."[1]

Such hesitations, however, did not hinder the development of many cooperative undertakings. On the contrary, even at the first conference, an agreement was reached to introduce equitable relationships among federations in matters of helping transients and newcomers in cities where they had not yet established residence. It will be recalled that this Transportation Agreement was effective in eliminating from the practices of the organized federations and relief agencies the undesirable method of passing on transients to the next city en route, rather than assisting them locally or returning them to their places of residence. The agreement led gradually to the principle that not only the city of origin of the traveling individuals or family had a continuing responsibility, but also that the city in which transients applied for help had related responsibility for his welfare, until a suitable plan could be effected. This was especially applicable to transients who were ill and to families with young children.

With the subsequent development of field service by the Conference, the promotion of training for Jewish social workers, and the establishment successively of the Bureau of Jewish Social Research, the National Appeals Information Service, and the Council of Jewish Federations and Welfare Funds, intercity cooperation increased both in scope and intensity in these and other matters.

The establishment of the CJFWF in 1932 coincided with the onset of the economic depression and of world-

353

wide anti-Semitism. Spurred by these problems, a network of regional organizations facilitated the meeting of communal leaders from cities in the same or adjacent states. Intercity planning and cooperation among large, small, and intermediate-sized cities were facilitated through national assemblies, regional conferences, intercity visiting, institutes, reports, publications, periodicals and other methods. The service program of the CJFWF was increased, and helped each federation to plan its programs with a knowledge of the experiences of other cities.

LOCAL FUNCTIONS

REPORTS AND STATISTICS

Basic information on local health, welfare and cultural developments is made regularly available to federations and their constituent agencies throughout the country and is constantly utilized for federation administration and planning. The information available from the CJFWF includes service and financial data, descriptions of programs and analyses of results, innovations and modifications in objectives, fund-raising techniques and results, and changing community attitudes.

Statistical data are collected and made available on five functional fields under Jewish auspices: hospitals, outpatient services, care of the aged, child care, and family service. Detailed information in the field of Jewish education comes from the American Association for Jewish Education, on the work of Jewish Centers from the National Jewish Welfare Board, on public relations from the National Community Relations Advisory Council, and on vocational services from the Jewish Occupational Council. Such data are developed for the Jewish field against the background and with the knowledge of trends in the total American welfare field. Governmental and national welfare offices are the sources of information on general welfare trends and developments.

CONFERENCES

The CJFWF and the national agencies mentioned hold annual or biennial national conferences and special meetings. In addition, there are national conferences of non-sectarian groups, such as the National Conference for Social Service (organized in 1873), the National Social Welfare Assembly (1945), the National Association of Social Workers (1955), United Community Funds and Councils (1918), The Family Service Association (1911), The Child Welfare League (1920), American Hospital Association (1899), and many other national associations. Members or associates of these bodies or participants in their programs include lay and professional representatives of Jewish federations and their constituent agencies. Local federations, as noted, are also likely to be enrolled as members of local councils of social agencies and to participate in state, regional and national conferences.[2]

STANDARD PRACTICE

Many principles, goals and standards have been brought forth at conferences of federations, but only on a few occasions have such formulations been accompanied by formal commitments. They have instead been voluntary affirmations on the part of conference delegates.[3] However, the results for all practical purposes have been the same. Through interchange of experiences and a basic readiness to undertake activities or policies which were successful in other cities, there has been achieved a rough approximation to agreement on

355

specific goals and standards. The natural desire for emulation, and the pride of having one's own community in step, if not in the lead, have resulted in tendencies toward common patterns throughout the country, though there are lags and minor differences due to the various sizes of Jewish population, regional factors or other local conditions.

The development of annual awards, conveying national recognition of superior performance by a community or agency, has been an additional factor in calling attention to standards of achievement worthy of emulation and in offering a platform of positive aspects of new developments or of appreciably successful changes in program.

Beginning with the 1942 General Assembly and annually thereafter, the Council has selected the best of the entries of campaign materials and items of interpretation submitted by member agencies. Awards are given in three classes: for large, intermediate and smaller cities. Each group is judged for the best set of campaign materials, year-round educational materials and best individual item. These awards have been given annually since that time. In 1953 the Council established the annual William J. Shroder Award to honor outstanding achievements in community organization and health and welfare service; and in 1956 it initiated the Edwin Rosenberg Award for leadership in community and national cooperation.[4]

REGIONAL AND AREA COOPERATION

Contacts between federations on a regional and national basis have stimulated service programs provided jointly by groups of federations and welfare funds. It was recognized that all services essential to community welfare could not be organized and maintained in every separate community. With a lack of sufficient resources to maintain a complete range of local services, or with too few problems of one kind to justify a concrete program, there was need for shared services on a regional and a national basis.

In addition to providing the financial support necessary for programs of nation-wide and overseas agencies, federations have taken joint action to meet special problems as they arose. Such cooperation in recent years has been especially notable in immigrant and resettlement needs developed jointly with the national agencies in this field, and in the development of special regional facilities for the care of children and of the aged and chronically ill.[5]

In addition to annual assemblies and regional conferences, special meetings have been initiated from time to time on the part of certain cities which have common problems due to similar complexities of structure and function.[6]

One of the major developments in intercity cooperation among large communities has been the Large City Budgeting Conference, organized in 1948, which has developed into a permanent and continuing project. This Conference, initiated by Baltimore and with a membership of twelve cities, has been extended to include a total of twenty-three communities. Through the utilization of the facilities of the CJFWF, special staff services and the activities of committees appointed by the LCBC, this group of federations is given an opportunity for a more intensive analysis of national agency programs and for a more extended process of consultation with the leaders of national agencies than is usually available to the individual community. The LCBC's reports and recommendations are made available to all member community organizations of the CJFWF.

The use of these various bodies for conference has yielded significant results in stimulating progressive developments in federation programs.

BASIC HEALTH AND MEDICAL PROGRAM PLANNING

The Tri-City Conference (New York, Chicago, and Philadelphia federations) held in 1946 stimulated interest in the development of the Jewish hospital along modern lines. At that conference Dr. George Baehr, then the president of the New York Academy of Medicine, urged the development of Jewish hospitals as centers for teaching and research and stressed the values of university affiliation for the attainment of high standards of care in Jewish hospitals.[7]

The benefits of coordinating and integrating various programs of medical care and in relating them to other programs of social service for individuals and families, especially for the aged and other special groups, was an important development stimulated by various federation meetings. The progressive quality of this development among Jewish medical and welfare institutions was acknowledged by the United States Public Health Service, which has made $185,000 in research funds available to the Council for a three-year study of the results and values of such coordination.

Intercity cooperation has also been a factor in stimulating federation interest in governmental programs of health and welfare and in exploring the availability of governmental funds for the construction of voluntary hospitals and for the care of dependent persons by other voluntary agencies.

CARE OF THE AGED

Since 1945 there has been greater recognition of the problems of the aged and chronically ill arising from the increase in their number in the general population. Simultaneously there has developed a deeper understanding of the basic needs of the aged and consequently a more intelligent use of health and welfare resources. The Council, through its Department of Social Planning, has taken an active interest and leadership in this field.

Beginning with important steps among Jewish agencies in New York and Chicago (including the development and strengthening of central planning for the aged, the coordination of institutional and family services, and the improvement of institutional standards), there has been a marked improvement of personnel and standards of care, better use of medical and case work services, and a strengthening of recreational and leisure-time programs for the aged and disabled in both institutional and other community forms of care throughout the country. There has also been a radical shift in the policy of homes for the aged through changes in their admission policies, which now tend increasingly to serve the chronically sick and the senile, and decreasingly the ambulatory.

Many communities now provide a variety of services suited to the needs of the aged. These range from help and facilities which are made available to persons in their own homes to intensive medical treatment in general hospitals or specialized medical institutions. The increased utilization of old-age assistance, and other forms of income available for the aged in their own homes or in special institutions from governmental sources, has also been stimulated through exchange of local experience.

CHILD CARE

In the field of child care, intercity cooperation has accelerated acceptance of the method under which family homes are used, while institutional care is restricted to selected children who have special problems. The implementation of this policy, as well as general improvement in methods of child care, has resulted in a considerable reduction in the number of children requiring care away from their homes at any given time.

These developments have greatly reduced the number of institutions needed for dependent Jewish children. The emphasis today is on providing facilities for a selected group of children best adjusted through group living, and for those emotionally disturbed requiring intensive treatment in a specialized environment. Since facilities of this nature can be undertaken effectively only in a few of the largest cities, which are able to obtain adequate funds and specialized personnel, they are being made available on a limited basis to other federations. For example, the regional child care agency located in Cleveland (Bellefaire) is being extensively utilized for special forms of child care by a large section of the United States.[8]

JEWISH FAMILY SERVICES

In the last twenty years Jewish family services have had to face the necessity of basically readjusting their traditional functions. With local, state and federal governments developing economic assistance services on a large and expanding scale, the family welfare agencies began to experience sharply reduced relief loads. The clientele of family service agencies had been drawn largely from among individuals and families in economic

need, but the efforts to help had gone beyond material
aid and had stimulated efforts to deal with other aspects
of family life, many of which seemed to be contributing
factors to dependency. Out of this experience in helping
families there developed the theories and skills of social
case work, adapting to their practice also some of the
knowledge being developed by modern psychology, psychiatry, and psychoanalysis. The reduction in the relief
role of the voluntary agencies made it possible to give
increased attention to these other aspects of individual
adjustment and social relationship.[9]

Since all Jewish family agencies were affected by
the new conditions, it was logical for their boards and
staffs to seek guidance through exchanging experiences
and judgments with other agencies. Responsibility for
helping recent immigrants and refugees continued temporarily as a sizable economic function for most Jewish
family service agencies, but this did not mean any lack
of progress toward other services. The psychological
and personal, as well as the economic, needs of the immigrant group called for mature case work skills based on
the newer psychological theories of human behavior and
social adjustment.

A division of responsibility in New York City, between the Jewish Family Service Agency, caring for
residents, and the National Refugee Service and its suc-
sor agency, the New York Association for New Americans, aiding immigrants, gave the Jewish Family Service
an opportunity to concentrate on a clientele not derived
exclusively from the dependent and lowest income
groups. In 1942 the New York JFS began the practice
of charging fees to those able to pay for its counseling
and case work services, thereby providing leadership in
broadening the scope of the Jewish case work agencies

beyond the marginal and dependent groups in the population.

Group consideration of these problems was facilitated by a number of activities undertaken by the Social Planning Department of the CJFWF. There was need for analysis by the agencies of their current activities and their future goals, as well as understanding of those changes on the part of the federations which were financing the family service programs.[10]

Committees of representatives of Jewish family agencies and of federations, working under the auspices of the Social Planning Department of the Council, have been concerned with the task of defining the rationale and the functions of Jewish family services. Similar but more general analysis and evaluation are being performed for the whole field of family services by the Family Welfare Association of America.[11]

COMMUNITY CENTERS

With the cessation of immigration at the time of World War I there was a complete redirection of the function of agencies offering cultural and recreational services. The new program was similar to that of the Settlement Houses, in that it helped new immigrants adjust to the requirements of the American environment and was followed by programs offering cultural and recreational services for American-born Jewish youth. This gave impetus to the "Jewish Center" movement and stimulated institutional building in the 1920s and again in the post-World War II period.[12]

During the war years, the use of the Centers for meeting the needs of servicemen in the home communities and related activities at military camps as part of the USO (United Services Organizations) were logical extensions of their previous functions.[13] Guided by the Jewish Welfare Board, their national association and service agency, local Centers addressed themselves to changing problems of administration, function and building. The relation of the Center program to services of other communal agencies, the planning of new Center buildings to follow or anticipate population movements, and the deficits of such programs not covered by membership and service fees, were questions discussed by groups of federations, and by representatives of the JWB and the CJFWF. The two national organizations established a joint commission which developed a statement of principles in 1958 on relations of federations and community Centers in program, financing and planning. The practice of utilizing a single executive, in small communities, for both the administration of the federation and of the Center, has led to the development of cooperative relationships on personnel between the JWB and the CJFWF.[14]

A current problem facing both the Center and the federation in large communities is the movement of the Jewish population to the suburban areas, making it exceedingly difficult for the membership, especially among the younger age groups, to utilize a communal building located in the city's center. A complicating factor is the current tendency of synagogues and other groups to operate and finance recreational and cultural services for members as an integral part of their own functions. This poses the question of whether it is more desirable to set up neighborhood extensions of a communally administered Center, or to concentrate on a program of centrally directed services and staff for a variety of units under different forms of sponsorship and administration. This involves, too, the question of what should be the relationships between the synagogues and other communal agencies. These questions are as yet unresolved in many cities.

JEWISH EDUCATION

There has been a gradual development of federation responsibility for programs of Jewish education. This has been marked by the growth of central bureaus for Jewish education fostered and financed by federations in many communities. There is no longer any question as to the responsibility of federation for Jewish education. Before the 1920s, when federations were concerned with welfare problems, it was assumed that education was the function of special groups. However, the Orthodox and Conservative groups had been establishing talmud torahs under general rather than single or joint congregational auspices, both for those children whose parents were able to pay and for other children whose Jewish education would have to be either free or obtained at reduced cost. It was when these schools sought philanthropic funds for their deficits from the community at large that federations were first influenced to undertake some limited financial assistance. Out of this grew a broader interest in Jewish education as a communal function, an interest accelerated and defined in part by surveys in communities conducted by the Bureau of Jewish Social Research, forerunner of the CJFWF. There were many issues to be resolved, however, before this attitude of communal responsibility through the federation could be more fully achieved.

Over the course of years, federations have been concerned with their role in Jewish education from many different viewpoints—financial responsibility, responsibility for curriculum and standards, division of responsibility between federation and others. These and other topics have been discussed at regional and national meetings, in the Large City Budgeting Conference, and in other ways, including exchanges of local surveys. An unresolved issue in some cities is the responsibility of federation for the all-day Jewish school which seeks to combine both secular and religious education as an integrated program; and here, too, federations have found a sharing of thinking, experience and judgment especially helpful.[15]

CHANGES IN THE STRUCTURE AND ADMINISTRATION OF FEDERATIONS

Intercity contacts have also influenced basic changes in the structure and administrative policies of federations. With federations limited initially to support of local welfare agencies, the financing of national and overseas agencies was not immediately absorbed into the federation program. With the increased importance of these needs in the 1930s, central fund-raising for non-local agencies was frequently undertaken by a welfare fund set up as a structure separate from the established federation, although often initiated by federation leadership. The upsurge of anti-Semitism and the need for self-defense similarly led to new organizations in many cities, such as councils of Jewish organizations, to deal in an overall way with public relations.

One reason for the development of new structures to deal with new or greatly enlarged problems derived from the fact that in many of the larger and intermediate cities the role of financing some types of local Jewish services had been transferred to or had been assumed by the non-sectarian community chests. For nearly two decades the federation in such cities had not been required to undertake direct campaigns to seek out and solicit Jewish contributors. In the smaller communities, which had not previously developed a federation, a joint local fund for overseas and national agencies was frequently the first general communal structure.

The additional structure of welfare fund or community council established in a number of the larger communities, with the initiative and cooperation of federation leadership, was frequently directed by the federation executive. These new agencies were seeking to enroll contributors on a mass basis and were drawing additional leadership from elements of the Jewish population that had not been prominent in the local federation. The organization of a delegate body from various Jewish associations and interest groups seemed an effective way of bringing into the new welfare funds and community councils a broader representation of religious and other Jewish group associations.

These new developments also paralleled changes that were taking place in the power structure of the Jewish community. It was recognized that many of the newer immigrants had materially improved their economic position. There was a new group among the business and professional people to be recruited for leadership in communal work and utilized as key personnel in fund-raising campaigns. The newer groups were also being drawn upon increasingly for important administrative committees (such as budgeting and allocation). Federations also began to involve this new leadership as board members of their affiliated agencies.

In order to make a place for these "up-and-coming" individuals, it was sometimes necessary to unfreeze the incumbent leadership by providing for greater rotation in office. The opening up of federation boards and the use of local interest groups as units in communal organization stimulated marked changes in the structure of central communal organizations. Mergers of the federation, the welfare fund and the community council began to occur. This tendency towards uniting the structures for communal work was first developed in Indianapolis, Buffalo, Kansas City, and other cities with intermediate-sized Jewish populations that had originally established two or more central agencies. Newark, following a general communal survey undertaken by the CJFWF, organized the Jewish Community Council of Essex County in 1945, becoming the largest city in the United States operating with a single unified structure for local, national, and overseas philanthropic and general functions.[16] Mergers followed in Boston, Cleveland, Los Angeles, San Francisco, Pittsburgh, and Philadelphia among the largest cities, and in a number of smaller areas.[17]

Systematic organization for communal planning was also increasing in the post-war period. The scope of federation responsibility for welfare was being broadened, and relationships with beneficiary local agencies began to take on more of the quality of cooperative planning. An outstanding example of development in central planning was the creation of the Social Agency Committee (the SAC), of Cleveland's Jewish Community Federation, in 1943, as its planning arm operating on a year-round basis with regular meetings and intensive activity.[18]

The acceptance of central planning as a regular function of the federation, in partnership with its constituent agencies, is now an accepted goal in community welfare programs. Progress toward the fulfilment of this objective continues to be a major part of the program of national and regional meetings of community representatives.[19]

Programs organized on a national basis concerned with some aspect of Jewish welfare have a history that is almost as long as that of local organization, going back to the first half of the 19th century.[20] The national agencies have varying functions and types of organization and structure. Most of the important national agencies were established by individuals in New York City, or originally from New York and nearby cities, who later enlisted a few key individuals from other parts of the country. Some of these national agencies have developed a membership recruited on a nation-wide basis, divided into local and regional chapters, such as the Zionist Organization of America, the American Jewish Committee, and Hadassah. Several other national agencies have been created through representation of a number of autonomous national organizations, such as the original American Jewish Congress, the Synagogue Council and the Council of Jewish Cultural Agencies (1960), or out of a coalescence of national and local units as in the American Jewish Conference (no longer in existence).

Whatever the initial form of structure, national agencies usually seek close relationships with local communities through local units or influential individuals. With the development of welfare funds, national agencies have been especially concerned with the fund-raising bodies of these cities.

National agencies with few exceptions seek support from all Jews and seek affiliation with welfare funds to achieve local responsibility for such support. Such affiliations involve negotiations concerning the amounts which the national agencies expect or hope to receive. National agencies which had previously been successful in establishing a substantial local supporting group were sometimes reluctant to give up independent fund-raising, while other agencies, whose programs did not have a wide popular appeal, welcomed inclusion. The development of satisfactory relationships between these agencies and the new forms of federated financing for national and overseas agencies represented by the welfare fund has been a gradual and complex process. In the thirty-five years of the existence of welfare funds, some of the difficulties have been clarified, while new problems have arisen.

There is great diversity in the various welfare funds in the number of national and overseas agencies included. A few of the largest are beneficiaries of practically all welfare funds, while some of the smaller agencies, especially in the religious and cultural fields, benefit from only a few. In between, there is a wide range of variation in the number of non-local beneficiaries and, similarly, in the number of independent campaigns for funds. There are the additional problems of developing full accord between national agencies and local welfare funds on such matters as local membership, ceilings on amounts of dues, solicitation for special projects, building fund campaigns, and the like. Some of these questions have been receiving the attention of special committees on national-local relations, which have been set up by the welfare funds under the auspices of the CJFWF.

The formation and growth of welfare funds coincided with the intensified needs of the major overseas agencies during the 1930s and 1940s. At that time, deep emotions and concern had been aroused on the part of

American Jews. As a consequence, fund-raising campaigns were undertaken with energy and enthusiasm in an effort to secure as large amounts as possible. But, while successful fund-raising results helped to resolve some of the questions of fund distribution, they did not exceed total needs and thus did not answer the question of what part each of the various national and overseas agencies should receive from the total funds raised.[21]

These major questions had many aspects, including: What part of the total raised should be appropriated to overseas, to national and to local programs? What factors should determine the amounts to be allocated to agencies and overall fields when more or less total funds have been obtained? What is the legitimate share of each of the several national and overseas agencies operating in the same or in related fields of work? Under what conditions should the welfare fund accept new applications from agencies which may or may not have been engaged in raising funds previously?

The high cost of national fund-raising and the lack of capital prevented many of the smaller national agencies from attempting to raise funds directly in all parts of the country. Their continuing attempts to interest welfare funds in adding them as beneficiaries, undertaken largely through correspondence, were futile or resulted in mere token grants. The decisions on distribution which a welfare fund made in the first years frequently set a formula for subsequent fund distribution. But many questions continue to be raised annually because of dissatisfaction with this decision on the part of the welfare fund, the beneficiary agency or, usually, of both.

Systematic attempts are continuing in the hope of arriving at better answers. For example, in the field of overseas programs, the UJA is accepted as the primary agency. But there is still no basic criterion to help local communities determine what additional funds for overseas programs should be channeled through the ten or more agencies which have staked out a claim in this field, and have been approved by the Jewish Agency's Committee on Authorization and Control.

Another major question has revolved about the respective merits of the several national community relations agencies. Group efforts to resolve this question through the NCRAC and other devices have been discussed in previous chapters. There are special problems of budgeting the cultural agencies (which led to a national study of this field by the CJFWF), the rabbinical seminaries, domestic and overseas religious institutions, and national health agencies. The reports of national and overseas agencies prepared by the CJFWF since its establishment have been a major aid in helping local communities arrive at decisions. The reports give basic objective fiscal and service data on a uniform basis. Council prepares budget digests annually which are sent to the member agencies of the Council and are used by individual members of budgeting committees. At the request of community budgeting groups, about 100,000 copies of such reports are provided annually, reflecting the wide use of this material. They include the current programs, finances and budgets of Israel and overseas agencies, traditional institutions in Israel, five groups of national community relations organizations, cultural, health and welfare, and national services, and religious agencies, and information on major regional service agencies. Special data are available on several hundred other national and overseas agencies that are not regularly included in any, or in more than a few, welfare funds, but which apply to the funds or to individual local contributors.

In addition to reports on individual, and on groups of, national and overseas agencies, the Council attempts, through special studies, to keep its member agencies informed of changing problems and developments. Concentrated effort has gone into keeping member agencies informed on the various fields, especially on Israel developments. A special service of the Council has been the issuing of reports called "Israel Fact Sheets," on economic and welfare problems which have a bearing on changing needs and conditions of philanthropic interest in Israel.

MAJOR AIDS TO BUDGETING

A major aid to local welfare fund decisions in the budgeting process was gained from observation of local experience elsewhere. Such information, enabling each welfare fund to compare its decisions with those of other cities, has been facilitated from the beginning of the organization of CJFWF, which has collected and published annually the allocations of welfare funds throughout the country.[22] A local welfare fund, by consulting these data, could compare the dollar allocations and the percentages of total funds being distributed to the different fields and agencies.

Such information, it should be pointed out, has been recognized as only a partial aid. Last year's decision is not necessarily a standard which can be viewed as ideal for today. There is no reason for assuming that the decision made in any other city, or in the aggregate of all cities, was either better or worse than a variant local judgment. The allocation of funds reflects the sifting of previous experience and the making of current local judgments. It also involves knowledge of local interests, affiliation of community leaders with various national and overseas agencies, as well as the study of objective data on agencies' needs, programs and finances.[23]

Out of the experiences of welfare funds have come tentative judgments on how some of the problems faced by them in fund distribution might be solved in part or in whole. It is generally accepted that among local communities there are sufficient differences in scope and degree of interest in the national and overseas programs to warrant diversity in fund allocations. It is similarly recognized that, apart from legitimate local differences in views and interests, many of the variations in the distribution of funds are not the result of design, but of accident. It has been recognized that the process of local welfare fund allocations might be improved through greater intercity cooperation and mutual understanding of the problems of, and joint action with, the national and overseas agencies. Some of the recent activities growing out of this recognition were:

1. Factual studies and analyses of fields of work, such as the CJFWF Special Overseas Studies.

2. Group meetings of representatives of welfare funds to tackle special problems, such as the Large City Budgeting Conference with representatives of national and overseas agencies.

3. The urging of cooperative relationships among agencies operating in the same general field, such as in agreements on principles and details of the separate efforts of the UJA and Israel Bonds in behalf of Israel.

4. Efforts to bring about a reduction in duplication

373

of agency programs, such as the recommendations leading to the establishment of United HIAS Service.

5. Basic research in fields inadequately understood and therefore underdeveloped, including some not originally integral parts of the philanthropic program, such as the survey of cultural and research agencies by CJFWF.

The fiscal and program relationships of local and national agencies inevitably draw attention to the structure and methods of administration of national programs. Administration of a national agency by a lay board is frequently attended by special difficulties. Unlike a local organization which is able to call frequently upon its lay board for regular and special meetings, a national agency administrative session may involve only that part of its membership resident in or near the city of its main office (usually New York). Many of the national agencies operate with large boards and have advisory councils widely scattered throughout the country. They therefore have difficulty in attracting sufficiently large or fully representative attendances, and accordingly do not assign meaningful administrative functions to such groups.

In many communities there may be individuals who maintain a direct interest in the work of a national agency with which they have been affiliated, and such individuals are frequently enlisted by the national agency to interpret its program to the local community and to strengthen the relationships between the national agency and the local welfare fund. But, however well-informed and well-intentioned such local spokesmen may be, they represent at best only a tenuous contact between the local welfare fund and the national administrative agency.

The most active form, in recent years, of intercity cooperation between welfare funds and national agencies has been through two major projects, the Large City Budgeting Conference and the CJFWF's Committee on National Local Relations.[24] Highlights of such developments have been referred to in this and previous chapters.[25] While a rough approximation to a *modus vivendi* has in recent years modified the problem of this relationship, there remain some unresolved questions that face both the national agencies and the local welfare funds. Some of these questions deal with the practical day-to-day operations and relationships; others involve more general issues of Jewish communal life and communal organization locally and nationally.[26]

PROPOSALS FOR NATIONAL-LOCAL RELATIONSHIPS

Various devices have been attempted or projected with the aim of effecting a closer integration of national agencies and local welfare funds. There is involved in these proposals a desire on the part of community leadership to participate in such matters as program planning, setting of campaign goals, and the fixing of operating costs of the agencies for which funds are being raised. A proposal which was under consideration for a period of years and received considerable response, was an evaluation of agency budgets and requirements by a presumably objective and impartial national committee. This proposal, known as the National Advisory Budgeting Plan, was projected during the period from 1940-1946 (see chapter VIII). Other suggestions have been advanced since then.

Another proposal which received attention was for the establishment of a national Jewish welfare fund. A resolution adopted at the CJFWF General Assembly in December 1949 stated:

Permanent and stable fund-raising structures exist locally in the Jewish welfare fund. Under emergency conditions, communities may need to develop extensions of such unified and stable fund-raising on a national basis.

What some leaders had in mind was a plan for a national campaign service and assistance to community campaigns on a welfare-fund basis. A major reason why such organization was not put into effect was that the threatened United Jewish Appeal split was healed in time; the UJA already had fund-raising machinery in operation (costing over three and a half million dollars) and had already taken action in many phases of stimulating and assisting fund-raising campaigns. The Campaign and Interpretation Department of the CJFWF has been providing services to local communities, including welfare fund campaign literature, radio and television programs, guides for campaign organization and other aids, geared to total welfare fund coverage—local and national as well as overseas.

LOCAL REPRESENTATION ON NATIONAL AGENCY BOARDS

There have been other specific proposals designed to bring national and local agencies closer together. On a number of occasions, one or more of the national agencies and some of the welfare funds have explored the possibility of effecting a systematic and formal type of local representation on the governing boards of national agencies. The aim has been to establish a closer liaison and to give local communities a greater voice in the operation of national organizations. Prior to the 1940s, the structure of the American Jewish Committee included a provision for corporate representation of supporting federations, as well as of affiliated national agencies. Similarly, for a number of years, the United Jewish

Appeal provided for representatives selected by a number of the large cities directly, and by the regions of the CJFWF for smaller cities, on some of its committees. In 1949, the United Palestine Appeal developed a procedure of obtaining 40% of its administrative body from local community and regional representatives, with the balance named by its constituent Zionist organizations. Other national agencies similarly have attempted, from time to time, to work out plans for local representation. Experience has demonstrated, however, that such plans have not achieved effective local participation in basic administration. While boards of directors and executive committees of national agencies may be large enough to give representation to a number of cities outside of the national agency headquarters, the day-to-day administration and the basic operations of the agency have been carried by a few individuals who could meet more frequently. There are likely to be few individuals in such an administrative body who reside outside the New York metropolitan region.

While the procedure of formal representation has not solved the desire for more intensive local participation in the management of the affairs of national agencies, efforts have continued to select board members from various parts of the country. A number increasingly have consulted the federations in selecting leaders from their respective cities.

RELATIONS OF FEDERATIONS WITH ISRAEL

Federations which support agencies and programs operating in or in behalf of Israel have developed close relationships with Israel. These relationships are channeled through the welfare agencies—the Jewish Agency and its constituents, the Joint Distribution Committee, the America-Israel Cultural Foundation, the Hebrew University, Technion, Pioneer Women, Hadassah, the Federated Council of Israel Institutions, and other agencies. Relationships of federations to Israel have been primarily with the United Jewish Appeal, which has been the recipient of the largest part of the funds raised and allocated to overseas programs. With its two major agencies operating in Israel—the United Israel Appeal and the JDC—the United Jewish Appeal receives approximately 95% of the funds which central community campaigns allocate for overseas and refugee needs. (In 1958 approximately 64% of all the funds raised went to overseas agencies and for refugee care.)[27]

The United Jewish Appeal has developed various methods for keeping the federations informed about developments in Israel and Israeli needs. This has included: the organization of conferences in Israel and in this country involving professional and lay leadership of federations, and organized publicity and publications prepared by the UJA and by its constituent agencies. Individual federation leaders visit Israel and report to their constituents, and the CJFWF and the Large City Budgeting Conferences are utilized for relating the federations to the needs and developments in Israel.

The problems and difficulties surrounding the establishment and the survival of Israel have been an important area of interest, have stimulated intensive fund-raising and have enlisted American Jews in a sustained program of help. As in the early stages of the Zionist movement, the development of Israel has continued to engender controversial issues, but these have now shifted primarily to questions of administration and fiscal operations rather than of objectives. The multiplicity of agencies attempting to raise funds for Israel causes, the lack of coordination of the welfare programs, the difficulties of long-time planning and the relation of voluntary responsibility to the responsibility of the State of Israel— these questions have been on the agenda of the federations and of their national service agency. Committees, conferences, studies and reports have brought information on such matters to the federations and have led to measures for improving the operations of the agencies and the relationships with the federations. On occasion, in addition to studies in Israel, the CJFWF has appointed representatives who have visited Israel and conferred with agency and governmental leaders on matters of mutual concern.

The National-Local Relations Committee of the CJFWF has undertaken to improve relationships between the federations and the recently reorganized Jewish Agency. Some sections of the community have for many years been critical of the lack of clarity as to what programs of the Israel agencies were exclusively philanthropic and devoted to social welfare purposes, and what activities involved political or partisan objectives. Such mingling of welfare and political objectives had been a natural concomitant of initial Zionist efforts in Palestine and had continued after the creation of the State of Israel. The Jewish Agency, originally established as an instrument of the World Zionist Movement and administered by Zionist party representatives, had continued to use some of the funds, received from the UJA through its constituent the United Israel Appeal, for grants to the Zionist agencies engaged in political as well as in welfare activities. The uses to which the funds derived through this channel were put were not clearly distinguishable from uses of funds derived from other sources and meant for political and similar purposes.

379

Since the reorganization of the Jewish Agency in 1960, several shifts have been in process or are being contemplated which would discontinue grants to agencies under specific Zionist party auspices. Cultural, educational and public relations activities are to be carried on by the American Zionist Council—which is to raise its funds directly for such purposes—rather than through the Jewish Agency. These proposed changes, presumably to take effect in 1960 and 1961, have been reported aimed at freeing the UJA from the charge that some of the funds were being used for political as well as welfare objectives. The Board of the CJFWF and the federations are continuing to concern themselves with these and related questions.[28]

STANDARDS OF OPERATION

Standards for the operation of national agencies have been only partly defined: a statement on standards was adopted by the CJFWF in 1954 and by a number of other agencies in the National Social Welfare Assembly.[29] Standards on fiscal operations and audits by public accountants have gradually been adopted through agreement between the Budget Research Department of the Council and the national agencies which submit reports to welfare funds.

The CJFWF organized an Institute of Controllers of Jewish communal agencies in 1951 which addressed itself to the problems of uniform accounting for the first time in the voluntary welfare field. The CJFWF also stimulated and aided the first study of this question undertaken by the New York Community Trust in 1957.[30]

XVII

The Future of Federations

The life of mankind and the future of social institutions is affected by a complex of variables, uncertainties and contingencies. As with weather conditions, but with less adequate aids to forecasting, we can only speculate on what may be the consequences of forseeable changes that are likely to have an influence on the growth and vitality of federations.

The basic postulate in this account of the federation movement is that the nature and the quality of voluntary social institutions is determined by two facets of group living: first, the element of group consciousness; and second, the nature of the needs and problems that will impel a group-conscious segment of the population to recognize them as requiring group action. An important corollary of this assumption is that needs that are common to a group of people may stimulate group consciousness and that group consciousness may in turn be a factor in producing group needs and group problems.

The federation movement has been an expression of Jewish group awareness. It has been developed in response to the impact of that awareness on group problems and group interests. During the sixty-five years of federation history there have been variations in the quality of group consciousness and changes in the nature and intensity of group problems. Speculation on the future of the Jewish federation, as on Jewish philanthropy as a whole, must necessarily involve speculation on the outlook for the continuation of group consciousness and of special group needs and problems.

In speculating on the future of federations we must exclude from our consideration such gross factors as new wars and world catastrophes, the possible resurgence of a virulent Nazi type of anti-Semitism or the collapse of the American economy. We may assume that these are among the possibilities but not among the probabilities of the future. Taking the optimistic approach, let us assume that current trend factors in American political, economic and cultural life will continue during the next two decades.

With these reservations in mind, it may perhaps be useful to explore the outlook for group consciousness, the nature of group problems and the environmental conditions that will influence the future of federations. Specifically, how are current trends likely to affect federation in the operation of joint services such as fundraising, budgeting, inter-agency and inter-group consultation, planning, and cooperation on matters of common interest and significance to the Jewish population?

INFLUENCES ON GROUP CONSCIOUSNESS—EXTERNAL FACTORS

The major influences on Jewish group consciousness deriving from the external environment have been political and cultural. The anti-Semitism, prejudice and discrimination of the surrounding population reinforced group consciousness over the centuries. Few have sought to escape these external pressures by withdrawing from the group, since prejudice in general circumscribes the possibilities of such withdrawal. Predominantly, Jews have found relief from the pressures of anti-Semitism through group affiliation.

Horace Kallen believes that "the safety, the freedom, and the equality for everybody which the American idea postulates" has been interpreted by Jews as an opportunity for

discontinuing association, atrophying remembrance and ignoring responsibilities. . . . Every so often, anti-Semitic aggression abroad, reverberating at home, arrests this flight of Jews from one another. . . . But when the acute anti-Semitism becomes chronic again, the internal dispersion resumes.[1]

In the lifetime of federations practically all phases of political anti-Semitism have been surmounted. Current legislative attacks on segregation and discrimination are helping to shrink the areas of social and economic discrimination, and to reduce the tensions arising from prejudice that are outside of the purview of political action.

There is general agreement among observers of the American scene that the current trend shows a lessening of prejudice toward all minority groups. The relaxation of tensions is overwhelmingly accepted as desirable. Now, only the irrational find comfort in an unfavorable environment, in the specious belief that it compels the kind of separateness they favor. On the other hand, there is no reason to assume that an atmosphere of freedom and equality cannot serve legitimate desires for maintaining group difference. Conditions today and those obtaining during the first decades after Emancipation and immigration to the New World are not comparable. There are stronger impulses toward preserving group culture and group identity today than in the days

when Jews were attempting to free themselves from
the restrictions of the ghetto by becoming "American-
ized" as rapidly as possible. There is more sympathy at
present with cultural conservatism than was prevalent
during the first three decades of the 20th century.

A modern Jewish group culture under conditions
of freedom is possible, Kallen believes, provided an effective educational program can be organized and maintained.

There are many contingencies, inside and outside the American
Jewish community, which make a bet on its survival a true
hazard. Only education can transpose this hazard from the blind
risk of animal faith to the calculated risk of human courage.[2]

While the general effect of prejudice has been for
Jews to close ranks, and its relaxation has been to increase social mobility, it will take considerable time,
perhaps several generations, for a more favorable environment to erase the strong memories of the virulent
anti-Semitism of the recent past. To conceive of an
environment completely freed from prejudices and discrimination can be an act of faith; it is not likely to be a
certainty for the next generation.

An external influence on the positive side of group
consciousness is the current tendency toward acceptance
of sectarianism. There is a wider tolerance for multiple
sectarian and denominational groups. There is greater
acceptance both outside and within the Jewish group for
maintaining Jewish group identity and Jewish group
association. The growing numbers and importance of
the Roman Catholic faith with their strong church and
group loyalties has helped to reinforce the acceptance of
sectarian groupings and sectarian organization among
the American population.

The general conclusion to be drawn concerning the

effects of the external environment on Jewish group consciousness is that the continuation of Jewish group association in the future will depend more on how Jews
react to the positive factors of acceptance and equality
than to the goads of discrimination and prejudice.

As far as the present situation is concerned, it seems
to this observer there has been no great departure from
religious affiliations. On the contrary, there are indications of a renewed interest in the Jewish past, increases
in the extent to which children receive a Jewish education (albeit of short duration) and more numerous synagogue memberships. The relaxation of group tensions has
for a time intensified rather than diminished Jewish philanthropic activity. There is little indication of slackening
of interest in the welfare field either in domestic or in
overseas problems. There are optimistic indications,
however, of widening social and cultural horizons, reflected for example in the questioning of the sectarian
aspects of Jewish philanthropy, and in an expanded interest in public welfare movements.

INFLUENCES ON GROUP CONSCIOUSNESS—INTERNAL FACTORS

There are cultural factors influencing group consciousness that arise from within the Jewish group. The
current trend in religious practices and in social interest,
habits and manners is toward greater homogeneity. This
encourages a reduction in group differences and group
conflicts and facilitates group cooperation. It is difficult
to determine whether a greater degree of group identity
is to be found among homogenous or heterogenous social
groups and whether the absence or presence of class and
social conflicts within the group serves to weaken or to
strengthen solidarity. Class and group conflicts, which
occur in societies that are homogenous in nationality,

religion, language and ethnic origin, will certainly detract from cooperation on many common projects—without necessarily lessening identification. To the extent that there is an increasing homogeneity of the American Jewish population, there is increasing group cooperation. This continuing trend towards homogeneity should strengthen cooperative activities in the field of welfare.

Among the major factors which have affected the homogeneity of the American Jewish population and which have been responsible for the growth of the federation movement, we may list the following:

A. Immigration and National Origins

More than a fivefold increase in Jewish population has occurred since 1895. There were wide divergencies in background, in cultural and other group interests, between the settled population of 1900 and the newer immigrants. In the 1890s a small and relatively well adjusted group, primarily descendants of or themselves immigrants from, central Europe, were being overwhelmed by immigrants from eastern Europe arriving at the rate of 100,000 a year. Today there is only a small trickle of immigrants; the Jewish population is predominantly native-born and the Jewish community is losing much of the variegated coloration which was originally traceable to the national origins of its mixed population.

For a long time, these differences in national origin and period of arrival made for a divided community. The separate elements of the Jewish population varied greatly, not only in religious adherence and practice, but in social and economic status and in ideological motivation. With time and changes in the character of the population, resulting from the processes of adjustment to American life and the inevitable replacement of the foreign-born by their native-born descendants, the task of reconciling group differences has become less difficult. Today residues of the old rivalries and group diferences persist, but these are no longer the major obstacles toward achieving full acceptance of the current purposes and functions of central communal association within the local community.

B. Cultural Trends

Although variations in religious denominations among Jews are likely to persist, there are evidences of a growing tendency toward more similarities than differences (except for a number of recent immigrants striving to maintain the Orthodoxies brought from their European homes). The old group rivalries among the denominations are diminishing, and there is greater acceptance of sect variations than in the first half of the 20th century.

The European immigrants of the 1890s and early 1900s were largely Orthodox in religious practice and proletarian and class conscious in their political outlook. Many, under the stimulus of the movements then taking place in eastern Europe, were oriented towards socialism and internationalism. In time, Zionism or Yiddish nationalism and conservative political doctrines were to gain greater influence. The cultural gap between those new immigrants and the settled and conservative older Jewish population was profound. Over the years the gap has been narrowing even between Reform and extreme Orthodoxy. As one manifestation, Conservative Judaism began to flourish and attract the second generation, some of whom had been reared in families that had given up their religious practices and rituals or had reduced them to a minimum. The sharp edges of ideological controversies in other areas were being blunted.

The forces of American acculturation (the common educational system and instruments of mass communication) have been of profound importance in overcoming the differences between the old and new generations. Of even greater significance has been the common traumatic experience of the thirties and forties, which intensified group identification and brought all elements closer together in recognition of a common problem.

A current factor of great significance in communal life is the group movement of Jews from the center of the city to the outskirts and the suburbs. Transference from one residential area to another, dictated by economic improvement and population pressures, has been characteristic of the entire period. However, the movement has recently become intensified and more widespread. This mobility has had a profound effect upon institutional planning and location of synagogues, Centers, and welfare agencies.

C. Economic and Social Adjustment

In 1895 there was a small relatively well-to-do and economically settled middle class group. The immigrants were largely a working class element, struggling to obtain an economic foothold, while facing low wages and long periods of unemployment. Today the Jewish community shows a rapid advance in its economic conditions and in its integration into American life. Standards of living have risen with the nation's remarkable progress in production and general prosperity. This has been reflected in a considerable shrinkage of the numbers and proportion of the population requiring economic assistance.

Occupational shifts and changes also have diminished the influence of proletarianism and Socialist doctrines on the American population as a whole. The American-born generation of Jewish immigrants from eastern Europe is beginning to resemble the older elements in the population in occupations, economic status and in religious interests. By the next generation the differences between these groups are likely to be even smaller.

CHANGES IN NEEDS AND PROBLEMS

The cultural, economic and social changes that have occurred in the American Jewish population have facilitated the cooperative movement in Jewish philanthropy. The increased homogeneity and increasing affluence of the group has facilitated communication and has made it possible to base federation on an increasingly large number of contributors, to increase their sense of identification with the community program and to change the character of the federation from a limited to a more widely representative group. This is evidenced in the composition of boards, the backgrounds and affiliations of officials and active workers, in the auspices of the beneficiary agencies and in the broadening of the local, national and overseas interests of federation.

These changes, however, have also been accompanied by changes in social problems and needs, which have radically affected the functions and interests of federation. With the dwindling of immigration, the dependent and marginal economic group is no longer the major domestic concern of the federation or its agencies. The tendency in this country has been away from voluntary, toward governmental, responsibility for the alleviation of poverty. Provisions for meeting economic need resulting from the death of the wage earner, from old age or from disability, are now acknowledged to be within the function of the federal, state and local governments. Like other Western nations, America is becoming what is called a "welfare state."

The extent of economic need among Jews, as for other established sections of the general population, has been diminishing as the initial period of immigrant adjustment has been succeeded by an improved occupational structure, by the improved earnings of labor, and by enhanced prosperity. More people have the resources with which to meet ill health and personal and family problems. Public assistance among Jews is lower than for most other groups; governmental social security measures, voluntary plans for health and medical care, labor union and employer retirement systems, fringe benefits and commercial insurance systems are adding to the economic security of Jews as of other Americans.

As indicated in previous chapters, federation and its agencies are deploying their philanthropic resources to group needs and to social problems other than those rising out of poverty. They are serving the middle class and the well-to-do as well as the remaining marginal economic classes with case work, recreational centers, hospitals and other types of institutional and service facilities. Hospitals, residences for the aged, the care of the chronically ill, case work and personal guidance agencies require group effort and group cooperation for their establishment and upkeep. A considerable number of consumers are able to pay the full per capita costs of the health and welfare services that they receive. Such services for the most part cannot be established or main-

tained on a commercial basis. Where they can be so
established, as in proprietary hospitals or nursing homes,
experience has indicated the superiority of philanthropic
over commercial ventures.

The shifting of the focus of federation from the
dependent group to the entire community has been a
gradual but a steady development, and the trend is certain to continue. There is still, however, the need for
voluntary philanthropy and group action in a vast area
of problems not yet met by government, and less adequately met by business enterprise.

In 1955, Dr. Maurice Hexter, executive vice-
president of the New York Federation, speculated on
the next twenty-five years in Jewish communal services.[3] He postulated the continuing expansion of the welfare state, growth of unionization and of labor's ability
to obtain the social services known as "fringe benefits"
in the labor contracts, increased suburbanization and
increased leisure, closer ties with Israel, and strengthening of the synagogues. He predicted the broadening of
programs for the care of the aged, who increasingly are
in need of medical as well as of residential care. Homes
for the aged he believed will come under the auspices of
hospitals and, like them, provide facilities for those able
as well as for those unable to pay the costs of their
care. Unions and the government would increasingly
provide economic security and economic assistance, and
voluntary agencies increase their programs of individual and family case work and counseling. There would
be an end of the child care institution, except for special
provisions for the emotionally disturbed child. The Jewish component in case work would become more evident, giving a sectarian basis for a service now largely
conceived in non-sectarian terms.

Hexter suggested that both synagogue and general community Center programs would continue; there would be an appreciable extension of camping programs and facilities. There would be an increased use of the synagogues as auspices for programs of Jewish education. In addition to the continuation of hospitals, Hexter predicted the development of medical schools under Jewish auspices. He did not foresee any reduction in the organization of the federation:

I believe [he said] there won't be much dispute with my prediction that certainly Jewish welfare funds will continue to grow, and that the Jewish federations will not be displaced by community chests. More and more . . . Jewish philanthropic institutions are looking for more and more of their support from Jewish sources rather than to the community chests. . . . Jews give more to Jewish causes than to general causes. The differential propensity is not due completely to better organized campaigns. It's in our blood. And it is constructive.[4]

We should note that except for religious education, welfare programs do not necessarily involve a sectarian component. It is also evident that many Jews obtain health and welfare services from sources that are not under Jewish auspices. Hexter indicates, however, that the desire for a Jewish environment is a potent factor in the demand for institutional services maintained under Jewish auspices such as in Jewish homes for the aged. He further states that the general community requirement for the care of a child who is separated from his own family is that he be placed with a family of his own religion.

Hexter believes that there are many Jews who seek identification with other Jews, and that this inclines them to prefer Jewish hospitals and Jewish case work agencies where they may find sentiments of identification with the client and his "ethnic past." They will select a community Center under Jewish auspices as a secular equivalent for the synagogue and send their children to Jewish camps for the purpose of cultural indoctrination.

There can be little dispute with the main points of Dr. Hexter's predictions, which it is to be noted rest in large measure on the persistence of Jewish group consciousness and Jewish group identity. We need to remember, however, that the social service programs especially in the medical and case work services have become less rather than more specifically sectarian, and that there is very little evidence of any reversal to sectarian objectives in their basic approaches. We must note that the non-sectarian character of services have qualified Jewish agencies for serving non-Jews as well as Jews, and that admittance policies rather than the nature of services limit the clientele of some case work agencies and recreational Centers to a Jewish clientele.

It is my own belief that we may anticipate a slow but gradual increase in the proportion of Jewish clients and patients who will utilize agencies under other than Jewish auspices, both because of individual choice and through factors independent of choice, such as the hospital affiliation of the patient's physician, or the truly non-sectarian character of the welfare agency. Without necessarily reducing Jewish interest and support of Jewish agencies, including those that serve non-Jews as well as Jews, we may also anticipate that the philanthropy of Jews will be extended increasingly to agencies and programs under other than exclusively Jewish auspices.

OVERSEAS NEEDS

We have also to consider the needs and the appeal of the programs for Jews overseas, and especially the needs and the appeal of Israel. It is likely that those needs that led to such tremendous increase in Jewish philanthropy in the early post-war years and were responsible for the establishment and growth of welfare funds will not disappear in the years ahead. Israel is not now an economically independent state and it would be overly optimistic to expect that, because progress is being made toward self-sufficiency, there will be a cessation of the need for American funds in the next ten or twenty years. For the year 1958, Jewish federations (including those which support national and overseas programs) allocated 62.5% of their annual philanthropic income to agencies engaged in aiding Israel.[5] The proportion is likely to remain large in the years ahead. Interest of the majority of American Jews in Israel has been basically philanthropic and cultural, eliciting feelings of pride in its establishment and concern for its maintenance and its future. This interest might be designated as "proprietary" and non-political and is likely to continue to be vigorously alive.

THE FUTURE FUNCTIONS OF FEDERATIONS

With the assumption that the foregoing factors, which have had a major effect on the nature of Jewish social and cultural life in this country, will continue— greater homogeneity, continuing prosperity and economic improvement, interest in Israel and the welfare of Jews in other lands, and a reduction in the external factors that create group tensions and negatively induced separatedness—it is anticipated that the Jewish federation will be developing under the following conditions:

1. A continuing expression of philanthropic interest in health, educational and welfare agencies under Jewish auspices, with increasing interest in con-

tributing to the support of programs under other auspices.

2. With a larger part of the Jewish population able to pay for services, and with federal economic security provisions and organized group resources for meeting costs of health and welfare services steadily mounting, the quality of services available under Jewish auspices will have to meet increasingly high standards and involve increasing costs.

3. With a wider choice of health and welfare services available for potential consumers, a diminished use of agencies solely on the basis of ethnic identification can be expected. Quality of services will play a major part in agency selection. Jewish agencies will be widely utilized only when they are among the best that are available to the consumer of health and welfare services.

4. While there may be increases in private practice in the case work and counseling field, following the pattern developed in general medical practice and in psychiatry, the importance of the medical center and of organized counseling and guidance services will increase rather than diminish.

5. Improving economic conditions and increased leisure will add to the demand for recreational Centers and services. While these may take the form of non-sectarian and commercial programs, private clubs and associations, the number of Centers related to the synagogues may also increase.

6. We may expect a greater interest in the arts and in scholarship, but philanthropic contributions to such projects may come, as they have in the past, much more from individuals, and foundations, than from communal funds.

7. With the increasing demand for opportunities in higher education and the shortage in facilities available for enrollment in colleges and universities, help from federal funds will be essential. We may expect Jewish philanthropy to become more interested in this field, with the possibility that one or more universities and medical schools under Jewish auspices may be added to the several now in existence. Like the institutions under other auspices these will be non-sectarian in student body; but the initiative and main sources of philanthropic funds will be derived from Jews, and the governing bodies will tend to become less completely sectarian.

8. Interest in Israel and in overseas needs will be sustained and will continue to require large amounts of philanthropic funds.

JOINT FUND-RAISING

Under these conditions active joint fund-raising, which has been the outstanding contribution of the federation movement in the past, is likely to continue. Contributors will be brought slowly to the recognition that they are responding not alone to the requirements of charity, but for their own and the general welfare. A major motivation arising out of group consciousness and identification will continue to be a concern for demonstrating the civic and social responsibility of the Jewish population and group pride in this demonstration.

ALLOCATION OF FUNDS

Concepts underlying the budgeting and allocation of funds by federations will continue to broaden. With the recognition that the services of agencies are intended to meet needs of all income classes, more funds will be allocated for the improvement of the quality of the services—by experimentation, demonstration and research.

Cultural and educational agencies will share increasingly in this broader function, and will agree to closer scrutiny of their purposes and results. Federations will become more concerned with the conceptual basis and objectives of the cultural agencies. A more minute study of aims, purposes, methods and results will also be given to the health and welfare agencies. All beneficiaries, including the national and overseas as well as the local agencies, will be held to a stricter accounting by federations as the trustee for the contributor.

SOCIAL AND COMMUNITY PLANNING

A deeper concern with needs (conceived more broadly than in the past) will receive greater attention in the planning and coordination of welfare and health services. There will be more attention to problems and less focus on agencies. Closer relationships will be established between the fund-raising apparatus and the operating bodies of the health and welfare services. Community planning will bring into a closer relationship the welfare activities of the synagogues and of other independent groups with the organized health, welfare and educational agencies under Jewish auspices.

Closer relationships for community welfare planning will be established with the community chests, the united funds and councils of social agencies. The

397

federation will receive greater recognition as the central instrument that can be used for a channel to the Jewish population for broad community and civic improvement.

The federations will give increasing attention to the health, welfare and educational functions of the local, state and federal governments and participate in the general associations for community welfare planning.

LEADERSHIP AND REPRESENTATION

The recruiting of a devoted and competent leadership—always a problem of federation—will be a continuing difficulty. The primary need of the federation is to raise the funds needed for its program, and as the bulk of the funds comes from a small well-to-do segment of the population, reality indicates that the administration will continue to come from their ranks, or from surrogates acceptable to this group. At the same time, federation must strive to be a symbol for the broad range of economic and social groups.

The growing homogeneity of the Jewish population will decrease the problems heretofore inherent in administrative representation. With the exception of the size of income, there will no longer be sharp differences among the members of a board who are willing to give to and work for the federation. It is usually found, however, that on such a board there will be a larger percentage of people from the upper and middle income group.

Exceptions may occur when the largest contributors prefer to remain on the sidelines and leave the conduct of affairs to others in whom they have confidence —through business, professional or social relationship. Accordingly, the composition of such a board might include proprietors of businesses or their executives, attorneys, representatives of organized labor, persons with income in the lower middle brackets, some outstanding professional leaders, or others with prestige in the community, as well as women who devote themselves to philanthropy and civic affairs.

The recruitment of leaders may be affected when outstanding personalities in the Jewish community find greater acceptance than previously in the civic affairs of the total community. Attracted to these opportunities for serving the community, some leaders find it difficult to devote their time to Jewish as well as to general civic matters. However many leaders most active in serving general programs are also very active in Jewish causes. In any event, the easing of restrictions against sharing the control of general communal organization with representatives of minority groups will not be rapid. Studies of the power structure of some American communities show a preponderance of leadership drawn from among the Protestant section of the community well beyond their numerical proportion.[6]

Increasingly, Jewish associations may have to meet the competition from other parts of the health and welfare field for leaders. The broadening of the range of interests and functions of federation will serve to facilitate the recruitment of leadership as does the recognition that experience in the Jewish welfare field is an enriching rather than a restricting experience and that the leaders in the Jewish welfare field are apt to receive general recognition for their public spirit and civic responsibility.

FEDERATION HISTORY

As this account of the federations has attempted to indicate, federations have had an eventful and on the whole satisfactory history. They have grown more rather than less important with the years. Given an environment of peace and prosperity, federations will function in the future as a form of Jewish organization adapted to serving Jewish needs according to the requirements of the New World and of democracy. One would have to look far indeed into the future to see federations disappearing, either through the complete assimiliation of the Jewish population, the shrinking of the field of voluntary action and voluntary initiative, the lack of a Jewish group consciousness and the absence of specific Jewish interests and needs.

It would take a radical turn of events, amounting to a revolution in American democratic organization or a world catastrophe, to upset current trends in the development of Jewish federations.

Acronyms

Notes

NOTES TO CHAPTER 1

1. For a comprehensive study of the history and structure of the Jewish community from biblical times to the American Revolution, Salo Wittmayer Baron, *The Jewish Community: Its History and Structure to the American Revolution*, is indispensible. It is published by the Jewish Publication Society (5706-1945), in three volumes. Of special interest to the subject of welfare are vol. I, chapters VII and VIII and vol. II, chapters XIV, XV, and XVI.

2. The history of Jewish philanthropy in relation to the Bible and Talmudic Law is also contained in Ephraim Frisch, *An Historical Survey of Jewish Philanthropy: From the Earliest Times to the Nineteenth Century* (New York: The Macmillan Company, 1924).

3. *Ibid.,* p. 9.

4. *Ibid.,* p. 23.

5. *Ibid.,* pp. 75-78.

6. *Ibid.,* p. 101: *Rules for the collection and distribution (of public charity funds) are laid down in the Mishnah and elaborated with painstaking care by later authorities.*

7. Baron, *op. cit.,* p. 208.

8. Baron, *ibid.,* p. 347.

9. Samuel C. Kohs, "Whither, the Jewish Family Agency?" *Jewish Social Service Quarterly* (New York: Jewish Communal Service), XXIV, no. 1 (Sept. 1947), pp. 153-159. "Why Jewish Family Agencies?" *The Reconstructionist* (New York: Jewish Reconstructionist Foundation), XXI, no. 15 (Dec. 2, 1955), pp. 8-15.

10. There was a sharp reversal of the attitude that no Jewish client should be on the public relief rolls after 1920, with the improvement of governmental relief systems beginning with the state programs of Mother's Aid and Old Age Assistance and their reinforcement under the 1935 federal Social Security Act.

11. Ludwig B. Bernstein, "Certain Phases of Community Life in Berlin

and Vienna," *Proceedings of the National Conference of Jewish Social Service*, 1924, pp. 289-307.

12. The earliest form of Jewish charity was on a congregational basis. The same form of organization for relief was also employed in the Christian community by the Christian churches which were originally offshoots from the Jewish community (Frisch, *op. cit.*, p. 40). However, organization of charity apart from church or synagogue develops in the modern period of history. *Growth in the number and influence of the voluntary benevolent organizations in the 16th, 17th and 18th centuries gradually removed the charities from the control of the official communal authorities . . . leading ultimately to complete detachment from ecclesiastical direction, which characterizes modern Jewish philanthropy* (Frisch, p. 164).

   See also p. 167 for further discussion of the transfer from religious and secular and voluntary direction for welfare programs.

13. Jacob Shatzky, "Institutional Aspects of Jewish Life in Warsaw in the Second Half of the 19th Century," *YIVO Annual of Jewish Social Science* (New York: YIVO), X (1956), pp. 9-44.

14. *Ibid.*, pp. 35-36: *The situation in Warsaw differed fundamentally from that in the cities of Western Europe, where the* kehillah *was, by and large, the parent organization of all major institutions in the city. Most Jews in Warsaw came in contact with the* kehillah *and its officials only in matters of hospitalization and burial. Aside from these, the influence of the* kehillah *in the life of Jews was minimal, particularly in everyday welfare problems, such as a small loan, assisting the needy, sick, and the like.*

15. Bernard H. Bloom, "Yiddish Speaking Socialists in America: 1892-1905, *American Jewish Archives* (Cincinnati: HUC-JIR), XII, no. 1 (April 1960), pp. 34-70.

16. *Ibid.*, p. 38.

17. *Ibid.*, p. 63.

18. *Ibid.*, pp. 66-67.

NOTES TO CHAPTER II

1. Excellent data on the development of social institutions during the Colonial period may be found in Carl Bridenbaugh, *Cities in the Wilderness: The First Century of Urban Life in America, 1652-1742* (New York: Alfred A. Knopf, 1955).

2. See Hyman B. Grinstein, *The Rise of the Jewish Community of New York.*

3. Harry L. Lurie, "Jewish Communal Life in the United States," *The Jewish People, Past and Present* (New York: Marstin Press, 1955), IV, 187-242. Herman D. Stein, "Jewish Social Work in the

United States," *American Jewish Year Book*, 1956 (Philadelphia: Jewish Publication Society), pp. 1-98.

4. See Harry L. Lurie, "The Development of Social Welfare Programs in the United States," *Social Work Year Book*, 1960 (New York: National Association of Social Workers).

5. From article by Joseph Jacobs, *AJYB* (1914-1915), p. 339. Estimate made by Mordecai M. Noah in 1818 was 3,000 Jews; in 1877 William B. Hackenburg of the United States Bureau of Census, in a survey based on "actual counts made in the smaller communities and careful estimates made in the larger ones," reported a Jewish population in the United States numbering 230,257.

6. Stuart E. Rosenberg, *The Jewish Community in Rochester*, 1843-1925, pp. 142-143: *When the German refugees began to immigrate to the United States in the 1930s they established their separate societies apart from the descendants of German immigrants who had arrived in this country before 1900.*

7. Jewish population statistics for the United States are invariably based on estimates rather than on census counts. Estimates have been published by the *AJYB*. See vols. IIL (1946-1947), vol. LIII (1954), and later volumes.

8. *The Jewish Communal Register of New York City*, 1917-1918. Published by the *Kehillah* of New York City, 1918, as reported in the "Directory of Jewish Local Organizations in the United States," *AJYB*, XXI (1919-1920), p. 330.

9. Computed from *AJYB*, XXI, 337-583.

10. From A. M. Isaacs, "Final Report of the Board of Delegates of American Israelites," made in 1879. Published in *Publication of AJHS*, XXIX (New York: 1925), pp. 83-116.

11. Max J. Kohler, "The Board of Delegates of American Israelites," *PAJHS*, 1925, pp. 75-137.

12. Grinstein, *op. cit.*

13. Ismar Elbogen, *A Century of Jewish Life* (Philadelphia: Jewish Publication Society, 5705-1945), pp. 326-354.

14. *Ibid.*, p. 326.

15. *Ibid.*, p. 326: *The Jewish immigration differed from the rest in that the newcomers were regularly penniless and dependent upon the assistance of their coreligionists. In the summer of 1881, even before the first reports of the pogroms had reached America, some hundreds arrived unexpectedly, and soon there were thousands of refugees in the harbors of New York, Philadelphia and Baltimore. . . . They came with their few possessions hastily bundled together—came, unlike most of the earler immigrants, together with their families. They aroused general and deep sym-*

pathy in the non-Jewish immigration officials as in the Jewish charitable establishments.

16. *Ibid.*, p. 328.

17. Benjamin Glassberg, "History of the Jewish Welfare Society," *JSS Quarterly*, III, no. 4 (June 1927).

18. *Ibid.*, pp. 34-35.

19. Abraham Oseroff, manager UHC, "Report of the United Hebrew Charities of New York and Subsidiary Relief Agencies," *The Jewish Communal Register* . . . , 1918, p. 994. See also *Fifty Years of Social Service* (the history of the UHC), published by the Jewish Social Service Association, Inc., 1926.

20. *Proceedings of the Fourth National Conference of Jewish Charities*, 1906, Philadelphia, pp. 71-72, remarks of Morris Jacoby, New York City.

21. By the year 1900 there were Jewish orphanages in 14 cities, homes for the aged in 12, and hospitals in 9 cities. Only in New York was there more than 1 institution in all of these fields. Chicago also at this time had 2 homes for the aged, 1 under Reform and 1 under Orthodox auspices.

NOTES TO CHAPTER III

1. Harry L. Lurie, "The Development of Social Welfare Programs in the United States," *SWYB*, 1960.

2. *Proceedings of the Third NCJC*, May 1904, New York, p. 27.

3. The National Conference of Jewish Charities was the first formally organized national forum for Jewish philanthropic agencies. Beginning in 1899, its membership was limited initially to regular organized Jewish Relief Societies. Federations, usually called at that time United Hebrew Charities, were eligible from the outset. Later other philanthropic agencies, such as orphanages and homes for aged, became members, but for several years the Conference was opposed to accepting individuals as such as members.

The National Conference of Jewish Charities was not organized for nearly a quarter of a century after the formation of the National Conference of Charities and Correction (1877), and was stimulated by the experience of Jewish members of the general Conference who recognized the need of the expanding system of Jewish charities for a forum for group consultation and discussion of common problems. The National Conference of Jewish Charities changed its name, subsequently, to the National Conference of Jewish Social Service and is now the National Conference of Jewish Communal Services.

4. *Proceedings of the First NCJC*, June 1900, Chicago, p. 13.

5. Three of the five original members of the Federation of Jewish Charities in Boston held a joint fund-raising campaign in January 1895. Their charity banquet raised "a goodly sum," the *American Israelite* reported on February 7, 1895, and looked forward to the actual federation for the "dispensing of charity, making it more general and thorough, and *by the enlarged resources pouring into one* treasury, the facilities for helping the needy will be greater."

A detailed history of Boston's Federation is contained in Barbara Miller Solomon, *Pioneers in Service:* The History of the Associated Jewish Philanthropies of Boston. From letter, January 12, 1956, received from Dr. Solomon: *This campaign did, in fact, determine the pattern of fund-raising for the little Federation officially established in April 1895. The five constituents agreed that thereafter the Federation would conduct joint fund-raising campaigns from which each society would receive a proportionate share. In return, the societies would hold no separate benefits without the permission of the Federation. At the same time, however, the Federation permitted each constituent to collect membership dues and personal gifts from the members of each particular agency. In the beginning the separate societies continued to have more personal appeal for some of the members, and the central fund which existed from the outset was far from adequate for maintaining the activities of the constituent societies.*

By 1904 the number of contributors to the Federated Jewish Charities (as it was known by then) had increased only slightly and distributions to the separate agencies still represented only one-third of their budgets. In that year, among other schemes which were tried to increase the central fund, the leaders proposed to stimulate larger direct donations to the Federation by making any person who contributed "the sum of fifty dollars or more" automatically a member of all the constituent societies without paying further dues to the separate agencies. Through this significant step, these philanthropists hoped to expand the Boston Federation's existing central fund.

6. Solomon Lowenstein, "Report on the Associated Jewish Philanthropies of Boston," survey published by Bureau of Jewish Social Research, August 1930.

7. At the 1902 NCJC, Judge Julian Mack stated that large givers gave federation 50% more than before. *Proceedings*, p. 26.

8. Morris O. Loeb, "Federation versus Consolidation of Jewish Charities in a City," *Proceedings*, 1900, pp. 42-44. Professor Loeb said in part: *To secure freedom of movement in all essentials coupled with a unity of purpose and concentration of effort, whenever needed, healthful supervision without arbitrary domination, our charities should follow the example of our country and adopt a system of federation of sufficient elasticity to meet the wants of*

the large as well as the small. No organization should be called upon to surrender its charter or its property; in fact, as an inducement for all organizations to join the federation without hesitation, it should be distinctly stipulated that any member could withdraw, if dissatisfied with the arrangement, after giving reasonable notice, without any forfeit of any kind.

As modified to suit the wants of an American Jewish community, this plan might advantageously take the following form. The various cooperating societies, whether incorporated or not, would retain their respective entities, no attempt being made to induce them to surrender their property or their individual subscribers, form of management, etc. They would agree, however, to place the solicitation of funds from the Jewish public into the hands of a general committee, say of 50 or 100, chosen perhaps for the larger part from among their own directors.

This central committee would be a small body of men especially chosen for their broad acquaintance with the needs of our institutions, and preferably containing some men not actively interested in any one particular society. It would be called upon to supervise the work of the general committee and to see to the proper distribution of the funds collected through it. Of course, the designated contributions are beyond its control; but, assuming that the amount of undesignated contributions be considerable, it would be called upon to apportion it. And herein would lie its most important and delicate function: for the fund should be distributed according to the amount of legitimate deficit appearing in the annual budget of the various societies, after the designated contributions have been distributed. By submitting their accounts to the criticism of this disinterested central committee, the various societies would give their subscribers the best possible guarantee of the economy and efficiency of their management.

9. *Proceedings of the Third NCJC*, May 1904, New York, pp. 169-171. In the same address, Senior stated: *From whatever point of view we regard it, federation offers undeniable advantages. If we take account only of finances, we shall find that in every city the subscription list has grown in numbers and amounts to proportions far in excess of those preceding federation. We shall find that these subscriptions do not decrease; that they do not represent amounts subscribed in moments of enthusiasm and afterward withdrawn, that they represent a permanent source of income which can be confidently counted upon and that their collection is easy and inexpensive. We shall find that the number of subscribers is largely increased and that, therefore, the popular interest in charity work is fostered.*

10. From Address of Welcome: William B. Hackenburg, president Jewish Hospital Association, Philadelphia, in *Proceedings of NCJC*, 1906, pp. 23-24.

11. Quoted from remarks of Max Herzberg of Philadelphia, president of the Third NCJC, 1904. *Proceedings,* p. 27.

12. Remarks of Louis Wolf, Philadelphia. *Ibid.,* p. 176.

13. Max Senior, president of United Jewish Charities, Cincinnati, at 1904 NCJC. *Proceedings,* p. 169.

14. *Ibid.*

15. *Ibid.*

16. Address of Professor Jacob H. Hollander at NCJC, Richmond Va. *Proceedings,* pp. 54-55.

17. *Ibid.,* pp. 54-55: *It was not long, moreover, before the situation was made more complex by the economic betterment of the new arrivals, and their eagerness to assume a part of the burden of relieving the needs of those who still lagged in the bitter struggle. Had the older community been wise it would have strained every nerve to have included within its resources this new force, whose potentiality in economic capacity and in philanthropic impulse was not then, and is not even now, fully appreciated. We should have so modified, enlarged, even reconstructed, our charitable agencies as to have found place and accorded welcome reception to those who, arising from prostration, clamored for a place at the wheel. But we did none of this. We took their money only when it could be given in the form in which we had been accustomed to assess it. We were slow in electing the newcomers to membership, and we were averse to giving even the foremost of them place in the institutional directorates.*

    See also Bloom, "Yiddish Speaking Socialists in America: 1892-1905," *American Jewish Archives,* XII, no. 1 (April 1960), pp. 34-70.

18. Hollander, *ut supra.*

19. Morris Goldstein, "Causes of Poverty and the Remedial Work of Organized Charity," *Proceedings of NCJC,* 1900, pp. 80-81: *There are, however, causes of poverty which in my estimation are the real causes of poverty. First, there are those able-bodied, but unfortunately not able-minded, applicants, who would rather peddle than work, and who, if they do consent to accept work, are surrounded by barriers which cause them to be undesirable acquisitions. It is not that they are unskilled or that they lack strength or ability—it is their custom of praying three times a day and of refusing to work on the Sabbath and holidays. It is not my intention to cirticize these habits, nor will the liberal minded censure them for their expression of religion, but as times and conditions have changed, they also must change their habits to fit the new conditions; otherwise, they meet with constantly increasing difficulties in maintaining themselves. A loss of from 3 to 4 hours a day for prayer will eventually lead to idleness*

and laziness. It prevents a man from fitting himself into the industries of the time, and the consequence is that the man remaining unemployed falls into the peddling nuisance.

This view, however, was opposed at the same conference by Mrs. S. Pisko—p. 86:
The question of these people not working on the Sabbath: Now, in this prosaic age we are prone to look upon this as something to be condemned. The contention is to support their families, and whether they have a Sabbath or not, they must work and take care of their families. But, to me, it seems that this is the old spirit of martyrdom in these people; it is something that they have stood for for a good many years, that they have suffered for, and it is a very serious question in my mind how this subject should be treated by Jewish charitable organizations. Shall we condemn these people because they will not work on their Sabbath? I do not think I can condemn a man for observing his Sabbath.

20. *"Jewish Communal Organization in America,"* report of committee. Solomon Lowenstein, chairman. *Proceedings of NCJSS*, 1923, pp. 191-192.

21. Excerpts from "Survey of Jewish Philanthropic Organizations in Philadelphia." Unpublished (in files of BJSR), 1920: *The work of the [Federation] at the time this survey was begun presented a type of organization and disorganization quite familiar in American cities up to within a few years. There were the old established societies, many of them formed decades ago, organized into a Federation, which sought to collect as large a contribution from the public as it was possible to obtain, and to distribute this amount as equitably as possible to its constituent societies. Each organization was autonomous and pursued its purpose under the Federation just as it had done before the era of the Federation, but with its income secured at less cost in money and energy to its directors. Outside of the Federation there existed numerous organizations that had comparatively lately come into being, and that for one reason or another were not taken within the fold of the Federation. The city as a whole was organized neither for the purpose of distribution nor for the coordination of its social activities, nor to meet the needs of the entire Jewish community. There had been even within the Federation itself no study of community problems and service which would indicate the lines along which development should be encouraged, where emphasis should be laid, or where previous emphasis should be relaxed.*

The newly organized Federation very soon, however, came to realize that if it was to carry on its work effectively, it would not only have to provide the means for the growing needs of the affiliated agencies, but would have to extend its scope and assume responsibility for the support of deserving nonaffiliated agencies as well as for the establishment and maintenance of new activities for which there was a need.

The Federation was confronted with the problem of its inability to admit new beneficiaries on account of lack of funds. In November 1901, the Jewish Sheltering Home for the Homeless and Aged applied for admission, and was refused on account of lack of funds.

In 1903, the Hebrew Orphans' Home established an institution in the downtown, or so-called ghetto district. The organizers of the new venture insisted upon a strictly Orthodox home, including the observance of dietary laws. An earnest endeavor was made by the Federation to have them abandon this project and unite with the Jewish Foster Home. (The attempt failed.)

When the Federation attempted to enlarge its constituency, the question always revolved about the financial status. Organized primarily for the purpose of raising funds for its members, the Federation had no machinery for the evaluation of the services of those agencies it was supporting, or for ascertaining the social needs of the community and making adequate provision for them. The result was a wavering policy, expressing itself in a number of instances in anxiety to enlarge its constituency, and discouraging, on the other hand, other organizations willing to join it.

The wavering policy of the Federation resulted also in another undesirable condition. New institutions and organizations grew up outside of the Federation. In their attempt to raise funds for maintenance they utilized methods which were against the very principle on which the Federation was established, and in many instances challenged the soundness of these principles by raising amounts sufficient for their needs. Such a situation undoubtedly hampered the normal and successful development of the Federation.

Notwithstanding the few isolated instances referred to above, the thought of an entire and complete Federation was uppermost in the minds of those most interested in the welfare of the community.

In December 1903 . . . a committee was appointed to confer with the representatives of the East-European community looking to a fuller cooperation in the work of charitable relief. The leaders of this community did not favor the plan and felt that the time was not ripe for such an amalgamation, nor did they think their constituency would support this idea.

In May 1911, a committee was appointed to consider the state of Jewish charitable work . . . and to make recommendations whereby the scope of the Federation would be so enlarged as to affiliate with itself such organizations as did not participate in the original Federation, and to consider and report on steps to

*be taken, looking to the avoidance of duplication and waste in
Jewish charitable effort . . .*

*A subcommittee reported that there were forty existing Jewish
charitable organizations in that city not affiliated with the Federation, that is, forty of a dignity at least sufficient to court investigation. A preliminary survey of the field, however, showed that
some few of these organizations were already non-existent; many
were mere duplications of existing charities; some were incapable
of rendering practical service; others were helpful only to those
who founded and operated them; some were unnecessary as dis-
tinctive Jewish charities; some had not yet attained to the growth
which would make them worthy of consideration; some, too,
were more or less antagonistic to the Federation and would not
desire admission if offered. The result of all of this was that the
committee had no difficulty in eliminating all but four, which
invited more serious investigation.*

*After considering each of them in some detail, the committee
reported adversely on the admission of any of them at the time.
It agreed that they were, in the main, worthy charities, although
not all of them, perhaps, necessary as separate institutions, and
it was reluctantly thought inadvisable to recommend their enrollment at that time as constituents. At least one, and possibly more
of the institutions, would not have been willing to join the Federation. And it was felt by some members of the committee that to
admit certain of them would be unjust to the institutions, as it
might seriously curtail their revenue at the time by preventing
them from soliciting other contributions; this for the price of
the comparatively small income which the Federation might then
be able to supply to them.*

22. Elbogen, *A Century of Jewish Life*, p. 328.

23. Harold Silver, "The Russian Jew and Charity," *JSS Quarterly*,
    IV (1927-28), p. 140.

24. *Ibid.*

25. *Proceedings of the NCJC*, 1918, pp. 10-11.

26. "Survey of Los Angeles Federation 1923," p. 15. Files of BJSR.

27. Louis H. Levin, "Social Work as a Profession," *Proceedings of
    Sixth NCJC*, 1910, St. Louis, p. 284.

28. *Ibid.*, p. 285.

29. "Jewish Communal Organization in America," *Proceedings of
    NCJSS*, 1923, p. 193.

30. *Ibid.*, pp. 193-194.

31. *Ibid.*, pp. 194-195: *During the period covered by the federation
    movement, it can easily be seen after even a cursory examination
    that even in those agencies which had been well established and*

had acquired an honorable tradition in pre-federation days, there has been a broadening of vision and of scope, taking full advantage of all scientific discoveries and applying more humane and intelligent treatment of all classes of dependents. There is today absolutely no comparison in the field of family welfare, medical social service, child care and delinquency with the conditions existing prior to the days of federation. There is an eager search for new methods and for scientific research. This is a positive achievement of federation and one for which it cannot be given too much credit.

The great shortcoming of federation has been that in many instances it has signally failed to organize the community. This is due to a variety of causes. In the first place, insufficiency of funds has too often restricted the federation activities to those agencies already existing at the time of its organization and compelled a great hesitancy in admitting new organizations, thus leaving outside the federation list worthy institutions deserving communal support, and compelling them to meet the tremendous competition of a centrally organized body enlisting the financial support of the great bulk of large givers in the community. For purely local reasons, frequently purely personal or institutional, organizations which should be included in the federation stand aloof, preferring to continue a selfish policy of isolation, because of assurance of adequate financial support, instead of pooling their interest with those of the community at large and thus bringing about a well-rounded program of work.

But the chief cause of failure to create a comprehensive federation must be sought in the lack of understanding and congeniality between the different national groups within the community itself. Too often the federation has been merely a federation of old-line institutions, ignoring completely or partially the new enterprises established by the more recent arrivals. Thus there has been created unnecessarily a lack of unity which is destructive of any true manifestation of communal life.

32. *Ibid.*, pp. 197-198.

NOTES TO CHAPTER IV

1. Derived from immigration statistics reported in annual volumes of *AJYB*.

2. Address of Max Senior, president, at First NCJC, 1900, Chicago. *Proceedings*, pp. 13-14.

3. *Proceedings of Fifth NCJC*, 1908, Richmond, p. 110.

4. Differentials between relief standards and policies of Jewish and of other family agencies were discussed in "Jewish Standard of Relief," a symposium, *JSS Quarterly* (Dec. 1925), pp. 79-104. Statistics in this symposium based on a study by John Slawson, pp. 86-104.

5. Samuel Joseph, *The History of the Baron de Hirsch Fund.*

6. From Michael Freund and George W. Rabinoff, "Jewish Communal Trends in the Intermediate Communities," *Proceedings of NCJC*, 1932, p. 77: *Credit should also be given to the Industrial Removal Office for its part in fostering federation development, particularly in the Middle West and South. In order to secure competent agents to receive and adjust their clients, the IRO subsidized organizations both for relief needs and for the salary of a worker.*

7. *Proceedings of NCJC*, 1900, p. 180.

8. Boris D. Bogen, "Persistence of Dependence as Indicated by Relief Statistics," *Proceedings of NCJC*, 1906, pp. 63-72.

9. *Proceedings of NCJC*, 1900, pp. 16-17.

10. Quoted from an address on East Side preventive work. *Proceedngs*, 1904, pp. 116-117.

11. Quoted from "A Survey of Jewish Recreation Activities, April 1920," Miscellaneous Reports 1916-1926. Files of BJSR.

12. Solomon Lowenstein, "Introduction to the Survey of Jewish Education in Boston," Boston Jewish Communal Survey by BJSR, 1930.

13. Statement by Judge Mack, in *Proceedings of NCJC*, 1906, p. 36.

14. *Ibid.: The experience of the committee which had anticipated the arrival of 500 of the Russian orphans of 1905, and had determined that they should not receive the congregate love and care of an institution, but the individualized affection of a Jewish home, the ready response that their appeal met with in all sections of the country is a sufficient guarantee that with the necessary funds—not more than it takes to maintain institutions—and right direction, no difficulty will be experienced.*

15. *Ibid: Cincinnati, ever in the lead, has sent no children to an orphan asylum in several years. There, as in some other communities, widows are granted pensions so as to enable them to keep their children at home, and not only to keep them, but to rear them. For the problem is only half solved if the allowance is so inadequate as to compel the mothers to join the ranks of the wage earners whose children, deprived of the parental care and oversight, are rapidly increasing the truant and the delinquent classes. Home is the place for the mother as well as for the child. If the number of her own children does not justify a living allowance, add to them by giving her the supervision of some full orphans. Two problems are thus solved at one stroke and rightly solved.*

16. Rabbi Coffee stated that *Massachusetts, for a quarter of a century, has boarded out children in private homes. At least 8 states*

are successfully doing this work; yet, this morning we heard the remark made that the system of boarding out children is yet in the experimental stage. Two years ago, 11 societies caring for dependent children in southern California gave up the institution plan and formed an agency for placing children in board. What has been discarded by the Christians as out of date was accepted as good enough by our Jewish people, who started soon after in Los Angeles an orphan asylum for Jewish children. Quoted from Proceedings of Sixth NCJC, 1910, St. Louis, p. 272. The "Christian" workers and agencies referred to were largely Protestant. The Roman Catholic groups adhered to institutional care for a longer time.

17. *Jewish Social Work Year Book.* Reports of BJSR, CJFWF, 1932 to date.

18. Brooklyn Jewry organized a Federation in 1909, but a larger part of New York City's agencies were located in the boroughs of Manhattan and the Bronx and were not federated until 7 years later. Efforts had been made earlier to federate the Manhattan, Bronx agencies and one philanthropist had offered a one million dollar fund (now the Heinsheimer Fund) to stimulate the development, but it had no success at that time.

19. I. Edwin Goldwasser, "Jewish Federation of New York City," *AJYB*, 1918-1919, p. 142.

20. *Proceedings of NCJC*, 1908, Richmond, p. 129.

21. "The Jewish Community of New York City," *AJYB*, 1909-1910, p. 45.

22. *Ibid.*, p. 44.

23. *Ibid.*, p. 48.

24. Julius Drachsler, "Coordinating, Standardizing and Research Institutions," *The Jewish Communal Register of N. Y. C.*, 1917-1918, pp. 1149-1151: *The first of these bureaus to be organized was the Bureau of Jewish Education (1910). Its task was to study the problem of Jewish education in this city, in all its varied aspects, and to help establish progressively higher educational standards. Similar organizations were instituted in quick succession: the Bureau of Industry (1914), to search out the factors that make for industrial disturbances in the economic life of the Jews in this city, and to harmonize conflicting interests of employer and employee; the National Council of Young Men's Hebrew and Kindred Associations (1914), the chief aim of which is to study the recreational and cultural needs of the Jewish youth, and to help in the development of YMHAs, YWHAs, Settlements and social centers; the Bureau of Jewish Statistics and Research (1914), whose aim is to gather facts on the most basic aspects of Jewish life in this country, such as immigration and vital statistics; the*

School for Jewish Communal Work (1914), the purpose of which is not only to train expert workers to carry on the manifold Jewish communal activities, but also to help formulate the underlying principles of Jewish life in America; the Bureau of Philanthropic Research (1916), organized to analyze the philanthropic problems of the Jewish community and to propose plans for the more efficient management and administration of the vast enterprises of the Jews in this city.

25. Harry Sackler, the executive secretary of the *Kehillah, The Jewish Communal Register* . . . , 1918, pp. 55-56: *However, one phase of the Kehillah's world receded into the background, owing to the all-absorbing activity of communal experimentation; namely, the expansion of the Kehillah organization from the point of view of numbers. The great mass of New York Jewry, while tacitly approving the work of the Kehillah, has not displayed an active interest in the formation of its policy and of its programme. This indifference on the part of the Jewish mass may be traced to a somewhat defective system of representation which considered the Jewish society as the only unit from which representation was allowed to the annual convention. The distribution of the Jewish population in Greater New York, creating densely populated Jewish districts at points widely remote from each other, was another contributing factor. As a central organization, the Kehillah was too far removed from the simpler elements of our population, who are impressed "only by a concrete, visible fact. Many of them had only heard of the existence of the Kehillah and most likely considered it as one of many good organizations.*

At the last annual convention, this phase of the problem was carefully gone into and the thorough-going democratization of the Kehillah decided upon. To afford the Kehillah an opportunity for doing the work of the democratization without let or hindrance, it was deemed best to sever the bureaus from the Kehillah and to give them an independent existence, so that all the energy of the Kehillah could be devoted to its main task: namely, the formulation of our communal problems and the coordination of the existing communal agencies which will bring about a conscious, organized and united community.

The plan of representation was the result of a careful study of the various constituencies which would make the Kehillah representative of New York Jewry in the widest sense.

26. Salo W. Baron, *The Jewish Community*, I, 26.

27. "List of Federated Jewish Charities in the U.S.," *AJYB*, XXI (1919-1920), pp. 584-586:

Before 1900	1900 through 1905	
		Detroit, Mich.
Boston, Mass.	Buffalo, N.Y.	Indianapolis, Ind.
Cincinnati, O.	Chicago, Ill.	Milwaukee, Wis.
Syracuse, N.Y.	Cleveland, O.	Omaha, Neb.

Philadelphia, Pa.	Memphis, Tenn.	Houston, Tex.
St. Louis, Mo.	Minneapolis, Minn.	Little Rock, Ark.
	San Francisco, Calif.	Los Angeles, Calif.
1906 through 1910	Nashville, Tenn.	Montgomery, Ala.
Atlanta, Ga.		New Orleans, La.
Baltimore, Md.	*1911 through 1915*	St. Paul, Minn.
Brooklyn, N.Y.	Akron, Ohio	Scranton, Pa.
Columbus, O.	Altoona, Pa.	
Dallas, Tex.	Birmingham, Ala.	*1916 through 1919*
Dayton, O.	Elizabeth, N.J.	New York, N.Y.
Des Moines, Ia.	Fort Wayne, Ind.	Oakland, Calif.
Kansas City, Mo.	Hartford, Conn.	Savannah, Ga.
Louisville, Ky.	Hot Springs, Ark.	

28. Salo W. Baron, "Effect of the War on Jewish Community Life," *JSS Quarterly*, XIX, no. 1 (Sept. 1942).

29. *Ibid.: The situation changed suddenly when the European Jews found themselves sharply divided through the belligerence of their respective countries. . . . America, long neutral, was thus placed in a position of extraordinary responsibility and had to take over many urgent tasks entirely on its own. For one example, the struggling Palestine settlement, which had theretofore been supported by a primarily European halukkah on the one hand, and a primarily European Zionist movement on the other, was plunged into misery by Turkey's entry into the war on the side of the Central Powers.*

At that crucial moment the American community assumed responsibility. The small and powerless Zionist federation gave way to the newly organized Provisional Committee for All Zionist Affairs under the leadership of Louis D. Brandeis and Shmarya Levin, who was then in America as the representative of the World Zionist Organization. The immediate result was effective assistance, through both relief and political action. To quote a subsequent report of the Zionist administration in Jerusalem: "in spite of all efforts made in Palestine to cope with the situation, the Jewish population would have succumbed had not financial help arrived from America." Moreover, the leadership thus assumed by the American community was co-responsible for the issuance of the Balfour Declaration and for the important decisions made at the Peace Conference and the League of Nations concerning international guarantees for a Jewish homeland in Palestine. . . .

On the European scene, too, it was American initiative in both the economic and political domains which greatly helped to reconstruct vast areas of war-stricken Jewish life. The Joint Distribution Committee, a new and in many ways original creation of American Jewry during the First World War, assumed the responsibility first for the immediate relief and, subsequently, for

417

the permanent economic reconstruction of millions of Jews in eastern and central Europe.

The decade of the war and early post-war years is unrivaled also from many other aspects of communal history . . . the federation idea, born and acted upon in Boston and Cincinnati before the war, received new stimulus. The largest of all federations known in the annals of Jewish history, that of New York City, was established in 1917, in the midst of the war turmoil. . . . It was merely as a crowning of that achievement that we witnessed in the last few years the rise of all-embracing local community councils and welfare funds culminating in the general Council of Jewish Federations.

NOTES TO CHAPTER V

1. For a brief history of the peace treaties and the work of the American Jewish Congress following World War I, see Elbogen, *op. cit.*, pp. 485-509 (chapter on Pogroms and Treaties of Peace).

2. Samuel A. Goldsmith "The Question of Financing Non-Local Jewish Philanthropies," *Proceedings of NCJSS*, 1924, Toronto, pp. 342-372.

3. Charles S. Bernheimer, "The Relation of Jewish Centers to Jewish Federations & Community Chests," *Proceedings of NCJSS*, 1925, Denver, p. 62.

4. Maurice B. Hexter, "Federation and Community Chests—Certain Present Tendencies in the Federation Movement in American Jewish Philanthropy," *Proceedings of NCJSS*, May 1923, Washington, pp. 127-137.

5. *Ibid.*, p. 136.

6. Samuel C. Blumenthal, "Experiences of Jewish Community Chests," *Proceedings of NCJSS*, 1927, p. 102.

7. "Communal Survey of Washington, D.C.," 1929, p. 1. Files of BJSR.

8. Excerpt from a survey made in 1923 by the BJSR, "Study of the Jewish Population of Cleveland," p. 12:
   [Duplication of agencies was attributed to] *a natural outgrowth of a system of communal organization in which one element, predominant largely because of its length of settlement, its earlier adaptation to American conditions and its greater wealth and industrial position, has undertaken to solve the various communal problems without the active cooperation of other elements in the community, probably much larger numerically, with very definite positions, differing from those of the other group with regard to traditions, elements and practices in Judaism, and with an increasing financial and industrial importance.*

9. Some of the problems of unorganized small communities, and the kind of recommendations which the surveyors were making

at that time to solve them are illustrated by excerpts from a survey of a community of approximately 7,500 Jews. From "Jewish Communal Survey of Trenton, N.J.," Files of BJSR, 1929, p. 17: *There is no agency today which represents the Jewish community. In consequence there is no organized leadership to voice the will of the community as to general policies which call for common action. There is misunderstanding on the part of the general community as to which Jewish agency should be dealt with in regard to specific problems which arise. In one instance an individual took the responsibility of advising the public authorities that the "Jews did not intend further to draw upon municipal relief funds" and the city officials acted on this instruction. This is a matter which should have been considered by a representative Jewish community body.*

One agency whose funds have come from the community and which serves a recognized communal purpose is conducted by a single individual. This would not be the case were a central representative community agency in existence.

The lack of a central Jewish body means that the Jewish community is not in position to secure the most effective results from general community resources. It is obvious that a body representing all elements could command more attention than can individuals or single organizations.

There is no means by which the Jewish community can deliberate and plan for Jewish community needs. The various projects which are now being considered by individual agencies should not be launched without the sanction of a body representing the community as a whole.

10. The president of one federation in a large city, Mrs. Siegmund Herzog, in 1928 expressed that idea as follows in "Trends in Federation Scope," *Proceedings of NCJSS*, 1923, p. 185: *Another tendency of marked significance in current federation functioning is in the direction of unification of philanthropic forces. No longer is it possible, much less desirable, if federation is to serve as a unifying community force, to restrict its interest and activities to the early Jewish settlers, excluding and ignoring societies of later origin which came into existence as instruments of protest. All other things being equal, the presence of unaffiliated Jewish social agencies in any community is an indication of the weakness of the existing federation. There can be no place in the vocabulary of federation, once it serves as the articulate will of the united Jewish community, for such words as German, Russian, Polish, American, Orthodox, Reform, etc. Federation must concern itself with the cross-section needs and desires of the entire Jewish community.*

Adequate representation on federation and agency boards and committees, a policy of rotation of office, giving leadership oppor-

tunity to the many, instead of confining to the few, will soon dispel a criticism, so often heard, that federation is a closed corporation serving vested and inherited interests. Proper representation on board and committees will in time break down many false barriers that now exist between organization and organization, as well as between individual Jew and Jew.

11. From Files of CJFWF. See also Israel S. Chipkin, "Jewish Education in the United States," *AJYB*, XXXVIII (1936-1937). On page 79 of this report, Dr. Chipkin lists the organization of central agencies for Jewish education as follows: New York (1910), Boston (1918), Philadelphia (1920), Baltimore (1921), Pittsburgh (1922), Chicago (1923), Cleveland (1924), Cincinnati, Detroit, St. Louis (1926), Indianapolis, Milwaukee (1929), Buffalo (1931).

12. Ben Rosen, director of Associated Talmud Torahs of Philadelphia, "Survey of Jewish Education, Camden, N. J.," 1929. In files of BJSR.

13. From "Social Work as a Profession," *Proceedings of NCJC*, 1910, Louis H. Levin described the situation as follows—p. 284: *The Jewish social worker generally has little social standing. In this respect we do not follow the custom of the goyim, among whom the profession of the social worker is as highly regarded as any other. We need only look at the National Conference of Charities and Corrections, to see the position that has been reached by the professional social worker, to understand to what dignity that profession has attained, and to see also how far Jewish social workers have to travel before the same dignity shall be theirs. The non-Jewish workers have obtained their position by brilliant achievement in constructive philanthropy, by a leadership at once intelligent, enlightened and effective, and their contribution to modern social ideas and expedients is universally acknowledged. The Jewish social worker can at least hope to share in this program of useful progress, if it be too much to expect him to make a like contribution to theoretical and practical charity administration.*

14. *Ibid*, p. 286.

15. Philip Bernstein, "A Study on Training for Jewish Social Work," prepared for the Committee on Training for Jewish Social Work, 1943.

16. *Proceedings of NCJSS*, May 1927, p. 149, in discussion of paper by Raymond Clapp: "What Have Been the Effects in Jewish Social Agencies of Membership in Community Chests and Councils of Social Agencies?"

17. The United Jewish Philanthropies of Des Moines has the distinction of being the first federation to assume substantial responsibility for raising funds for non-local appeals (1914). Other federations had also been allocating funds from their annual campaigns

to a selected number of national agencies in lieu of independent campaigns.

18. In Harry J. Sapper, "The Experience of a Community in Funding National and International Philanthropies," *Proceedings of NCJSS*, 1927, pp. 106-107, Oakland, California, described its plan as follows:

1. Local groups agreed to give up their money-raising activities for any agency included in the budget, and to lend the cooperation of their forces to the united appeal.

2. The budget was to include as many beneficiaries as usually made appeals in the community, either through local auxiliaries, itinerant collectors, the medium of the mails or local appeal chairmen.

3. A campaign organization was to be created and was to consist of the usual officers, committees on budget, publicity, advance gifts, branch houses, appraisals, speakers, women's cooperation and an army of 160 workers, each group to consist of a major and 10 lieutenants.

4. Beneficiaries were to be notified of their inclusion in the budget and were to be requested to refrain from indulging in any form of solicitation in the community and also to advise the organization of any gift received during the year from a resident of the community.

5. An educational campaign was to be launched through the medium of organization periodicals and the presentation of the cause at social and religious gatherings, and particularly through the literature of the Fund. Workers were to be trained in selling the cause at special meetings called for that purpose.

6. Donors were to be guaranteed against local solicitation for outside agencies and in return were to be requested to refrain from giving to any outside appeal, and furthermore, to direct the solicitor or letter to the Fund.

19. The following excerpt is from an early welfare fund report on its 1927 campaign—Paul Goldblatt, "The Experience of the Jewish Community Chest in Harrisburg," *Proceedings of NCJSW*, 1927, pp. 128-129; *Keren Kayemeth with its Jubilee Book annual Flag Day, Golden Book, Purim Shalach Mones and other special holiday collections, is still presenting problems to us. Once again, we faced the necessity of forcing a definite understanding between the United Palestine Appeal and one of its constituent organizations. Strangely enough, there was no agreement between the two organizations at first. . . .*

Our contributors felt also that in giving "once a year for all Jewish causes" they would not be solicited again. Many resented these methods and it has been difficult to overcome their objections.

20. In 1917, Rabbi Mordecai M. Kaplan described the condition in New York City in "Affiliation with the Synagogue," *Jewish Communal Register* . . . , 1917-1918, pp. 120-121: *It is a matter of common experience that the synagogue and the temple do not hold the Jewish young men and young women. To a very great extent this is due to the fact that economic conditions prevent attendance at religious services.*

What are some of the truths that stand out as significant? The first and foremost is the fact that the synagogue has lost hold on more than one-half of the largest Jewish community in the world. . . . It is evident that the density of population, economic conditions, and length of stay in this country have so rapid an effect upon synagogue affiliation that we cannot but infer that the synagogue owes its existence more to the momentum of the past, than to any new forces created in this country that make for its conservation and development.

21. "Jewish Communal Organization in America," *Proceedings of NCJSS*, 1923, p. 197.

22. "The Presidential Address," *ibid.*, May 1927, p. 10.

23. Morris Waldman, president of the National Conference of Jewish Social Service in 1928, stated this opinion in "The Presidential Address," *Proceedings*, p. 14: *The trend in American Jewish philanthropy is toward diminishing emphasis upon provision for dependents and delinquents. This does not mean that Jewish communities will cease to deal with the problems of disease and dependency and delinquency.*

Hospitals, child care work and relief will continue to reflect the major items of our budgets, but the items for the positive elements in Jewish life will grow larger. Support and encouragement will be increasingly given to education, to primary and secondary schools, teachers' training schools and theological colleges. Whatever is of value in the spiritual heritage of the Jewish people will be conserved and further developed. Jewish art and music will, less and less, be permitted to languish in the garrets of impoverished artists. Jewish writers and philosophers will, less and less, be obliged to depend on penny-a-line contributions to struggling publications. More and more, the renascence of the Jewish spirit, which has infected our communal enterprises, will envisage these precious potentialities and will regard them as legitimate claimants for the liberal support of the whole community.

24. *Proceedings of NCJSS*, 1928, p. 22.

NOTES TO CHAPTER VI

1. From annual reports in files of BJSR and CJFWF.

2. "Service Trends in Jewish Social Agencies," *Notes and News* (New York: BJSR of CJFWF), no. 17 (Sept. 29, 1933), p. 8. The statistics of relief of the family agencies were significant during this period. In July 1930 these agencies reported approximately 4,400 families on relief, and relief expenditures of $164,000. By July, 1933, relief costs and relief clientele had almost tripled (12,188 families and expenditures of nearly $400,000 a month).

3. *Notes and News*, no. 25 (Dec. 20, 1934), p. 10.

4. *Ibid.* Federations in 13 large cities reported a decline in contributions and community chest receipts from $8,830,000 in 1930 to $5,950,000 in 1933.

5. "Planning Jewish Child Care Services," May 1953. CJFWF report on social planning. This marked trend has continued with a gradual decline in the number of Jewish child care institutions and in the number of children receiving institutional care. Various factors account for the decrease in the number of dependent children beginning during the depression and continuing through the 1950s: the growing competence of services for children, the sharp decline in the birth rate, and the greater stability of family life indicated by a reduction in the problem of desertion, are considered to be among some of the elements involved.

6. By 1939 there were 24 local vocational service bureaus, and federations and welfare funds were spending 4% of their incomes on these local services.

7. *Notes and News*, no. 3 (May 29, 1931), p. 7. The New York Federation made an initial grant of $75,000 to Brooklyn.

8. *Notes and News*, no. 1 (March 20, 1931), p. 4. Federations and welfare funds were distributing their funds as follows: 96.1% went for the support of local activities; 2.6% was contributed for nonlocal regional and national agencies, and 1.3% for international and foreign causes.

Of the local disbursements, appropriations for medical service took 31.5% of the total, the other functional fields following with family welfare 26.5%, child care 14.5%, leisure-time 10.1%, Jewish education 6.3%. Appropriations for all other types of local work, 10.8%.

9. From "Report of Committee of Five," *Notes and News*, June 1932, p. 1.

10. From Ben M. Selekman, "Federations in the Changing American Scene," *AJYB*, XXXVI (1934-1935), pp. 67-68: *The federation movement . . . proved on the whole an efficient money-raising mechanism. From the growing subscription totals of their annual campaigns, federations were able to amplify progressively the budgets voted to their constituent agencies. They became the means of linking the prosperity and status achieved by American*

Jewry during the first 30 years of the current century—years perhaps unparalleled during any other period of the Diaspora—with recognized community responsibility for the disadvantaged and under-privileged.

Beyond this, however, the record remained unsatisfactory and confused. Without the primary powers of the central organization, federations could not impose order in our complex development. They could not effectively study, plan in terms of needs and resources, integrate existing agencies, or launch new ones. In community after community, haphazard building programs multiplied new hospitals and added new centers. By the same token they multiplied mortgage indebtedness. With characteristic American confidence in continuing prosperity, sponsors laid cornerstones before assuring initial cash payments, or providing for amortization and operating budgets. Meanwhile the rapid shifts in Jewish populations made for constantly changing needs. Expensive and elaborate institutions, built primarily to serve Jewish clienteles, found themselves catering to non-Jewish groups. Other institutions became obsolete in terms of developing social work standards. Still others unnecessarly duplicated functions already served by existing agencies. Even in the fund-raising process, unhealthy features appeared. Too great reliance was placed on large donors without any serious attempt to develop the potential balance weight of mass support. When general community chests were formed, some federations joined before their communities were really ready for such a move. The results proved unfortunate, bringing insufficient contributions from the Jewish group, and a weakened sense of Jewish community consciousness.

Nevertheless, until the full effects of the depression began to make themselves felt, federations proved able to continue in their established, if inadequate, ways. Until 1931 they maintained their growing rate in the collection of funds. But, since that year, they have suffered a decrease in income approximating roughly 30% per annum. If we could drift without hazarding actual shipwreck before the depression, we can hardly afford to take such chances any longer. The almost catastrophic influences of the past four years have so affected the whole federation position as to make imperative a reconsideration of scope, objectives, function and structure.

Weaknesses and limitations ascribed to federations were also summarized in 1937 in a report on Jewish community organization in the United States by Dr. Maurice J. Karpf, "Jewish Community Organization in the United States." From pp. 136-137: *The federations are facing the greatest challenge and severest test. Many factors conspired to weaken them. Federations, as a rule, obtained their greatest power through the purse rather than from the sanctions resulting from constructive and representative leadership. With a more limited purse has come, therefore, a diminu-*

tion of power and influence. Federations have been accused of being arbitrary, undemocratic, nearsighted, timid, or cowardly, visionless, interested mainly in charity, leaderless, provincial, mechanical in their approach and method, dominated by an assimilationist point of view, being supported by and appealing to comparatively small numbers, and [of] having failed to develop the cohesiveness, organization, and other characteristics of an intelligent, wisely planned and representative Jewish community. While all these charges cannot be leveled at all federations, it must be admitted that most federations have some of these shortcomings, and that some of them would have to plead guilty to most or all of the charges if they had the necessary objectivity and insight to see themselves as they are seen by others.

Nevertheless, when all is said and done, federation is the most important single organization in the Jewish community. It has in it elements of strength, at least potential strength, which no other organization in the Jewish community has. In its representativeness, unrepresentative as it is; in its community mindedness, narrowly conceived as it may be; in its financial resources, limited as they are; in its leadership, one-sided and conservative as that may be; in its catholicity of interests, circumscribed as they are said to be; and in its status before the non-Jewish world, there lie possibilities heretofore unrealized and assuredly unequaled by any existing Jewish organization in the United States.

11. Selekman, *op. cit.*, pp. 85-87.

12. Information in files of CJFWF.

The popularity of the idea of a central welfare fund was not limited to communally organized bodies. In some cities the project was utilized by special segments of the Jewish population as a device for collecting and distributing contributions. The fur industry in New York City, for example, established a chest for the philanthropy of its members. Labor unions collected funds from its members, as did the public school teachers in New York City who formed the Jewish Teachers Community Chest. The educational group established the Keren Ami Fund for collecting from children in Jewish schools. Students on some college campuses established Jewish welfare funds, as have some fraternal organizations.

Statistics of the funds raised by the overseas and national agencies are incomplete, but probably less than $4,000,000 was being raised by all of them in 1931 and 1932. By 1942, the major organizations had raised over $21,000,000; in 1943, $28,000,000, and by 1945 it was estimated that the total raised by the national and overseas agencies had increased to over $55,000,000 (from files of CJFWF).

The special character of welfare funds as a fund-raising instrument for national and overseas agencies, as distinguished from the local federations, is indicated in the report of the distribution of

425

the welfare fund dollar in 1939. In that year, about 71.4% was spent for overseas needs, 8.4% for national and regional agencies, 20% on local costs—largely for increased needs of immigrants and refugees who had come to this country—and for employment and vocational services which had been stimulated by the needs of the depression, and 2% for local group relations programs (from Notes and News, no. 62 [June 1940], p. 19).

Combining the financial reports of federations and welfare funds, 97 cities in 1941 showed total aggregate appropriations of $22,-500,000, of which $3,600,000 was derived from community chests. Of the total funds spent by welfare funds and federations (other than for administration, contingencies and reserves) about 63% was being expended for local costs and 37% for overseas, national and regional services and for special refugee costs (Ibid.).

13. Louis Kraft "Servicemen and Veterans," *AJYB*, IIL (1046-1947), p. 165.

14. The pros and cons of joining war chests is indicated in the following excerpt from "Community War Chests Organizing," *Notes and News*, April 23, 1942, pp. 3-4: *There are practical difficulties in reaching conclusions with regard to Jewish organizations within the new war chests, applying not to the ordinary local services encompassed in federations, but rather to the activities usually included in Jewish welfare funds, which were non-existent at the time of the last war chests.*

The Jewish welfare fund interests are more specifically Jewish in scope and go beyond the local philanthropic or even war relief purposes which, it is anticipated, will be the core of the new war chests. Welfare funds include Jewish cultural, religious, civic-protective and other national activities which may be questioned as proper obligations of the general community.

Some war chests will consider it desirable to include the Jewish welfare fund as an entity, if for no other reason than to eliminate independent appeals, and in recognition of the status and broad gauge of Jewish interests. Other war chests will scrutinize the welfare fund and include only those agencies that are essentially philanthropic in character, such as the national health agencies, JDC, UPA, NRS, ORT, HIAS, etc.

Other vital points which merit consideration at the present time are the problems of (1) retaining leadership interest and financial support for those parts of the Jewish program which may not be included in the war chests, and (2) the re-establishment of specific Jewish community interest after the war in the causes that have been included in the war chest.

15. *Ibid.*

16. Irving Lipsitch, *Proceedings of NCJSS*, May 1927, p. 146.

17. H. L. Lurie, "A Decade of Jewish Organization," *Notes and News*,

Oct. 2, 1942, p. 5: *Fears have been expressed that a war economy and war taxation will diminish the resources, divert the leadership and weaken Jewish community organization. Inter-sectarian cooperation through community war chests and the outlook for governmental direction of voluntary agencies through the President's War Appeals Control Board are held by some to be indicative of radical changes that may weaken Jewish organization. In the opinion of the writer these fears are groundless. As Jews, we organize and build and maintain activities and institutions as an expression of our will to solve vital problems. As long as these problems are real we shall continue to seek solutions and ways in which we can make group progress toward our religious, social and cultural objectives.*

18. From Summary of Fund-Raising and Budgeting Session at 1944 General Assembly, *Notes and News*, Feb.-March, 1944, p. 16: *Last year's Assembly (of CJFWF, 1943) dealt at length with the advisability of war chest joinder. With the passage of a year, the point was reached at which evaluation of chest campaign experience became possible.*

Representatives of about fifty communities who attended the session heard Abe Srere, president of the Jewish Welfare Federation in Detroit, present the opinion of eight agencies whose campaigns had been merged with chests.

All regarded the experience as worthwhile, particularly in the development of better community relations. The opportunity for a large job of interpreting the Jewish community to the general public was recognized in each case. At the same time Jewish contributors, accustomed always to meeting communal obligations, gave generously, thus helping to raise the level of gifts generally.

As for Jewish federation receipts, all agreed that they were definitely in line with amounts that could have been expected through independent campaigns.

These factors, Mr. Srere pointed out, picture the credit side of joinder. A possible disadvantage, it was felt, lay in the fact that a diminution of interest in and knowledge of Jewish causes on the part of members of the Jewish community could result.

19. "War Chest Reconversion," *Notes and News* (Oct.-Nov. 1945), p. 13.

20. Information in files of CJFWF. The growth of welfare funds is indicated in a 1939 report which showed that the income of welfare funds had nearly doubled in three years. Results were due not only to increased giving on the part of those who renewed their pledges from year to year, but to large increases in the number of contributors who responded to the pressing needs at home and abroad. For example, in one city contributors who had numbered 5,047 in 1930, and had declined to 3,330 in 1933 owing to the depression, had increased to 19,080 six years later.

21. From 1931 to 1943 the total of Jewish immigration to the United States again showed an upward trend with a reported net increase of 173,259 during this twelve-year period.

22. "Facing Community Problems," a summary of the 1936 General Assembly in *Notes and News*, no. 33 (Feb. 20, 1936), p. 10.

23. Sidney, Hollander, "Federations Face 1938," *Notes and News*, no. 45 (Dec. 1, 1937), p. 5.

24. In Cleveland a merger of federation-welfare fund and community council structures took place in 1951 into one overall central agency responsible for the varieties of communal functions which had previously been carried on by separate bodies. Similar mergers had previously taken place in other cities—for example, in Kansas City and Hartford.

25. Max Simon, president of the Cleveland Jewish Community Council, "Unifying Jewish Group Activities," *Notes and News*, no. 34 (April 8, 1936), pp. 3-4: *A question frequently raised in the preliminary discussions concerned the power such a Council would wield over the member organizations. The constitution specifically states that the action of the Council need not be binding upon any member. To have taken any other point of view would have been to disregard the reality of the situation. In the first place, only on such a basis would most of the groups become affiliated with the Council. Secondly, even if a police power clause were inserted, it would be meaningless. For the only power of compulsion the Council could have is the power of public opinion.*

If we believe that Jewish life in this country presents us with a unitary problem which can be solved by a set of decrees representing the residual judgment derived from combining the judgments of carefully selected representatives, then the Council could be established on the basis of a particular philosophy of Jewish life. If, however, we believe that Jewish life is an endless series of problems, some soluble and others not, then we must recognize that the essential need is for building up a method of group association which might result in a better understanding of these problems and conflicts.

26. Samuel A. Goldsmith, "Jewish Community Organization," *Notes and News*, no. 36 (July 1, 1936), pp. 3-5.

NOTES TO CHAPTER VII

1. William J. Shroder, "The Relationship of National Agency Programs to Local Community Organizations," *JSS Quarterly*, Sept. 1941, p. 12.

2. "Toward A National TB Program," *Notes and News*, no. 49 (May 19, 1938), pp. 3-4.

3. From information in files of CJFWF.

4. The National Coordinating Committee in 1938 organized a National Resettlement Committee for the purpose of achieving a more effective distribution of the refugees arriving at New York City, the major port of entry. The National Resettlement Committee cooperated with the federations and welfare funds which assumed responsibility for the care of refugees sent to their communities. In 1938, the efforts of the National Coordinating Committee for Refugees were endorsed both by the JDC and the UPA and were beginning to be a larger factor in welfare fund allocations.

5. William J. Shroder, "A Three-in-One Campaign," *Notes and News*, no. 53 (Jan. 11, 1939), pp. 3-4.

6. "UJA Dissolved," *Notes and News*, no. 65 (Jan. 15, 1941), p. 10; and James L. White, "They Wanted a UJA," *Notes and News*, no. 66 (March 19, 1941), pp. 8-9.

7. "Regional Resolutions," *Notes and News*, II, no. 2 (Dec. 1944), p. 2.

8. The President's War Relief Control Board had, by 1945, been active in reducing the number of foreign war relief agencies from 300 to 87, and had been instrumental in the establishment of the National War Fund which had been conducting a combined annual campaign since 1943 for the United Service Organization, War Prisoners' Aid, and for major foreign relief agencies. The UJA and other Jewish overseas organizations had not joined the National War Fund, since their campaign goals were relatively greater than those of the beneficiary agencies of the National War Fund.

9. Milton P. Firestone, "General Jewish Council Reviewed," *Notes and News*, Feb. 1940, p. 11; also "Assembly Demands Defense Unity," *Notes and News*, Feb. 1943, pp. 13-15.

10. Philip Bernstein, "Issues Facing the GJC," *Notes and News*, March 1941, pp. 15-17.

11. "Congress Withdraws from GJC," *Notes and News*, May 1941, p. 11.

12. "A National Program on Anti-Semitism," *Notes and News*, I (n.s.), no. 4, p. 18.

13. From statement prepared by NCRAC 1947:
Created March 20, 1944 pursuant to a recommendation of the General Assembly of the Council of Jewish Federations and Welfare Funds, the NCRAC operates within the framework of the following Aims and Objectives which have been adopted by the Plenary Session and subscribed to by all its member agencies:

   1. To study, analyze and evaluate the policies and activities of the national and local agencies.
   2. To ascertain the problem areas from time to time.

3. *To ascertain the areas of activities of these organizations and to conduct a continuous inventory of their projects.*
4. *To serve as a coordinating and clearance agency for projects and policies, to eliminate duplication and conflict of activities, and to recommend further projects to member agencies.*
5. *To seek agreement on and formulate policies. Such policies once formulated and adopted, it is expected that the affiliated organizations will adhere to such policies and will not engage in any activities in contravention of such policies.*

14. "Turn Spotlight on Budgeting," *Notes and News*, Dec. 1940, pp. 13-14.

15. Jacob Blaustein, "The Advisory Budget Service," and Harry Greenstein, the Discussion, both *Notes and News*, March 1941, pp. 10-14.

16. "Regional Resolutions," *Notes and News*, II (n.s.), no. 2. (Dec. 1944), p. 2. Cf. Resolution adopted at 1944 General Assembly, *Notes and News*, IV (Feb.-March, 1944), p. 17: *Resolved: that the Board of Directors of the Council of Jewish Federations and Welfare Funds be asked to reconsider the subject of national budgeting.*

17. "National Advisory Budgeting," *The Jewish Community*, I, no. 1 (March 1946), pp. 4-6.

18. Isador Lubin, "Overseas Study Launched," *The Jewish Community*, II, no. 3 (June-July, 1947), pp. 3-6.

19. See Report of first Large City Conferences, *The Jewish Community*, Dec. 1948, on conference held in Pittsburgh, Oct. 23-24, 1948; several of these conferences were held in subsequent years.

20. Herbert R. Abeles, "No Double Standard in Trusteeship," in *The Jewish Community*, VII, no. 2 (June 1952), pp. 3-7.

21. Members of the LCBC in 1958 included:
Atlanta Jewish Welfare Fund
Baltimore Jewish Welfare Fund
Boston Combined Jewish Appeal
Buffalo United Jewish Federation
Chicago Jewish Welfare Fund
Cincinnati Jewish Welfare Fund
Cleveland Jewish Community Federation
Dallas Jewish Welfare Federation
Denver Allied Jewish Community Council
Detroit Jewish Welfare Federation
Hartford Jewish Federation
Houston Jewish Community Council
Jewish Federation Council of Greater Los Angeles
Kansas City Jewish Federation and Council
Miami-Greater Miami Jewish Federation
Milwaukee Jewish Welfare Fund

Minneapolis Federation for Jewish Service
Newark Jewish Community Council of Essex County
Philadelphia Federation of Jewish Agencies
Pittsburgh United Jewish Federation
Rochester United Jewish Welfare Fund
St. Louis Jewish Federation
San Francisco Jewish Welfare Federation

22. "Large Cities Confer on Agency Budgets," *The Jewish Community*, IV, no. 3, pp. 10-11.

NOTES TO CHAPTER VIII

1. "Jewish Population of New Orleans," report of a local study prepared by CJFWF, April 1954. Ben B. Seligman, "The American Jew—Some Demographic Features," *AJYB*, LI (1950), pp. 3-52. Ben B. Seligman, "Changes in Jewish Population in the United States 1949-50," *AJYB*, LII (1951), pp. 3-16.

   In a study made in New Orleans in 1953, it was found that the Jewish population was predominantly native-born. Those born abroad constituted only 17% of the total population and were to be found primarily in the older age groups. In the age group under 25, the foreign-born were only 3% of the total.

   While New Orleans perhaps had a smaller settlement of immigrant Jews than other communities, studies in several cities find that between 70% and 80% of American Jewry were born in this country. With the normal aging processes, the proportion of the foreign-born is bound to decline.

2. In the New Orleans study, it was found that there was an increasing tendency for the native-born to reach at least the undergraduate level of college. In the 21-40 age group, more than 7 out of 10 had progressed beyond the high school level. This is to be compared with 40% of college attendance for those in all ages no longer attending school. For the total group, an additional 40% had attended or been graduated from high school. The number without formal education was almost non-existent. While the proportion that had received higher education may not be as great in the large centers of Jewish population, the impression is that the trend is generally in this direction.

3. From "Tables of Receipts of National Jewish Agencies" *AJYB*, vols. 52-61 inclusive, and supplementary information in the files of CJFWF.

4. *Ibid.*

5. Harold Glasser, "DP's—The End," in *The Jewish Community*, IV, no. 2, pp. 7-9.

6. One additional instance of temporary difficulty related directly to the UJA did, however, arise. In 1948, there was an internal conflict within the leadership of the United Palestine Appeal which,

for a time, threatened to disrupt that organization and its relationship to the UJA. A group organized as a "Committee of Contributors and Workers" challenged the structure and the activities of the UPA and its two constituent member agencies, the Keren Hayesod and the Keren Kayemeth. After protracted negotiations and discussions in which a committee of the CJFWF served as conciliators, a final settlement was reached by the Board of the UPA in February 1949. Since that time, there has been no difficulty within the internal structure of the United Jewish Appeal which has impinged on the work of the local welfare funds.

7. "Institutions of Hebrew Learning in Israel," memo from CJFWF, February 16, 1953.

8. Press release issued jointly by HIAS and USNA, January 28, 1954.

9. From information in files of CJFWF.

10. Table prepared from information in series of articles in *AJYB* on Jewish communal services, vols. 52-61 inclusive.

11. The figures used in this table are *inclusive* of the Greator New York Fund. Grants from the Fund to the New York Federation ranged from less than $700,000 to more than $1,400,000 during the period 1949 through 1958.

12. Arnold Gurin, "Financing of Jewish Communal Programs," *AJYB*, LV (1954), pp. 126-140.

13. Stanley C. Myers, "Israel Conference Analyses Problems," *The Jewish Community*, V, no. 3, pp. 3-6. "Communities Expand Efforts for Israel," *ibid.*, VI, no. 1, pp. 6-8.

Distribution of Net Amounts Budgeted by Jewish Federations and Welfare Funds to the United Jewish Appeal and Other Major Fields of Service 1945-1959

(Amount of Dollars Given in Thousands)

YEAR	TOTAL	United Jewish Appeal (a)	Other Over- seas	Total Over- seas (a)	National Agencies	Local Agen- cies (a)
1945						
Amt.	$ 49,456	$ 29,416	$2,150	$ 31,566	$3,630	$14,260
%	100.0	59.6	4.3	63.9	7.3	28.8
1946						
Amt.	112,135	86,875	2,965	89,840	3,670	18,625
%	100.0	77.5	2.6	80.1	3.3	16.6
1947						
Amt.	134,925	96,962	3,235	100,197	7,220	27,508
%	100.0	71.8	2.4	74.2	5.4	20.4
1948						
Amt.	172,483	125,239	4,289	129,528	8,790	34,165
%	100.0	72.6	2.5	75.1	5.1	19.8

1949					
Amt.	133,937	81,297	3,492	84,789	7,392	41,756
%	100.0	60.7	2.6	63.3	5.5	31.2
1950					
Amt.	118,204	68,976	2,845	71,821	6,892	39,491
%	100.0	58.4	2.4	60.8	5.8	33.4
1951					
Amt.	110,910	67,017	2,748	69,765	4,857	36,288
%	100.0	60.3	2.5	62.8	4.5	32.7
1952					
Amt.	99,420	57,516	2,607	60,123	4,565	34,732
%	100.0	57.9	2.6	60.5	4.6	34.9
1953					
Amt.	96,244	56,836	2,335	59,171	4,686	32,387
%	100.0	59.1	2.4	61.5	4.9	33.6
1954					
Amt.	89,592	50,347	2,244	52,591	4,414	32,567
%	100.0	56.2	2.5	58.7	4.9	36.4
1955					
Amt.	88,810	51,010	2,313	53,323	4,421	31,059
%	100.0	57.4	2.6	60.0	5.0	35.0
1956					
Amt.	107,806	68,033	2,624	70,657	4,640	32,504
%	100.0	63.1	2.4	65.5	4.3	30.2
1957					
Amt.	115,658	73,767	3,005	76,772	4,633	33,029
%	100.0	63.8	2.8	66.6	4.0	28.6
1958					
Amt.	99,671	58,443	2,870	61,313	4,488	32,928
%	100.0	58.4	2.9	61.3	4.5	32.9

NOTE: Individual amounts do not add to total in all instances because of rounding and undistributed amounts.

This table is based upon estimates for all welfare funds and federations derived from statistical series which includes over one hundred reporting agencies. It does not include welfare fund receipts used for fund-raising costs, administration, contingencies, shrinkage, reserves.

Where capital funds are raised in the central campaigns, these are included in allocations to local or overseas beneficiaries, except for New York Federation capital campaigns of 1945 and 1949 which in those years were run concurrently with campaign for operating funds.

(a) UJA allocations made to New York Association for New Americans have been subtracted from United Jewish Appeal and Total Overseas columns and added to Local Agencies column.

NOTES TO CHAPTER IX

1. Saul Cherniak and Albert Gordon, "Relationship of Synagogue and Community," at 23rd General Assembly, CJFWF, Nov. 18-21, 1954. Samuel H. Rubiner and Ralph Simon, "Community-Synagogue Relationships," at 24th General Assembly, CJFWF, Nov. 10-13, 1955. Myron B. Blanchard, "The Effect of Social Trends and Population Mobility on the Jewish Center," *JSS Quarterly*, Fall 1955, pp. 49-60.

2. See "Small City Services Grow," a symposium in *The Jewish Community*, June 1955, p. 7; and "Small Community with Big Record" (Norristown community organization develops model integrated program), *ibid.*, Feb. 1955, p. 12.

3. "Post-War Capital Fund," *Notes and News*, II (n.s.) no. 1 (Oct.-Nov. 1944), p. 15; and "Fund-Raising Prospects for 1945," *ibid.*, II (n.s.), no. 4 (April 1, 1945), pp. 7-8. Also "Guidepost and Pitfalls," *The Jewish Community*," III, no. 2 (June 1948), pp. 3-6.

4. Information derived from the annual reports of the CJFWF, "Jewish Social Work," and secured from American Association for Jewish Education and National Jewish Welfare Board.

5. Study of Coordination of Health Services for Patients with Long-Term Illness—Preliminary Reports: IV. Coordination of Personal Health Services: A Study of Relationships Between General Hospitals and Institutions for Long-Term Care, May 1959 (revised ed.); V. Chronic-Disease Hospitals and Related Institutions, March 1959; VII. Jewish Family Service Agencies and Vocational Service Agencies: Their Role in the Care of the Chronically Ill and Disabled, August 1959; VIII. Jewish Homes for the Aged: Organization, Functions and Relationships, Sept. 1959; X. The Role of General Hospitals in the Care of Patients with Long-Term Illness, Feb. 1960; XV. Basic Factors in Planning for Coordination of Hospitals and Institutions for Long-Term Care, Oct. 1960.

6. S. P. Goldberg, "Jewish Communal Services: Programs and Finances," CJFWF, 1957 and 1960 eds.

7. *Ibid.*

8. R. M. MacIver, "Report on the Jewish Community Relations Agencies," NCRAC, Nov. 1951, New York.

9. "Climax in Community Relations," *The Jewish Community*, VII, no. 3 (Oct. 1952), pp. 4-61; also "Jewish Community Relations," *ibid*. For a full report, see Selma G. Hirsh, *AJYB*, LIV (1953), pp. 162-177.

10. Roland Baxt, "Jewish Vocational Services," *AJYB*, LV (1954), pp. 103-104.

11. Michael Freund, "The Training Bureau for Jewish Communal Service," CJFWF, 1956. "School for Communal Service," *The Jewish Community*, II, no. 1 (Jan. 1947), p. 24.

12. L. W. Neumark, "Planning Before Emergencies," *The Jewish Community*, VII, no. 2, pp. 9-11; and CJFWF reports on the Advisory Committee on Social Planning.

13. "Cultural Foundation Elects Officers," *The Jewish Community*, Oct. 1960, p. 17.

14. Sidney Z. Vincent, study director, "National Jewish Cultural Services in America: Appraisals and Recommendations 1959," study by CJFWF. David Zeff, "The National Jewish Cultural Study," *AJYB*, 1960, pp. 149-164.

NOTES TO CHAPTER X

1. See, for example, R. M. MacIver, "Report on the Jewish Community Relations Agencies," NCRAC (March 1951), section I, p. 3: *We shall, however, from time to time speak of the "Jewish Community" as a way of denoting the people of Jewish origin in a particular locality or in the United States as a whole. We use this term for lack of any other convenient designation, but it should be clearly understood that there is not and should not be any implication that the Jewish groups constitute communities in the strict sense of the word.*

2. For an extensive historical treatment of Jewish communal organization, throughout history, see Salo W. Baron, *The Jewish Community: Its History and Structure to the American Revolution*, 3 vols.

3. For a discussion of this topic by representatives of sectarian organizations in the field of social welfare, see "Social Services Under Catholic, Jewish and Protestant Auspices in the Total Welfare System" (a report on the Great Lakes Institute sponsored by Community Chests and Councils of America, Inc., July 1948): *In the case work field there is a division of family and child care services on strictly sectarian lines. In the group work field we see demands that church settings be used. In community organization we find ourselves concerned with a further fragmentation of social work. We have the problem of unifying the community and we see division being created.* Introductory remarks (p. 2) by Chairman Robert H. MacRae. Other speakers outlined the necessity for and the desirability of social welfare programs under sectarian auspices.

4. Joseph Willen, "The Responsibility of Jewish Agencies to Today's American Community," General Assembly paper, CJFWF, Nov. 1959, with discussion by Mrs. Charles Lakoff and Lewis Cole.

5. *Ibid.*

6. Benjamin B. Rosenberg, "Jewish Agencies and Jewish Responsibilities," General Assembly paper, CJFWF, Nov. 1960.

7. See Will Herberg, *Protestant-Catholic-Jew:* An Essay in American Religious Sociology (Garden City, N.Y.: Doubleday Co., 1955).

8. An example of this trend is reflected in the topics discussed at recent General Assemblies of the CJFWF which include the communal organization of Jewish education, relationships with synagogues, and similar subjects.

9. Morris Axelrod, "Urban Structure and Social Participation," *American Sociological Review* (New York: American Sociological Society), Feb. 1956, pp. 13-18.

10. Alvin Chenkin and Benjamin B. Goldman, "The Jewish Population of New Orleans, Louisiana, 1953: A Demographic Study," CJFWF.

11. Religious preferences by households in New Orleans are given as Reform, 57.2%; Conservative, 4.9%; Orthodox, 29.3%; and "none" or "no answer" 8.6% (*ibid.,* p. 41). In a population study of Greater Lynn, Mass., made in 1956, population estimated at 10,400 Jews, 76% of all households reported at least one membership in congregations and 17.5% "which did not hold membership in a congregation indicated preferences for adherence to a particular religious group." The two groups combined gave as their affiliation or preference Conservative, 45.6%; Orthodox, 37.8%; Reform, 8.7%. Information concerning native and foreign born was not obtained in the Lynn study, but it is generally assumed that the foreign born element is a large fraction of its population and that the group is much closer to its European antecedents than in New Orleans. The high proportion of congregational affiliations and preferences in these two cities, in different sections of the country but of similar size, would tend to support the assumption of the large extent of religious affiliation among Jews at least in the smaller cities. (Report published by the Jewish Community Federation of Greater Lynn, Massachusetts 1956.)

12. It is difficult to determine statistically whether the total number of local Jewish group associations is increasing or declining in relation to size of population. In the early years of large-scale Jewish immigration, there was an efflorescence of associations with small memberships (congregations, *hevras,* relief societies, *Landsmanschaften,* fraternal associations, etc.) based largely on the town or area from which the immigrants derived. Some vestigial aspects of these first efforts at Jewish group association remain, but there is on the whole a tendency for their disappearance or (as in the case of congregations) amalgamation with others into a new form of association. New kinds of association have come

into existence and there have been large growths in the membership of a number of groups which have emerged as the dominant
associations in certain areas of interest (for example, Hadassah
and Council of Jewish Women chapters, B'nai B'rith lodges, etc.).

In addition to participation in congregations, the New Orleans
study provided data on participation in some other groups, as
follows:

	Number	Male Age 15 and Over	Number	Female Age 15 and Over
		Percentage of Group Participation		
B'nai B'rith	912	26.9	530	14.1
Jewish Community Center	676	20.0	721	19.2
Council of Jewish Women	—	—	1,224	32.5
Hadassah	—	—	1,234	32.8
Other Zionist Organizations	371	11.0	125	3.3
College Fraternity	600	17.7	381	10.1
American Council for Judaism	97	2.9	121	3.2
Number in Age Groups	3,388		3,762	

13. New York City may be an exception to this general condition.
The total number of contributors to the New York Federation
or to the New York United Jewish Appeal falls considerably
below the total of membership of all synagogues. In the case of
Federation, this may be due to the policy of not soliciting employees, considered as the potential contributor of the Greater
New York Fund.

From Rabbi Isaac N. Trainin, "Jewish Communal Civics: A Program for Federations and Welfare Funds," *Journal of Jewish
Communal Service*, Summer 1956, p. 347: *Let us examine the
situation in Greater New York (including the 5 boroughs, Nassau
and Westchester). Here perhaps two and one-half million Jews
reside. Yet, both the Federation of Jewish Philanthropies, supporting 116 institutions, and the United Jewish Appeal of Greater
New York, probably do not receive more than 120,000 to 150,000
unit contributions each.*

14. Grinstein, *The Rise of the Jewish Community of New York*,
pp. 4-5: *Several factors stand out in a consideration of the effect
of the American environment on the religion and culture of New
York Jewry . . . The laws of New York on burial, on marriage,
and especially on the incorporation of religious societies pro-
foundly affected Jewish practice. Among the results of these laws
were the new concept of a minister in the house of God and the*

intrusion of democracy into the Jewish community to break down the barriers of the several social classes existing therein.

A less direct, but equally prominent, influence was the broad concept of liberty which existed in America. The early separation of Church and State gave each man the right to worship or not, as he chose. . . . Secession after secession was a natural development among the synagogues of New York. Jewish organizations of purely cultural or social nature, having no connections with the synagogue or with religion as such, soon came into being. Individual Jews lived inside or outside the Jewish community without molestation. It became equally impossible for the community to control ritual, dietary, and reform tendencies.

Grinstein also reports on numerous incidents of unwillingness of some of the congregations in New York City to cooperate on matters of vital importance.

NOTES TO CHAPTER XI

1. Though federation was considered a segment of Jewish community organization, it was early recognized as a cementing force. A statement by a federation executive in 1925 is indicative of that attitude: *Whatever the defects of the present federation plan may be, we have not yet evolved a better method of welding the community together, at least for purely humanitarian purposes* (Ludwig Bernstein, "Issues in Jewish Social Service," *Proceedings of NCJSS*, 1925, p. 6).

2. Dr. Alexander M. Dushkin, "Programs of Jewish Community Organization in the Light of Changing Trends," *Proceedings of NCJSS*, June 1933, p. 26.

3. A position which offered a theoretical basis for central Jewish communal organization was stated by the 1933 president of the NCJSS, I. M. Rubinow, in "The Credo of a Jewish Social Worker," *Proceedings*, June 1933, p. 17:
First there is the relation of the Jew as a citizen to the American scene; also (2) the relation of the individual Jew to his Jewish community; (3) the relation of the Jewish community to the American nation of which it constitutes an integral part; and finally, (4) the relation of American Jewry to the Jewish people of the world. Every one of these relationships is as should be, a matter of greatest importance to the individual Jew as well as to each Jewish communal group, no matter how isolated—no matter how small. None of them can be disregarded, none of them relegated to the rear.

4. William J. Shroder, "Programs of Jewish Community Organization in the Light of Changing Trends," *Proceedings of NCJSS*, June 1933, p. 31: *I do not feel that there is a possibility of a real Jewish community in America. I doubt very much if there is a real Jewish community in Europe, although we seem to concede in*

our discussion this evening that they have Jewish communities because they have a technical legal form supported by taxation. To me, a community means background, a common need and a common purpose to satisfy that need, together with a sufficient desire to devote to the satisfaction of that need at the sacrifice of whatever else may be involved . . . to make its satisfaction possible. Now, if I am correct in that idea of a community, then when we are talking about Jewish communities, we are talking about non-existent units of society.

5. Solomon Lowenstein, "Programs of Jewish Community Organization in the Light of Changing Trends," *ibid.,* June 1933, p. 26.

6. George W. Rabinoff, "The Need of Reorganizing Jewish Communal Life From the Federation Point of View," *ibid.,* May 1934, pp. 72-74. *In America, the Federation has been a voluntary agency, assuming certain limited philanthropic functions on behalf of the Jews resident in a community. It never attempted to speak or to act for all Jews. Even within its limited scope, concern for the philanthropic and in some degree for the cultural needs of the Jews, Federation had not succeeded in enlisting the full support of all classes of Jews, either in finances or in leadership. However, it had established its place; it had demonstrated that divergent groups could come together on a working platform without violence to their individual viewpoints; it had aspired to effective utilization of Jewish communal resources to meet communal problems through a centralization of financial and policy-making interest and responsibility.*

. . . conscious of the differences among our people, we seek a platform of harmony between the divergent elements. Through the democratic processes of discussion and education, controversial issues are resolvable into those factors which can be dealt with communally, and those which cannot be reconciled in such a program. Group survival is accepted by all the elements. Practical considerations dictate the necessity of cooperation within this minimum framework. We can attain this goal most readily by the extension and modification of the one mechanism with which we have already experimented, the Federation; the Federation as a centralized community agency to serve the Jewish group, the leaders democratically designated, alert to the crosscurrents of Jewish life, flexible to meet changing conditions, firm in their acceptance of the basic principle of an integrated Jewish group within the American milieu.

7. Mordecai M. Kaplan, "The Organization of American Jewry," *ibid.,* June 1935, pp. 52-71.

8. Notes 8 through 13 in the text are quotations from, or paraphrases of, Dr. Kaplan's proposals.

14. "What the Assembly Faces," *Notes and News,* Jan. 15, 1941.

15. Rabbi Silver, "The American Jewish Community in Wartime and After," *Proceedings of NCJSW*, May 1944.

16. From *Notes and News*, Nov.-Dec. 1943: *For many years our Jewish communities have organized themselves to meet their communal needs and community obligations with complete recognition and acceptance of* two basic principles: *(1) that united community action can be achieved in all fields where there is a common desire to act together for the benefit of Jewry generally and the community in particular; (2) that all individuals and groups in our communities can work together effectively with full recognition that there are differences of opinion and belief in many areas. . . .*

    Under the stress of present conditions, it becomes increasingly difficult to forget differences in order to do together those things which can and should be done together. This may result in hasty action inimical to your long-term obligations. Recognizing this, the Council of Jewish Federations and Welfare Funds, by formal action of its Board of Directors, has authorized this word of reaffirmation of its basic principles:

    WE URGE UPON ALL COMMUNITIES THE NECESSITY OF NOT PERMITTING CONFLICTS IN SOME AREAS TO DESTROY WHAT HAS BEEN ACHIEVED BY COOPERATIVE ACTION, AND TO CONTINUE, AND TO EXPAND THEIR COMMUNITY ORGANIZATIONS FOR THE BETTERMENT OF OUR PEOPLE HERE AND THROUGHOUT THE WORLD, AND FOR MAKING THEIR CONTRIBUTION TO AMERICAN LIFE.

17. *Notes and News*, Dec. 2, 1940.

18. *Ibid.*

19. *Notes and News*, Jan. 15, 1941.

20. Samuel A. Goldsmith, "Organizational Structure of the American Jewish Community," *JSS Quarterly*, Fall 1952.

21. Some of the more important of these changes have been described by the writer. Lurie, "Jewish Community Organization—Functions and Structures," *JSS Quarterly*, Sept. 1949: *The functions we developed for overseas needs served to bring together for co-operative efforts large sections of our Jewish population who had previously not found equally compelling incentives for participation on purely domestic matters; the importance of this influence on our Jewish communal organization cannot be overemphasized.*

    In recent years . . . a continuing cultural evolution . . . has tended to erase some of the sharper intra-group conflicts which had made community organizations of the past only a theory and not a fact. Gradually, because of the urgency of needs, there has developed a tendency toward mutual acceptance . . . a change from a benevolent paternalism to the creation of a composite leadership body which may symbolize, if it does not actually represent, a variety of Jewish groups that have achieved the ability to express themselves in meaningful ways in community affairs. Leadership is changing, in some cities more rapidly than in others. With a diminution in the importance of segmental group values among the younger population, intermarriage among the descendants of the older and newer immigrants, the shift, for many of the younger age groups, from Orthodoxy to Conservatism or Reform, the desire for participation in the older, established synagogues by the children of the newer immigrants, and similar factors have tended to create a more acceptable formula for broader participation in the management of communal affairs, and therefore for a more homogeneous community. See also chapter XVII.

22. *Ibid.*

23. Henry L. Zucker, "Functions of the Jewish Community Agency: A Practical Approach," *JSS Quarterly*, Fall 1953 (*Proceedings* issue).

24. Goldsmith, *op. cit.*, pp. 8-9.

25. Zucker, *op. cit.*, p. 43.

26. Isidore Sobeloff, "Jewish Community Organization: The Past—Current Trends—Directions," papers, 23rd General Assembly, CJFWF, Nov. 1954, p. 11.

NOTES TO CHAPTER XII

1. "Report on Small Cities Executives Institute" (summary of papers and discussions), sponsored by NJWB and CJFWF, Aug. 28-Sept. 1, 1955; and Allan Bloom, "Problems of Jewish People in the Small Community and Programs to Meet Their Needs," CJFWF, July 1955. See *supra* notes 1 and 2, chapter IX.

2. A considerable part of the data utilized in this chapter has been derived from the following publications of the CJFWF:
   1. "Central Community Organization in Large Cities," 1949, 26 pages.
   2. "Central Community Organization and Planning in Intermediate Communities," 1950, 25 pages.
   3. "Central Jewish Community Organization and Planning in Small Communities," 1952, 24 pages.

   See also Samuel A. Goldsmith, "Organizational Structure of the American Jewish Community," *JSS Quarterly*, Fall, 1952, pp. 1-9.

3.   *Central Agency Structures of Selected Cities**

	Number of Agencies	Number of Cities
A. Cities with less than 5,000 Jewish Population		
1. Individual Memberships Only	4	
2. Beneficiary, Constituent or		

* Based on studies of CJFWF, 1949 and 1952.

Participating Agencies Only   8
3. Both Individual and Agency Memberships 18
                                         ——
                                  Total   30 (a)   30 (a)

B. Cities with Jewish Population of from
   5,000 to 40,000
   1. Individual Memberships Only   3
   2. Beneficiary, Constituent or
      Participating Agencies Only   4
   3. Both Individual and Agency Memberships 36
                                         ——
                                  Total   43 (b)   34 (b)

C. Cities with Jewish Population from
   40,000 to 375,000
   1. Individual Memberships Only   3
   2. Beneficiary, Constituent or
      Participating Agencies Only   3
   3. Both Individual and Agency Memberships 15
                                         ——
                                  Total   21 (c)   11 (c)

D. New York City (d)
   1. Individual Memberships Only   0
   2. Beneficiary, Constituent or
      Participating Agencies Only   2
   3. Both Individual and Agency Memberships 1
                                         ——
                                  Total   3   1

(a) As of 1952.
(b) As of 1950.
(c) As of 1949.
(d) Includes the New York Federation, the New York United
    Jewish Appeal, and the Brooklyn Jewish Community
    Council.

A. List of cities with less than 5,000 Jewish population included in
   table:

Altoona, Pa.	Flint, Mich.	Newburgh, N.Y.
Bessemer, Ala.	Ft. Wayne, Ind.	Newport News, Va.
Benton Harbor, Mich.	Harrisburg, Pa.	Peoria, Ill.
Binghamton, N.Y.	Jacksonville, Fla.	Port Chester, N.Y.
Canton, O.	Lancaster, Pa.	Portland, Me.
Davenport, Iowa	Long Beach, Calif.	Poughkeepsie, N.Y.
Duluth, Minn.	Nashville, Tenn.	Savannah, Ga.
Elmira, N.Y.	New Britain, Conn.	Schenectady, N.Y.

| Shreveport, La. | Stockton, Calif. | Tulsa, Okla. |
| Sioux City, Iowa | Tampa, Fla. | Waco, Texas |

B. List of cities (5,000 to 40,000 Jewish population) from which information was derived includes:

Atlantic City, N.J.	Indianapolis, Ind.	Rochester, N.Y.
Bay Cities, Mich.	Lynn, Mass.	St. Paul, Minn.
Bayonne, N.J.	Memphis, Tenn.	Schenectady, N.Y.
Buffalo, N.Y.	Minneapolis, Minn.	Seattle, Wash.
Camden, N.J.	New Haven, Conn.	Springfield, Mass.
Cincinnati, Ohio	New Orleans, La.	Syracuse, N.Y.
Dallas, Texas	Norfolk, Va.	Toledo, Ohio
Dayton, O.	Oakland, Calif.	Trenton, N.J.
Denver, Col.	Omaha, Neb.	Wilkes-Barre, Pa.
Elizabeth, N.J.	Passaic, N.J.	Wilmington, Del.
Hartford, Conn.	Paterson, N.J.	Worcester, Mass.
Houston, Texas	Portland, Ore.	Youngstown, Ohio

C. List of cities included (40,000 to 375,000 Jewish population):

Baltimore	Detroit	Pittsburgh
Boston	Los Angeles	St. Louis
Chicago	Newark	San Francisco
Cleveland	Philadelphia	

By the end of 1956 the number of 21 communal agencies in these 11 cities had been reduced by mergers to 17.

4. By-Laws of Federation of Jewish Philanthropies of New York, adopted June 24, 1917 as amended May 9, 1949.

5. *Ibid.*

6. By-Laws of the United Jewish Appeal of Greater New York as amended (1955).
The three constituents of the New York UJA are the JDC, the United Israel Appeal, formerly known as the United Palestine Appeal, and the New York Association for New Americans which, since the organization of United HIAS, is the successor to the National Refugee Service in this arrangement.

7. By-Laws of Brooklyn Jewish Community Council.

8. Excerpts from a letter dated 1956 written by a well informed observer of the affairs of the Brooklyn Jewish Community Council:
Originally the Brooklyn Jewish Community Council had more or less active participation of the 800 or so group organizations which it claims as members. They sent delegates to an annual assembly, participated in neighborhood councils, and received and acted upon reports of their delegates to the Brooklyn JCC. The ... Board ... has nearly a hundred members and is fairly representative of major groups in the community. The member organizations still respond fairly well to the call for an annual meeting or for a conference on matters of current interest, such as support for Israel.

443

The Council was originally supported in a large part by subventions from the American Jewish Committee and the Anti-Defamation League; some funds for special projects were also contributed by a local Jewish leadership group called the Men's League. The arrangement with the American Jewish Committee and the ADL became a source of mutual dissatisfaction a few years ago. In 1948 the executive director attempted to establish an independent fund-raising campaign, but finally settled for an arrangement with the New York UJA which provided that funds earmarked for the BJCC be given through the American Jewish Congress. The successor executive (about 1950-1953), tried to increase the UJA subsidy and when this was impossible he again attempted an independent campaign. The campaign was carried out, but raised only a very small sum, and the Council had to cut its staff to one professional worker and one clerk.

In terms of function the agency has maintained a program under two major headings: Community Relations and Internal Jewish Affairs. The program has been handled as well as it is possible for one professional to handle the load.

9. "Pilot Studies in Jewish Community Organization Summary," published by Committee on Community Organization, CJFWF, 1955.

NOTES TO CHAPTER XIII

1. Goldsmith, "The Organizational Character of the American Jewish Community," *JSS Quarterly*, Fall 1952, p. 1.

2. There are some exceptions, such as the Philadelphia Federation which is supported by the United Fund and Community Chest. In most other cities the federation of local beneficiary agencies is an integral part of a combined Jewish fund-raising program which organized support through direct campaigns and also as a constituent of community chests. A number of local agencies known as "community councils," such as in Detroit and Washington, D.C., do not raise funds independently, but are beneficiaries of the local federation-welfare fund.

3. There are one or more Jewish welfare and cultural agencies that are not affiliated with Jewish federations or community chests in some communities, but it is mainly in New York City and to a lesser extent, in a few of the other largest communities that there is any number of local welfare agencies with sizable budgets that are not beneficiaries of federations or chests.

4. Rudi Walter and Henry L. Zucker, "Study of Endowment Fund Programs of 13 Large Jewish Federations," Community Federation of Cleveland, Nov. 1959. See also Robert L. Smith, "The Legacy Program of the New York Federation," 24th General Assembly, CJFWF, Nov. 13, 1955.

5. The Budget Research Department of the CJFWF in 1960 prepared

digest reports on 88 overseas, national and regional agencies (distribution over 95,000 copies annually); issued 6 "Israel Reports" (distribution over 10,000 copies) on special aspects of selected programs in Israel; maintained a checklist of over 300 traditional institutions (yeshivot, etc.) in Israel; sent out information on 300 agencies not covered in the Budget Digests, in response to 677 requests; provided technical and consultative services at hearings and in the preparation of reports on 10 agencies for the Large City Budgeting Conference; issued an annual report on "Jewish Communal Services: Programs and Finances"; worked on questions of budgeting practices (i.e., pre-campaign budgeting arrangements, information on special budgeting problems of communities, financial relationships between federations and community chests, advice on tax provisions affecting philanthropy); served on the Jewish Agency for Israel Committee on Control and Authorization of Campaigns; provided information on the technical aspects of staff pension arrangements; provided consultation on office operations, machines, forms and insurance coverage; and filled speaking engagements at request of communities, on overseas and national developments, before leadership groups, governing boards and allocations committees.

6. "Jewish Population of the United States," articles in *American Jewish Year Books*.

7. Year books on Jewish social services have been published by CJFWF since 1930, analyzing service and cost trends in family service and child care, service to the aged, hospitals and clinics, and related programs.

8. "Planning for Federation Programs—Medical Centers, Jewish Community Institutions, Community Center Programs," *Proceedings* of Third Annual Conference of the Jewish Federations of New York, Chicago, Philadelphia: Social Surveys, 1948, CJFWF (mimeo), 75 pp. "A Guide for Use in Local Planning," 1949, 29 pp. "Planning Health and Welfare in the Jewish Community," a statement of the principles of social planning, prepared by Social Planning Advisory Committee, CJFWF, 1951. Mrs. Charles Lakoff and William C. Treuhaft, "Planning for the Changing Local Budget Dollar," at 20th General Assembly, CJFWF, 1951.

9. See, for example, "Central Community Organization in Large Cities," CJFWF, 1949, pp. 14-17; "Central Community Organizations and Planning in Intermediate Communities," pp. 10-11; and "Community Organization in Small Cities" (advance report and papers presented at 1959 General Assembly).

10. See Resolutions adopted at CJFWF 1960 General Assembly on social legislation. Also, "Guidelines for Local Federation Action on Tax-Supported Health and Welfare Programs, CJFWF, May, 1959.

NOTES TO CHAPTER XIV

1. A variation is the constituent agency of federation which does not receive funds from the federation but from a non-sectarian community chest. In some cities one or more agencies receiving support from community chests may not be members of the federation.

2. In New York City, for example, the majority of Jewish homes for aged are not constituents or beneficiaries of the Federation but hold membership in the Central Bureau for the Aged, organized by Federation for cooperative planning by both the affiliated and unaffiliated agencies serving the Jewish aged. Similarly, non-affiliated Jewish institutions and agencies for children have joined several of the affiliated agencies in the New York Jewish Child Care Council which receives funds from the Federation.

3. William Avrunin, "Jewish Social Services," *SWYB*, 1960, p. 342.

4. *Ibid.*

5. See "Statement of Principles on Jewish Center Purposes," adopted by annual meeting of National Council of JWB, May 1948. (Quoted in *AJYB*, 1956, pp. 263-264.)

6. Oscar I. Janowsky, *The JWB Survey* (New York: Dial Press, 1948).

7. Grace L. Coyle, "Social Group Work," *SWYB*, 1954, p. 481.

8. Elias Picheny, "Tasks Ahead in the Jewish Center Field," *Journal of Jewish Communal Service* (New York: National Conference of Jewish Communal Service), Fall 1956, pp. 104-116. See also *supra*, chapter X.

9. David M. Goldenberg, "Practice of Group Work in a Synagogue Center," *JSS Quarterly*, Winter 1954, pp. 233-239.

10. Bernard Carp, "The Philosophy of Fee Charging in the Center," *JSS Quarterly*, Spring 1955, pp. 359-367.

11. Sidney Z. Vincent, "Summary of Jewish Education Study in Cleveland, Ohio," *AJYB*, 1956, p. 223.

12. S. P. Goldberg, "Jewish Communal Services," *AJYB*, 1958. Tables 6 and 6A. See also "Community Responsibility and Planning for Jewish Education," an outline for discussion of this topic prepared by CJFWF for 1953 General Assembly.

13. Vincent, *op. cit.*, p. 224.

14. "Community Responsibility for Jewish Education," papers by Morris Garvett, Oscar I. Janowsky, Louis Kaplan, at General Assembly, CJFWF, Nov. 1954, p. 12.

15. The CJFWF has been close to this progressive development in Jewish homes for the aged through its Social Planning Department, especially after 1940. Some of the more recent CJFWF re-

ports which are informative on these trends include the sections on Homes for the Aged in annual *Yearbooks of Jewish Social Services* and the following:

"New Trends in Services to Older Persons," 1949

"Administration of Homes for the Aged, Selected Papers on Management and Program Planning," 1952

"Per Diem Costs in Jewish Homes for the Aged," 1952-1953

"Financial Assistance to the Aged in Institutions, Effect of Social Security Amendments," 1953

"Home Care for the Aged," 1954

"Sheltered Workshops," 1954

"Services to the Aged in Jewish Case Work Agencies," 1954

"Services to Senile Persons in Jewish Homes for the Aged," 1954

"Financial Requirements for Admission to Jewish Homes for the Aged," 1956

"The Small Home for the Aged, Cost and Staffing," 1956

"Apartment House and Residence Club Projects for Older Jewish Persons," 1957

"The Development of New Non-Institutional Programs and Resources for the Aged," 1957

"Institutional Services for the Jewish Aged—The Essentials of a Program for the Intermediate-Size Jewish Community," 1957

"Jewish Community Responsibility for Services to the Disturbed Aged," 1957

"Planning for the Aged in the Small Community," 1957

"Psychiatry in a Home for the Aged," 1957

"The Future of the Institutional Programs for the Aged," 1958

"Regional Institutional Services for the Jewish Aged," 1958

"Guidelines for Institutional Services for the Aged in the Small Community," 1959

16. *YBJSS*, 1960, CJFWF.

17. "The Jewish Hospital—Today and Tomorrow," summary of a workshop, CJFWF, 1954, Table II.

18. *Ibid.*, p. 1.

19. *Ibid.*, p. 2.

20. Published reports derived from this research include:

"Organization of Personal Health Services in Homes for the Aged," Nov. 1959.

"Residents of Homes for the Aged: Their Health Conditions and Health Needs," Feb. 1959.

"Prolonged Stay in General Hospitals: A Study of Two Hundred Patients," June 1959.

"Coordination of Personal Health Services: A Study of Relationships Between General Hospitals and Institutions for Long-Term Care," May 1959 (revised ed.)

A HERITAGE AFFIRMED

"Chronic-Disease Hospitals and Related Institutions," March, 1959

"Patients on Home Care: Their Characteristics and Experience," July 1959

"Jewish Family Service Agencies and Vocational Service Agencies: Their Role in the Care of the Chronically Ill and Disabled," Aug. 1959

"Jewish Homes for the Aged: Organization, Functions and Relationships," Sept. 1959

"Disabled Clients of Family Service Agencies and of Vocational Service Agencies," Jan. 1960

"The Role of General Hospitals in the Care of Patients with Long-Term Illness," Feb. 1960.

"Nursing Service in Homes for the Aged," April 1960

"Medical Social Service in the General Hospital: Contributions to the Care of Long-Term Patients," June 1960

"Social Service in Homes for the Aged," Aug. 1960

"Characteristics of Patients in Chronic-Disease Hospitals," Sept. 1960

"Basic Factors in Planning for Coordination of Hospitals and Institutions for Long-Term Care," Oct. 1960

21. "The Jewish Hospital . . . ," *op. cit.*, p. 2.

22. *Ibid.*, p. 4.

23. There are no recent statistics on the extent to which Jewish patients use hospitals other than those under Jewish auspices, where these exist. Studies in the 1930s indicated that from one-half to two-thirds of Jewish patients were receiving care in general hospitals under public, proprietary, non-sectarian or Christian denominational auspices. On the other side of the picture, 41 Jewish general hospitals reporting in 1957 to the CJFWF had 38.4% Jewish patients, with a range of 9.3% to 70.9%. (*YBJSS*, 1958, CJFWF, Table H-I.)

24. *YBJSS*, 1958, CJFWF, reported tables on Jewish family services.

25. "Jewish Communal Services: Programs and Finances," Table 6. The total expenditures of medical care and cultural and recreational agencies are much greater than those of the case work agencies because of greater proportion of income available from membership and service fees.

26. A special agency for child care service is to be found in Chicago, Cleveland, Los Angeles, Minneapolis, Newark, New Haven, New York, Philadelphia, St. Louis, and San Francisco. A number of these represent mergers in previous years of two or more children's agencies. Newark has 2 and New York City 9 specialized children's agencies. Regional agencies initially established by B'nai B'rith are located in Atlanta, Cleveland, and New Orleans. An institution for asthmatic children, formerly a national home for dependent children, is located in Denver.

27. In 1929, institutions housed a population of over 5,000 children, declining to 1,100 by December 31, 1959.

28. On December 31, 1959, reports from 55 child care agencies showed a total of 1,669 children in foster homes, 1,105 in institutions maintained by the agencies, 967 under care in homes of parents or relatives, 150 under direct supervision of another agency and 278 under other forms of care (guardianship, etc.).

29. *YBJSS*, 1960, CJFWF, p. 6.

30. Maurice B. Hexter, "The Next Twenty-five Years in Jewish Communal Service," *JSS Quarterly*, Fall 1955, p. 37: *The number of children who do not require special services is, in my judgment, apt, for a few years more, to continue to decline still further. The rise in the birth rate a number of years ago will be reflected in the agencies some 10 years from now and we should take stock now to determine whether the institutional resources for our children's needs are ample.*

31. See article on Jewish social work by William Avrunin, *SWYB*, 1960.

NOTES TO CHAPTER XV

1. See F. Emerson Andrews, *Attitudes Toward Giving*. N.Y.: Russell Sage Foundation, 1953; and Harry L. Lurie, "Private Philanthropy and Federated Fund-Raising," *Social Service Review* (Chicago University Press), March 1955, pp. 64-74.

2. CJFWF has had in operation for many years a Campaign and Community Interpretation Department for services to its member agencies. Its activities have included a training film for campaign workers, an instruction kit for solicitors, developed cooperatively with 15 national and overseas agencies, guides on house organs, year books, annual meetings, initiation of a basic guide for communities, and advice to local communities on varied aspects of interpretation.

3. See "Pilot Studies in Jewish Community Organization," report of the Committee on Community Organization, CJFWF, 1955.

4. Stanley C. Myers, "Are Community Organizations Keeping Pace with the Communities?" Report to 24th General Assembly, CJFWF, Nov. 10, 1955.

5. *Ibid.*

6. *Ibid.*

7. *Ibid.*

8. "Leadership Development; Community Experience and Guide Lines," CJFWF, 1959.

9. Excerpts follow from a discussion of "The Synagogue and Jewish Welfare Activities" at the 1935 General Assembly of the National CJFWF held in New York City Jan. 3-6, 1935.

Rabbi De Sola Pool (Rabbi of the Spanish and Portuguese Synagogue, New York City): *With the growing complexity of Jewish communal life in the big city . . . and the inadequacy of the synagogue to comprise the totality of the Jewish community, these welfare activities have been virtually removed from the environment and sponsorship of the synagogue. . . . The removal of all these interests has had a seriously weakening effect on the synagogue—with the transference to secular agencies—the synagogue is left impoverished, denuded, and a failing influence in communal Jewish life throughout the country. . . . It has had an almost equally unfortunate effect on the nature of Jewish welfare activities.*

Rabbi Ira Eisenstein (Associate Leader of the Society for the Advancement of Judaism): *The foundation of Jewish organization must . . . be . . . in that community interest which all must share, namely, the advancement of the complete welfare of the Jewish people. . . . The unit of Jewish life can no longer be the congregation, for the congregation by its very character divides.*

Rabbi De Sola Pool: *There must be a reversion from the traditional Protestant concept of the separation of the church from social service, to a positive Jewish philosophy of welfare work. The much needed synthesis between welfare and synagogue can be brought about through a number of steps. The simplest and most direct measure would be organization of local community councils in which both synagogue and other communal organizations shall be represented . . .*

Ira M. Younker (a vice-president of CJFWF): *I believe the Council of Federations is seeking the formula for such unity. The Council, as such, has no prejudices. This meeting (and others) are indications that we seek to bring the synagogues into our conferences through their representative rabbis.*

10. See Assembly Papers:
    Saul Cherniak and Albert Gordon, "Relationship of Synagogue and Community," 1954
    Samuel Rubiner and Ralph Simon, "Community-Synagogue Relationships," 1955
    Lawrence Weinstein, "Small Cities—A Total Program," 1955
    Benjamin B. Rosenberg and Mark H. Tanenbaum, "Federation-Synagogue Relationships," papers at 1959 Assembly.

11. "Central Community Organization and Planning in Intermediate Cities," CJFWF, 1950.

12. See 1959 CJFWF publications: "Guidelines for Local Federation on Tax-supported Health and Welfare Programs," and "Public Welfare Developments."

13. "Are Community Organizations Keeping Pace with the Communities?" A statement on this subject was made by Sidney Hollander at the 1955 CJFWF Assembly:

Assuming that the activities now being carried on were all really needed in days gone by—it doesn't follow that they're needed now. Even if they are, it again doesn't follow that the Jewish community has to be providing them . . . [upon consideration of] *the establishment of Social Security and significant changes in the scope, the standards, and the attitudes of the non-sectarian voluntary agencies in our communities.*

I've heard the stock arguments against utilization of the non-Jewish services, voluntary and tax-supported. Yes, their standards are sometimes lower than ours. It may be that some Jews are not too comfortable using these other services, implying, of course, that all who use ours are completely at ease.

"Jews wish to be helped by Jews," we're told, ignoring the fact that both the non-sectarian and public services are already employing Jewish personnel, and would gladly use more. . . .

Assuming though that these comments are all valid, does it mean that we must continue permanently to maintain services paralleling those which our own funds help support? Neither the patterns nor the standards of the public services, nor the voluntary non-Jewish ones are fixed and immutable.

Their standards can be raised, their performance made acceptable, their staffs sufficiently Judaized, if and when we demand it. Existing deficiencies should be a challenge to our social conscience, rather than an excuse for duplication. Should standards considered inadequate for Jews be tolerated for others either?

There are certain areas of Jewish life for which only the Jews can be responsible, and the Jewish federations must concern themselves with them. What disturbs me is the tremendous expenditures of funds for services that we know in advance we cannot hope to meet adequately from Jewish funds alone, rather than to stimulate the provision of those services through public sources, not only for Jews but for all.

When it comes to areas like the treatment of mental health, when it comes to medical care, . . . *to care for the aged, which are increasingly calling on us for more and more funds, as they have a right to do as long as we support them, it seems to me that those needs can only be met at the expense of other services that are dominantly and predominately Jewish with which we should be concerning ourselves.*

Aren't there sufficient real Jewish needs in a community with which the community should be concerned, rather than divesting and diverting its funds to services that seem no longer to be needed?

See also discussion of sectarianism and non-sectarianism in chapter X.

NOTES TO CHAPTER XVI

1. *Proceedings of Second NCJC,* 1902 (address of president, p. 12).

2. A few of the topics under discussion (selected at random) in recent national conferences in which Jewish federations and/or their constituent agencies participated were:

"Jewish Communal Organization in Latin America, South Africa, Western Europe"

"Care of Emotionally Disturbed Children"

"Community Planning for Education, Recreation, and Cultural Services"

"The Jewish Community and the Synagogue"

"Religion and the Public Schools"

"The Use of Public Funds by Sectarian Agencies"

"Federation's Responsibility for Hospitals, etc."

3. For example, the by-laws of the CJFWF have this provision concerning actions and resolutions adopted at General Assemblies of CJFWF: *The General Assembly shall consist of accredited delegates of member organizations, . . . decisions (of the General Assembly) shall be binding upon the Board of Directors but not upon the member organizations of the Council, except as each member organization adopts such decisions as its own . . .* (Article III, Sec. 1 of By-Laws.)

4. The William J. Shroder Award, established in 1953 as a memorial to the first president of the Council, William J. Shroder, annually honors two organizations under Jewish auspices for their achievements in the fields of social welfare, communal organization or group relationships. The aim of the award is to cite for their achievements a local, regional, national or international agency through whose specific development the entire community derives ultimate benefits. The Edwin Rosenberg Award was established by CJFWF for the recognition of outstanding leadership in advancing the ideal of greater cooperation in Jewish communal service programs.

5. Developments of intercity cooperation on a regional basis in recent years include:

A. The establishment in New York State region of a committee aimed to assume responsibility for assisting wartime refugees permitted to come to the United States outside of the quota laws but held at Ft. Ontario, N.Y., pending further possibilities of adjustment (*Notes and News,* Nov. 1944).

B. The establishment of a regional community relations program in the Southwest in 1945.

C. Arizona Health survey sponsored by the Southwest Regional Health Committee in 1946.

D. Regional survey of the need for the care of the aged in Georgia, South Carolina and Florida.

E. Regional survey in five southern states concerning most

suitable use of the facilities of the Atlanta Children's Home.
F. Regional support agreements, between communities and regional institutions for the aged in the South and elsewhere.

6. For a number of years, beginning in 1949, the Council organized large city planning conferences to which were invited about 30 of the larger cities. Such conferences gave an opportunity on a more intensive basis than was available at General Assemblies or regional meetings to discuss the basic problems of various financing plans and of local communal organizations. With the extension of the Large City Budgeting Conference in 1952, LCBC has taken the place of these *ad hoc* large city gatherings.

A special project was first developed in 1946, the Tri-City Conference of New York, Chicago, and Philadelphia, where lay and professional leaders met annually to discuss such problems as the development of Jewish hospitals, division of psychiatry in hospitals, and social agencies, the recreational and cultural programs of federation, etc. Four of these conferences were held, the last in 1949.

There have also been, from time to time, institutes and seminars of federation executives of small, intermediate and large communities, for the consideration of common problems.

7. See George Baehr, M. D., "The Role of Jewish Hospitals," *The Jewish Community*, June-July 1947, pp. 12-14.

8. During the fiscal year 1958-1959, children under care of Bellefaire were residents of Cleveland and of 32 organized and 14 unorganized communities—"Bellefaire Regional Child Care Service," Council report, April 1960.

9. For a description of social case work, see article, "Social Case Work," *SWYB*, 1960.

10. See "A Jewish Community Looks at its Case Work Services," survey of Springfield, Mass., CJFWF, 1952; Joseph B. Cowett and Mrs. Sol W. Weitman, "Why Jewish Family Service," *The Jewish Community*, Nov. 1952, pp. 10-12; Robert Morris, "The Future of the Small Family Service Agency under Jewish Auspices," CJFWF, 1956; "Values of Jewish Family Service to the Client and the Community," a rationale for the Jewish family agency, CJFWF, 1954.

11. "Scope and Methods of the Family Service Agency," report of Committee of Family Service Association of America, 1953, and "Family Social Work," *SWYB*, 1960.

12. Benjamin Rabinowitz, "A History of the YMHA," *PAJHS*, XXXVII (1948), New York: American Jewish Historical Society.

13. 'Social Planning for Defense," *Notes and News*, Dec. 2, 1940, pp. 3-4. "The Home Front in Three Cities," *ibid.*, June 16, 1942, pp. 11-14. "JWB with the Troops," *ibid.*, July 9, 1943, pp. 10-11.

14. Elias Picheny, "Tasks Ahead in the Jewish Center Field," *Journal of Jewish Communal Service*, Fall 1956, pp. 104-116. "A Statement of Principles Concerning Relationships Between Jewish Community Centers and Jewish Federations," CJFWF and NJWB, 1958.

15. For recent discussions of federations' responsibility for Jewish education see Morris Garvett, Oscar I. Janowsky and Louis L. Kaplan, "Community Responsibility for Jewish Education," at 23rd General Assembly, CJFWF, Jan. 1955; and Discussion Outline on same subject prepared for the 22nd General Assembly, CJFWF, Nov. 1953.

16. Daniel Shiman, "Newark Sets Up Joint Council," *The Jewish Community*, Jan. 1947, pp. 5-7.

17. The Edwin Rosenberg Award given at the 1956 General Assembly recognized the achievement of the two Philadelphia agencies in consummating their merger.

18. The committee was composed of one lay representative and the executive of each of the federation's beneficiary agencies, along with ten representatives of the community-at-large, plus the officers of the Federation. The SAC with a full-time secretary, working through numerous subcommittees, concerns itself with the relationship between agencies, standards of service and priority of needs, and seeks to maintain a balance of service from a total community perspective. It keeps close contact with the budget, fund-raising, interpretation, and other phases of federation activity. See also L. W. Neumark, "Planning Before Emergencies," *The Jewish Community*, June 1952, pp. 9-11.

19. "Communities Are Maturing," *The Jewish Community*, March 1949, pp. 19-20. H. L. Lurie, "Intermediate Cities Change Scope," *The Jewish Community*, V, no. 2 (May 1950), pp. 12-14.

20. H. L. Lurie, "Jewish Communal Life in the United States," *The Jewish People—Past and Present*, IV (New York: Jewish Encyclopedic Handbooks, 1955).

21. "Budgeting Principles and Practices," CJFWF, July 1953.

22. Special Budget Workbooks are prepared by the CJFWF annually for a number of welfare funds in communities ranging in size from 1,200 to 30,000 Jewish population.

23. The CJFWF collects and distributes annually to its member agencies the statistics on welfare fund grants in four categories, to non-local beneficiaries:
    A. The welfare funds which distribute $500,000 and over,
    B. Welfare fund granting from $200,000 to $500,000,
    C. Welfare fund granting from $100,000 to $200,000,
    D. Welfare fund granting under $100,000 to non-local beneficiaries.

notes

There are also studies published of fund distribution to local agencies in all major fields of service. The studies are on four groups of cities:

A. Over 40,000 Jewish population
B. 15,000 to 40,000
C. 5,000 to 15,000
D. Under 5,000

24. Annual and interim reports are issued by LCBC and by the Committee on National-Local Relations through the CJFWF.
25. See *supra*, chapter VII.
26. See *supra*, chapter XI.
27. "Jewish Communal Services: Programs and Finances," CJFWF, Jan. 1960.
28. "Highlights," bulletin on CJFWF Board of Directors meeting, June 13, 1960.
29. "Standards of Fund-Raising Practice for Social Welfare Organizations," prepared by the Committee on Current Financing Factors of the National Social Welfare Assembly:

A. *Board*. Responsible direction of this organization is in the hands of an active voluntary board, serving without compensation, holding regular meetings, and exercising effective administrative control.

B. *Program*. The agency maintains an active and necessary program. Objectives are being pursued with careful regard: (a) to the welfare of the persons served by the program; (b) to efficiency of operation, and (c) to consultation and cooperation with other organizations, and particularly those in the same or related fields.

C. *Finances*. Fiscal operations of the agency are conducted in accordance with a detailed annual budget prepared and approved at the beginning of the year, with such current changes as may be authorized by the Board of Directors. At the year's close an audit is made by an independent certified public accountant or trust company, showing all income, disbursements, assets, liabilities, endowments, reserves and surplus in reasonable detail.

D. *Ethical Methods of Promotion*. The agency does not mail unordered tickets or commerical merchandise with request for money in return. The telephone is not used for soliciting funds from the "general" public. No arrangements are entered into to raise funds on a commission basis.

E. *Fund-Raising Costs*. The agency is pledged to honest reporting of fund-raising costs, and to the development of improved standards of recording such costs. Fund-raising costs are disclosed to contributors and to the general public in the report mentioned below.

F. *Report*. The agency prepares annually a report which in-

455

cludes a full account of activities, names of board members and chief administrative personnel, and a complete audit report, with appropriate detail, including the cost of fundraising. Information regarding finances and program is available to the contributors and the general public.

30. See Louis Englander, "Accounting Principles and Procedures of Philanthropic Institutions," New York Community Trust, 1957. See also "Institute of Controllers of Jewish Communal Agencies," by S. P. Goldberg, secretary of Institute. CJFWF report, Nov. 27, 1951.

NOTES TO CHAPTER XVII

1. Horace M. Kallen, "American Jews, What Now?" *JSS Quarterly*, XXXII, no. 1 (Fall 1955), pp. 12-29.

2. *Ibid.*, p. 29.

3. Maurice B. Hexter, "The Next Twenty-five Years in Jewish Communal Service," *JSS Quarterly*, XXXIII, no. 1 (Fall 1955), pp. 30-48.

4. *Ibid.*, p. 47.

5. S. P. Goldberg, "Jewish Communal Services: Programs and Finances," CJFWF, Jan. 1960, Table 3.

6. Floyd Hunter, *Community Power Structure*: A Study of Decision Makers (University of North Carolina Press, 1953).

On the History of The Jewish Communities in the United States and Canada

The United States

Regional Broches, Samuel. *Jews in New England*. Part I: Historical Study of the Jews in Massachusetts, 1650-1750; part II: Jewish Merchants in Colonial Rhode Island. New York: Bloch Publishing Company, 1942.

Huhner, Leon. *Jews in America in Colonial and Revolutionary Times*. Studies of New York, New England, South Carolina, Georgia and Virginia. New York: Gertz Brothers, 1959.

Marcus, Jacob Rader. *Early American Jewry*. Vol. 1: The Jews of New York, New England and Canada, 1649-1794; vol. 2: The Jews of Pennsylvania and the South, 1655-1790. Philadelphia: Jewish Publication Society, 1951, 1953.

Tarshish, Allan. "Jews in South Carolina, North Carolina and Virginia, 1695-1950." Unpublished (American Jewish Archives, Cincinnati).

"The Historic Aspect of New England Jewry, 300 Years." Supplement of Tercentenary issue of Jewish Advocate (Boston), January 27, 1955.

"Trail Blazers of the Trans-Mississippi West," *American Jewish Archives* (Cincinnati), VIII, no. 2 (Oct. 1956), pp. 59-130.

Alaska Glanz, Rudolf. *The Jews in American Alaska, 1867-1880*. New York: privately published, 1953.

Arkansas Shain, Samson A. "The Story of Arkansas Jewry, 1836-1953." Unpublished (American Jewish Archives).

California Glanz, Rudolf. *The Jews of California*: From the Discovery of Gold until 1880. New York: privately published, 1960.

LONG BEACH Hartmann, Sidney A. *The History of the Long Beach Jewish Community*. Jewish Community Council of Long Beach, 1957.

LOS ANGELES "History of Jews in Los Angeles." In preparation. The American Jewish History Center. Scheduled for 1962.

OAKLAND "Historical Summary of Jewish Activities in Oakland for the Past 50 Years." Unpublished (Jewish Welfare Federation, Oakland), 1926.

SAN FRANCISCO Voorsanger, Jacob. *The Chronicle of Emanu-El*: Being an Account of the Rise and Progress of the Congregation Emanu-El which was founded in July 1850. San Francisco: 1900.

Zarchin, Michael M. "Glimpses of Jewish Life in San Francisco." San Francisco: privately issued (mimeo), 1952.

Colorado Kauvar, C. E. Hillel. "The Colorado Jewish Community, 1859-1953." Unpublished (American Jewish Archives).

Uchill, Ida Libert. *Pioneers, Peddlers and Tzadikim*. Denver: Sage Books, 1957.

DENVER Breck, Allen DuPont. *A Centennial History of the Jews of Colorado, 1859-1959*. (University of Colorado, Dept. of History Series: "The West in American History," no. 1.) Denver: Hirschfield Press, 1960.

Connecticut Marcus, Jacob Rader. "Light on Early Connecticut Jewry," *American Jewish Archives* (Cincinnati), Jan. 1949, pp. 3-52.

HARTFORD Feldman, Abraham Jekiel. *Remember the Days of Old*: An Outline History of the Congregation Beth Israel, 1843-1943. Hartford: Congregation Beth Israel, 1943.

NEW HAVEN Osterweis, Rollin G. and Siskin, Edgar E. (eds.). *Congregation Mishkan Israel Centennial Volume, 1840-1940*. New Haven: 1940.

Reznikoff, Charles. "New Haven; The Jewish Community: A Portrait Sketch," *Commentary* (New York), Nov. 1947.

NEW LONDON Sulman, Esther with Goldstein, Leonard J. *A Goodly Heritage*: The Story of the Jewish Community in New London, 1860-1955. Privately published, 1957.

NORWICH Goldberg, Arthur and Gordon, Mrs. Isaac. "The Jew in Norwich: A Century of Jewish

Life." Norwich: Tercentenary Research Committee (mimeo), 1956.

Florida Proctor, Samuel. "Pioneers of Jewish Settlement in Florida, 1765-1900," *Proceedings of the Conference on the Writing of Regional History of the South* (New York), 1956, pp. 81-115.

MIAMI Lehrman, Irving. "The Jewish Community of Greater Miami, 1896-1955," *Proceedings of the Conference on the Writing of Regional History of the South,* 1956, pp. 116-130. American Jewish History Center, New York, 1956.

Simonhoff, Harry. "History of the Jewish Community in Miami," *Under Strange Skies.* New York: 1953.

Illinois
CHICAGO Bregstone, Philip P. *Chicago and Its Jews*: A Cultural History. Chicago: 1933.

Gutstein, Morris A. *A Priceless Heritage*: The Epic Growth of Nineteenth Century Chicago Jewry. New York: Bloch Publishing Company, 1953.

Hutler, Albert A. "The Story of Jewish Communal Life in Chicago." Chicago: Chicago Jewish Youth Assembly (mimeo), 1942.

Levitats, Isaac. "The Story of the Chicago Jewish Community," Chicago: Board of Jewish Education (mimeo).

Meites, Hyman L. (ed.). *History of the Jews of Chicago.* Chicago: Jewish Historical Society of Illinois, 1924.

Rawidowicz, Simon (ed.). *The Chicago Pinkas* (Heb. and Eng.). Chicago: College of Jewish Studies, 1952.

The Sentinel *Presents 100 Years of Chicago Jewry.* Chicago: *Sentinel,* 1948.

Iowa Glazer, Simon. *The Jews of Iowa*: A Complete and Accurate Account of Their Religious, Social, Economic and Educational Progress in this State. Des Moines: 1904.

Wolfe, Jack. *A Century with Iowa Jewry*: From 1833 through 1940. Des Moines: 1941.

DES MOINES Rosenthal, Frank. *The Jews of Des Moines*: The First Century. Des Moines: Jewish Welfare Federation, 1957.

Kentucky
LOUISVILLE Compiled by the Jewish Historical Society of

New Orleans. *A History of the Jews in Louisville*. The Society, 1903.

Louisiana Kaplan, Benjamin. *The Eternal Stranger*: A Study of Jewish Life in the Small Community. (A sociological study of Jewish life in 38 small Louisiana communities.) New York: Bookman Associates, 1957.

Shpall, Leo. "The First Synagogue in Louisiana," *Louisiana Historical Society*, XXI, no. 2 (April 1939).

NEW ORLEANS Feibelman, Julian Beck. *A Social and Economic Study of the New Orleans Jewish Community*. Philadelphia: privately published, 1941.

Shpall, Leo. "Early Jewish Philanthropy in New Orleans," *Jewish Forum* (New York), XXXVIII, nos. 1, 3, 7, pp. 14, 52, 114.

SHREVEPORT "Survey of Historical Records of Congregation Agudath Achim, Shreveport, 1890-1939." Unpublished (American Jewish Archives; copies from the Dept. of Archives, La. State University).

Maine
PORTLAND Band, Benjamin. *Portland Jewry*: Its Growth and Development. Portland: Jewish Historical Society, 1955. Supplement One (covering years 1955-1960), 1961.

Maryland Glushakow, A. D. (ed.). *A Pictorial History of Maryland Jewry*. Baltimore: 1955.

BALTIMORE Blum, Isidor (ed.). *The Jews of Baltimore*. Baltimore Historical Review Publ. Co., 1910.

Cahn, Louis F. *The History of Oheb Shalom*, 1853-1953. Baltimore: Oheb Shalom Congregation, 1953.

Rubenstein, Charles A. *A History of Har Sinai Congregation of the City of Baltimore*. Baltimore: Har Sinai Congregation, 1918.

Massachusetts
BOSTON Broches, Samuel. *Historical Study of the Jews in Massachusetts, 1650-1750*. Jews in New England—6 monographs. New York: Bloch Publishing Company, 1942.

———. "A Chapter in the History of the Jews of Boston," *YIVO Annual* (New York), IX (1954), pp. 205-211.

Fifty Years of Jewish Philanthropies in Greater Boston: Boston: Associated Jewish Philanthropies, 1945.

Neusner, Jacob. "The Impact of Immigration and Philanthropy upon the Boston Jewish Community, 1880-1914," *PAJHS* (New York) XLVI, no. 2 (Dec. 1956), pp. 71-85.
————. "The Rise of the Jewish Community of Boston, 1880-1914." Unpublished (Harvard University Archives).
Solomon, Barbara Miller. *Pioneers in Service: The History of the Associated Jewish Philanthropies of Boston.* Boston: Associated Jewish Philanthropies, Inc., 1956.

CAMBRIDGE Mann, Arthur (ed.). *Growth and Achievement:* Temple Israel, 1854-1954. Cambridge: Riverside Press, 1954. (Containing by Lee M. Friedman, "1854—Boston and Its Jews."

Michigan Franklin, M. M. "Jews in Michigan," *Michigan History Magazine*, XXIII, no. 1 (1939).
DETROIT Katz, Irving I. and Marcus, Jacob Rader. *The Beth El Story:* with a History of the Jews in Michigan before 1850. Detroit: Wayne University Press, 1955.
Weinberg, S. D. *Jewish Social Services of Detroit:* A History of Its Welfare Institutions, Agencies and Activities (Yiddish). Detroit: Jewish Welfare Federation, 1940.

Minnesota Plaut, W. Gunther. *The Jews of Minnesota:* The First Seventy-Five Years (Series: "American Jewish Communal Histories," no. 3.) New York: AJHS, 1959.
DULUTH Eldot, Walter. "Jews of Duluth, Minn." Unpublished (American Jewish Archives), 1955.
MINNEAPOLIS Danenbaum, Ruby. "A History of the Jews of Minneapolis," *Reform Advocate* (Chicago), Nov. 16, 1907, pp. 7-40.
Gordon, Albert I. *Jews in Transition:* A Sociological Study of the Jewish Community of Minneapolis. University of Minnesota Press, 1949.
ST. PAUL Frankel, Hiram D. "The Jews of Saint Paul," Special Minnesota Edition of *Reform Advocate* (Chicago), Nov. 16, 1907, pp. 41-53.
Plaut, W. Gunther. *Mount Zion, 1856-1956:* The First Hundred Years. St. Paul: Mt. Zion Hebrew Congregation, 1956.

New Jersey Haberman, Joshua O. "The Jews in New Jersey, 1702-1953." Unpublished (American Jewish Archives).
ATLANTIC CITY "The Story of Beth Israel Congregation in

461

Atlantic City, N.J., 1890-1951." Unpublished, Beth Israel Congregation (American Jewish Archives).

ELIZABETH
(Eastern Union County)

Gale, Joseph (ed.). *The Development of a Jewish Community*. Elizabeth: Jewish Culture Council of Eastern Union County, 1958.

NEWARK
(Essex County)

Gelbart, Gerson; Kohn, Sylvan H. and Rudavsky, David. *A History of the Jewish Community in Essex County, N.J.* Newark: Jewish Education Society of Essex County, 1955.

Kussy, Nathan. "An Early History of the Jews of Newark," *The Jewish Community Blue Book of Newark*. Newark: Jewish Community Blue Book Publ. Co., 1926.

PASSAIC

Jewish Roots: A History of the Jewish Community of Passaic and Environs. The Tercentenary Committee of the Jewish Community Council of Passaic-Clifton and Vicinity, 1959.

New Mexico
LOS ALAMOS

Shinedling, Abraham I. *History of the Los Alamos Jewish Center, 1944-1957*. Los Alamos: privately published, 1958.

New York
ALBANY

Silver, Louis. "The Jews in Albany, New York, 1665-1914," *YIVO Annual*, IX (1954), pp. 212-246.

BUFFALO

Adler, Selig and Connolly, Thomas E. *From Ararat to Suburbia:* The History of the Jewish Community of Buffalo. Philadelphia: Jewish Publication Society, 1960.

ITHACA

Goodstein, Anita Shafer. "A History of the Jews of Ithaca." Mimeo (American Jewish Archives), 1955.

NEW YORK

Fifty Years of Social Service: The History of the United Hebrew Charities of the City of New York. New York: Jewish Social Service Assn., 1926.

Grinstein, Hyman B. *The Rise of the Jewish Community of New York, 1654-1860*. Philadelphia: Jewish Publication Society, 1945.

Joseph, Samuel. *History of the Baron de Hirsch Fund:* The Americanization of the Jewish Immigrant. Philadelphia: Jewish Publication Society, 1935.

Oppenheim, Samuel. "The Early History of the Jews in New York, 1654-1664," *PAJHS*, XVIII (1909), pp. 1-91.

Pool, David de Sola and Pool, Tamara. *An Old Faith in the New World:* Portrait of Shearith Israel, 1654-1954. New York: Columbia University Press, 1955.
"The Kehillah," *Jewish Communal Register.* New York: Kehillah of New York, 1918.

NEW YORK- Abelow, Samuel P. *History of Brooklyn Jewry.*
BROOKLYN Brooklyn: Scheba Publishing Co., 1937.
ROCHESTER McKelvey, Blake. "The Jews of Rochester: A Contribution to their History during the Nineteenth Century," *PAJHS,* XL, no. 1 (Sept. 1950), pp. 57-73.
Rosenberg, Stuart E. *The Jewish Community in Rochester, 1843-1925* (Series: "American Jewish Communal Histories, no. 1.) New York: Columbia University Press for AJHS, 1954.

UTICA Kohn, S. Joshua. *The Jewish Community of Utica, New York, 1847-1948* (Series: "American Jewish Communal Histories," no. 2.) New York: AJHS, 1959.

Ohio Bernheim, Isaac W. *History of the Settlement of Jews in Paducah and the Lower Ohio Valley.* Paducah: 1912.

CINCINNATI Brickner, Barnett R. "The Jews of Cincinnati." Unpublished Ph.D. dissertation (University of Cincinnati), 1920.
Heller, James G. *As Yesterday, When It Is Past:* A History of the Isaac M. Wise Temple, 1842-1942. Cincinnati: K. K. B'nai Yeshurun, 1942.

CLEVELAND Reznikoff, Charles. "History of Cleveland Jewry." In preparation. The American Jewish History Center. Scheduled for 1962.

COLUMBUS Rabin, Phillip Haskell. "A Study of American Jewish Community Backgrounds: A Description of Jewish Organizations and the Jewish Community Council in Columbus, O., 1830-1942." Unpublished, Ohio State University (American Jewish Archives).

Oklahoma Levenson, Joseph. "The Story of Oklahoma Jewry, 1864-1953." Unpublished (American Jewish Archives).

Oregon Suwol, Samuel M. *Jewish History of Oregon, from 1840.* Portland, Ore.: privately published, 1958.

PORTLAND Apsler, Alfred and Nodel, Julius J. *The Ties Between:* A Century of Judaism on America's

Last Frontier. The human story of Congregation Beth Israel, Portland, Ore., the oldest Jewish congregation in the Pacific Northwest. Portland: Temple Beth Israel, 1959.

Pennsylvania

EASTON   Trachtenberg, Joshua. "An American Jewish Community: Easton, Pennsylvania, on its Two Hundredth Anniversary," *PAJHS*, XLII, no. 2 (Dec. 1952), pp. 193-206.
———. *Consider the Years:* The Story of the Jewish Community of Easton, 1752-1942. Easton: 1944.

PHILADELPHIA   Davis, Edward. *The History of Rodeph Shalom Congregation, 1802-1926.* Philadelphia: 1926.
Morais, H. S. *The Jews of Philadelphia:* Their History from the Earliest Settlements to the Present Time, a Record of Events and Institutions and of Leading Members of the Jewish Community in Every Sphere of Activity. Philadelphia: 1894.
Whiteman, Maxwell and Wolf, Edwin, 2nd. *The History of the Jews of Philadelphia:* From Colonial Times to the Age of Jackson. Philadelphia: Jewish Publication Society, 1957.

PITTSBURGH   Feldman, Jacob S. "The Early Migration and Settlement of Jews in Pittsburgh, 1754-1894." United Jewish Federation of Pittsburgh and the Pittsburgh Council of B'nai B'rith (mimeo), 1959.
Pine, Kurt. "The Jews in the Hill District of Pittsburgh, 1910-1940: A Study of Trends." University of Pittsburgh.

Rhode Island

NEWPORT   Gutstein, Morris. *To Bigotry No Sanction:* A Jewish Shrine in America, 1658-1958. New York: Bloch Publishing Company, 1958.
———. *The Story of the Jews of Newport:* Two and a Half Centuries of Judaism, 1658-1908. New York: Bloch Publishing Company, 1936.
Pool, David de Sola. "The Touro Synagogue: Aspects of the Missing Half-Century of its History, 1850-1900," *PAJHS*, XXXVIII, no. 1 (Sept. 1948), pp. 57-76.

PROVIDENCE   *Rhode Island Jewish Historical Notes,* published since 1954 by the R.I. Jewish Historical Association. Presents history of Jews of the state, particularly those of Providence.

South Carolina Elzas, Barnett A. *The Jews of South Carolina: From the Earliest Times to the Present Day.* Philadelphia: J. B. Lippincott, 1905.

CHARLESTON Reznikoff, Charles with Engelman, Uriah Z. *The Jews of Charleston: A History of an American Jewish Community.* Philadelphia: Jewish Publication Society, 1950.

Tobias, Thomas J. *The Hebrew Orphan Society of Charleston, S. C., Founded in 1801: An Historical Sketch.* Charleston: privately published, 1957.

South Dakota Colman, Blanche. "Early Jewish History of the Black Hills." Unpublished (American Jewish Archives).

Texas Cohen, Rev. Henry. "Settlement of the Jews in Texas," *PAJHS*, no. 2 (1894), pp. 9-19.
———. "The Jews in Texas," *PAJHS*, no. 4 (1895), pp. 9-19.

HOUSTON Cohen, Anne Nathan. *Congregation Beth Israel of Houston, Texas, 1854-1954.* Houston: privately published, 1954.

Tennessee
MEMPHIS Wax, James A. "The Jews of Memphis, 1800-1954," *The West Tennessee Historical Society Papers*, III (1949), pp. 39-89.

Utah Watters, Leon L. *The Pioneer Jews of Utah: History of the Jews in Utah until the 1880s.* (Series: "Studies in American Jewish History," no. 2.) New York: AJHS, 1952.

Washington Levine, Raphael H. and Robinson, Michael. "History of the Jews of the Pacific Northwest." Unpublished (American Jewish Archives).

Virginia
PETERSBURG Ginsberg, Louis. *History of the Jews of Petersburg, 1789-1950.* Petersburg: 1954.

RICHMOND Ezekiel, Herbert T. and Lichtenstein, G. *The History of the Jews of Richmond, 1769-1917.* Richmond: 1917.

Through the Years: A Study of the Richmond Jewish Community. Tercentenary Committee of the Richmond Jewish Community Council, 1955.

West Virginia Shinedling, Abraham I. "The History of the

Jews of West Virginia, 1840-1953." Unpublished (American Jewish Archives).

BECKLEY Pickus, Manuel and Shinedling, Abraham I. *History of the Beckley Jewish Community and Congregation Beth El, 1895-1955* (including Raleigh and Fayette counties). Beckley: 1955.

Wisconsin Gartner, Lloyd and Switchkow, Louis J. "History of Jews in Wisconsin." In preparation. American Jewish History Center. Scheduled for 1961.

FOND DU LAC Sumberg, Alfred D. "History of the Jewish Community of Fond du Lac, Wisconsin, 1790-1954." Unpublished (American Jewish Archives).

MADISON Swassensky, Manfred. *From Generation to Generation:* The Story of the Madison Jewish Community, 1851-1955. Madison: privately published, 1955.

MANITOWOC Sumberg, Alfred D. "History of the Jewish Community of Manitowoc, 1890-1954." Unpublished (American Jewish Archives).

MILWAUKEE Levitats, Isaac. "The Story of the Milwaukee Jewish Community." Milwaukee: Bureau of Jewish Education (mimeo), 1954.

Switchkow, Louis J. "The Jewish Community of Milwaukee, Wisc., 1860-1870," *PAJHS*, XLVII, no. 1 (Sept. 1957), pp. 34-58.

Canada

Hart, Arthur Daniel. *The Jew in Canada:* A Complete Record of Canadian Jewry from the Days of the French Regime to the Present Time. Toronto: 1926.

Rhinewine, A. *Der Yid in Canada.* Two vols. Toronto: 1925, 1927.

Rosenberg, Louis. "Some Aspects of the Historical Development of the Canadian Jewish Community," *PAJHS*, L, no. 2 (Dec. 1960), pp. 121-142.

————. "Two Centuries of Jewish Life in Canada, 1760-1960," *AJYB*, LXII (1961), pp. 28-52.

Sack, Benjamin G. *History of the Jews in Canada.* Montreal: 1945.

Wilder, H. E. "An Outline of the History of the Jews in Canada," *Israelite Press* (Winnipeg), 1932.

Wolf, Martin. "Jews of Canada," *AJYB*, XXVII (1925-26), pp. 154-229.

Manitoba   Chiel, Arthur. *Jewish Experiences in Early Manitoba*. Winnipeg: Manitoba Jewish Publications, 1955.

LONDON, ONT.   "The Growth of London's Jewish Community," *Jewish Standard*, Sept. 7, 1934.

REGINA, SASK.   "History of Regina's Jewish Community," *Jewish Post* (Winnipeg), Sept. 1928.

TORONTO, QUE.   "Highlights of Toronto's Jewish History." Toronto: Joint Committee on Centennial Celebration (mimeo), 1957.

"Toronto Jewry: An Historical Sketch." Canadian Jewish Congress and United Jewish Welfare Fund of Toronto. Centennial Research Committee (mimeo), 1957.

Index

Addams, Jane, 36
Acculturation, 18, 89, 233. *See also* Immigrants
Adoption, agency service, 326
Advisory Committee on Social Planning, 206
Advisory National Budgeting, 150; opposition to, 155-156
Aged, Jewish care for, planning for, 193; homes for, 193, 313-314, 315, 316, 317; federation role in, 313; inter-federation planning for, 359
Agro-Joint, 92
Agudath Israel, 179
Alliance Israélite Universelle, 43
America-Israel Cultural Foundation, 378
American Association for Jewish Education, activities of, 207; information services of, 354. *See also* Education, Jewish
American Fund for Israel Institutions, 176
American Hospital Association, 355
Americanization, effects of on Jewish life, 216-217. *See also* American Jewry; Education of immigrants; Immigrants in the U.S.
American Jewish Committee, 144, 368; and the Joint Defense Appeal, 146; withdrawal from NCRAC, 202; federation representation on, 376

American Jewish Conference, 144, 149, 154, 368; purpose of, 91; and the UJA, 141; withdrawal of from General Jewish Council, 146-147; opposition to, 167; organization of, 248, 249
American Jewish Congress, 238, 241
American Jewry, and federations, 3, 158; class divisions, 17; overseas relief activities, 29, 165; relief activities, 86; importance in world Jewry, 86-87, 111, 166; and Jewish communal welfare organization, 87, 215; effects of World War II, 110-111; and anti-Semitism, 111, 117-118, 132; rescue and rehabilitation programs, 165; fundraising efforts, 165, 169; effects of internal migration, 166-167; solidarity of, 167; changes in, 168-169, 386-387; inter-sectarian life of, 217, 225-226; acculturation of, 216-217, 386
Anti-Defamation League, 144, and the JDC, 146; withdrawal from NCRAC, 203
Anti-Semitism: effects on American Jewry, 90, 117-118, 132, 233-234; and European Jewry, 110, 117; in Germany, 117; and the JDC, 117; effects on Jewish communal organizations, 229, 382-383; easing of, 383
Associations, Jewish, rivalries among, 227

469

creasing concern with, 201; 306-307; federation support of, 202; and the NCRAC, 308; and the ADL, 308; and the American Jewish Committee, 308; and the MacIver Report, 308
Conferences for inter-federation cooperation, 355
Constitution, of the U.S., and Church-State separation, 21-22. *See also* Colonial America
Council of Jewish Cultural Agencies, 368
Council of Jewish Federations and Welfare Funds, 135, 253; JDC-UPA cooperation, 137; and overseas agencies, 139; and Israel's financial needs, 188; Institute on Overseas Studies, 188; and coordination of Jewish health services, 193-194; Advisory Committee on Social Planning, 206; and Jewish culture in the U.S., 207-208; and federations, 231, 293, 353-354; and Jewish communal organization, 248; symposium on community harmony, 251-253; budgeting and research committees, 293; information function, 297, 354, 371-372, 454; Committee on Leadership Development, 339-340; Social Planning Department, 362
Council of National Tuberculosis Institutions, 135, 138
Curtis, Jerome N., 250

Dallas, "functional" federation of, 40, 273
Delinquency, in American Jewry, 70-71
Denver Home for Consumptives, 43
Depression, the, effects of, 109, 111-112
Des Moines, Ia., United Jewish Philanthropies in, 420
Desertion, of family, problem

among Jewish immigrants, 66-67; federation efforts to combat, 68; government attitudes toward, 68-69
Detroit, Mich., 42, 95; Jewish welfare fund, 105; community council, 127; building of Jewish hospitals, 191; study on Jewish group association, 226; *Kehillah*, 83
Diaspora, the, Jewish welfare activities in, 8
Displaced Persons Act, 175
"District Service," experimentation with, 58

East-European Jewry, 11, 12; metropolitan welfare organizations of, 13; in post-World War II Europe, 91. *See also* Immigrants, Jewish, to the U.S.
East-European Jews, in America, welfare programs of, 15, 50, 52; and German Jews, 15, 49; and socialism, 16; dissensions among, 17; fraternal and labor organizations, 17; and federations, 55, 235
Education, of immigrants, Jewish community groups for, 71, language instruction, 71; and youth programs, 71; attitudes of immigrants towards, 71, 72; improvements in, 72. *See also* Americanization
Education, Jewish, early federation attitudes towards, 73; federation support of, 74, 75, 100, 206, 207, 290, 309, 311, 312, 364; communal interest in, 90; increased enrollment in, 195; community planning for, 206; and the AAJE, 207; denominational programs for, 309; all-day schools for, 310; quality of, 312; integrated structure for 312
Educational Alliance, 72

Overseas agencies, Jewish, centralized support of, 136, 137, 176; welfare fund allocations to, 137; budgetary problems 138, 139; multiple campaigns, 156; post-World War II dissensions, 167; expanded activities of, 172, 173
Overseas relief, 91-93. *See also* Overseas agencies, Jewish

Pale of Settlement, 13
Palestine White Paper, 173
Pennsylvania, 20
Peoples Relief Committee, 92. *See also* JDC
Personal service, 61-62
Philadelphia Federation, 41, 191, 272, 367; early fund-raising, 42-43; original affiliated agencies, 43; *Kehillah*, 83
Philanthropy, inter-faith, 16; in Warsaw, 14; denominational associations, 24
Philanthropy, Jewish, shift to mutual aid and self-help, 192
Pioneer Women, 176, 378
Pittsburgh, Pa., first federation, 42; hospital construction, 191; merger of communal organizations, 272, 367
Poor-Relief, 23, 83
Prisoners' Aid Bureau, 71
Protestant Church, 218
Public welfare, federation concern with, 349

Quakers, treatment of in Colonial America, 10
Quebec, French Catholics in, 20

Reform Judaism, 16
Reformed Church, New York, 20
Relief, government programs, 90; changing Jewish attitudes, 90; decreasing emphasis on, 118

Relief agencies, Jewish, early multiplicity, 32, 61; mergers, 32, 33; inadequacies of, 38; early methods, 61; and immigrants, 61, 67-68; and "scientific" policies, 63; and war refugees, 126. *See also* Federations, Jewish
Relief assistance, Jewish, 64-68
Religious schools, Jewish, 310
Resettlement of Jewish immigrants, 64-65; and the Industrial Removal office, 64-65. *See also* Immigrants, Jewish
Revisionists, 179
Rosenberg, Benjamin B., 222-223
Russia, 29

St. Louis, Mo., 42; campaign for hospital, 191
San Francisco, 95; first federation, 42; Jewish welfare fund, 105; merger of communal organizations, 272, 367
Scholarship funds, 328
School for Jewish Communal Work, 103
Scots Charitable Society, Boston, 22
Seaside Home for Children: *see* Philadelphia Federation
Sectarianism, in America, 218, 223; Willen study of, 219-221; effects on Jewish group consciousness, 384
Selekman, Ben, 118
Senior, Max, 37-38, 41-42, 62
Sephardic synagogues, 22
Settlement movement, 36
Settlements, Jewish, 90; and immigrant education, 72; shortcomings of, 72-73
Shearith Israel Congregation, New York, Hebrew Benevolent Society, 23
Shroder, William J., 108, 124, 139, 141, 248, 249
Silver, Abba Hillel, 249
Simon, Max, 128

community relations organizations, 147. *See also* National Community Relations Advisory Council

Willen, Joseph, 219-221

William J. Shroder Award, for community service, 356, 452

Winfield Tuberculosis Sanatorium, Chicago, 68

Wolf, Louis, 42

World War I, effects on Jewish immigration rate, 59

World War II, general effects of, 121-122; effects: on social welfare agencies, 122; on Jewish communal organizations, 121-125, 126

Yeshiva University, social work program, 206

Young Women's Union for Care of Children: *see* Philadelphia Federation

Youngstown, Ohio, 191

Zionist Organization of America, 368

Zucker, Henry, 256, 258

The Jacob R. Schiff Library of Jewish Contributions to American Democracy